A
Carmarthenshire
Anthology

A Carmarthenshire Anthology

Lynn Hughes

A New & Revised Edition

CYHOEDDWYR
DINEFWR
PUBLISHERS

Copyright © Introduction & Selection Lynn Hughes 1984
Translations © as listed on p. 433.

First published 1984 by Christopher Davies Publishers.

Published in 2002 by
Dinefwr Publishers
Rawlings Road, Llandybie
Carmarthenshire, SAl8 3YD

A CIP catalogue record for this book is
available from the British Library.

ISBN 1 904323 02 2

Printed and bound in Wales by
Dinefwr Press Ltd.
Rawlings Road, Llandybie
Carmarthenshire, SA18 3YD

Cover design by Nicholas Thirkell.
Photograph of Ystradffin, Rhandirmwyn, 'David Price Jones a'i stên'
is from the DC Harries (Llandilo) Collection by permission of
The National Library of Wales.

Contents

III. SAINTS & SINNERS

IV. HEROES & THE CRACHACH

V. BITS OF CHARACTERS

VI. SOME BLAGGARDS

VII. ANCIENT MONUMENTS & HOLY PLACES

VIII. HOUSES GREAT & SMALL

IX. WAR & STRIFE

X. WORK & PLAY

XI. EVERYDAY LIFE

XII. WILDLIFE

XIII. HUSBANDRY

XIV. RIVERS & LAKES

† denotes translation. A key to the translators appears on page 433.

Key to Illustrations

Foreword

From early days the geographical area of Carmarthenshire has always enjoyed a separate entity. Although, throughout the Middle Ages, the land was a loose collection of commotes and lordships, it retained its own individuality, fashioned largely by topography and economic interests, so that when the area became a shire during the years 1536-40, its intrinsic character and traditions were not unduly violated by resultant changes. This character has persisted, the inherited attitudes still flourish; a character which, seemingly, a radical recent reorganisation in local administration failed to efface.

Such distinctiveness is well illustrated here in this anthology compiled for us by Lynn Hughes. His selections reveal him to be a man of wide horizons, familiar with all aspects of Carmarthenshire life, as acquainted with writers of ancient times as he is with his contemporaries. Anthologists are inclined occasionally to emphasize romantic aspects of our past, to highlight the spectacular and momentous. Here, however, we have an investigation of all features of Carmarthenshire society 'saints and sinners' alike – and descriptions by observers who call out to us across the ages and evoke a bygone world like Giraldus Cambrensis and James Howell whose volumes, richly gemmed with anecdotes, have tinted our minds, and like Prys Morgan and Geraint Jenkins whose matter-of-fact methods contribute preciseness to their more modern narratives.

The wide scope of the compiler's detective work is indicated by the titles of the fifteen sections comprising this anthology: they reveal his catholicity. Present-day authors as well as those who lived over a millennium ago are called to bear witness to the Carmarthenshire scene, from Pliny to Heather James, from Leland to Gomer Roberts, from Lewys Glyn Cothi to Wil Ifan, from the *Mabinogion* to D. J. Williams, from Hywel Dda to Pat Molloy, and from Merlin the Magician to Gilbert Chaldecott. Not that all verdicts are favourable by any means. For instance, the comments of tourists are refreshingly frank, if sometimes prejudiced. Whether such observations raise a smile or a frown is immaterial, for no aspect of life should be ignored or disguised. In *A Carmarthenshire Anthology* the witnesses are marshalled and allowed to have their say. Happily, the great majority sing a paean of praise, and the reader will be well content. Some extracts included are refreshingly given at length, so that not only is the book a source of 'lucky dips' for the random reader, but it will undoubtedly become a useful work of reference for scholars, an Open Sesame for our delectation, which it will be a joy to possess.

Francis Jones
November 1984

Introduction

The Character of Carmarthenshire

The magnificence of Carmarthenshire, extends from her proud abutting vans high in the east upon the Black Mountain, shouldering Breconshire and commanding views down over miles and acres in square meadows, bushy woodlands and winding river valleys to the estuaries at Loughor, Llanstephan and Laugharne – and the golden flats of Cefn Sidan and Pendine sands.

The horseshoe of brown hills that defends and encloses these milk-and-honey lands – by way of the Betws mountain and the Black – circling from Llanddeusant to the Sugar Loaf and Eppynt, the wild hills above Rhandirmwyn and Rhydcymerau, Mynydd Pencarreg and Mynydd Llanybydder, across to Trelech and down to Crymych, separates us from our Cardiganshire cousins and the strangers, our neighbours in Glamorgan and Brecon. Strangers too lie to the south and the west: the sea and Pembrokeshire – equally alien to the pastoral people of the interior, though having trading and tribal allegiances with the coastal people around Carmarthen Bay, including those of north Gower.

In fabulous times gone by, when the borders of Wales stretched beyond Cumbria to the lowlands of Scotland and Welsh was the language of the greater portion of the Island of Britain, a breed of Carmarthenshire men held sway whose gifts in leadership have seldom been equalled. We need to be fiercely proud of them.

Urien, whom we read about in Taliesin's poem of the sixth century, is said to have been a Knight of Arthur's table and the founder of a castle at Carreg Cennen. This is legend. That Rhodri Mawr (Roderick the Great) was at Dinefwr we know, and that his stature as a ruler is comparable with Alfred is self-evident. Hywel Dda, his grandson, 'head and glory of all the Britons', was the only British King to have deserved the accolade 'the Good', we may presume in recognition of his fair-mindedness and his humanity – as evidenced in the body of law he had formulated by the time of his death around 950 A.D., after consultation with the crowned heads of Europe.

> 'Hywel son of Cadell prince of all Wales saw the Welsh misusing the laws and called to him six men from every Cantref in Wales to the White House on Tâf. These were to be the wisest men in the realm, four of them laymen and the other two clerks. This was the reason for bringing the clerks: lest the laymen should set down anything that might be against the Holy Scripture.'

This Christian urbanity and sense of intellectualism was inherited by Rhys ap Tewdwr, Hywel's grandson, who was the last of the rulers of Deheubarth to style himself King. The eisteddfodau which Rhys proclaimed at Dinefwr, the royal palace of South Wales, and later at Cardigan, were *the* social and cultural event of the Celtic calendar. Poet/singers who came in peace from Ireland, Brittany, Cornwall and even the Hebrides, competed with the bards from all corners of Wales. They were entertained for forty days.

> 'Every dainty meat and drink, every disputation in wisdom, and every amusement of vocal and instrumental music was provided. He welcomed bards and minstrels and maintained all games of phantasy and illusion.'

A place in immortality would have been reserved for Rhys ap Tewdwr if only for his remarkable children. For them the chroniclers and the bards reserve an especial hyperbole. Princess Nest was possessed of a legendary beauty: so much so that it is said men came from far and wide and hid in the bushes for days to catch just a glimpse of her. She was brought up in Dinefwr's whispering groves and given in marriage to the castellan of Pembroke, Gerald de Windsor, at the age of thirteen. Comparisons can be made with Helen and Cleopatra. Her beauty was the cause of war. King Henry I of England fell in love with her and she bore him a son. Among her other offspring were the Geraldines who conquered Ireland – from whom the FitzGerald Kennedys, first men of the United States, claim descent. Her grandson was that outstanding historian and travel-writer Giraldus Cambrensis.

Nest's brother was Rhys ap Gruffudd, who became known as The Lord Rhys. As statesman and military tactician even in this august succession, there is no-one to compare with him. Exiled to Ireland as a boy, he returned to Ystrad Tywi and drove out the combined might of the English and the Normans, together with their native collaborators, and reached an accommodation with the King whereby, as justiciar of

Deheubarth, he held the balance of peace between the warring factions in the southern half of Wales until his death of the plague in 1197.

Never was more dismay felt or expressed by the princes' chroniclers or their bards than is apparent at the death of

> 'the man who was the head and the shield and the strength of the South and of all Wales and the hope and the defence of all the race of the Britons . . . conspicuous for the force of his mind . . . counsellor of the magnates, warlike against the strong, protection of the vanquished, assaulter of fortresses, attacker in battles, arrayer and ruler of armies, overthrower of hosts . . . the arm of prowess, the hand of generosity, the eye of reason, the light of worthiness, the height of magnamimity, the substance of might.'

Though Llewelyn and Owain Glyndŵr were to follow him in later generations, men from different tribes but cast in a similar mould to the Dinefwr men, there was to be, as it turned out, no holding the overwhelming opposition that threatened. With the death of Rhys there passed a glory, the era of the Kings of Deheubarth was truly over. The princes would not hold for long, their power divided; their nature divisiveness.

There was, however, one yet to come – to flare up like an afterglow – the fire having been kicked apart. Rhys Gryg had a spark of his father's warlike genius: Rhys Gryg, the hoarse, croak-voice, Rhys the stammerer. As some men of his class were wont to be preoccupied with going out after stags, wolves or foxes, Rhys left his bed most mornings for thirty years in pursuit of Normans. He burned castles and fought battles for a pastime. In one week all those on Gower he razed to the ground – including poor Swansea. Harassed by his brothers, nephews and cousins, he languished in dungeons, lost and regained castles and possessions as if in some great game of cards. Tenacious, he was a terrier of a man:

> Proud croak voice, with cruel dented sword
> Passionate in anger, harsh in battle
> Warmongering, blade-thrusting lion
> Bloody spear always at the slant.

Characteristically, he died wounded in battle. His years of aggressive roistering, of struggle to regain his castles in the Vale of Towy to shut out the Norman, over. Leading a host from the West they came under fire. He was in process of laying a three-month siege against Carmarthen where they had built a bailey bridge across the Towy. A naval force came up with the tide to demolish the bridge and the great and brave Rhys Gryg was struck by an arrow from an arrow-shower. They carried him to Dinefwr where he was attended by his physician, Rhiwallon of Myddfai, whose mother in legend was the Lady of the Lake of Llyn-y-Fan.

Rhys died. He lies in St David's Cathedral. In effigy he is a very little man, the great Rhys Gryg, son of Rhys ap Gruffudd, The Lord Rhys.

Such martial, back-bone qualities are not so fashionable today among our leaders, but it is as well not to forget that they are there in the breeding of Carmarthenshire people, famous though we are for mild manners, gentleness.

Llanelli people, they say, are the *nicest* people in the British Isles. Nowhere is the traveller's question generally met with kindlier helpfulness. In shops you are made to think that you and the assistant have spoken before. These are country people living in a town by the sea and, though fate has been cruel to them in recent years, there is little of that gritty cynicism in them that besmirches other industrial communities.

Laugharne people have a strange reputation in-land which infects, to a lesser extent, their neighbours in Pendine, Pembrey and even Burry Port where things have happened that outrage the chapel standards of the holy meadows. It is a whispered thing about women in men's caps and hob-nailed boots smoking pipes on the doorstep, of children with no known fathers, feuds, fights, secret burials: the curled lip, the tribal curse, the cover-up. Easy to blame the Irish, the Flemish, the French or the Armada, for none of it is true, not any longer. It is still talked about though, white-eyed in the lamplight or on the edges of funerals. Our prejudices are precious to us.

They say Llandovery is an Irish town; Llandeilo is snobby; the best view of Carmarthen is over your shoulder as you climb Llangunnor hill. Kidwelly is a place that was; Trelech is the end of the world. When you've seen the world and Betws you've seen the lot. You only go to Llanstephan to die; there's more of value underneath Ammanford than above ground. They say . . .

But there *is* a Carmarthenshire face and a Carmarthenshire voice. Some of the best language is spoken in Carmarthenshire and some of the worst. The talk in Carmarthen town can be as good as that of Dublin city. Dylan Thomas's voice was a Carmarthenshire voice, the voice of his ancestors through his father and his great uncle, the poet and preacher, Gwilym Marles. Some of Dylan's finest writing is tuned to his Carmarthenshire experience and his Carmarthenshire voice.

North of the Towy and into the hills facing Cardiganshire, the Welsh is like the honey off the heather. No wonder – if Glyn Cothi's ghost still roams there and if Dafydd ap Gwilym, as many say, came to Talley to rest 'above the shining waters'. Here, Williams Pantycelyn rode by to his house at Pentre Tŷ Gwyn composing those hymns for choirs of angels, while the Charles brothers from St Clears – and Howell Harris – charged with fire congregations of believers who knew they were listening to the language of heaven.

Gwenallt and D. J. Williams opened the chapters of their lives in Rhydcymerau and Llewelyn Williams's Llansadwrn, like Richard Vaughan's Llanddeusant, was alive to a conversational tradition which is at its best in narrative. There are country men in those hills today practically incapable of sustaining a conversation without. ''Rwy'n cofio 'slawer dydd, bachan,' I remember long ago, boy . . . and then the story rolls. It is an old, old tradition – naturally intellectual in approach – and theatrical. No wonder we have produced so many preachers, teachers, advocates, broadcasters, poets, writers, actors too . . . the wonder is we didn't produce more.

To live in Carmarthenshire is to have a sense of history: for it totally surrounds us. At every corner a castle or a tower or some ruin, once complete, stands in reminder of the great and of the infamous who have gone before. There *have* been some very wicked ones, too, people who need not be forgotten. We can boast cheats and murderers as black as any blaggard that walked. The Llandovery men who followed William Williams through the snow to assassinate the undoubtedly villainous William Powell were mainly led and blinded by a quirk of hero-worship still to be seen today in the agricultural community. A natural leader will ascend who decides the style of dress, the make of tractor and the price of cattle.

It is a pity that this leadership did not more often dictate a sense of taste in things visual, particularly architecture. There are few places outside Ireland where the natural beauty of farmhouses and cottages in the countryside is being more senselessly blemished than in rural Carmarthenshire today. Pebbledash (and worse) the 'nice little bungalow' and the double-glazing window, plastic doors and frames have played havoc in the last fifteen years. The men behind the Atcost barn, the tower silo, the hedge-flail, the JCB and chain-saw have a lot to answer for – as do the Forestry Commission. The face of this our most dear and beautiful county is being disfigured – by us. It would not be allowed elsewhere.

This visual illiteracy (or a dyslexia) is perhaps our most curious character fault. Surrounded as we are by so much natural beauty maybe we have no requirement to create our own. Our native painters too are few – Thomas Brigstocke, Morland and his father B. A. Lewis – all from Carmarthen – J. D. Innes, of Scots ancestry but a native of Llanelli, and Carey Morris, born into an artisan family in Llandeilo Fawr, are all we have to talk about and very little are they known in their native place. Surely, if its literature is the chief glory of a nation its art should share an equal glory too?

Politically Carmarthenshire has always been the most uproarious county. From the era of the Princes of Deheubarth to the present day the seat of government in London has needed to keep a watchful eye on marginal Carmarthen. Rhys ap Thomas defected and tilted Richard III at Bosworth in 1485, so bringing the Tudors into power and greatness to Britain. He was much rewarded but not much liked for it. Never was there an election quite like Sir William Paxton's in 1802 when £15,690.4.2d was spent on breakfasts, porter, ribbons and whisky. It did as much as anything, Old Sarum included, to usher in parliamentary democracy. Carmarthenshire has always been steadfastly radical and full of surprises. When Lady Megan Lloyd George won the seat for Labour, most of the older people thought they had cast a Liberal vote and when Gwynfor Evans won for Plaid Cymru in 1966 it was a triumph for originality.

The great estates now have broken up, all in our time. Most of the social goals of radical politics have been won. The struggle for individual freedom runs deep in the minds of the men and women of our county. The fighting spirit of Rhys ap Gruffudd and Rhys Gryg runs in the blood of our writers and thinkers. William Vaughan, the pioneer of that ill-fated migration to Newfoundland, saw a vision of individual and democratic opportunity. The educationalists Griffith Jones, Llanddowror, Madam Bevan and William Williams M.P. for Coventry were as one with the Methodists and the sisters of Rebecca who fought for spiritual, mental and economic freedom. Glory to them and those gentle fighters who reside in Merlin's fortress.

Lynn Hughes
September 2002

I

The Land
& Early People

1. CARMARTHENSHIRE

Carmarthen hills are green and low
And therealong the small sheep go
Whose voices to the valley come
At eve, when all things else are dumb.

Carmarthen hills do in their arms
Hold many quiet white-walled farms;
The cattle feed by Towy banks,
Silken, sleek, with dappled flanks.

And Towy river, men have said,
Is the loveliest river God has made.
From Twm Shon Catti's cave its way
Lies silver to Carmarthen Bay.

The roads between the villages
Are shy and shadowy with trees,
And every turn to left or right
Opes a new picture of delight.

And hazel boughs are everywhere,
And autumn time, if you go there,
On any roadside hedge you'll find
The brown nuts nodding to the wind.

Dudley G. Davies

2. *Old Red Sandstone*

The fossils of the Old Red Sandstone include the first vascular plants found in South Wales, and (in any number) the first fishes. In the Lower Old Red Sandstone jawless ostracoderms, in some ways comparable with living lampreys, reached their acme in a variety of armoured types. In the Upper Old Red Sandstone true bony fishes are found in diagnostic genera . . .

At Capel Horeb near Llangadock *Thallomia breconensis*, an early vascular plant showing well-preserved stomata, occurs in an interbedded lens of shale.

Overlooking rocks are dominantly red and fine-grained, and constitute the Downtonian Red Marls, over 2,000 ft. thick. In detail they are alternating mudstones, siltstones, and fine sandstones, many of the beds displaying current rippling and fine cross-bedding. Despite their red colour they contain occasional layers of fossils including brachiopods and molluscs, and many beds were reworked by scavengers and burrowers. Their general characteristics suggest they were deposited in the brackish waters of wide delta flats not far above sea-level, where waves and currents moulded the beds, and where periodic incursions of the sea allowed the formation of marine or near-marine intercalations. Towards or at the top of the group, and continuing for about 100 ft. into the overlying Ditton Series, impersistent bands of nodular and conglomeratic calcareous 'cornstones', probably the product of desiccation, are rich in fish remains, and as the *'Psammosteus'* Limestones (with *Traquairaspis* [*Psammosteus anglicus*]) form a widespread marker of great use in mapping.

Along the escarpment face of the Black Mountains, the Brecon Beacons, and the Fans the Red Marls are followed by a group of sandstones, reaching 2,000 to 3,000 ft. in thickness, that (like the Marls) persist with little change for many miles along their outcrop. They range from siltstones and flaggy mudstones to grits and some conglomerates, and they display a rhythmic alternation of coarse and fine beds through many hundreds of units that gives them a characteristic appearance in the scarp face. They fall into two distinct formations, the Senni Beds below, with dark green chloritic layers interbedded with red, and the Brownstones above, uniformly dark red and purple. The differences in colour may be due to a richer organic content in the Senni Beds, which have yielded not only the last of the pteraspids but also a flora of some variety including *Psilophyton, Dawsonites,* and *Gosslingia* – whereas the Brownstones have as yet yielded no fossils. In places the sequence above the Red Marls is uniformly brown or purple, and a lithologically recognisable group of Senni Beds cannot be distinguished from the Brownstones, probably because of lateral passage of green beds into brown.

T. Neville George.
British Regional Geography, H.M.S.O.
(Third Edition) 1975

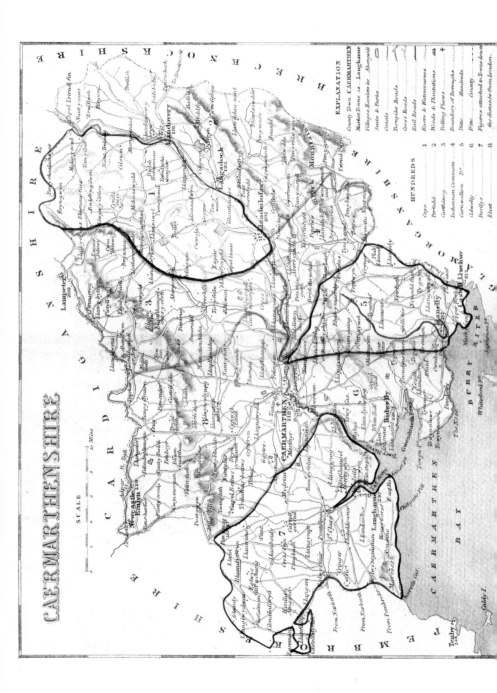

CAERMARTHENSHIRE

SCALE

10 Miles

EXPLANATION

County Town CAERMARTHEN
Market Towns as Laugharne
Villages Hamlets &c Aberystil
Seats & Parks
Canals
Turnpike Roads
Cross Roads
Rail Roads
Rivers & Watercourses
Woods & Plantations
Folding Places
Boundary of Boroughs
Ditto. Hundreds
Ditto. County
Figures attached to Towns denote
the distance from London.

HUNDREDS

1 Cayo
2 Perfeld
3 Carthinoy
4 Iscenmen Cemmaets
5 Carnwellon Do
6 Carwelly
7 Derllys
8 Elvet

BRECKNOCKSHIRE

CARDIGANSHIRE

GLAMORGANSHIRE

PEMBROKESHIRE

CAERMARTHEN BAY

BURRY RIVER

3. *Caermarden-shire*

Caermardenshire, so-called from the chief town *Caer-marden*, lieth bordered upon the North with Cardigan-shire; upon her East, by Brecknock and Glamorgan-shires; upon the South, with a Bay upon the British Seas; and upon the West with *Pembroke-shire*.

The form of this County is long, and shooteth itself from the Southwest into the North and by-East, betwixt whose furthest bounds are thirty-five *English* miles, and in her broadest part twenty; the whole in circumference about one hundred and two miles.

This Shire is not altogether so pestered with hills as her bordering neighbours are: and those that she hath, neither so high nor so thick and therefore is better for Corn and Pasturage, yea and in Woods also, so that for victuals this Country is very well stored, which the stomach does as well digest, the air being wholesome, temperate, and pleasing.

Anciently these parts were possessed by the *Dimetree as Ptolemie*, *Gildas*, and *Ninius* do name them: though *Plinie* holds opinion that they were part of the *Silures*, with whom no doubt they were subdued by the *Romans* yoke by *Julius Frontius*, when he struggled with the rocky hills in those southern parts. And this county is accounted by writers to be the very strength of South-Wales. In the West thereof, at *Killmanlloid* (as it should seem) their Legions kept, where lately an earthen Pot hoarded with store of *Roman Coins*, was by the spade digged up, being stamped upon imbased silver, from the time of *Commodus* unto the first *Tribuneship* of *Gordon* the third, which fell in the year of Christ two hundred and forty-three: and amongst these were the coins of *Helius Pertinax*, *Marcus Orellius*, *Antonius Diadumenius*, *Julius Versus Maximus*, the son of *Maximus of Coelius Balbinus*, of *Clodius Pupienus*, of *Aquilia Severa*, the wife of Heliogabalus, and of *Sall Barbia Orbiana*, pieces rarely found.

The commodities of this shire chiefly consist in Cattle, Pit-coal, Fowl and Sea-fish, whereof the salmon is common among them, and that of such greatness as no place is better furnished there-with than the shire-town of *Caer-marden* is.

Which Town by *Ptolemy* is called *Maridunum*; by *Antoine* the Emperor, *Muridunum*, by the *Britaines Caerfirdhin*; and by us *Caermarden*. It is pleasantly seated upon the South-west side of the River *Towy* that runneth thorow the middest of this Shire, and falleth South from hence into the *British Sea*, where before times was a convenient Haven for ships arrivage, but now is sore pestered with Sands and Shelves: notwithstanding some small vessels ascend up River, even unto the Bridge of this Town, being in circuit one thousand and four hundred paces. The inhabitants of this place do not a little glory in their *Merlin*, who (as they say) was therein born, the son of a bad Angel, or of an *Incubus* spirit, the *Britaines* great *Apollo*, whom *Geffrey ap Arthur* would rank with the *sooth-saying Seer*, or rather with the true *Prophets* themselves; being none other than a mere *Seducer* and *phantastical* Wizard, which howsoever *Alani de Insulis* in his commentaries hath laboured to unlock those dark and hidden Similes, wherewith his book is pestered and full, yet was it not without cause forbid the reading by the *Councell* of *Trent*, as vain, and not worthy of countenance or credit.

At the entrance of the *Normans*, this Town was brought under obedience, and for a long time was distressed with the calamities of war, yet afterwards was made by the *English* Princes the *Chancery* and *Exchequer* for all *South Wales*; and this day is yeerely governed by a *Mayor*, who ever after this is an *Alderman* and justice of the Peace, two *Sheriffs* elected out of sixteen *Burgesses*, all of them in skarlet, a sword bearer, a *Town-clerk*, and two *Sergeants* with *Maces*: from whence the *Pole* is raised 52 degrees 15 minutes in Latitude, and for Longitude is the degree 15 and 30 minutes from the first point in the West, according to Mercator.

East from this place are the ruins of *Carreg Castle*, which stood mounted on a high hill, under the which many vaults and spacious caves far into the ground are seen, wherein is thought the people unable to fight, were therein secured in time of their wars. Where also is a well.

This Shire is watered with twenty-eight Rivers and Riverets of name, strengthened with ten castles, traded in six Market Towns, divided into six hundreds, wherein are seated fourscore and seven Parish-Churches . . .

John Speed. *Atlas* 1611

4. *Llandeilo Flags*

Llandeilo flags, distinguished by the presence of the *Asaphus Buchii* and *A. tyrannus*, and underlying the great mass of Caradoc sandstone, are exhibited on the left banks of the rivers Sowdde and Towy below Llangadock. They extend thence by Tan-yr-allt, Pen-y-banc and Pomprenarreth, to the low hills of Pentref and Tir-wyn-fach, where they strike across the Towy, occurring in great force at Llandeilo and in Dynevor

Park. From Llandeilo to Caermarthen, this formation is seen on the right bank of the river, chiefly in detached and broken masses, near Llangathen and Llanegwad, the only places where I have detected the rock on the left bank being at Golden Grove and at Capel Dewi. Beyond the latter point the calcareous matter thins out, and does not reappear till we reach Clog-y-frain, on the borders of Pembrokeshire, though the course of the formation is traceable at intervals by its organic remains, as at Pensarn, &c., near Caermarthen.

By consulting the map, it will be seen that between Llangadock and Caermarthen, a space about fifteen miles in length, and from half a mile to two miles in width, these Llandeilo flags have been singularly thrown about with divergent strikes and reversed dips. At their north-eastern end a transverse section from Tan-yr-allt, to Blaen-dyffri-garn, passes over the low hills of Pen-coed, Pen-llan, and Tyr-y-garn, exposing beds of black calcareous flagstone, occasionally very pyritous, and more or less charged with trilobites, alternating with thickish bedded strata of grey, quartzose sandstone and dark shelly grits. These flagstones have a prevailing direction to the south-west, and dip in opposite directions, i.e. both north-west and south-east, at high angles. In following the strata to the south-west, they are subjected to several breaks, by one of which they are deflected to the north-north-west, or nearly at right angles to their prevailing strike; but they resume their south-westerly direction, and range with tolerable regularity along the western flanks of Cairn-goch and Carreg-cegin, plunging at one or two spots at high angles beneath the overlying sandstone. At Pompren-arreth, the subordinate beds of grit thinning out, the blackflags and shale are exposed in a thickness of nearly half a mile in highly inclined strata, (70° to 80°) on the banks of the brook, extending eastward to the waterfall. Many casts of trilobites occur in these beds, and also bands of stone sufficiently calcareous to be burnt for lime.

The prevailing strike is here 30° south of west, whilst at Pentref and Tyr-wyn-fach, only one mile nearer Llandeilo, beds charged with the same trilobites, are wrenched from the prevailing strike and range, in vertical positions to the west, and even 10° north of west. If we trace the beds to the westward across the valley of the Towy, we again meet with them greatly developed at Llandeilo, but in the very first ledge on the eastern side of the town they recover their south-westerly strike. This direction is however maintained a very short distance, for in the space occupied by even the high road, the same beds are broken off and trend on one side to the west, dipping 80° to the north, or nearly at *right angles* to the beds observed upon the other. In most of the quarries in and about Llandeilo, the number of dislocations to which the flags have been subjected is truly surprising, the strata being for the most part in vertical or highly inclined positions. In one of the chief quarries of Dynevor park, the beds are thrown so completely out of the prevailing direction, as to strike E.S.E. and W.N.W., dipping 70° N.N.E., whilst in Bird's Hill they bend round from 15° W. of N. to true *N.W.*, S.E., though in the Llangathen and Grongar Hills, the old strike of N.E., S.W. is resumed. In fact the beauty of Dynevor Park depends upon these dislocations, by which the surface has been diversified and thrown into separate knolls now wooded to their summits.

The prevailing flagstone, in beds from two to four inches thick, is dark-grey or indigo colour when extracted, but it weathers to a light ashen hue, the surface being in some parts covered with a profusion of casts of the *Asaphus Buchii*, other organic remains being rare. The calcareous flags are very generally traversed by veins of white calcareous spar, from one-tenth to half an inch wide, which usually divide the beds into rhomboids. These flags occasionally, as at Grüg, about three quarters of a mile north-west of Llandeilo, pass down into thicker masses of sub-crystalline, dark, impure lime-stone, having an east and west strike, and a dip of 45° to the north. They contain encrinites, a few casts of shells, *Asaphus Buchii* and *A. tyrannus*. The beds have a corrugated surface, due to the mass being composed of small irregular concretions, and this structure is partly occasioned by the unequal dissemination of sand and even of small pebbles in the calcareous matrix. The true flag-like structure of the Llandeilo flags is not discernible in any of these beds. The Grüg quarries exhibit the oldest calcareous beds of this formation, as they lie to the west and north-west of the flags, and the same nodular limestones occur in Llangathen and Grongar Hills in similar positions, rising from beneath the younger strata and graduating on their western flanks into the rotten slates and greywacke grits of the inferior or Cambrian System, in which (in this district) all traces of fossils are lost.

To the south-west and west of Llandeilo the flagstones are found on both banks of the Towy in distorted masses, none of which have a continuous strike for more than a few hundred paces. Below galena diverge from the chief mass, to the sides of the rider quartz rock; and a rich bunch of ore was worked out on its opposite or south-eastern face.

The red vein is further removed from the rider rock, and has its name from the lead being coated with the hydrate of iron. At the spot where this vein was cut by the comet vein, the ore thickened for a short distance to six feet, much exceeding the average width of this and the other veins. Besides these principal veins there are several cross lodes.

In one part of the works the ore is found in apparently regular beds, forming thin laminæ in a true greywacke grit, composed of small pebbles of quartz and felspar, with a base of black slate. These beds, some of which are metalliferous and others not, have an united thickness of forty to fifty feet, and dip away from the rider rock or the north-west, at an angle of about 25°. Their position is between the red and the comet veins.

The levels enter the hill about 500 feet above the adjoining valley of the Towy, and the most extensive are from 1,000 to 1,200 feet in length. These works are effectually drained by an adit, whose mouth is a little above the rivulet at the base of the hill; and from which is a constant flow of ferruginous water.

Here, as in the country of Shelve, are remains considered to have been Roman mines, which, having been placed upon the steepest side of the hill, and where the ore probably cropped out, were, it is conceived, worked by water? (See further observations below, on the Roman mines of Gogo-fau.)

It is quite evident that mines, situated like those of Nant-y-moen, where vertical shafts or steam-engines are not required, the whole being drained by an adit, must always be of high value, and accordingly I found the works in full activity in 1833, a period when, from the low price of lead, so many mines had necessarily been abandoned.

The ore of Nant-y-moen is for the most part of excellent quality, the varieties called 'potter's ore' and 'steel ore' being abundant, as well as 'small ore', a mixture of the two former.

R. I. Murchison. *The Silurian System* 1839

5. *Dyer Criticism*

The vale of Towy is still less a scene of cultivation than that of Usk. The woodland views are more frequent; and the whole more wild, and simple . . .

In this vale, the river Towy, tho it frequently met us, and always kept near us; yet did not so constantly appear, and bear us such close company, as the Usk had done before. Some heights too we ascended; but such heights as were only proper stands, from whence we viewed in greater perfection the beauties of the vale.

This is the scene, which Dyer celebrated, in this poem of *Grongar-hill*. Dyer was bred a painter; and had here a picturesque subject: but he does not give us so good a landscape, as might have been expected. We have no where a complete, formed distance; tho it is the great idea suggested by such a vale as this: no where any touches of that beautiful obscurity, which melts a variety of objects into one rich whole. Here and there, we have a few *accidental* strokes, which belong to distance; tho seldom masterly: I call them *accidental*; because they are not employed in producing a landscape; nor do they in fact unite in any such idea; but are rather introductory to some moral sentiment; which, however good in itself, is here forced, and mistimed.

(*Dinevawr-castle*) also is taken notice of by Dyer in his *Grongar-hill*; and seems intended as an object in a distance. But *his* distances, I observed, are all in confusion; and indeed it is not easy to separate them from his foregrounds.

The landscape he gives us, in which the castle of Dinevawr makes a part, is seen from the brow of a distant hill. The first object, that meets his eye, is a wood. It is just beneath him; and he easily distinguishes the several trees, of which it is composed:

> The gloomy pine, the poplar blue,
> The yellow beech, the sable yew,
> The slender fir, that taper grows,
> The sturdy oak, with broad-spread boughs.

This is perfectly right: objects so near the eye should be distinctly marked. What next strikes him, is a *purple-grove*; that is, I presume, a grove, which has gained its *purple-hue* from distance. This is, no doubt, very just colouring; tho it is here, I think, introduced rather too early in the landscape. The blue, and purple tints belong chiefly to the most removed objects; which seem not here to be intended. Thus far however I should not greatly cavil.

William Gilpin. *Observations on the River Wye and Several Parts of South Wales* 1770

6. ABODE OF RAVEN AND TOAD – DYNEVOR

Gaudy as the op'ning dawn,
Lies a long and level lawn
On which a dark hill, steep and high,
Holds and charms the wand'ring eye!
Deep are his feet in Towy's flood,
His sides are cloath'd with waving wood,
And ancient towers crown his brow,
That cast an aweful look below;
Whose ragged walls the ivy creeps,
And with her arms from falling keeps;
So both a safety from the wind
On mutual dependence find.
'Tis now the raven's bleak abode;
'Tis now th' apartment of the toad;
And there the fox securely feeds;
And there the pois'nous adder breeds
Conceal'd in ruins, moss and weeds;
While, ever and anon, there falls
Huge heaps of hoary moulder'd walls.
Yet time has seen, that lifts the low,
And level lays the lofty brow,
Has seen this broken pile compleat,
Big with the vanity of state;
But transient is the smile of fate!
A little rule, a little sway,
A sun beam in a winter's day,
Is all the proud and mighty have
Between the cradle and the grave.

John Dyer, from *Grongar Hill*

7. *Cockshot Rock and High-grade Anthracite*

Proceeding through Brynamman and taking the road to Llangadog (A4069), one begins the long ascent of the Black Mountains. Approaching the locality it is worth pausing and looking back to see the marked hollow of the softer lower half of the Coal Measures, with the harder Pennant sandstones forming the plateaux to the south. Within the main hollow a subsidiary ridge (between Brynaman and Gwaun-Cae-Gurwen) is due to a thin but tough quartzite band called 'the Cockshot Rock'. The lower coals of this region and others further west in Carmarthenshire are high-grade anthracite coals. These have a very high carbon (and a low volatile) content, the gases having been largely driven off. Heat is believed to be the chief mechanism in the formation of anthracite, but the source of that heat is the subject of several conflicting theories. One theory says there is an igneous mass beneath this part of the coalfield. The presence of mineral veins (copper, lead and zinc) near Carmarthen and Kidwelly is cited as support for this theory. Another theory attributes the extra heat to the 'load' of higher Coal Measure strata above the rocks now seen. It is suggested that there was once another 8,000 feet of Coal Measures above those of this north-western portion of the coalfield. The third theory attributes the heat to friction caused by thrusting along the Carreg Cennen Disturbance. This frictional heat would affect those coals of the coalfield nearest to the thrust plane, that is the coals of the north-western portion of the main coalfield.

T. R. Owen, *Geology Explained in South Wales*

8. *Carmarthenshire's Parts*

Reckoned in early mediaeval terms, therefore, Carmarthenshire includes (i) Ystrad Tywi, but without Gower; (ii) Emlyn Uch Cuch, i.e. above the river Cuch; and (iii) Y Cantref Gwarthaf, i.e. the upper-most cantref of Dyfed, but without Efelffre. Of these, the second, being itself a commote, underwent no sub-division, but the other two were divided into a number of smaller units. At some period previous to the Norman Conquest, Ystrad Tywi properly so called was separated into Y Cantref Mawr and Y Cantref Bychan, i.e. the Great and the Little Cantref, two names which point clearly to an original unity broken up for convenience of administration. The course of the river Towy, from Ystrad Ffin to Abergwili, was adopted as the dividing line, a boundary which could cause no confusion or dispute, save for the vagaries of a stream which, flowing over alluvial flats, was liable without warning to change its bed in time of flood. Cantref Mawr (the article was usually dropped) answered well to its name; it stood high among the cantrefs of Wales, both in its area and in the number of its commotes; Cantref Bychan was only small by comparison with its neighbour, and stretched along the south bank of the Towy for some forty miles. Both names appear in the oldest portions of the *Liber Landavensis*, and the evidence is that both were well established and generally known in the reign of Henry I.

In addition to these two cantrefs, Ystrad Tywi was generally assigned a third. Had we only the testimony of the lists upon which to depend, we might suspect an artificial arrangement, made by the compilers for their convenience. But, in two passages in the oldest portion of the Mabinogion, Ystrad Tywi is said to contain three cantrefs, so that the association of a third district with the Great and the Little Cantref must be regarded as of long standing. Suspicion, however, rests upon its name, as given in two of the lists, viz., Cantref Eginog. This form is nowhere else to be found, and certainly had no popular currency.

About the time of the Norman Conquest, Cantref Mawr was divided into the seven commotes of Mallaen, Caeo, Maenor Deilo, Cetheiniog, Widigada, Mabelfyw, and Mabudrud. In the Pipe Roll of Henry I for the year 1130, there appears under 'Chærmerdin' a certain 'Blehien de Mabuderi', from which it may safely be inferred that the sevenfold division had by that time been carried through. The same conclusion is suggested by the statement of Giraldus Cambrensis that, in the reign of Henry I, Gruffydd ap Rhys, lineal heir to the kingdom of South Wales, had been reduced to the single commote of Caeo in Cantref Mawr. Thereafter, the commotes played a leading part in the history of the country, and it will be well to indicate more precisely their situation.

Mallaen was the easternmost of the seven, and extended from Fforest yr Esgob (which was in Ceredigion) to the church of Llanwrda. It corresponded to the present parishes of Cilycwm and Llanwrda, together with the township of Ystrad (in full, Ystrad Mynys), which, although in the parish of Llandingad, is situated on the right bank of the Towy, and thus fell within the limits of Cantref Mawr. The names of 'Mynydd Mallaen' and 'Rhiw Mallaen' still perpetuate the memory of this commote. It was a wild, remote region, thickly forested, and typical of those wooded fastnesses in which the men of Cantref Mawr successfully defied the foreign invader. To the west lay the commote of Caeo, with a name derived, it may be, from the personal name Cai. This included the parishes of Llansawel and Cynwyl Gaeo (so called to distinguish it from Cynwyl Elfed), with the township of Mynachty (a grange of Talley Abbey) in the parish of Llanycrwys. The name would seem to be of long standing in this region; there was a Caer Gaeo, not far from Pumsant, which is mentioned in the *Liber Landavensis*, and in the Black Book of Carmarthen one of the traditional graves of ancient warriors is located 'in the Plain fo Caeo' (*ig gwestedin caeav*).

When we come to Maenor Deilo, we reach the heart of Ystrad Tywi and the seat of its historic capital. It comprised the parishes of Llansadwrn, Talley, and Llandyfeisant, with as much of the parish of Llandeilo as lay on the north side of the Towy. The name was obviously taken from that of the hamlet or township of Maenor Deilo, in the parish of Llandeilo, which lay between the Towy and the eastern Dulais, in the neighbourhood of Capel Bach (or Capel Isaf).

Sir J. E. Lloyd, *A History of Carmarthenshire*

9. *Ossiferous Caves*

Without doubt the most interesting ossiferous cave in West Wales is the Coygan, near Laugharne, in Carmarthenshire. It is excavated from an outlying hill of mountain limestone, which stands about a mile from the sea, flat marsh land and sand burrows intervening. There can be little doubt that in comparatively recent days the sea washed the foot of this hill. The entrance to the Coygan is extremely low and narrow, but soon opens out into a lofty and extensive chamber. So far as I know there has been no discovery of Neolithic remains in this cave. It was deemed by the late Professor Rolleston to be the most perfect instance of a hyæna den he had met with. We found hyæna bones in position, and their coprolites in great quantities, apparently as fresh as though they had been voided recently; the other remains were similar to those found in Black Rock and Caldy, but were more plentiful, in good condition, and much scored by teeth marks.

In addition to these ordinary cave bones, I had the good fortune to find under rhinoceros bones which were overlaid by stalagmite a piece of bone, whittled and rounded into the shape of an awl, lying alongside of two flint flakes, one of which had indubitably been manipulated, the other was a pebble which had been broken, whether by natural or artificial means it is impossible to say; these are in the Tenby Museum, and constitute the sole proof of the presence of Pleistocene man in West Wales discovered by me.

A second cave not far from this was laid open in 1858. The bones on the surface were recklessly destroyed, but fortunately a fall of *debris* prevented the floor being broken up, and it was afterwards examined by Professor Boyd Dawkins. He obtained numerous bones and teeth of young wolves representing a litter, and two metatarsals of bisons cemented together into a compact mass. The Rev. G. N. Smith and myself dug from the same source lion, mammoth, rhinoceros (*tichorinus*), horse, hippopotamus, wild boar, Irish elk, red deer, reindeer, and *bos primigenius*. I saw no trace of coprolites, but still from the tooth-marks on some of the bones am disposed to think that it was a wild beasts' den in Pleistocene times. Professor Boyd Dawkins's young wolves would surely have been dispersed had they been carried into the cave by a torrent. I found no Neolithic remains; but as they would have been on the surface, they may have been shovelled overboard when the cave was discovered in 1858.

Edward Laws. *Little England Beyond Wales* 1888

10. *Caermarden-shire*

Caermarden-shire, is plenteous enough in Corn, stored abundantly with Cattaile and in some places yieldeth pit coal for fewell. On the East side it is limited with Glamorgan and Brecknock-shires, on the West with Pembrock-shire, on the North with Cardigan-shire severed by the river Tivie, running between, and on the South with the Ocean, which with so great a Bay or Creek getteth within the Land, that this Country seemeth as it were for very feare to have shrunk back, and withdrawn itself more inwardly.

Upon this Bay, Kidwelly first offereth itself to our sight, the Territory whereof, Keinai the Scot his sonnes held for a time, until they were driven out by Cuneda the Britan. But now it is counted part of the inheritance of the Duchy of Lancaster by the heiress of Maurice of London or de Londres: who making an out-road hither out of Glamorganshire, after a dangerous war made himself Lord hereof, and fortified old Kidwelly with a wall and castle to it, which now for very age is grown to decay and standeth, as it were, forlet and forlorne. For, the inhabitants having passed over the little river Vendraeth Vehan, built a new Kidwelly, enticed thither by the commodity of the haven; which notwithstanding at this day being choked with shelves and bars, is at this present, no great use. Whiles Maurice of London invaded these Parts, *Guenliana* the wife of Prince Gruffin, a stout and resolute woman in

the highest degree, to recover the losses and declining state of her husband, came with displayed banner into the field and fiercely assailed him, but the success not answerable to her courage, she with her son *Morgan* and other men of especial note (as Girald recordeth) was slain in battle. By *Hawis* or *Avis* the daughter and heir of Sir Thomas of London: this passing fair and large patrimony, together with the title of Lord of Ogucon and Kidwelly came unto Patrick Chaworth, and by his son Patrich's daughter, unto Henry Earl of Lancaster . . . A few miles beneath Kidwelly, the River *Tovie*, which *Ptolomy* calleth *Tobius* falleth into the sea, after he hath passed through this region from North-East to South, first by *Lanadiffry*, so called, as men think, of Rivers meeting together, which *Hoel* the sone of *Rhese* overthrew for malice that he bare unto the English: then by *Dinevor*, a princely Castle, standing aloft upon the top of an hill, and belonging unto the Princes of South Wales whiles they flourished: and last of all by *Caer Marden* which the Britans themselves call *Caer-Firdhin*, *Ptolomy* Maridunum, *Antonine Muridunum*, who endeth his journeys there, and through negligence of the transcribers is in this place not well used. For they have confounded the *Journeys* from *Galena* to *Isca*, and from *Maridunum* to *Viriconum*. This is the chief City of the Country, for meadows and woods pleasant, and in regard of antiquity to be respected; compassed about very properly, as Giraldus saith, with brick walls, which are partly yet standing upon the famous river *Tovie*, able to bear small ships, although there now be a bar of sand cast up against the very mouth thereof.

William Camden, *Britannia*

11. *Daughters*

A daughter, after she is baptised, until she is seven years old, is not entitled to take an oath. From when she is born until she is twelve years old it is right for her to be at her father's platter. From twelve years old on, her breasts and pubic hair develop and she menstruates, and she is then of age to be given to a husband; and from then on, even if she does not take a husband she is entitled to control what is hers, and it is not right for her to be at her father's platter unless he himself wishes it. And the father is not bound to pay amobr for his daughter unless he is himself her bestower, for every bestower of a woman is bound to pay her amobr unless he takes sureties for paying it from him to whom she is given. If it happens that a woman is taken clandestinely from her father's house to another house, and there slept with, the man of that house is bound to pay her amobr, unless he takes sureties from the man who took her clandestinely.

At twelve years old it is right for a woman to menstruate, as we have said above. And from twelve to fourteen years old it is right that she should not become pregnant, and from fourteen until she is forty it is right for her to conceive, and from then on galanas does not fall on her and she gives no oath that she will not have children, since it is undoubted that she will not.

Hywel Dda, The Law †

12. *Dialects*

Use of the voiceless consonants p, t, c, for intervocalic b, d, g, as in *bwpach* (bwbach), *oti* (ydyw), *rhacor* (rhagor), extends almost as far west as the Glamorgan county boundary. Isolated instances of this change occur in the Aman Valley, as in the words *eclws* (eglwys), *llytrew* (llwydrew), and *cardetwyn* (cardydwyn). The dialect of East Carmarthenshire, however, is essentially Central-Southern; Gwentian features were introduced recently, when a closer connection was established between the Aman Valley and West Glamorgan with the development of coal-mining. The immigration of tinplate workers from the Swansea Valley in the last quarter of the nineteenth century had a similar slight effect on the dialect.

The Demetian dialect of West Carmarthen has been modified considerably by contact with Central-Southern, though there are marked distinctions between it and the latter. The tendency to drop final consonants as in *gily* (gilydd), *angla* (angladd), *llony* (llonydd), which may be due to rapid articulation of words in combination, peculiarities in vowel and consonant changes such as the change of *y* into *w* as in *cwmryd* (cymryd), *cwmint* (cymaint), and the use of dental for labial in certain words such as *twddu* (tyfu), *plwyddi* (plwyfi), *addanc* (afanc), are general features of Demetian. In Pembrokeshire, South Cardiganshire, and the extreme west of Carmarthenshire there are other phonetic developments, such as *we* for *oe*, as in *wes* (oes), *crwes* (croes), i for y, as in *cifoeth* (cyfoeth), *mini* (mynydd), and w for f, as in *cewn* (cefn), *llawnu* (llyfnu), which are not frequently heard in districts speaking Modified Demetian.

---

† (throughout book) denotes translation. A key to the translators appears on page 433.

A peculiar phenomenon of the dialect of Llanelly and the neighbouring villages of Llwynhendy, Llangennech, and Hendy is the use of the third person in familiar conversation. This practice also occurs, though less generally, in the west of the county around Llanboidy and Trelech. In Carmarthen town and the surrounding districts there is a marked tendency for the accent to fall on the ultima in words like *yno*, *yna*, *yma*, *yco* and consequently the final vowel is lengthened and the pitch of the voice rises. A distinctive feature of the dialect to the west of Pumsaint and as far north as Tregaron is the obscure y in *hyn*, *grym*, *tyst* and other monosyllabic words.

Various agencies for the anglicisation of the language have been active at different periods. Carmarthen is a typical example of a castle town which has been under foreign influence since the twelfth century, and has remained, to a great extent, alien in outlook and sympathy to this day. In later years, the establishment of educational institutions on English models and the resultant growth of a peculiar notion that the mother tongue was a social handicap have had the same effect. The extension of railways during the nineteenth century through territories which were hitherto purely Welsh has introduced a definite anglicising factor into the life of towns such as Whitland and Llandovery, whilst the immigration of Englishmen from Lancashire and elsewhere into the mining valleys of East Carmarthenshire and the general effects of industrialisation have likewise weakened native culture considerably. Loss of old descriptive and expressive words and phrases, and ruthless borrowing of English ones in their place, mark a decline of vitality in the spoken language.

Along the coastline from Pendine to Laugharne English is the native tongue, where it was introduced by Teutonic invaders early in the twelfth century. This English settlement is an extension of that of South Pembrokeshire. The Gower Peninsula was colonised about the same time, and linguistic evidence favours the supposition that the settlers there and in South Pembrokeshire were of common origin. A third settlement was made in the extreme south-east of Ireland, where specimens of the same dialect [Iola] can still be collected.

These settlements must be regarded as early Teutonic colonies, which succeeded in ousting the Welsh from their native territory. There remained, however, a sprinkling of the Welsh interspersed with the foreign settlers, who left traces of their language in the new tongue. Innumerable words in common use in this dialect of English are borrowed from Welsh, and a detailed study of the prevailing Welsh element would be work of historical importance, as well as linguistic interest . . .

In phonology and vocabulary, the English spoken in each of these settlements is similar. The people speak rapidly and in falsetto; there is a tendency to broaden the vowels, and the use of initial z for s, and v for f is significant. It was thought that the language was derived from Flemish, and brought to Wales by Flemings who had settled in England sufficiently long to acquire the English tongue. Analysis of glossaries of the dialect tends to prove that comparatively few words are definitely Flemish or Low German in origin. The dialect is similar in many respects to Southern English, as spoken across the Bristol Channel.

The outlook of the people through the centuries was seaward. Their maritime activities established contacts for the purposes of trade and commerce with English and foreign parts. Such an intercourse must have had its influence on the life of this foreign colony, though it does not appear to have produced at any period a strong stimulus to mental or spiritual awakening. Intellectually and culturally, these settlements remained largely in isolation, whilst their life was separated from that of the neighbouring Welsh by an artificial boundary, resulting from a deep consciousness of wide national differences.

T. Gwynn Jones, *A History of Carmarthenshire*

13. FROM THE TOP OF THE BLACK MOUNTAIN

There below the Cuckoo Bend the God-head is measured,
His chapter of grasslands divided by hedgerows
Nurturing a variety of greenery in verse-field and verse-field,
Enjoying the luxury of boundaries for once.

Beyond, His gospel in the county fatlands
Presses its sufficiency beneath the horizon.
This is the land of Dewi, Tybie, and Teilo,
The mature Deheubarth of their indivisible harmony.

But the boy in me wants to leap on the mountains
And stride the hills to Aman unchecked
To fondle my loved one's locks with my soul
And ravish her with my coming, as a roe or a young hart.

Derec Llwyd Morgan †

II

Some Legends, Folklore & Customs

1. *The Lady of the Lake, the Legend of Llyn-y-van Fach*

When the eventful struggle made by the Princes of South Wales to preserve the independence of their country was drawing to its close in the twelfth century, there lived at Blaensawdde near Llanddeusant, Carmarthenshire, a widowed woman, the relict of a farmer who had fallen in those disastrous troubles.

The widow had an only son to bring up, and Providence smiled upon her, and, despite her forlorn condition, her live stock had so increased in course of time that she could not well depasture them upon her farm, so she sent a portion of her cattle to graze on the adjoining Black Mountain, and their most favourite place was near the small lake called Llyn-y-van Fach, on the North Western side of the Carmarthenshire Vans.

The son grew up to manhood, and was generally sent by his mother to look after the cattle on the mountain. One day, to his great astonishment, he beheld, sitting on the unruffled surface of the water, a Lady; one of the most beautiful creatures that mortal eyes ever beheld, her hair flowed gracefully over her shoulders, the tresses of which she arranged with a comb, whilst the glassy surface of the water served for the purpose of a mirror. Suddenly she beheld the young man standing on the brink of the lake, with his eyes on her, and unconsciously offering to her the provision of barley bread and cheese with which he had been provided when he left his home.

Bewildered by a feeling of love and admiration for the object before him, he continued to hold out his hand towards the lady, who imperceptibly glided near to him, but gently refused the offer of his provisions. He attempted to touch her, but she eluded his grasp, saying

Cras dy fara!	Hard baked is thy bread!
Nid hawdd fy nala.	'Tis not easy to catch me.

and immediately dived under the water, and disappeared, leaving the love stricken youth to return home, a prey to disappointment.

The young man told his mother about the extraordinary vision he had seen. She advised him to take some unbaked dough or 'toes' the next time in his pocket, as there must have been some spell connected with the hard baked bread, or 'Bara cras' which prevented his catching the lady.

Next morning, before the sun had touched the peaks of the Vans, the young man was at the lake, not for the purpose of looking after his mother's cattle, but looking for the same enchanting vision he had witnessed the day before.

Hours passed on, the wind was hushed, and the clouds which had enveloped the mountain had vanished, when to his inexpressible delight, the object of his search again appeared to him as before, and seemed much more beautiful than when he first beheld her. His hand was again held out to her, with the unbaked bread, which she refused, saying,

Llaith dy fara!	Unbaked is thy bread!
Ti ni fynna'.	I will not have thee.

Next his mother suggested that his bread should this time be but lightly baked, as most likely to please the mysterious being.

The following day his vigil at the lake lasted till evening when, to his astonishment, he beheld several cows walking along its surface, with the lake maiden following behind them.

As she approached the land, he rushed to meet her in the water. On this occasion she did not refuse the moderately baked bread he offered her; and after some persuasion she consented to become his bride, on condition that they should only live together until she received from him three blows without a cause

Tri ergyd diachos.	Three causeless blows.

And if he ever should happen to strike her three such blows, she would leave him for ever. To such conditions he readily consented, and would have consented to any other stipulation, had it been proposed, as he was only intent on then securing such a lovely creature for his wife.

Thus the lady of the lake was engaged to become the young mortal man's wife, and having loosed her hand for a moment, she darted away and dived into the lake.

Soon there emerged out of the lake *two* most beautiful ladies accompanied by a hoary headed man of noble mien and extraordinary stature, but having otherwise all the force and strength of youth. This man addressed the bewildered youth, in accents calculated to soothe his troubled mind, saying that as he proposed to marry one of this daughters, he consented to the union provided the young man could distinguish which of the two ladies before him was the object of his affections. This was no easy task as the maidens were such perfect counterparts of each other, that it seemed quite impossible for him to choose his bride, and if perchance he fixed upon the wrong one, all would be for ever lost.

Whilst the young man narrowly scanned the two ladies, he could not perceive the least difference between the two, and was almost giving up the task in despair, when one of them thrust her foot a slight degree forward. The motion, simple as it was, did not escape the observation of the youth, and he discovered a trifling variation in the mode with which their sandals were tied . . .

'Thou hast chosen rightly,' said her father, 'be to her a kind and faithful husband, and I will give her, as a dowry, as many sheep, cattle, goats, and horses, as she can count of each, without heaving or drawing in her breath. But remember that if you prove unkind to her at any time, and strike her three times without a cause, she shall return to me and shall bring all her stock back with her.'

The young couple were soon married, and afterwards went to reside at a farm called Esgair Llaethdy, somewhat more than a mile from the village of Myddvai, where they lived in prosperity and happiness for several years, and became the parents of three sons.

There was a christening to take place in the neighbourhood, to which the parents were specially invited. When the day arrived the wife appeared very reluctant to attend the christening, alleging that the distance was too great for her to walk. Her husband tauntingly tapped her shoulder, saying 'go! go!' (*dos, dos*) when she reminded him of the understanding upon which she consented to marry him: that he was not to strike her without a cause; and warned him to be more cautious for the future.

On another occasion when they were together at a wedding, in the midst of the mirth and hilarity of the assembled guests, who had gathered together from all the surrounding country, she burst into tears and sobbed most piteously. Her husband touched her on her shoulder and enquired the cause of her weeping. She said 'now people are entering into trouble, and your troubles are likely to commence as you have the *second* time stricken me without a cause.

Years passed on, and their children had grown up, and were particularly clever young men. In the midst of so many wordly blessings at home the husband almost forgot that there remained only *one* causeless blow to be given to destroy the whole of his happiness and prosperity.

It however so happened that one day they were together at a funeral, where, in the midst of the mourning and grief at the house of the deceased, she appeared in the highest and gayest spirits, and indulged in immoderate fits of laughter, which so shocked her husband that he touched her saying 'Hush! Hush! don't laugh.' She said that she laughed 'because people when they die go out of trouble,' and, rising up, she went out of the house, saying, 'The last blow has been struck, our marriage contract is broken, and at an end! Farewell!' Then she started off towards Esgair Llaethdy, where she called her cattle and other stock together, each by name. The cattle she called thus:

Mu wlfrech, Moelfrech,	Brindled cow, white speckled,
Mu olfrech, Gwynfrech,	Spotted cow, bold freckled,
Pedair cae tonn-frech,	The four field sward mottled,
Yr hen wynebwen	The old white-faced,
A'r las Geigen,	And the grey Geigen,
Gyda'r Tarw Gwyn	With the White Bull,
O lys y Brenin;	From the court of the King;
A'r llo du bach,	And the little black calf
Sydd ar y bach,	Tho' suspended on the hook,
Dere dithau, yn iach adre!	Come thou also, quite well home!

They all immediately obeyed the summons of their mistress, even the little black calf which had been slaughtered, became alive again and walked off with the rest of the stock at the command of the Lady. This happened in the spring of the year, and there were four oxen ploughing in one of the fields, to these she cried,

Pedwar eidion glas	The four grey oxen,
Sydd ar y maes,	That are on the field,
Deuwch chwithau	Come you also
Yn iach adre!	Well home!

Away the whole of the livestock went with the Lady across Myddvai Mountain, towards the lake from whence they came, a distance of above six miles, where they disappeared beneath its waters, leaving no trace behind except a well marked furrow, which was made by the plough the oxen drew after them into the lake, and which remains to this day as a testimony to the truth of this story.

The sons, it is stated, often wandered about the lake and its vicinity, hoping that their mother might be permitted to visit the face of the earth once more, as they had been apprised of her mysterious origin.

Once, at a place near Dôl Howel, at the Mountain Gate, still called Llidiart y Meddygon, The Physicians' Gate, the mother appeared suddenly, and accosted her eldest son, whose name was Rhiwallon, and told him that his mission on earth, was to be a benefactor to mankind by relieving them from pain and misery, through healing all manner of their diseases; for which purpose she furnished him with a bag full of Medical Prescriptions and instructions for the preservation of health. That by strict attention thereto, he and his family would become for many generations the most skilful Physicians in the country. Then promising to meet him when her counsel was most needed, she vanished. But on several occasions she met her sons near the banks of the lake, and once she even accompanied them on their return home as far as a place still called Pant-y-Meddygon, The Dingle of the Physicians, where she pointed out to them the various plants and herbs which grew in the dingle, and revealed to them their medicinal qualities or virtues, and the knowledge she imparted to them, together with their unrivalled skill soon caused them to attain such celebrity that none ever possessed before them. And in order that their knowledge should not be lost, they wisely committed the same to writing, for the benefit of mankind throughout all ages.

And so ends the story of the Physicians of Myddvai, which has been handed down from one generation to another, thus:

Yr hen ŵr llwyd o'r cornel,	The grey old man in the corner,
Gan ei dad a glywodd chwedel,	Of his father heard a story,
A chan ei dad fe glywodd yntau	Which from his father he had heard,
Ac ar ei ôl mi gofiais innau.	And after them I have remembered.

Rhiwallon and his sons became Physicians to Rhys Gryg, Lord of Llandovery and Dynevor Castles, 'who gave them rank, lands, and privileges at Myddvai for their maintenance in the practice of their art and science, and the healing and benefit of those who should seek their help,' thus affording to those who could not afford to pay, the best medical advice and treatment, gratuitously.

Of the above lands bestowed upon the Meddygon, there are two farms in Myddvai parish still called Llwyn Ifan Feddyg, the Grove of Evan the Physician; and Llwyn Meredydd Feddyg, the Grove of Meredith the Physician.

William Rees, Tonn*.
Adapted from the Introduction to
The Physicians of Myddfai 1843

2. *Shadow Insult*

It chanced to come to the ears of a jealous king of Wales that a young man of those parts, most exalted in reputation, nobility of character, race and beauty, and most prosperous in affairs and person, had dreamed that he slept with the queen. The king declared himself undone, was as enraged as if the act had been real. He seized the man by guile and, had not respect for his kindred and fear of vengeance restrained him, would have tortured him to death. The king refused bail and demanded instant judgment.

The royal claim for compensation [sarhaed] was referred to a learned judge who ruled that 'This man accused of dreaming that he abused the queen does not deny the charge.' Had the offence confessed been real, it is certain that sarhaed of 1,000 kine would have had to be paid. But as it was a dream it was ordered therefore that the offender should set 1,000 kine in the king's sight on the bank of the lake of Behthen, in a row in the sunlight, so that the reflection of each cow may be seen in the water. 'Their reflection only shall belong to the king and the kine to him that owned them before. For a shadow insult the king's entitlement is shadow compensation'.

Walter Map, *De Nugis Curialium* † (c.1190)

---

* Written down by Mr William Rees, of Tonn, near Llandovery, from the oral recitations of the late Mr John Evans, tiler, Myddvai; Mr David Williams, mason, Morfa, Myddvai; (about 90 years old) and Mrs Elizabeth Morgan, of Henllys Lodge, near Llandovery, a native of Myddvai.

3. *Medical Recipes*

For swelling or pain in the dorsal spine: grind the root of the celandine and the fennel and garlic and vinegar or wine and butter, poultice it round your neck and that will reduce the pain and the swelling.

Trophining

There are three places in the head where disease develops, one is the scalp, the second is the cranium (skull), the third is the dura mater. The scalp is healed by cautery and bleeding. The cranium is healed by opening the head as far as the cranium. The dura mater is healed by opening the head as far as the dura mater. Then take two parts of betony and a third part of violet, together with salt butter. Mix them together and apply it to the wound. That will take away the poison from the dura mater, if inflammation and infection arise in it. From then the scalp be opened until the end of the ninth day, let there be a covering (damp covering) on the bone. That is what shall be done in the case of an old head wound.

For a new blow or wound on the head, the sooner it be opened the better, lest blood congeal on the dura mater and set up an inflammation. When the one be removed from the dura mater, take the violet and fresh butter and beat them together; and if violet be not available, take the white of an egg and linseed and beat them together and apply it to the wound until it forms a scar and then make an ointment of herbs and butter and wax and apply it to it, until it be better.

The fee of the doctor for that work which he does in his mercy is a pound without sustenance, or nine score pence with sustenance.

Here are the things that are good for gangrene: take a black toad which is only able to crawl and beat it with a stick until it becomes furious and so that it swells until it dies, and take it and put it into an earthenware cooking pot and close the lid on it so that the smoke may not escape nor the air get into it, and burn it in the pot until it is ashes and apply the ashes to the gangrene.

For toothache: Take the bark next to the ivy tree and the leaves of the honey-suckle and pound them together well in a mortar, and press them through a cloth into the two nostrils with the belly uppermost and that will get rid of it.

Break up seeds of poppy in wine to cause a man to sleep well.

Soporific

This is a potion which when taken causes man to sleep when he be opened up; wherever the wound may be, this potion eases the pain. Take the juice of opu-tebagia, the sea holly, the papaver, namely the poppy, mandragore, rood ivy, blackberries, hemlock, lettuce, each one in equal amount. Let them be mixed in a clean earthenware dish and left in it, and let this potion be made during the Dog days, and when preparation is being made to open the patient, cause him to stare as long as possible and after that let some of the mixture be put in his nostrils and he shall sleep without the pain. When you wish to awake him, press a sponge in vinegar and push it into the nostrils.

Triads

The three most difficult treatments for a doctor: an injury to the lungs, an injury to the milk glands and to a knee.

The three best potions for reducing temperature: apple juice, and goat's milk and spring water.

Three bones in man, if they break they will never knit, and not one of them is found in a man at his birth: a tooth, and the patella and (the fontanelle of) the cranium.

The three thick indispensables: liver and kidney and heart and this is the reason they are so called, it is proven, that wherever a hurt touches one of them, it cannot be cured, but death will come at once.

The three thin indispensables: the membrane of the brain and the small intestine and the vesicle, and it is for the same reason that they are indispensable as the others.

The three lingering wounds: the hip joint, and the marrow of a rib, and the lung, since once pus has formed in anyone of those it is proven that no doctor knows when it may heal him until he see him well.

A Heptad

There are seven enemies to the eye: weeping and watching and a discharge and drunkenness, and adultery, and a dry membrane and smoke.

Question and Answer

What is the most difficult treatment? Extracting a piece of bone without harm from the brain.

What is the least difficult treatment? Scratching the hand until it hurts and then spitting on it and rubbing it.

Calendar
(a)   Good days for bloodletting.
        March 6th, April 1st, 9th, May 28th
(b)   Bad days for bloodletting
        May 30-31, whoever has blood let on these days will be blind.
        July 15th. Beginning of bad days for bloodletting.
        September 6th. End of bad days.

Instructions
Blood should be let until the colour change, for if it appear black when
it runs, let it run until it be red. If it be thick, let it run until it be thin.
If it be watery let it run until it be thick.

Quinzy
In case of quinzy, let blood from beneath your tongue or beneath your
two arms and from the vein of the head and put a plaster of mallow,
linseed and a little butter without salt around your neck and at the base
of your tongue.

The Physicians of Myddfai

4. *Culhwch and Olwen*

Arthur overtook him again in Pelumiawg, and there the boar killed Madawg son of Teithion, Gwyn son of Tringad son of Nefedd, and Eiriawn Penlloran. From where he went to Abertywi and he made a stand there. That is where he killed Cynlas son of Cynan and Gwilenhin, king of France. From there he went to Glyn Ystu, and there the men and hounds lost him.

Arthur summoned Gwyn son of Nudd, and asked him if he had any information about Twrch Trwyth. He replied that he hadn't. Then all the huntsmen began to hunt the swine as far as Dyffryn Llychwr, where Grugyn Gwallt [*recte* Gwrych] Ereint silver-bristles and Llwydawg Gofyniad the claimant rushed out upon them. Such was the slaughter of huntsmen that not one of them escaped alive except one man. What Arthur did then was to bring his hosts to where Grugyn and Llwydawg were, and let loose upon them all the hounds that had been required by Ysbaddaden. As soon as they had the boars at bay, Twrch Trwyth came and rescued them. From the time they had come across the Irish Sea until then, he had not seen them. Then the men and dogs came upon him, and he took flight as far as Amanw Mountain. There one of the piglets was slain, and mortal battle was joined. Twrch Llawin was killed and then another of his pigs by the name of Gwys. From there they fled to Amanw Valley, and there boar and sow alike were killed; none of his brood was left alive save Grugyn Gwallt [*sic*] Ereint silver-bristles and Llwydawg Gofyniad the claimant.

From there they went to Llwch Ewin, where Arthur overtook him. He gave battle there, and slew Echel Morddwyd Twll of the pierced thigh, Arwyli son of Gwyddawg Gwyr and many men and hounds besides. From there they went to Llwch Tawy.

Grugyn Gwallt [*sic*] Ereint silver-bristles left then, and made for Din Tywi. From there he went to Ceredigion with Eli and Trachmyr and a host of others besides in pursuit. He went as far as Garth Grugyn where he was killed among them, and he killed Rhuddfyw Rhys and many others besides.

The Mabinogion

5. *Merlin, Incubus Offspring*

In the end Vortigern summoned his magicians, asked them for their opinion and ordered them to tell him what to do. They all gave him the same advice: that he should build for himself an immensely strong tower, into which he could retreat in safety if he should lose all his other fortresses. He surveyed a great number of places in an attempt to find a site suitable for this, and in the end he came to Mount Erith. There he assembled stonemasons from different parts of the country and ordered them to build a tower for him. The masons gathered and began to lay the foundations of their tower. However much they built one day the earth swallowed up the next, in such a way that they had no idea where their work had vanished to.

When this was announced to Vortigern he consulted his magicians a second time, to give them a chance of explaining the reason for it. They told him that he should look for a lad without a father, and that, when he had found one, he should kill him, so that the mortar and the stones could be sprinkled with the lad's blood. According to them the result of this would be that the foundations would hold firm.

Messengers were immediately sent out through the different parts of the country to find such a person if they could. They came to a town which was afterwards called Kaermerdin and there they saw some lads playing by the town gate. They went to look at the game. Tired by their journey, they sat down in a circle, still hoping to find what they were seeking. At last, when much of the day had passed, a sudden quarrel broke out between two of the lads, whose names were Merlin and Dinabutius. As they argued, Dinabutius said to Merlin: 'Why do you try to compete with me, fathead? How can we two be equal in skill? I myself am of royal blood on both sides of my family. As for you, nobody knows who you are, for you never had a father!' At this word the messengers looked up. They examined Merlin closely and asked the standers-by who he was. They were told that no one knew who his father had been, but that his mother was daughter of a king of Demetia and that she lived in that same town, in St Peter's Church, along with some nuns.

The messengers lost no time. They hurried off to the governor of the town and ordered him in the King's name to send Merlin and his mother to Vortigern. When the governor knew the object of their errand, he immediately sent Merlin and his mother to Vortigern, so that the King could do what he wanted with them. When they were brought into his presence, the King received the mother with due courtesy, for he knew that she came of a noble family. Then he began to ask her by what man she had conceived the lad. 'By my living soul, Lord King,' she said, 'and by your living soul, too, I did not have relations with any mortal man to make me bear this child. I know only this: that, when I was in our private apartments with my sister nuns, someone used to come to me in the form of a most handsome young man. He would often hold me tightly in his arms and kiss me. When he had been some little time with me he would disappear, so that I could no longer see him. Many times, too, when I was sitting alone, he would talk with me, without becoming visible; and when he came to see me in this way he would often make love with me, as a man would do, and in that way he made me pregnant. You must decide in your wisdom, my Lord, who was the father of this lad, for apart from what I have told, I have never had relations with a man.'

The King was amazed by what he heard. He ordered a certain Maugantius to be summoned to him, so that this man could tell whether or not what the woman said was possible. Maugantius was brought in and listened to the whole story, point by point. 'In the books written by our sages,' he said to Vortigern, 'and in many historical narratives, I have discovered that quite a number of men have been born in this way. As Apuleius asserts in the *De deo Socratis*, between the moon and the earth live spirits which we call incubus demons. These have partly the nature of men and partly that of angels, and when they wish they assume mortal shapes and have intercourse with women. It is possible that one of these appeared to this woman and begot the lad in her.'

When he had listened to all this, Merlin went up to the King and asked: 'Why have my mother and I been brought into your presence?' 'My magicians have advised me,' answered Vortigern, 'that I should look for a fatherless man, so that my building can be sprinkled with his blood and thus stand firm.' 'Tell your magicians to appear in front of me,' answered Merlin, 'and I will prove that they have lied.'

The King was amazed at what Merlin said. He ordered his magicians to come immediately and sit down in front of Merlin. 'Just because you do not know what is obstructing the foundations of the tower which these men have begun,' said Merlin to the magicians, 'you have recommended that my blood should be sprinkled on the mortar to make the building stand firm. Tell me, then, what lies hidden under the foundations. There is certainly something there which is preventing it from holding firm.'

The magicians, who were terrified, said nothing. Merlin, who was also called Ambrosius, then went on: 'My Lord King, summon your workmen. Order them to dig in the earth, and, underneath, you will find a pool. That is what is preventing the tower from standing.' This was done. A pool was duly found beneath the earth, and it was this which made the ground unsteady.

Ambrosius Merlin went up to the magicians a second time and said: 'Tell me, now, you lying flatterers. What lies beneath the pool?' They remained silent, unable to utter a single sound. 'Order the pool to be drained,' said Merlin, 'and at the bottom you will observe two hollow stones. Inside the stones you will see two Dragons which are sleeping.'

The King believed what Merlin said, for he had told the truth about the pool. He ordered the pool to be drained. He was more astounded by Merlin than he had ever been by anything. All those present were equally amazed at his knowledge, and they realized that there was something supernatural about him.

Geoffrey of Monmouth.
The History of the Kings of the Britons c.1150

6. MERLIN THE MAGICIAN

Forthwith themselues disguising both in straunge
    And base attyre, that none might them bewray,
    To *Maridunum*, that is now by chaunge
    Of name *Cayr-Merdin* cald, they took their way:
    There the wise *Merlin* whylome wont (they say)
    To make his wonne, low vnderneath the ground,
    In a deepe delue, farre from the vew of day,
    That of no liuing wight he mote be found,
When so he counseld with his sprights encompast round.

And if thou euer happen that same way
    To trauell, goe to see that dreadfull place:
    It is an hideous hollow caue (they say)
    Vnder a rocke that lyes a litle space
    From the swift *Barry*, tombling downe apace,
    Emongst the woodie hilles of *Dyneuowre*:
    But dare thou not, I charge, in any cace,
    To enter into that same balefull Bowre,
For fear the cruell Feends should thee vnwares devowre.

But standing high aloft, low lay thine eare
    And here such ghastly noise of yron chaines,
    And brasen Caudrons thou shalt rombling heare
    Which thousand sprights with long enduring paines
    Doe tosse, that it will stonne thy feeble braines,
    And oftentimes great grones, and grieuous stounds,
    When too huge toile and labour them constraines
    And oftentimes loud strokes, and ringing sounds
From vnder that deepe Rocke most horribly rebounds.

The cause some say is this: A litle while
    Before that *Merlin* dyde, he did intend,
    A brasen wall in compas to compile
    About *Cairmardin*, and did it commend
    Vnto these Sprights, to bring to perfect end.
    During which worke the Ladie of the Lake,
    Whom long he lou'd, for him in hast did send,
    Who thereby forst his workemen to forsake,
Them bound till his returne, their labour not to slake.

In the meane time through that false Ladies traine,
    He was surprised, and buried vnder beare,
    Ne euer to his worke returnd againe:
    Nath'lesse those feends may not their worke forbeare
    So greatly his comaundement they feare,
    But there doe toyle and trauell day and night,
    Vntil that brasen wall they vp doe reare:
    For *Merlin* had in Magicke more insight,
Than euer him before or after liuing wight.

Edmund Spenser,
The Faerie Queene, Book III Canto III

7. *Fairies*

Pant Shon Shenkin, it must be here remarked, was a famous place for the Carmarthenshire fairies. The traditions thereabout respecting them are numerous. Among the strangest is, that a woman once actually caught a fairy on the mountain near Pant Shon Shenkin, and that it remained long in her custody, retaining still the same height and size, but at last made its escape.

Another curious tradition relates that early one Easter Monday, when the parishioners of Pencarreg and Caio were met to play at football, they saw a numerous company of Tylwyth Teg dancing. Being so many in number, the young men were not intimidated at all, but proceeded in a body towards the puny tribe, who, perceiving them, removed to another place. The young men followed, whereupon the little folks suddenly appeared dancing at the first place. Seeing this, the men divided and surrounded them, when they immediately became invisible, and were never more seen there.

Wirt Sikes. *British Goblins* 1880

8. *Owen Lawgoch*

Owen Lawgoch, a personage dear to the Welsh legend of the district, and his men had their abode in a cave on the northern side of Mynydd Mawr, and while there Owen used, we are informed, to water his steed at a fine spring covered with a large stone, which it required the strength of a giant to lift. But one day he forgot to replace it, and when he next sought the well he found the lake. He returned to his cave and told his men what had happened. Thereupon both he and they fell into a sleep, which is to last till it is broken by the sound of a trumpet and the clang of arms on Rhiw Goch: then they are to sally forth to conquer.

Sir John Rhys. *Celtic Folklore* 1901

9. *The Legend of Llynllech-Owain*

Connected with Llynllech-Owain there is a pretty legend, which Sir Lewis Morris has put into verse. Here it is: The lake lies darkly clear amid the folded hills, and on its quiet waters float white water lilies. Once, where the lake now stands, a magic well lay several feet below the ground. It was a boon of the fairies, and to the well the shepherds at noon drove their sheep in summer to quench their thirst. But before anyone could make use of the wonderful water, a slate or stone that covered it had to be removed, and, when the necessary water had been obtained, the stone had to be replaced.

One hot day, weary and thirsty, Sir Owain, a brave knight of Arthur's Court, came journeying that way towards his old home. Not only was he weary and tired, but so, too, was his faithful steed. As a boy he had been fond of going to the well, and, on looking around, he was delighted when his eyes fell on it. Both man and horse drank long and deep from the bubbling spring, and then sank in slumber.

In a kind of waking dream, he seemed to hear the sound of a rushing stream, which he imagined was hemming him round. Opening his eyes, he was greatly surprised to see that the pasture lands had vanished. Then, he remembered that he had neglected to seal up the well. There, all around, he saw a waste of waters, where before had been pasture land with herds upon it. So alarmed did he become by what he had done, that he hurried away to hide in a cave.

In that cave he is said to be awaiting his fated hour, when Arthur shall come to arouse him from the deep slumber into which he has fallen. When that time comes, the place that knows the lake now will know it no more. The cave where Owain is believed to have hidden himself is known as the cave of Owain Lawgoch, and is in the limestone rocks of Dinas, Llandebie.

D. Morgan, *The Story of Carmarthenshire*

10. *Ghost Ladies of Llandawke and Cwmbiddy*

There is now only the mysterious part of its history to relate. It is said the foundress of the church, whose unhappy fate I have described, used to appear in Llandawke Lane, and that she does so still. There is a legend of a young lady, in Queen Elizabeth's time, being murdered and buried by her lover in the lane leading to the church. Another legend tells of a bride murdered on her wedding day at Llandawke, and thrown into the pond behind the church, which she afterwards haunted, and that she was buried under the kennel of the old manor house. Her husband was murdered at the same time. His body was found outside the church door, without marks of violence, but quite dead. In both cases jealousy caused the deeds. Fifty years ago people used to declare they saw the murdered bride leaning over the gate by the part where she met her death; sometimes in the twilight, dressed in white, with a broad lilac sash tied with a large bow behind; a very large straw hat and lilac ribbons. A clergyman related to me that an inhabitant of the parish told him that his wife as she passed Cwm Biddy to milk the cows used continually to meet a lady in a large straw hat standing by the gate.

Mary Curtis,
Antiquities of Laugharne, Pendine, and their Neighbourhoods

11. *Ghost Funeral*

Walking down the dark lane to Alltwen, I had the feeling that I had taken this same journey a long, long time ago. The sounds of voices in front of us and the noise of feet and hoofs struck some answering chord in my mind. I looked at Justin and realized that this was no dream. He was here at my side, the top of his head on a level with my eyes. He was very quiet, and once or twice he half lurched against me, heavy from the drink that was in him. The air was not as oppressive as it had been earlier in the evening, but perhaps that was only my fancy, and because it was so fresh after the tobacco smoke and the warm reek of the bar.

'Are you coming?' shouted someone in front of us.

'Carry on,' shouted Justin.

We were going down into the dip of the lane when I felt something heavy and stifling come upon me. I found myself struggling for breath, and through it all I heard the tramp tramp of feet. I thought at once of the Toili and began to tremble. It was so dark now that I could only see the shape of Justin at my side. I put out my hand and touched him. Without a word he took my hand, his grip cool and firm.

'What's up?' he asked at length, because I was still trembling.

I took a deep breath. Of course, it was nothing. The tramp of feet was still there, the crowd in front of us pressing on in silence towards Alltwen.

'It's all right,' I said. 'It was coming out into the fresh air after drinking. You know how it is.'

'Lucky you were not on rum and beer,' he laughed.

Once out of the dip, I felt better. But the experience had frightened me. Was it some augury of what the night held in store for us, or was it just my anxiety affecting my nerves and imagination?

Ahead of us we could now see Alltwen with its stark high firs around it. The barn was a score or more yards away from the buildings, and while Dai went to the house for some lanterns, we caught up with the rest of them and tethered the horses to the railings.

*   *   *

Old Howells stopped filing, and sat on the anvil. He was staring past me, the candle-light shining on the sweat on his forehead. Outside, the wind whined through the oak trees and a lick of rain beat against the window and the closed door. The others were all listening; Dico was all eyes, his moustache bristling around his half-opened mouth.

'It was pitch black; you know how it is when you come out of the light. So I walked slowly, not thinking of any thing in particular till I felt myself sweating. Sweating, mind, and it was a cold night. I was in a wabbling of sweat . . . I felt I could hardly breathe . . .'

'Y Cyheurath!' muttered old Prosser. 'I've felt it, too!'

'Yes! "Y Cyheurath", the "Toli",' said Howells. 'I knew it . . . I was in a funeral!'

'Did you hear it, too?' asked Dico. His deep voice trembled as he spoke.

'Hear it? Yes. I got to the side of the road. I could hear the feet going by; dozens of them! I tell you, I could hardly breathe. I felt I was caught in a great crowd . . . And, then, I heard the heavy tread of the bearers, and I could feel that the coffin was passing me.'

Old Howells wiped his face with his hands; he was sweating, and his eyes were staring in front of him as if he were still seeing what he was describing.

'I pressed myself against the hedge, and in a few minutes the air was light again; I felt I could breathe more easily. By now, they were getting near to the river, and I stood there waiting for the noise. Then it came, the Cyheuraeth. You know it, Prosser, like a thousand cats in torment.' He turned to me: 'You always hear that sound when they cross the water, even if it is only a little stream. Enough to make your blood run cold it is. Well, I knew then that old Jeffre would be going feet first that way in a few days . . . Yes, it was him all right, and when the doctor pulled up outside here two days after, I looked at him and said: "Well, I suppose you have come to say that Jeffre Tomos is gone!" You should have seen his face!'

'Tell me,' I asked him, 'You are sure you heard it you say? What if you only imagined it?'

Old Howells came over to me and put his hand on my shoulder. 'I heard it, Edwin. And others here have heard it . . . Pray God that you will never hear it. If you do, you will never be the same after. Look at me now. I'm not afraid of any man or animal; but, I tell you, there are certain roads around here that I wouldn't walk after dark if you gave me a sovran for every step I would take. As they say: "Better for a man the ill he knows, than the ill he knows not" . . .'

Richard Vaughan, *Moulded in Earth*

12. *The Phantom Fiddler of Green Bridge Cave*

Pendine is now a seaside village with wide and firm sands that have become famous for landspeed attempts. Nearby is a haunted cave.

Green Bridge Cave was once entered (so runs the story) by an old fiddler who thought he had found a temporary shelter for the night. He lit a candle to enable him to find his way into the dark interior and he went on deeper and deeper into the cave; his candle must have gone out and he either lost his way or fell but, at all events, he was never seen again and his body was never found. There are those who say they have heard him sometimes, playing his fiddle – a thin, far-away melody that is heard for a moment and then it is gone, only to return again and then again become inaudible: almost as though the old fiddler is trying to lead people to him – or lure them to their death as he died, alone, lost and sad in echoing darkness with only his fiddle for company.

When I was in the vicinity in June 1978 I met a man who told me he had personal experience of the haunting of Green Bridge Cave. He was walking past the cave one evening with his wife when they both heard the sound of a fiddle. It was very faint and at first they thought it was a trick of the wind but then, as they stopped and listened, they could make out a definite tune. They went into the cave and for a moment the music sounded louder but then it became faint again and although he had wanted to pursue the matter and see whether he could discover where the music came from, his wife was apprehensive and in the end they walked away, the soft sounds of a fiddle ringing in their ears.

Peter Underwood, *Ghosts of Wales*

13. *Corpse Candles*

It is ill jesting with the Corpse Candle. Persons who have endeavoured to stop it on its way have come severely to grief thereby. Many have been struck down where they stood, in punishment of their audacity, as in the case of William John, a blacksmith of Llanboidy. He was one night going home on horseback, when he saw a Corpse Candle, and his natural caution being at the moment somewhat overcome by potables, he resolved to go out of his way to obstruct its passage. As the candle drew near he saw a corpse upon a bier, the corpse of a woman he knew, and she held the candle between her forefingers, and dreadfully grinned at him. Then he was struck from his horse, and lay in the road a long time insensible, and was ill for weeks thereafter. Meantime, the woman whose spectral corpse he had seen, died and was buried, her funeral passing by that road.

A clergyman's son in Carmarthenshire, (subsequently himself a preacher), who in his younger days was somewhat vicious, came home one night late from a debauch, and found the doors locked. Fearing to disturb the folk, and fearing also their reproaches and chidings for his staying out so late, (as many a young fellow has felt before and since), he went to the man-servant, who slept in an outroom, as is sometimes the custom in Welsh rural districts. He could not awake the man-servant, but while standing over him, he saw a small light issue from the servant's nostrils, which soon became a Corpse Candle. He followed it out. It came to a foot-bridge which crossed a rivulet. Here the young man became inspired with the idea of trying an experiment with the Corpse Candle. He raised the end of the foot-bridge off the bank, and watched to see what the ghostly light would do. When it came to the rivulet it seemed to offer to go over, but hesitated, as if loth to cross except upon the bridge. So the young man put the bridge back in its place, and stayed to see how the candle would act. It came on the bridge, and as it passed the young man it struck him, as with a handkerchief. But though the blow was thus light and phantom-like, it doubled the young man up and left him a senseless heap on the ground, where he lay till morning, when he recovered and went home. It is needless to add that the servant died.

Wirt Sikes, *British Goblins*

14. *The Sin-Eater*

The superstition of the Sin-Eater is said to linger even now in the secluded vale of Cwm-Aman, in Caermarthenshire. The meaning of this most singular institution of superstition was, that when a person died, the friends sent for the Sin-Eater of the district, who, on his arrival, placed a plate of salt and bread on the breast of the deceased person; he then uttered an incantation over the bread, after which, he proceeded to eat it – thereby eating the sins of the dead person; this done, he received a fee of two-and-sixpence – which, we suppose, was much more than many a preacher received for a long and painful service. Having received this, he vanished as swiftly as possible, all the friends and relatives of the departed aiding his exit with blows and kicks, and other indications of their faith in the service he had rendered. A hundred years since, and through the ages beyond that time, we suppose this curious superstition was everywhere prevalent.

Paxton Hood.
Christmas Evans, Preacher of Wild Wales 1881

15. *Sin-Eating*

One of the customs of the inhabitants of the Two Mountains in the old days was performing the ritual of Eating Sins. When a man died years ago the first thing to do was to send at once for the Sin-Eater. As a rule, he was a poor man, some dirty rascal with whom nobody in the district deigned to have any relationship. And he lived on his own apart from everyone else. When he had reached the house, he was taken to the room where the corpse of the dead man lay. There a plateful of salt was laid on the chest of the corpse, and a slice of bread on top of that. He'd whisper some strange words over the bread and then he'd eat it voraciously together with a draught of beer to wash it down.

People believed in those days that the poor fellow by eating the bread, took upon himself all the sins of the dead man. Turning to the Bible (Leviticus xvi) we see that the children of Israel had a very similar custom: the people chose two billy-goats, one to sacrifice on the altar, and the other to release into the desert. Here is the custom in the words of the Bible: 'And let Aaron place his hands upon the head of the living goat, and confess all the iniquities of the children of Israel, and all their transgressions in all their sins, and let him put them all on the head of the goat, and turn it out in the hand of a fit man into the wilderness.'

Something similar to this scapegoat (as they call it) was the fate of the Sin-Eater. He was given a shilling or half a crown after eating the bread from the corpse, then he was led out through the door with a curse or two to follow him and instructions not to darken the door henceforth. He had finished his detestable work, and nobody wanted his company thereafter. A pity for him!

Gomer M. Roberts, *Tales of Two Mountains* †

16. *Legends of Kidwelly*

A Welsh chieftain, either by marriage or arms, had become possessed of Kidwelly. His name was Elider Ddu, and he had two sons, Gruffydd and Rhys, and a beautiful daughter called Nest. Besides these there was an orphan niece named Gwladys. Now Elider was bound for the Crusades, and taking with him his younger son Rhys, he left the elder Gruffydd in charge of the castle and its inmates. The castle proved an easier charge than the two women; for peace, as it happened, was having a brief reign in South Wales at that particular time.

At Margam, in Glamorgan, there then lived one of the Mansel family, Sir Walter, young, handsome, and gallant. He had conceived an affection for the fair Nest, which she returned, but the lord of Kidwelly was a Welshman, and Sir Walter a Norman, and Elider forbade the young man the house. But when this unfeeling parent had gone to the Holy Land, the lover, though he could not visit Kidwelly, where the elder brother still kept guard, could readily find means of meeting the fair Nest in the country round. Unfortunately, Gwladys was also in love with Sir Walter, and consequently very jealous of her cousin. She soon discovered that Nest had secret meetings with Sir Walter. To complicate matters, Gruffydd was in love with Gwladys, and this crafty maiden, who had snubbed him hopelessly, now thought to use him to help her in her revenge. So, pretending to be kind to him, she told him her tale of Walter and Nest, and wrought him up to such a pitch of fury that he agreed to join her in a dark scheme of vengeance against the Norman.

An evil ruffian about the castle, called Meurig, was now sent for, sworn to secrecy, and given his instructions. The next meeting of the lovers was by some means found to be the bridge over the tidal portion of the Gwendraeth. And as Sir Walter came forward to greet his lady-love, an arrow whistled from a reed bed and pierced his side. The villain Meurig then rushed from his hiding place, and before the eyes of Nest, hurled Walter's body into the rushing tide. The young woman, over-come with horror, flung herself after her lover, and they were both washed downwards to the sea.

Their bodies were found by fishermen, and Gruffydd and Gwladys made up a tale of accidental drowning. There were those, however, who had seen the arrow wound near Sir Walter's heart, but they were very poor people and durst not whisper of it. Gruffydd now asked Gwladys to marry him, but she turned from him with scorn, and called him a murderer. Then Gruffydd, in despair, followed his father and brother to the Holy Land, taking the villain Meurig with him. Rhys, however, returned and married Gwladys, but her brain gave way when rumours got abroad that a white spectre was seen at nightfall hovering about the Pont-y-Gwendraeth. On being approached this spectre vanished, with a piercing scream, into the dark waters of the river. The bridge acquired the name of Pont-yr-Yspryd-Gwyn, 'the bridge of the white spirit', and it bears it to this day.

D. Morgan, The Story of Carmarthenshire

17. Beating the Bounds

The head of the Corporation is the Portreeve. Elected for six months, he assumes office on Big Court Day, the first Monday after the festival of St Michael and All Angels, and, if re-elected, at the May Court held on the Monday after Low Sunday. Wearing a chain of golden cockle shells, the symbol of what was once the main local industry, he presides at the Town Hall once a fortnight over the 'Court Leet' and 'Court Baron' of Talacharn. Under him sit the Grand Jury of 21 members, with the Foreman as their chief. Chosen by the out-going Portreeve, the Foreman, in consultation with Portreeve and Recorder, appoints out of the Grand Jury, two Common Attorneys who are responsible for the collection of the rents. From the remaining 18, are chosen by lot 4 Constables, who in olden days would maintain law and order in the Township, and still share for their pay the rental of the Constable's Field.

Sitting in the Court on the right of the Foreman, just as the Common Attorneys sit on his left, is the Recorder, who acts as Clerk and is the only permanent official. Every Portreeve after six months of office becomes an Alderman of the Corporation.

On the Burgess Roll are over 450 'Burgages', the senior 76 of whom hold for life 'strangs' or plots of land of varying rentals, separated by a ridge, known as a 'landscar'.

Every year the Portreeve appoints the Bailiff whose duty is to open the Court with the traditional 'Oyez! Oyez! Oyez! Draw near all ye members of Her Majesty's Court Leet and Court Baron. Gentlemen of the jury answer your names.' He also has to terminate the Court with – 'Oyez! Oyez! Oyez! All ye that have attended may now depart hence and appear here this night fortnight at 7 p.m. sharp. God save the Queen.'

The first Sunday after the Michaelmas Court (Big Court) is Portreeve Sunday. The Portreeve invites the Corporation and on being prominent citizens to breakfast with him and then they accompany him to Morning Service at St Martin's Church. At one time he also regaled them with a Banquet where all the toasts had to be drunk in 'punch' according to ancient custom.

The Whit-Monday of every third year witnesses the Common Walk, or the Beating of the Bounds, involving a cross-country journey of over 20 miles on foot – following the exact course directed by the 700 years old Charter. En route are 24 'Hoisting Places' such as Green Back, Moldin Bit, Bramble Back, Halfpenny Furse, Oat meal and Cheese, and Feather-bed Lane. Woe betide the luckless spectator who fails to give the correct name of the hoisting place, for he or she is straightway turned upside down, and given three strokes with the Constable's staff on the place which nature has provided for the purpose. Thus are the boundaries kept from age to age.

The castle is in ruins; the 'Barracks' and the 'Butts' and 'Warriors Lane' are now mere names – but Laugharne is confident in her destiny, for did not the old magician, Merlin, prophesy long ago:

> Kidwelly was;
> Carmarthen is;
> But LAUGHARNE shall be
> The greatest city of the three.

J. I. Thomas, *A Laugharne Mixture*

18. CUTTY WRAN

The little wren is the hero;
There is much ado about him;
There is an inquest on him tonight
in every place.

The rogue has been caught,
who last night was so proud,
in a fair white chamber,
with his eleven brothers.

His tower has been broken,
the hero has been caught;
he has been wrapped in a sheet
on a fair chequered bier.

Ribbons of every colour
are about the wren;
ribbons thrice turned
are on his head for a covering.

Carmarthenshire Wren Song

III

Saints & Sinners

1. *The Cult of St Teilo*

If we possessed no ancient information whatsoever regarding St Teilo and were forced to make an appraisal of his work based on the number and distribution of the churches dedicated to him, we would realise at once that he must be placed in a different category from that of St Padarn. Many of his churches lie beyond the zone of Roman influence, whether civil or military, in South Wales. They are most numerous in western Carmarthenshire and eastern Pembrokeshire, while his traditional *podum* was located at Llandeilo Fawr in the former county. It would appear that an extension of his cult took place eastwards both along the coastal route towards Kidwelly, Llandeilo Penybont, Gower, and Merthyr Mawr near Bridgend, and also along the well marked Roman road running eastward from near Llandovery into the Vale of Usk, for, just to the eastward of Abergavenny, we have a cluster of Teilo dedications at Llannarth, Llandeilo Gresynni and Llandeilo Porth Halog, all in Monmouthshire. Roman roads branching off to the northward from the main west to east route may have led to the foundation of Llandeilo'r Fân in Brecknockshire and Llandeilo Graban in Radnorshire. It is clear from the overall picture that the orientation of the distribution pattern is definitely west to east and not south to north as would appear to be the case with St Padarn.

Another marked feature brought out by the distribution of the Teilo dedications is that they are clearly in keeping with a diffusion radiating from Llandeilo Fawr – the traditional centre of his cult and not from Llandaf as the Norman protagonists of their newly created See in the twelfth century would have us believe in the *Liber Landavensis*. We are, however, fortunate in that we possess written evidence of the cult of St Teilo reaching back at least three hundred years before the appearance of either the long and elaborate 'Life' of the saint contained in the Book of Llandaf, or the recension of it now included in the British Museum Ms. Vesp. A.xiv. The early evidence is found in the famous gospel-book known as the Book of St Chad now at Lichfield Cathedral. The gospels themselves would appear to have been written in Ireland before the year 700. Subsequently, they became the property of a church of St Teilo, and while in its possession certain entries of considerable historical value were made in the margins of its pages. Sometime after 850 it passed into the possession of Lichfield Cathedral. The marginal entries are in Welsh and record gifts and agreements made 'on the altar of Teilo'. They tell us nothing about St Teilo himself; their significance lies in showing that even in the ninth century there was an active cult of the saint, and that the community in the monastery where the book was located was of the Celtic type governed by an abbot-bishop who called himself Bishop of St Teilo. We are not told where this important monastery was, but an examination of the place names referred to in the Welsh entries makes it clear that it was at Llandeilo Fawr in Carmarthenshire.

E. G. Bowen.
The Settlements of the Celtic Saints in Wales 1954

2. *The Miracles of Teilo*

Now the miracles which we know to have been performed by him, we commit to writing and memory; for by being silent with respect to the miraculous power of God, and the saints, we are grievously deficient in duty; but by publishing it, we perform it. He had three packhorses, who without any one attending them, went to the wood, and when loaded by the woodmen, returned in a similar manner without a driver, and thus served the brethren daily. It is said that he raised one from the dead on the river Cowin, who was named Distinnic. That one sick of the palsy was by him healed in the church of Radh, before all the people, on the Sabbath day, and with whatever disorder the sick were afflicted, they were healed of it by the laying on of his hands. But they, who in any way injured him, either were long tormented, or immediately died; as an audacious woman who offended him, expired before all the people. Also a certain petty king, named Gwaeddan, violated his refuge in one of his churches, commonly called Llandeilo Fechan, and as he was raging there and committing this act of violence, he immediately, in the same cemetery, vilely lost his life; and those who acknowledged their crimes, immediately recovered their health, and were pardoned through means of his prayers.

On the night of his decease, there arose a great dispute between the clergy of three of his churches, each asserting its authorities and privileges for obtaining his body; one, of which was Pennalun, and which claimed because it was there his ancestors had been buried, and therefore, the proper place by hereditary right; the second church, which was situated on the banks of the Towy, claimed it because it was the place of his residence, where he lived retired, and because he there gloriously ended his life; the third was Llandaff, and urged its claim on account of its having been his Episcopal see, of its privileges and dignities, its consecrations and obedience, and of the unanimous voice of all the diocese, and especially because of its former state, and the appointment of St Dubricius, and other fathers. But at length, attending to the advice of discreet men, they had recourse to fasting and prayer, that Christ, the great judge, who is the true authority, and privilege of holy persons, should declare by some manifest sign, to which of them he would be pleased to commit the holy body of the Saint. And in the morning, a certain elder, looking towards the place where the body was, spoke with a loud voice, saying,

> Our prayer, brethren, has been heard by the Lord, who deprives no one of his reward: Arise, and behold what things have been done by Christ the Mediator between God and man, that our dispute might be settled; and as in the life, so in the death of the holy confessor Teilo, miracles should be performed.

For, lo! they saw there three bodies, to which there was the same dimensions of body, the same beauty of countenance, (what more?) they had the lineaments of the whole frame, without any difference. So peace being restored, each with their own corpse returned homewards, and they buried the different bodies in those several places with the greatest reverence.

Liber Landavensis, ed. W. J. Rees

3. St Teilo Flees the Plague

In the year 547 appeared the Yellow Plague. The account of the breaking out of this terrible pestilence is curious. It was preceded by the appearance of a vaporous column sweeping over the land, one head in the clouds, and the other trailing along the ground. All who came within its course sickened to death, and the contagion spread, affecting beasts as well as men. No medicines were of any avail that is no wonder considering what medicines were then in use – and physicians perished with the patients. The ravages of the plague were so terrible that the country was well-nigh depopulated.

Teilo, in a dire fright, resolved on flying along with his community.

He took with him a number of other bishops as timorous as himself, and a great many men and women as well, and escaped into Cornwall, where the king, Gerennius or Geraint, received him honourably, and constituted him his confessor. Geraint made him promise to visit and communicate him when he lay on his deathbed. But Teilo would not remain in Cornwall; and there he has left the scantiest trace of his presence. He crossed over to Armorica and visited St Samson at Dol.

S. Baring-Gould & J. Fisher.
Lives of the British Saints, Vol. IV 1913

4. THE MARTYRDOM OF BISHOP FARRAR

Burned by Bloody Mary's men at Caermarthen.
'If I flinch from the pain of the burning, believe
not the doctrine that I have preached.'
(His words on being chained to the stake.)

Bloody Mary's venomous flames can curl:
They can shrivel sinew and char bone
Of foot, ankle, knee, and thigh, and boil
Bowels, and drop his heart a cinder down;
And her soldiers can cry, as they hurl
Logs in the red rush: 'This is her sermon.'

The sullen-jowled watching Welsh townspeople
Hear him crack in the fire's mouth; they see what
Black oozing twist of stuff bubbles the smell
That tars and retches their lungs: no pulpit
Of his ever held their eyes so still,
Never, as now his agony, his wit.

An ignorant means to establish ownership
Of his flock! Thus their shepherd she seized
And knotted him unto this blazing shape
In their eyes, as if such could have cauterized
The trust they turned towards him, and branded on
Its stump her claim, to outlaw question.

So it might have been: seeing their exemplar
And teacher burned for his lessons to black bits,
Their silence might have disowned him to her,
And hung up what he had taught with their Welsh hats:
Who sees his blasphemous father struck by fire
From heaven, might well be heard to speak no oaths.

But the fire that struck here, come from Hell even,
Kindled little heavens in his words
As he fed his body to the flame alive.
Words which, before they will be dumbly spared,
Will burn their body and be tongued with fire
Make paltry folly of flesh and this world's air.

When they saw what annuities of hours
And comfortable blood he burned to get
His words a bare honouring in their ears,
The shrewd townsfolk pocketed them hot:
Stamp was not current but they rang and shone
As good gold as any queen's crown.

Gave all he had, and yet the bargain struck
To a merest farthing his whole agony,
His body's cold-kept miserdom of shrieks
He gave uncounted, while out of his eyes,
Out of his mouth, fire like a glory broke,
And smoke burned his sermon into the skies.

Ted Hughes

5. *The Bishop's Conkerbin*

We had a Welsh maid, Hannah, who taught us Welsh on the sly, and
told us queer stories about the old house (in Nott's Square). In the wine
cellar was a deep well which she said was bottomless, and out of it the
water was drawn by an iron chain-and-bucket. You know how anything
like a dark cavity with water in it can fascinate a child, and what was
strange, the first bucketful that came up was always tinged with red,
either from the rust of the chain or some iron in the soil. Hannah told

us the last bishop to live in the palace was a very wicked man, and as bishops in those days were not allowed wives, he kept a 'conkerbin'. But that led to scandal, and the bishop, not knowing how to get rid of her, sent her to the well one day for water, followed her down the steps of the cellar, and stabbed her in the back. Her blood ran into the well, and its water was for ever afterwards a rusty red. Now this story left us – me and my sister Bess – with a feeling of terror mixed with curiosity about the dark cellar and the deep well. The smell of wine barrels and the cobwebbed bottles stored in racks added a keener relish to the cellar.

Ernest Rhys, *Wales and England Wed*

6. 'Jumpers'

All five leaders of the movement were very young men. They furthered their cause by itinerant preaching and organising 'societies'. Howell Harris was possessed of immense energy and great physical endurance. He went on extended tours on horseback through the thirteen shires, travelling 150 miles a week and preaching twice or oftener every day, sometimes at midnight or early in the morning in out of the way places to avoid molestation. Their greatest orator was Daniel Rowland, who attracted crowds varying between two and four thousand to his monthly communion services at Llangeitho. He drove a highly emotional and imaginative people to frenzy by his descriptions of hell. John Gambold, who had now become a Moravian, describes how they 'would leap and jump for joy, and clap their hands crying Halleluia, Gogoniant'. 'This,' he adds, 'would continue for hours after the preacher would be over, and some fell to the ground exhausted.' Similar scenes were witnessed at Howell Davies's meetings. They won for the Methodists the name of 'Jumpers' and brought them into disrepute with some of their warmest friends. William Williams was found to have a peculiar genius for writing hymns. He began to print his hymns in 1744, and in all he wrote over a thousand. They were emotional and sensuous, like the hymns of the Moravians, and were conducive to religious revival. Their excellence caused them to be adopted by other denominations, and through them the spirit of methodism permeated the dissenting bodies and greatly increased the popularity of their services. These hymns have become part of the most precious heritage of the Welsh nation. Peter Williams wrote voluminously on doctrinal matters, and on his missionary tour in 1747 was the first Methodist minister to penetrate Anglesey.

Moderate opinion was scandalised by the excesses of the Methodists. Their exhorters were molested and their meetings were broken up, often at the instigation of the squire and the parson. This happened frequently in north Wales, for there their unpopularity was aggravated by the fact that all the exhorters were detested southerners. Peter Williams was imprisoned by Sir Watkin Williams Wynn of Wynnstay in his dog kennels. Often the exhorters were arrested as vagabonds, and there were frequent attempts to press them into the navy.

David Williams, *A History of Modern Wales*

7. *Riotous Assembly*

March 9, 1741. To Llangendeirne 6 miles abt 4 discoursed with an uncommon power & sweetness in Welsh & especially English. Many Gents & Servants hearing tandem Sir Ed. Mansel & Mr Gwynne of Wempa's wife and son (Richard Gwynne, son of Thomas Gwynne of Gwempa, entered St. John's College, Oxford, 1737) rode up asking the people had they nothing to do but to come here to be deluded by such a fellow, then ordered them to go away, & turning to me with great bitterness said he would send me away if I would not go that moment & rode on to me. I desired the people to make way for him, told him I would behave toward him as became to a Gent, but that he was mis-informed of me, that I did not delude the people was a member of the Est. Church. Still he rode on seeking a Constable, & the ch. Warden charging me never to come to his Parish again. I said I broke no law. The young gent with him then sought for the Constables to send me to Jayl. I asked what law did I break. They said, here is a Riotous Assembly. I said there was no Riot unless they made it so. Then an old gent came up to them while he was charging me as a bad character & said You & I should not cast a stone at him & I said Sir I could call you to account for defaming me, he asked him if he did not fear a judgement come from God on him – would he draw the curse of all these poor people on him. He asked if they had got a Church & Parson without hearing such a mad creature on fields – he said he had never heard so much from the Minister, & did not Xt. preach on the Mount. I at last turned to exhort the People with an uncommon Power to cut

& lash all to Pieces, never had more Power in my life, in English & Welsh abt. Adulterers & (he being a Common one) if we were here in Cockfighting we should have their Company, but as we were on the Lord's work they must come & hinder but that God saw from his Holy Place & took notice of this. "Remember" shall it behold to us in Hell how we spent our Time here, did the Ch. of England give us leave to swear & to whore & (they sometimes hearing & sometimes laughing but they could not go away) that I would come as soon as possible again, told them to read Acts 9, that Xt. would soon ask them Saul Saul why persecutest thou me, when he was full of human Authority (I becoming hoarse with the great straining) my voice being now lift up like a Trumpet indeed never had more Authority & Power. Gave out the hymn "Give me Thy strength &" part of it in Welsh. Then they went away & I went to prayer & exhorted sweet again. Now the Lord gave the victory over the Devil quite. Went to a Gent's House where I had so much carnal love & Respect that I know not what to do. 7 toward *Bolahaul* 3 miles via seeing great lights in the firmament, thought of the last Day. Exhorted in Welsh & English to pt 10. Could not give over.

Howell Harris, *Diaries*
from Tom Beynon, *Cwmsêl a Chefn Sidan*

8. *Williams Pantycelyn*

Although the cultural patriots thought of the Methodists as instruments of Anglicization, the Methodist leaders cultivated Welsh, producing a varied culture in that language. William Williams of Pantycelyn was one of the most energetic Welsh writers of the century. Williams greatly admired the homely verses of the seventeenth-century Vicar Pritchard of Llandovery which were memorised by the peasants all around him; he admired John Milton and imbibed a great quantity of English Puritan literature, as well as general knowledge from the current periodicals of the day. Williams of Pantycelyn wrote English perfectly well (his English hymn 'Guide me, O, thou great Jehovah' is known throughout the world) but chose to cultivate a most flexible Welsh style that was lively, practical, colloquial and popular. However much the Morris brothers and the scholars might scorn it, Pantycelyn and the Methodists made the greatest contribution in the century to Welsh writing. Pantycelyn himself produced about ninety books, many of them admittedly pamphlets and translations or adaptations. His practical moral advice, expressed in common-sensical, sometimes witty, prose could reach the illiterate masses through the talks of the leaders of the Methodist *seiat*. His widest audience, however, was reached through the hymns he composed by the hundred.

A few early-eighteenth-century Dissenters had tried to write lyrical hymns on the model of Isaac Watts, but it was Pantycelyn's energy and inspiration which completely transformed the scene. His words are mostly commonplace, his style familiar, personal and easily memorised. To the lilting and trilling melodies which Handel and Gay gave to love-songs for Vauxhall Gardens, Pantycelyn gave words of profound conviction and noble simplicity. His hymns had unprecedented success; indeed his collection of hymns *Môr o Wydr* (Sea of Glass) in 1762 virtually caused the second wave of the Methodist revival in that year. Robert Jones of Rhos-lan tells us that hundreds of people gathered at a place called Lôn-fudr in Llŷn in 1762 and carried on singing and singing for three days and three nights, as though they were in a modern open air pop festival. Pantycelyn was always looking for catchy numbers out of England to which to write his hymns. Nothing could be better than one of the song-tunes to which he wrote words 'Lovely Peggy – Moraliz'd', as a symbol of the way of life transformed by Methodism.

If one estimates the prose works of Williams of Pantycelyn, one sees prodigious efforts by him to serve the needs of the reading public which had appeared even before Methodism. His prose works broke new ground in Welsh, his *Ductor Nuptiarum* (the only pompous thing about it is the Latin title) advocated common sense in matters of sex and marriage; his *Templum Experientiae Apertum* was a guide on how to conduct a Methodist discussion group, the *seiat* being the 'Temple of Experience'. As the evangelical movement went into its second and third generation, at the end of the eighteenth century, men felt an urge to produce what they thought of as historical accounts of the movement, either histories of the local 'causes' or of Protestantism as a whole. Through Pantycelyn's influence, the lyric hymn took on its classic form in Welsh, a deeply personal outpouring of passion or emotion, and the hymn-like elegy, generally produced as an obituary for fellow-members of the *seiat* or the denomination, came to replace that most traditional of all the forms of Welsh poetry, the funeral ode or *cywydd marwnad*.

Pantycelyn also produced reams of poetry, which was never meant to be sung, a long verse account of the world's religions, and, most extraordinary, a long allegoricial novel in verse on the adolescent crises and subsequent spiritual development of an individual called *Theomemphus*.

Prys Morgan, *The Eighteenth Century Renaissance*

9. GUIDE ME, O THOU GREAT JEHOVAH

Guide me, O thou great Jehovah,
Pilgrim through this barren land;
I am weak, but thou art mighty,
Hold me with thy powerful hand:
Bread of heaven, bread of heaven,
Feed me till I want no more.

Open now the crystal fountain,
Whence the healing stream doth flow;
Let the fire and cloudy pillar
Lead me all my journey through:
Strong deliverer, strong deliverer,
Be thou still my strength and shield.

When I tread the verge of Jordan,
Bid my anxious fears subside;
Death of deaths, and hell's destruction,
Land me safe on Canaan's side:
Songs of praises, songs of praises
I will ever give to thee.

Musing on my habitation,
Musing on my heavenly home,
Fills my soul with holy longing:
Come, my Jesus, quickly come;
Vanity is all I see;
Lord, I long to be with thee!

William Williams, Pantycelyn

10. *Wesley in Wales*

Saturday, 20. We took horse at four, and rode through one of the pleasantest countries in the world. When we came to Trecastle, we had rode fifty miles in Monmouthshire and Breconshire; and I will be bold to say all England does not afford such a line of fifty miles' length for fields, meadows, brooks and gently rising mountains, fruitful to the very top. Carmarthenshire, into which we came soon after, has at least as fruitful a soil, but it is not so pleasant because it has fewer mountains, though abundance of brooks and rivers. About five I preached on the Green at Carmarthen to a large number of deeply attentive people. Here two gentlemen from Pembroke met me, with whom we rode to St Clears, intending to lodge there. But the inn was quite full so we concluded to try for Laugharne, though we knew not the way and it was now quite dark. Just then came up an honest man who was riding thither and we willingly bore him company.

Friday, 26. We designed to take horse at four, but the rain poured down so that one could scarce look out. About six, however, we set out and rode through heavy rain to St Clears. Having then little hopes of crossing the sands, we determined to go round by Carmarthen, but the hostler told us we might save several miles by going to Llanstephan ferry. We came thither about noon, where a good woman informed us that the boat was aground and would not pass till the evening; so we judged it best to go by Carmarthen still. But when we had rode three or four miles, I recollected that I had heard speak of a ford which would save us some miles' riding. We inquired of an old man, who soon mounted his horse, showed us the way, and rode through the river before us.

John Wesley. *Journal* August 1763

11. *Sectaries & Jumpers*

Llandilo War, June 19

Letter VII

Madam,

Though it is considered but twenty-four miles from Swansea to this place, yet we lengthened it to twenty-six by turning out of the road to examine the Ruins of Caraigcenin Castle; you will with difficulty believe that we could perform so long a journey on foot, and yet afford time to satisfy our curiosity. We noticed as we walked several chapels spread over the country, and we knew that in *this* particularly the sectaries were various: but is it true, Madam, that the Jumpers are so called, because when any one of them from fancied inspiration sees the Saviour, and springs up to touch him, that then the whole assembly in the same manner strive who shall first lay hold of the feet or the robes of the Lord? or that the person who wishes to be initiated among them, be the sex or age what I may, is immersed as if on the borders of Jordan? I hope, on my return to London, you will fix my opinion as to these circumstances.

(Maundet de Penhouet) *A Pedestrian Traveller* 1797

12. *Power over Lust and True Xtian Brotherly Love*

Howell Harris *Diaries*

March 10, 1741. Towd Carmarthen 1 mile there discussed in English to many hundreds in the Castle Green. The Lord made them all civil and opened my mouth sweetly on Luke iv. 18. poste. heard the greatest persecutors were satisfied, was sent for to a House to eat, he was pleased with everything but my saying of Bala and of myself. Ladies and all seemed touched, hope a door is opened here. Towd. Cefnygarn in Llanarthney, there pt. 11 discoursed to pt. 1. in a Battle with Satan & the flesh almost all the time resting in the House to 3, slept a little much tired.

May 10, 1741. Llanddowror. Towd. Llandevaelog 4 miles on foot. Sang in the boat over the River there discoursed to abt. 9 had great power indeed. At 11 to bed sorely tired having had great power given me over Lust and had true Xtian Brotherly love.

from Tom Beynon, *Cwmsêl a Chefn Sidan*

13. 'O Fryniau Caersalem'

The youngest brother of Rev. David Charles, of Carmarthen (Thomas Charles), has the Christ-given honour of having written one of the foremost hymns in the language. He was born in 1762; and, like his brother, he was under spiritual impression from early childhood. During the days of his apprenticeship he learnt by heart the whole of Young's *Night Thoughts*. A book, and an English book, was also the means of helping him to final decision for Christ – the sermons of Ralph Erskine. He spent several years of his young manhood in Bristol; and all these English influences served him well in after years, enabling him to preach effectively in both languages. He preached several times with and for Rowland Hill in Gloucestershire; and twice at least he occupied the famous pulpit of Surrey Chapel. He was a true builder of the churches; and early Methodism in Wales owed a great deal to his soberness and wisdom.

He wrote several hymns, but one has singled itself out from among the rest. The biography of '*O fryniau Caersalem ceir gweled*,' like that of the 'Miners' Hymn', can only be written in the light of the Homeland. The poet had heard 'the shout of them that triumph', and he was no longer afraid of the weariness and perplexity of his pilgrimage in the desert. Some day he would reach the cloudless hills of Zion, and look back on the meanderings of the journey, to find that it was the nearest way home.

> From the hills of the Beautiful City
>   The way of the desert is clear;
> What joy will be there in reviewing
>   The journey's meanderings here!
> To look on the storms as they gather,
>   On terrible death and the grave;
> While we shall be safe with the Father,
>   In peace on love's shadowless wave.

While dying lips have murmured in anticipation this joy of the heavenly retrospect from the hills of the City, the gate of pearl has opened to many a soul; and the faltering strain of earth has glided imperceptibly into the choral song of seraphim and saints redeemed.

H. Elfed Lewis. *Sweet Singers of Wales* 1887

14. *On hearing Daniel Rowlands Llangeitho preach*

On Jan. 20th, 1773, I went to hear Mr Rowlands preach at New Chapel. His text was Heb. iv. 15. A day much to be remembered by me as long as I live. Ever since that happy day I have lived in a new heaven and a new earth. The change which a blind man, who receives his sight, experiences, does not exceed the change which at that time I experienced in my mind.

> The earth receded and disappeared,
>   Heaven opened to my eyes,
>   My ears with sound seraphic rang.

It was then I was first convinced of the sin of unbelief, or of entertaining narrow, contracted and hard thoughts of the Almighty. I had such a view of Christ as our High Priest, of His love, compassion, power and all-sufficiency, as filled my soul with astonishment, with joy unspeakable.

Thomas Charles, *Diary*

15. *Griffith Jones, Llanddowror*

Griffith Jones was born at Cilrhedyn, Carmarthenshire, in 1684, and was presented to Llanddowror in 1711 by Sir John Philipps of Picton Castle in Pembrokeshire whose sister he married nine years later. His concern for the plight of the poor, who were neglected and untaught in an age when rectors, and even bishops, were more often than not absentees, and curates badly paid, overworked, and sometimes even illiterate themselves, was such that although ministering faithfully to his own two cures, he distributed books for the S.P.C.K. and travelled to wakes and fairs to preach, inaugurating a local revival. One of his sermons as an itinerant preacher was the means of converting Daniel Rowland, who became one of the founders of Welsh Methodism.

His great work of religious education began in 1731. In a 'Letter to a Friend' in October 1739 he explains his reason:

> 'It came to be discovered here how deplorably ignorant the poor people are who cannot read . . . The melancholy discovery of the brutish, gross and general ignorance in things pertaining to

salvation, gave great thoughts of heart and painful concerns . . .
it occurred at length to set up Welsh Charity Schools.'

When he began work, there were Charity schools in existence in
some parishes, but only for the young, and conducted in English.
Realizing how little these did to help the Welsh-speaking poor, he
opened his travelling schools to men and women of all ages, and taught
them in their native Welsh. His exquisite tact, and understanding sympathy, are shown in his description of the way in which he encouraged
the older people, who, 'being old in ignorance, were ashamed to be
thus taught and catechized publicly'. He encouraged them by distribut-
ing a dole of bread provided with part of the money communicants
gave at the Sacrament and then

> 'Being come together and placed orderly in a row to receive the
> bread, a few plain and easy questions were asked them, with
> great tenderness and caution not to puzzle or give them cause to
> blush, having instructed, and made private interest with the best
> disposed of them beforehand to lead on and encourage the
> others.'

The leaders of the Church gave him little encouragement complain-
ing that his work was encouraging Dissent, but some of the ordinary
clergy were ready to invite him to set up a school, and with the backing
of Sir John Philipps, Sir John Thorold, and other enlightened gentlemen and, of course, Madam Bevan, who carried on the work after his
death, the work progressed. Although these Circulating Schools were
not the first attempt to educate the poor people of Wales, they were
incomparably the most successful and far-reaching, and it is estimated
that before his death over 150,000 people, between the ages of six and
seventy years of age, had learned to read at these schools.

He awoke in the Welsh peasantry the Celtic hunger for knowledge,
so that in future not even semi-starvation could prevent them taking
advantage of any opportunity to become literate, and set an example
which Thomas Charles and others followed, until the Compulsory
Education Act made their work unnecessary. He lived and died a poor
man, but it was truly said of him that 'Few men in any age or country,
in so humble a position, have exercised a wider or nobler influence'.

Maxwell Fraser, *Introducing West Wales*

16. *Lying, Cheating and Unchastity*

There is no difference of intelligence between the small farmers and the labourers; both are in general very ill instructed. The Sunday-schools have in many instances knocked up the day-schools, where the latter are not gratuitous. The mass of the people possess nothing like general information; a small farmer would not, in 9 cases out of 10, know whether Africa was not a town or a parish; they cannot keep accounts so as to be intelligible to any but themselves. In the neighbourhood of posting-towns English is understood; but in the remoter districts not at all.

The general ignorance shows itself particularly in the vices of lying and cheating, and unchastity is quite a remarkable feature of the county. At Revivals, when such meetings occur, a great stimulus and opportunity for immorality is given; the parties attending them are under strong excitement, and often do not separate till a late hour. These Revivals are less frequent than formerly; there has not been one for five or six years; they are confined to a sect; the last was among the Independents; no educated man joins in them; but something of the same results accompany the common prayer-meetings.

Good secular education is the only basis on which parties can be united in school. From Mrs Bevan's schools, which are gratuitous, the poorest Dissenters often keep their children away, on account of the religious instruction enforced; in Cardiganshire they are even attempting to set up opposition schools to Mrs Bevan's.

Where schools are held in parts of Dissenting chapels, this is not done in the spirit of proselytism, but only for convenience sake.

The peasantry are generally very poor, and possess few comforts; but they are economical, and more cleanly than a stranger would think. The woman has the entire management of the house, and this she generally does well; she can generally sew and knit, and is very industrious.

Education is the only thing wanted for Wales; the country is paralysed for want of it; Wales might be worth double what it is, if the people were more educated; they are above their education, owing to their natural intelligence.

Nov. 6, 1846. Llandingat

(Signed) DAVID OWEN (Brutus)

Testimony to Commissioners of Enquiry into the
State of Education in Wales 1847

17. *The Tinker of Llandovery*

Moses by his alacrity and silent obedience, seemed to understand the spirit he had to deal with, but not in the least suspecting him to be Twm. Off he ran with his enormous present, and immediately returned; when our hero accompanied him to the shop of an old curmudgeon of an ironmonger, whose face, hardly distinguishable behind his habitual screen of snuff and spectacles, seemed of the same material as his own hard ware. The man of rags was quite in luck, and, as instructed, followed his benefactor into the shop in silence. Twm examined the culinary ware, with all the caution of an old farm wife, asking the prices of various articles, and turned up the whites of his eyes in the most approved puritanic fashion, expressive of astonishment of such excessive charges. Old hammerhead indignantly repelled the insinuation, and swore that cheaper or better pots were never seen in the kitchen of a king. 'Then you must mean the king of the beggars,' quoth Twm, 'for you have nothing here but damaged ware.' 'Damaged devil! what do you mean?' roared the enraged ironmonger. 'I mean,' replied Twm Shôn Catty, with provoking equanimity, 'that there is scarcely a pot here without a hole in it; now this which I hold in my hand, for instance, has one.' 'Where? where?' asked the fiery old shopkeeper, holding it up between his eyes and the light; 'if there is a hole in this pot I'll eat it: where is the hole that you speak of?' 'Here!' bawls the inexorable hoaxer, pulling it over his ears, and holding it there, while Moses took the wink from his patron, and walked off with a most choice article, which he had selected from the whole lot.

Loudly roared the hardwareman, but his voice was drowned in the fatal cavity. Having tied his hands behind his back, Twm left him howling and sweating beneath the huge extinguisher, and made as he took his departure, this consolatory and effective exit speech – 'had there not been a hole in it, how could that large stupid nob of yours have entered such a helmet?'

T. Llewelyn Pritchard,
Adventures and Vagaries of Twm Shôn Catty,
A Wild Wag of Wales

18. THOMAS AP MORGAN

He was a poet, it was the greatest fault
that he did not receive life: woe to Jesus!
from his court he went at the time of the feast,
and with his dwelling at Cynwyl:
a minstrel in his inlet
am I that he is not alive in the world.
From fair seed are shoots obtained,
and to summon men to receive wine:
and great vast splendid gifts,
and payment and a court once more;
and feasts like those of lords,
and notable amiable men for us.
Arousing Caio will I find
the old pedigree of the highest part:
where I was once understanding the world,
they will grow yet again.
There was an agreement here concerning Thomas
to provide fair heirs, without malice;
cold is the fear on his spouse,
if cold the frost under the snow:
crying for the descendant of Owain was she,
a bitter mournful cry it was.
His removal (God leaves her)
turned the day into sadness for her:
I ask a boon of the highest grace,
that there be heaven here for Thomas.

Ieuan Brechfa,
from *Elegy for Thomas ap Morgan* † NLW 728, 5-8

19. *Thomas Lewis, Talley*

Anyone who knows the road from Ammanford to Lampeter can imagine
what the country looks like this early July, with sunshine filtered through
green leaves and the singing of birds.

There were trees all the way, but it was at Dynevor that they came to
meet us in a solid phalanx. This must surely be one of the most over-

whelmingly beautiful spots in the whole of Wales, the trees bearing down on you from the brow of the hill, while the very road beneath you is upheld by a rainbow of a bridge, a rainbow drained of all colour that you may concentrate on its perfect shape, and rebuilding itself in the glass of Towy, like Browning's thrush, 'singing its song twice over'.

One cannot dwell on all that was seen as we hurried by on that road. I knew the lane on our left that ended in Talyllychau Abbey, and the dreaming mere, but at the time my mind was too full of a roadside smithy that we had just passed.

For every one Welshman who knows the ruined abbey there is a score that cherishes that blacksmith's forge, for it was there that Thomas Lewis hammered out the hymn that is sung in hundreds of Welsh Communion services: and one need not apologise for using the hammer-and-anvil metaphor in referring to the composing of this hymn.

It may be crude in its workmanship, it may be hard in its theology, but it has certainly known the white heat of a fervent devotion. It is a hymn about the cruel scourging that 'ploughed up a back that was so fair', about the 'nailing to a cross-beam', about being 'stricken down by His Father's sharp-edged sword'.

Wrth gofio'i riddfannau'n yr ardd,
   A'i chwys fel defnynnau o waed:
Aredig ar gefn oedd mor hardd,
   A'i daro gan gleddyf ei Dad;

In recalling his agony in the garden,
   With his sweat like beads of blood:
Scoring a back so fair,
   Being struck by his father's sword;

Wil Ifan, *Here and There*

20. *Dafydd Jones, Caio*

The second drover to leave his imprint on the literature of his country was Dafydd Jones, of Caio, one of Wales's foremost hymn-writers. He was noted as a drover who regularly visited Maidstone and Barnet fairs, as well as those of other towns. He achieved a mastery of, and fluency in the English language, sufficient to enable him to translate with ease. He will always occupy a high place in the history of Welsh hymnology as the translator of the hymns of Isaac Watts, several of which are contained in the denominational hymnaries in use at the present day. His conversion to Christianity is reminiscent of Saint Paul for its dramatic element. He was not until then conspicuous for a religious way of life, but returning from one of his droving enterprises, when about six miles from the village of Llanfairmuallt, where stood the chapel of Troedrhiwdalar, his attention was caught by the sounds of the hymn-singing coming from the Chapel, and it was the Sabbath. He was prompted to enter the Chapel, a circumstance that became the turning point of his life. From that time, he became an ardent and devout convert to the Christian Faith, and was moved by a deep repentance for, and absolute renunciation of his former way of life. In one of his poems referring to his conversion is manifest the new-found joy in his embracing of Christianity. He became a faithful member of the Independent Chapel of Crugybar, where he was buried in 1777.

P. G. Hughes, *Wales and the Drovers*

21. BYDD MYRDD O RYFEDDODAU

There'll be a myriad revelations,
At morning's break of dawn,
When the ocean's children
Bid farewell to grief;
All in their white robes together,
And in their newfound grace –
Like unto their Lord and Master
Coming ashore from the grave.

David George Jones, Llanarthney †

22. *The Revival*

Saturday night, however, I went to the meeting again, in that I felt that there were some herbal scented mountain breezes playing lightly and vitally through the place. The redeemed sang wonderfully and happily.

'Thanks unto Him . . .
Forever for remembering us, dust of the earth'

I said to myself, 'I'll join in singing 'Thanks unto Him', not that I had myself received the blessing, but that so many others had. Then, at last, some heavenly delight came through to me, something comparable to what Job felt when he prayed selflessly for his friends. Having gone home, and sat, totally quiet and undisturbed, I saw that salvation comes from *belief*, not through striving and agonising through praying all night on my part, but through someone else's striving on my behalf in the garden and on the cross; yes; by leaning on Him with his bloodied sweat and pain in death. O! What a release! What heavenly peace! I *believed*, because I was able to see unambiguously the ways through life. Well! Well: so simple, so near. So plain! So free! So loving in its conditions is the way of salvation: There's no need to aspire to the heavens or to descend to the depths to achieve it. The word is close at hand, and this is the word of the Faith. O heavenly revelation! A pity its simplicity is such a barrier to the rich and the intelligent and everyone.

But now, what was to follow? It was necessary to work out the new vision, whatever the cost. Some good brethren who worked energetically in the town, came and told me I would have to be baptised – by immersion of course – and by separation, that is to say separation from the church's teachings, as all the churches were lost since they had no experience of salvation, yes separation and joining with them. I have great respect for these Brethren who were so faithful to the gospel before the Revival. They had had some amazing converts, some from the deepest ditches of drunkenness, and some from more mysterious depths. But I did not feel free to follow them. For one thing, I remembered that the Holy Spirit had not confined Himself to those who were dipped in water. Had He not acknowledged and worked mightily through John Wesley and Whitfield, Daniel Rowland, Howell Harris and Pantycelyn and many others? No, I could not see that immersion in baptism was essential to a life of following Christ. The argument did not hold water.

Nantlais Williams, *O Gopa Bryn Nebo* †

23. Of Flatterie Glozingly Intermingled

Of Flatterie

Flatterie is hardly discerned from friendshippe, by reason that in every motion of the minde it is glozingly intermingled with it, but in the deedes they are meere adversaries for flattery differenteth from it in all verutous actions. This a wise man will soon espie, and that especially by these tokens: First, a flatterer is accustomed to praise a man before his face and yieldeth his consent with him in all matters, as well bad as good. Secondly, a flatterer is wont to comment the deformity of his friend, when he is present, and to admire his stammering voice. Thirdly, a Flatterer, when a man hath need of him, turneth his back. Fourthly a flatterer will take upon him at first to contradict a man, & by little & little he will yield as vanquished and will shake hands with him: these be the properties of a Flatterer, of whom let every honest man beware; for (as the Poet sayeth) *wicked poison lurketh under the sweetest honey.* And it is better to fall among a company of crowes, than to come among Flatterers because they will not peck a man till he be dead, whereas Flatterers will not spare to devour a man being alive.

William Vaughan. *The Golden Grove Moralised* 1600

24. *Rudd's Arithmetic*

Anthony Rudd acquired Aberglasney in 1594 when he, a Yorkshireman and Fellow of Trinity College Cambridge, left his Deanship of Gloucester to become the first resident Bishop of St David's. He it was who built the Palace of Abergwili, though he hardly lived there himself. He threw out a chapel at Llangathen and reconsecrated one in Aberglasney, still known as Rudd's Chapel. Above the house is a well, of Roman origin, called Rudd's Bath House. In his will he left money for four poor men from Llandeilo to buy land and build almshouses. One of these was at Llyshendy on the Bethlehem road.

Rudd was one of the great preachers of his age. And it was this which led to his downfall. He preached on one occasion before Elizabeth I who was so impressed with him that she intimated to Whitgift that Rudd should succeed him as archbishop. But the 'sneaking Tribe of Flattery' heard of it. When Rudd was asked to preach again they advised him that as Her Majesty, grown old, was weary of 'the vanity of wit and eloquence' Rudd ought rather to modulate his performance. The good bishop took it to heart and delivered a dismally plain sermon, choosing for his text, 'O teach us to number our days'. He always preached from the Psalms. Imprudently, he implied that even the beauty of a queen was subject to the ravages of time. Bess took it most ill. She rose. 'Enough of your arithmeticking master Rudd,' she said. And Rudd heard no more of Canterbury. 'Transient is the smile of Fate'. He died in 1615.

Bishop Anthony Rudd lies inside the church at Llangathen; he and his wife in effigy. His hands are not clasped in prayer. Sinister over dexter, the hand is covered which should have worn the Episcopal ring of Canterbury. 'So we mistake the future's face,/Eyed thro' hope's deluding glass.'

Lynn Hughes. *The Curse of Grongar Hill*
from the *Western Mail Weekend Magazine* 1977

25. *The Countess Canonised*

If we look on her as a Wife, she was chaste and loving, fruitful and discreet, humble and pleasant, witty and compliant, rich and fair; and wanted nothing to the making her a principal and precedent to the best wives in the world, but a long life and a full age.

If we remember her as a Mother, she was kind and severe, careful and prudent, very tender, and not at all fond: a greater lover of her children's souls than of their bodies, and one that would value them more by the strict rules of honour and proper worth than by their relation to herself.

Her servants found her prudent and fit to govern, and yet open-handed and apt to reward; a just exactor of their duty, and a great rewarder of their diligence. She was in her house a comfort to her dearest lord, a guide to her children, a rule to her servants, an example to all.

Jeremy Taylor.
Funeral Oration for Frances, Countess of Carbery,
Golden Grove 1650

26. *Don't Drink and Drive*

We have come across, and shall come across, several absent-minded little obelisks which surprise us simply because they have managed to survive at all. Clearly someone thought it worthwhile to set them up in the first place, when hearts perhaps were full of a recent sorrow, and posterity's indifference to it was unthinkable. Yet time, which cures and obscures so many griefs, which thins out old families, and brings new horrors to eclipse old ones, has seen to the downfall and disappearance of so many unprotected monuments that it is a pleasure to be able to comment on a veteran: one with a most apposite message for today's car drivers. The sturdy 'Mail Monument' near Llandovery, commemorating an 1835 disaster, says, in effect, 'If you drive, don't drink; if you drink, don't drive'; but the command is of more than slogan length:

> THIS PILLAR IS CALLED MAILCOACH PILLAR AND ERECTED AS A CAUTION TO MAIL COACH DRIVERS TO KEEP FROM INTOXICATION AND IN MEMORY OF THE GLOUCESTER AND CARMARTHEN MAIL COACH WHICH WAS DRIVEN BY EDWARD JENKINS ON THE 19 DAY OF DECEMBER IN THE YEAR 1835, WHO WAS INTOXICATED AT THE TIME AND DROVE THE MAIL ON THE WRONG SIDE OF THE ROAD AND GOING AT A FULL SPEED OR GALLOP MET A CART AND PERMITTED THE LEADER TO TURN SHORT ROUND THE RIGHT HAND AND WENT DOWN OVER THE PRECIPICE FOR 121 FEET WHERE AT THE BOTTOM NEAR THE RIVER HE CAME AGAINST AN ASH TREE WHEN THE COACH WAS DASHED INTO SEVERAL PIECES.

Correct, you see, to the nearest foot; utterly explicit concerning that nasty little short turn round to the right hand, and the kind of tree which shivered the mail coach to bits. Yet, although four passengers have their names inscribed in full, there are less formal mentions of 'a lad of the name of Kernick' and 'a person of the name of Edwards' who surely might as well have remained anonymous. The rest of the inscription, apart from an informative note concerning the mason and the 1930 restoration by the postal authorities, has charm but not much grace. In any part of the world its compiler might well be accused of having taken a drop of something to keep out the cold . . .

> I HAVE HEARD SAY, WHERE THERE IS A WILL, THERE IS A WAY, ONE PERSON CANNOT ASSIST MANY BUT MANY CAN ASSIST A FEW, AS THIS PILLAR WILL SHOW.

. . . all very acceptable to the forty-one subscribers who gave £13.16.6. toward this warning to wanton drivers, but unfair to the eight out of ten monuments which testify that one certainly can assist many!

Sir Hugh Casson, *Monuments*

27. *Saint Sarah*

Truly Sarah was a Wonder-child. She died alone, quietly, bravely, in what agony of thirst and suffering we may only guess. She never called for her parents, she never weakened in her determination not to betray their wicked fraud, even though it meant dying the lingering death she was enduring. Properly guided, and spiritually nurtured and cared for, she could, I feel sure, have grown up into a real saint, whom it would be a refreshing experience to visit and solicit her prayers. In her life and her brave death she had given proof that she had a complete mastery over the cravings and appetites of the flesh. She could endure the departure and abandonment of her parents Without one murmur. She could fast for long periods, for it is generally conceded that she managed to live on very, very little. She could be loyal and faithful to the last breath; she never gave anybody away, she would die rather than betray those who expected her not to betray them. Are there missing any qualities essential to the making of a saint? I do not think so. At this early age she had expressed grave anxiety about the state of her soul.

D. Parry-Jones, *My Own Folk*

28. '*To The Fasting Girl*'

'I saw people sitting by the fire in the kitchen as I was going out. The father said they were strangers from Aberdare, waiting their turn to go and see the child. They were five or six in number,' and such it seems was the case nearly every day at one time.

Pencader Station was at that period a comparatively unimportant station, although now a somewhat important junction of the Great Western and Manchester & Milford Railway Companies. The fasting girl of Lletherneuadd, however, effected an appreciable difference in the traffic, as the trains of the Carmarthen and Cardigan Railway were very frequently full of passengers who had come from long distances for no other object than to see the remarkable little girl. It is asserted that nearly the whole town of Carmarthen must, at one time or other, have made the pilgrimage to the shrine of the fasting girl. The station at Pencader, consequently, often presented a lively appearance, and the sight of men and boys wearing large caps, on which were attached strips of paper with the words: 'Guide to Lletherneuadd' or 'To the Fasting Girl', written in large letters thereon, unmistakeably pointed out the place as the proper spot for detraining. A picturesque walk of some two miles over hill and dale, brought the visitors to the lone farm of Lletherneuadd, and to the object of their quest.

These visitors, not only brought money to the place, but also presents of clothes, finery, books, or flowers, and the child was then bedecked with these things in the most grotesque fashion. Sometimes she had a victorine about her neck, and a wreath about her hair, and at other times she had ornaments and a jacket on, with her hair nicely dressed with ribbons, and enclosed in a wreath of flowers. When the Rev. W. Thomas, M.A.,* and Mr John Jones, solicitor, of Llandyssul, called at one time, 'she had a silk shawl, a victorine round her neck, a small crucifix attached to a necklace, and little ribbons (one blue on the right) above the wrists. She was lying on her back, a child's comb in her hair, which was brushed back and lying down on the sides. She had drab gloves on, whilst 'her bed was nearly covered with books – picture books especially.'

There is, no doubt, that the parents made a rich harvest during the last year of the little girl's illness, and the father himself admitted that 'many persons left a shilling or sixpence behind them.' In all probability, hardly a visitor would depart without leaving something behind, and the evidence of reliable witnesses goes to show florins, half-crowns, and even crown pieces were frequently given by individual visitors, and it was currently reported about April, 1869, that two English lady visitors left their offerings of two pounds in gold.

This 'oiling of the palm' seems to have an immediate effect on the parents, who became more gracious, and invited questions and examinations, which were not previously permitted. They, however, had generally too much modesty to receive the offerings themselves, and directed visitors to place their gifts on the breast of the little girl, stating that she and not they received them. Some, however, objected to this course, and found that the money, on such occasions, would be accepted in the usual way.

It would be interesting to know, approximately, the number of visitors who went to see the girl, but at this distance of time it has become impossible, as it is also improbable that we shall ever know the exact means by which Sarah was fed.

* 'Gwilym Marles' – Dylan Thomas's Great Uncle.

The personal testimony of those living near at the time, goes to show that she was visited by thousands, not only from the various counties of Wales, but also from England.

Anon. *Sarah Jacob, the Welsh Fasting Girl*, Pencader 1904

29. *Sarah Davies's Death Scene*

April   4th   Up all night casting brass, being the second night without rest.

         6th   Took Miss Davies and her brother for an airing in a phaeton.

     10th   J. Thomas returned.

     16th   Sarah Davies attained her 21st year at 6 this morning.
Sent a pattern book to the Exhibition for William Lewis, by rail.

May   5th   7 p.m. Sarah Davies after suffering from cough and difficulty in breathing, became perfectly free from pain. I was supporting her in nearly a sitting posture, she said 'Now I am dying, call Mother'. I desired her brother, who was in the room, to call his mother from the next room. She then said 'Mother, I am dying. Don't vex yourselves after me Mother, if you do you displease me. Blessed be the Lord for taking me. I am going to a place of bliss. I now see Heaven open before me, together with my Saviour and the God I worshipped from my youth. A description of what I now see is not given me to reveal to you if it were in my power but some things are given me to reveal for your good. Never more doubt the existence of a future state. Oh! where are those who doubt? I wish they were here now.' Speaking to me, she said, 'You see God revealed in this creation, in the beautiful flowers, in hill and valley, in all around you. If not enough, all is now clearly laid before me and I have authority to tell you never have the slightest doubt again.' She then told her mother and brother never to forget my kindness to her 'but the Lord will reward him and his children when my body is reduced to dust. Much that I tell you I speak not of myself, but I have authority to tell you. You may think from many things I do, or you may, hear me say that I am deranged but I am not indeed.' She then advised us respecting our future conduct in life, and desired me not to forget her mother, and saying she wished her father had been present to see her dying. She then said 'The sun is setting and it is getting dark, but it will soon be light again,' offering up a short prayer and singing several scraps of hymns, desired that she should be buried at Bethel, Cwmpedol, in the brook near which chapel she had been baptised when 12 years of age. Said what was to be done with her clothes, books, letters, etc., requested that I should make her coffin and design for headstone, and that the little flowers she was so fond of in life should be planted on her grave. All of which I promised to do. She then took us each by the hand commencing with her mother, telling me that I was the best friend she had on earth, and that I and her brother Evan were to have a lock of her hair to keep, and then desired each of us to kiss her, and not to give way to sorrow when she was gone. She asked Ellen, my servant, if she had seen anyone dying so happily before, and said 'You may all die thus if you do as I have told you.' She did not forget the children but kissed each, desiring them to be good to their father. 'I have now told you all, do not forget, so I shall lay myself down to die,' stretching her arms over the bed-clothes and playing her fingers, she continued with her eyes closed for about 5 minutes when, opening them she said 'I am not to die now, I shall yet see my father.' I told her we had not sent for him, and asked if we should do so she said yes, but it did not matter when, that the Almighty had promised she should see him 'and perhaps I may see Evan too stay a bit' closing her eyes for a few seconds she said 'Yes, I shall see my brother, too.' (I then sent for her father to Gelli, and her brother from Swansea). She said 'I shall live as long as I now wish. Do you know what inspiration is?' I said I knew the meaning of the word. 'Well,' said she, 'I am now inspired, I could tell you anything. I see all your faults past and present, every one of you. I can now see myself clearly. Where is Dr Prothero? I could tell him something of my disorder, that may be of benefit to him. I shall now recount my own faults.' Speaking to me she said 'I ought to have married you two years ago, I ought indeed, but I am following your poor Ann to the grave so I should have been no comfort to you. But what is this world with all its pleasures, its beautiful flowers, with man lord of creation, his quarrels and his wars spoiling the face of the earth. If he saw what I now do how different would he act. My past life is laid out as a map, it is as one day, but it is getting dark again, I have sinned.' I said 'No, you cannot sin now.' She said 'Yes, I have indeed, by saying that I should be talked of in ages yet to come, (a remark she made when she said she was inspired) but it will get still lighter yet. Here you see me receive the reward of my transgressions. This is my hell. There is no more pain for me but what I suffer here, and that won't be long. I am only now beginning to live.' It was about 9 o'clock. She seemed to enjoy intense pleasure, saying that she was perfectly free from any pain, she was clapping her hands and breast and singing praises to her Redeemer, and thanking and blessing us for our kindness to her, desired us to thank the Revd J. W. Pugh and Dr Prothero for their kindness to her. Soon after, the cough came on again.

6th She spent a sleepless night. Her father came about 8, and her brother Evan about 11 a.m. At 6 p.m. after Suffering much in the course of the day she desired us to kiss her again and wishing us goodbye said she had no further wish to live, and desired me to place her in an easy position to die. Shortly afterwards she asked me how long I thought she had to live, that she was anxious to go. I said about ½ an hour or ¾. She said 'Thank the Lord', and at 7 p.m. she breathed her last.

Perhaps the most striking thing about this death-bed scene is the fact that it was recorded, not by a writer deeply moved at seeing a person dying, for the first time, but by a man who had watched his small son and young wife die, and who must have acquired some degree of cynicsicm in his occupation of Undertaker. Even allowing for the personal involvement emotionally, it must have affected him greatly. Sarah Davies's prediction that she would be talked about in ages yet to come has certainly come about.

7th	Made her coffin, oak, covered with grey cloth and padded. Placed an account of her death in a stone jar in the coffin.
10th	Saturday. Left at 1 p.m. following her remains to Aberdauddwr. Mr T. T. Williams, her mother and cousin in a car following the hearse, her father and brother in another car, etc.
11th	Stayed at Aberdauddwr.
12th	Went in the morning to see the grave, and attended the funeral at 10 a.m. At 12 strewed flowers on her grave.

Ed. R. T. Jenkins,
The Diary of Thomas Jenkins of Llandeilo 1826-1870

30. *Your Sin Will Find You Out*

A Welsh boy bach was going to be a preacher. Joseph was his name. In his twentieth year he was summoned by Adah to petty sessions.

'He is the data of my female child,' said Adah.

The justices were parson church and other churchers.

'Say your say, Joseph,' said parson.

'Two times my age she is,' said Joseph, 'and too young was I to know she was teaching me bad.'

'For teacher you had the best looking mare in my parish,' said parson. 'Pay half a crown a week.'

The Big Man liked Joseph and spoke to him in the language of the Garden of Eden, which was Welsh.

'Blockheads are churchers,' he said. 'Their religion is in their back heads. Do not pay the wench.'

'All right you are,' said Joseph.

Then Adah sent a policeman after him, and he was afraid and cried out:

'Big Man, remember me!'

'A hiding courter is soon forgotten,' said the Big Man. 'I will make you, Jos bach, a preacher in a hurry.'

'I have not been to college for the B.A.'

'I will give you the soap religious. Open your mouth.'

Joseph opened his mouth and the Big Man put soap in his pipe neck.

'Now your voice is bubbles and suds,' said the Big Man.

Joseph spoke and it was so.

'Warn you I do,' said the Big Man. 'Sin once more and I will dry the soap and slap bang you into Hell. Go and wash my people on the high hills, where Adah cannot find you. Do not let her catch you, Jos bach, because there is no remedy in Heaven for the fury of a cheapened woman. Run full fast from here in the night and nobody will see how you go. So long.'

Capellers knew that Joseph's going was Adah's doing, and the big heads broke the woman from capel, and without a capel, bareness. She left the place.

In the thirty or so years that passed, Joseph grew into a great loose bearded man of strength and friendliness, and he carried the medicine into houses which were far from capels, and he saw no woman for whom he would fall into Hell. People called him Pilgrim because he came and departed singing the hymn that begins

> 'A pilgrim in a foreign land,
> Both near and far I roam,
> Expecting every moment to see
> My Data's glorious home.'

In the heavy heat of a June Sunday evening he came to a remote house. He looked at it and knew the plan of it: a loft reached by a ladder and two rooms for humans, a longish room for cows, the end a henroost and dairy. Hens pecked and two pigs snouted in its courtyard; two cows were lying in a field, as cows do before rain. Joseph sang his hymn in a deep belly voice and no person appearing, he went into the henroost. He was breaking eggs and swallowing them when a voice surprised him.

'Who you are?' said the voice.

'Drato, Big Man, why you did not give me a sign?' He answered:
'Pilgrim bach am I.'

'Heard have I of you,' said the voice.

The speaker was a lusty woman under a canopied chimney. Her
knees clasped the pole of a scythe and she was stoning the blade of it.

Joseph walked to her and watched her.

'A heavy hand is for cutting, old woman,' he said, 'not sharpening. I
will sharpen.'

He separated the blade from the pole and began to stone it.

'Seed you have scattered, old woman,' he said. 'What is your mowing? What is your crop for the crooked man with the crooked pole to
harvest?'

The woman mumbled sorrowfully:

'Brambles and thorns, dandelions and thistles are my harvest.'

Joseph cut a hair of his beard with the blade.

'Death's scythe is no keener,' he said.

Caradoc Evans, from *Your Sin Will Find You Out*

31. *Low Cunning*

In my day-school (in Cayo, Llandilo Fawr) some of the very poorest
have paid thus much: (from 1½*d.* to 2*d.* per week). There is a considerable desire among them to educate their children. But no good school
can be maintained by children's pence alone. In the country districts an
endowment of (certainly not less) from 15*l.* to 20*l.* per annum would
be requisite to ensure a permanent school. In this neighbourhood
(though all do not reside in my parish) the Earl of Cawdor and Lord
Dynevor, William Peel, Esq., of Taliaris, Mrs Du Buisson of Glynhir,
Mrs Cross of Abermarles, and John Lloyd, Esq., of Danyrallt, all maintain schools of their own; and of the 24*l.* which is paid annually
(exclusive of children's payments) to Morgan and Ann Lockyer in the
town of Llandilo, about 20*l.* is raised in subscriptions, 10*l.* of which I
receive from the Honourable Col. Trevor, M.P., alone. But there is
nothing, or next to nothing, in the shape of *general* subscription for the
education of the poorer classes.

The state of morals among the labouring population is bad; habitual lying and low cunning are very commonly met with, and unchastity is so prevalent that great numbers of the young women are in the family-way previous to marriage; and this sin, I fear, is very lightly regarded. There is also a great deal of drunkenness, where poverty does not prevent it. In this respect nothing can be more pernicious than the number of beer-houses with which this neighbourhood is infested. Many of these houses are kept by the worst characters. The facility of obtaining licences is an evil for which some remedy is imperatively demanded.

In their habits the labouring classes are particularly dirty. This arises in great measure, no doubt, from their poverty, and the low rate of wages which, until lately, they have been in the habit of receiving, so that it was quite impossible for them to have decent clothes or convenient houses. Pigs and poultry are frequently allowed to come inside. The flooring is generally bare earth; not even prepared with lime. There are rarely any privies. Neither light nor ventilation is well provided for. There are not usually more than two rooms. Cupboard-beds are those most commonly used, which are shut up as soon as the occupants quit them, and never opened again until night. The use of linen until lately, either by day or night, was almost unknown; it is now, however, coming more into fashion among the young people. Still, amidst so low a standard of morality, and such squalid poverty, there is a very general feeling that some degree of instruction would enable them to better their condition. This appears principally in their eagerness for their children to learn English; *e.g.* in my school I have the elder children taught to read their Bibles in Welsh (being their mother-tongue), as well as in English. Parents, however, have objected that 'their children can learn Welsh at home'.

I am of the opinion that the character of the schools in Wales is far from what could be desired. It is almost impossible to find an efficient teacher, owing to there being no training-schools, though happily that deficiency is now about to be supplied. When I first opened my school at Llandilo I paid 40*l*. a-year to a master, but he had never been trained, and consequently his mode of teaching was entirely without system, yet he was the best I could procure. In some of the schools maintained by private individuals children are well taught, but it is in consequence of the numbers being comparatively small, and great attention being frequently paid to them by those individuals and their families . . .

Of *general* information, I am of opinion that the amount possessed by the poor is very scanty, but among the class above them, such as farmers and shopkeepers, some few are well informed.

The majority of the poor in the country districts in Carmarthenshire and Cardiganshire can speak little or no English, nor have they any means of learning it. In the towns, however, there are few probably who do not know enough to make themselves understood, and many can speak fluently.

(Signed)   J. W. Pugh (Vicar of Llandilo)

Commissioners of Enquiry into the State of Education in Wales 1847

32. MRS JONES, LLANELLY

Her placid eye, where sparkling joy refines,
Benignant with alluring lustre shines.
His locks, which in loose ringlets charm the view,
Float careless, lucid from their amber hue.
A myrtle wreath her rosy fingers frame,
Which from her hand his polished temples claim;
His temples fair a streaking beauty stains,
As smooth, white marble shines with azure veins.
He kneeled; her snowy hand he trembling seized,
Just lifted to his lip, and gently squeezed;
The meaning squeeze returned, Love caught its lore,
And entered at his palm through every pore.
    Then swelled her downy breasts, till then inclosed,
Fast-heaving, half-concealed and half-exposed.
Soft she reclines; he, as they fall and rise,
Hangs hovering o'er them with enamoured eyes,
And, warmed, grows wanton. As he thus admired,
He pryed, he touched, and with the touch was fired.
Half-angry, yet half-pleased, her frown beguiles
The boy to fear; but at his fear she smiles!
The youth less timorous and the fair less coy,
Supinely amorous they reclining toy.
More amorous still, his sanguine meanings stole
In wistful glances to her softening soul;

In her fair eye her softening soul he reads:
To freedom freedom, boon to boon, succeeds.
With conscious blush the impassioned charmer burns,
And blush for blush the impassioned youth returns.
They look, they languish, sigh with pleasing pain,
And wish and gaze, and gaze and wish again.
'Twixt her white, parting bosom steals the boy,
And more than hope preludes tumultuous joy;
Through every vein the vigorous transport ran,
Strung every nerve, and braced the boy to man.
Struggling, yet yielding, half-o'erpowered, she pants;
Seems to deny, and yet, denying, grants.
Quick, like the tendrils of a curling vine,
Fond limbs with limbs in amorous folds entwine:
Lips press on lips, caressing and caressed;
Now eye darts flame to eye, and breast to breast.

All she resigns, as dear desires incite,
And rapt he reached the brink of full delight.
Her waist compressed in his exulting arms,
He storms; explores, and rifles, all her charms;
Clasps in ecstatic bliss the expiring fair,
And thrilling, melting, nestling, riots there.
How long the rapture lasts, how soon it fleets,
How oft it pauses, and how oft repeats,
What joys they both receive and both bestow –
Virgins may guess, but wives experienced know.

Richard Savage,
from '*Verses to Mrs Jones, on Valentine's Day*' 1742

IV

Heroes
& the Crachach

1. *Dialogue of Merlin and Taliesin*

Myrddin   How sad I am, how sad,
          For what befell Cedfyw and Cadfan!
          The battle was flashing and tumultuous,
          Shields were bloodstained and shattered.

Taliesin It was Maelgwn that I saw in combat,
          The retinue is not silent before the host.

Myrddin   Before two men in two groups they gather,
          Before Errith and Gwrrith on pale white steeds,
          Slender bay horses without doubt will they bring,
          Soon the host with Elgan will be seen,
          Alas for his death, they have come a great journey.

Taliesin One-toothed Rhys, whose shield was a span,
          To thee there came the blessing of battle.
          Cyndur has fallen, beyond measure will they grieve,
          Generous men, while they lived, have been slain,
          Three men of note, greatly esteemed by Elgan.

Myrddin   Over and over, in throng upon throng they came,
          From yonder and yonder there came to me fear for Elgan;
          In his last battle they slew Dywel,
          The son of Erbin, and his men.

Taliesin Maelgwn's host, swiftly they came,
          Battle-warriors in the glitter of slaughter.
          It is the battle of Arfderydd whence comes the cause,
          Throughout their lives they are preparing.

Myrddin   A host of spearsmen in the bloodshed of battle,
          A host of mighty warriors, mortal will they be,
          A host when broken, a host when put to flight,
          A host retreating, under attack.

Taliesin The seven sons of Eliffer, seven proven warriors,
          Will not avoid seven spears in their seven battle-sections.

Myrddin	Seven blazing fires, seven opposing armies,
	In every first onset Cynfelyn will be among the seven.
Taliesin	Seven piercing spears, seven rivers full,
	With the blood of chieftains will they swell.
Myrddin	Seven score men of rank lapsed into madness,
	In the forest of Celyddon they perished;
	Since it is I, Myrddin, after Taliesin,
	Whose prophecy will be correct.

The Black Book of Carmarthen* †

2. *Dawn Patrol*

At dawn, since I couldn't sleep, and it was such a lovely morning, I decided to get up and go on lone patrol. An hour later I was crossing the lines over Ypres at 15,000 feet. There were no Huns around or any of our machines, as far as I could see.

I climbed steadily in the direction of Roulers. Played around all over the place for a while. The sun was rising in a blaze of glory. I wondered if any Huns were approaching me from its direction. I couldn't see, because of the glare. Even when I put my fingers up against the glass, to lessen the glare, I couldn't see much better. Anyway, as I was at more than 18,000 feet, I did not get unduly worried.

At about 7.30 am, I spotted a V-formation of nine scouts at 10,000 feet, climbing south-west from the direction of an aerodrome east of Armentièrs. I got around behind them, unseen. Then, having made sure no other Huns were about, I very excitedly pulled back my throttle and dived on the last machine. When I got to a hundred yards off, I pressed

---

* Note: This poem, the first in the Black Book of Carmarthen (*c*.1250), is probably to be dated *c*.1050-1100. The first six speeches appear to deal with an attack against Dyfed by Maelgwn (of Gwynedd) in the early part of the sixth century. Ancient genealogies preserved in Dyfed show Elgan and Dywel ab Erbin to have been contemporaries of his. The remainder of the poem refers in prophetic form to the battle of Arfderydd (Arthuret, near Carlisle), *c*.573, for which the battle in Dyfed is seen as a preparation, and is therefore deemed to have been 'caused' by the later northern battle. The final stanza refers to the *gwyllon* of the Caledonian Forest, whose madness was one of the results of the battle. Myrddin is here made to claim the authorship of the poem but the exact meaning of the phrase 'after Taliesin' is uncertain.

A. O. H. JARMAN

the triggers. Nothing happened! I'd forgotten to pull up the charging handles of the gun gear, my Constantinesco, a necessary step before firing my Vickers gun. Unhappily I had also forgotten to cock the Lewis gun, which was fixed on to the centre section of the top plane.

Quickly I pulled my stick back, pushed my throttle open wide and zoomed, at the same time pulling up the handle, cocking the guns. It was a terrifying moment. When I looked over the side of the cockpit, I expected to find myself above a hornet's nest. Not a bit of it! The Huns were just ahead, still in the same peaceful formation. As on many occasions at this time of the morning, I found the pilots only half awake. The roar of their engines drowned the noise of mine.

I was in a quandary. Should I immediately dive and scrap the lot, probably getting shot down for my trouble, or should I follow them until they got closer to our own lines before having a go at them? I decided the latter tactics would give me the better chance of getting away with it. I followed behind the formation, taking up a position about 150 feet and dead behind the last man on the right. It was an eerie, uncanny situation in which I did not feel too happy, although I had created it myself.

I found myself well-nigh flying in a German formation, but had the consolation of knowing that none of the enemy suspected my presence, because I could see the back of their helmet heads. They were concentrating, not unnaturally on activities in the direction of the line straight ahead. I decided that if I thought I was spotted, to take a quick shot at the craft just in front, zoom up, have a crack at another, and then make my escape. Besides, I wanted to meet my King. That was something I did not want to miss. Every loyal citizen longs for that honour, and I might not get another opportunity. And as luck would have it, my hesitation did not end in the failure it deserved.

I followed behind the formation, about 500 feet above and dead behind the last man on the right. They flew over towards Bethune, then made an old man's turn back towards Bailleul. They were Fokkers. Most of them had black fuselages, with different-coloured tails. The fellow directly below me had a white tail. They all looked half asleep. Not even the leader had a single look behind him. I don't know whether it was because he was leaving the protection of his tail to the others.

The nervous strain was tremendous. I had an awful feeling that I was being led into a trap; that other Huns were coming at me from the sun. If there were, I was as blind to their presence as the lad in front of me was to mine. I was terribly excited as I followed. My heart was fairly thumping. Though I kept looking behind, I could see nothing. That made me more confident that the Fokkers could not see me, even if they looked behind.

Suddenly, in front and below, I spotted Hun 'Archie' firing at an RE 8 only a few thousand feet below over Merville. It was from No. 4 Squadron and engaged in taking photographs. I thought to myself: 'What a sportsman. You're asking for trouble, my lad.' And sure enough, he was. Two of the 'sleeping' birds dived simultaneously in his direction.

Now was my time for action, and quick, too, if I were going to save the RE 8. I dived full-throttle after them. My heart was thumping in my mouth, my whole body in a state of tremendous tension.

Fortunately, the RE pilot saw the Fokkers coming at him. He nose-dived for our lines. This gave me a little more time to get nearer to my birds, who were flying very close together. I fired from about two hundred yards, as I feared they would get a long shot home on the RE 8, and I was anxious to distract their attention. I succeeded. It was a straight shot.

On hearing the rattle of my machine guns, and seeing tracer and Buckingham bullets flash past, the two Fokkers quickly turned and collided. Then, firmly interlocked, they started going down in a sort of slow, weird spin. I could see the pilots struggling as I dived and fired into the already doomed mass. There was a streak of ominous smoke, followed by a tongue of flame, and soon both craft were enveloped in a blaze which must have quickly ended the agonising moments of the two German pilots. Horrible though the sight was, it held my gaze for a few precious moments which might easily have resulted in my own end.

The remainder of the flight came down on me. Suddenly I found tracer bullets shooting past and dangerously near. Things looked very awkward for a few moments, but, madly firing in all directions, I succeeded in getting away from all hostile aircraft except one, which remained to do battle until the line was reached. I easily got away from him.

Crossing the lines at Meteren, I joined the RE. We waved rejoicingly at each other. The old RE wagged his tail. I hastened back, as it was past eight o'clock. On the way, I had a terrible reaction. The tenseness of the episode so affected my nerves that I crashed on landing, turning a somersault on the ground. Extricating myself from the machine, I was greeted with anything but bouquets.

From the crash I dashed to get ready for parade. All the others were ready. It was decided that we should wear the old RFC uniform. As I had none, I borrowed Giles's breeches, boots and tunic, and Clem's cap and Sam Browne. A handkerchief was my only possession. Thus dressed in borrowed plumes and very nervous, I appeared before my King.

The officers were all lined up, ready for His Majesty's arrival. I can't imagine what he must have thought of our uniforms. There were about half a dozen sorts. He shook hands with all, and when he came to me he stopped and chatted for about five minutes. He was very interested in my opinion of the Hun machines and pilots. When I said that one Britisher was worth three Huns he laughed loudly. I was quite taken aback by his geniality. What a lovely laugh he's got. Plumer and Horn, who accompanied him, also laughed, but Webb-Bowen had a face like a sour apple.

When the King left me, he said: 'I wish you the best of luck, and a safe return.' This kind remark has touched me very much. Now I shall fight like hell.

My stammering was very bad while I was speaking to His Majesty, but he didn't seem to mind. Old Plumer seemed to be tickled by it and had a twinkle in his eye all the time. One amusing incident happened while the King was looking at my medals. Pointing at the silver rose in my DFC, he asked 'What's that?'

I replied: 'Bar to my DFC, sir'.

'So!' said his Majesty, looking somewhat surprised. 'You've got an MC, DFC and bar. How many enemies have you brought down?'

The importance of the occasion accentuated my stammer, with the result that I could not express the number '33' clearly.

I started, 'Th . . . th . . . th . . .'

His Majesty soon observed my difficulty, and with his usual kindness, tried to help me along. However, it only made things worse.

'Thirty!' suggested the King.

I shook my head. 'Th . . . th . . . th . . .' I started again.

Thirty-five?' he interpolated.

Again I shook my head, and stammered away, 'Th . . . th . . . th . . .'

His Majesty tried to put me at my ease by looking away for a moment. This did the trick, and eventually out came my figure, 'Thirty-three, sir.'

Ira Jones. Adapted from
Tiger Squadron and *An Air Fighter's Scrap-book*

3. Nest and Owain

Owain stared blindly at her. Her beauty last night had excited him as would that of any lovely woman – then the anger that followed had filled every corner of his being with a different passion. But now that he had her in front of him again – submissive, helpless, yet infinitely more desirable – he felt different from any other moment in his whole life.

He wanted her – not only because she was the most beautiful woman he had ever seen – but because some magic had just touched him. Some spell had fallen on him, compounded of animal attraction, the drama of the moment and the ecstatic fulfilment of an almost dream-like situation. He had fallen in love not only with Nest, the woman, but with the awareness that he was playing a role straight out of mythology, with the handsome young prince rescuing the maiden from the clutches of an ogre . . . this capture of a Norman's Welsh wife crystallized into a moment of triumph that must be marked by some even greater ecstasy.

He held out his arms and pulled her to him. With his face buried in her dark hair, he groaned into her neck, 'Nest, why did you not meet me again ten years ago . . . though I was then but a boy. Oh, Nest, Nest.' The last words were almost as if he were in pain and she could not tell if it was anguish or sheer, unbridled desire.

A husband and a royal lover had taught her well enough to recognize uncontrolled passion, but never had she felt so urgently wanted . . . and this time by a young man of her own kind, a prince and one who had so obviously capsized emotionally within the space of five minutes.

She shivered, partly with a sudden chill, partly from the nearness of Owain . . .

He looked eagerly at her, his face alive with expectation.

'Nest, then you feel what I feel . . . I know it! There is something between us that needs no human lips to frame. In the minutes we have been together, some bond has been tied between us. I have never felt like this before, though God knows, I have dallied with girls in plenty.'

She gazed steadily at him, knowing exactly what he was trying to say. He had pulled off his helmet and the unruly auburn hair wreathed down on to his forehead. The strong features were flushed and the smear of dried blood and the smuts did nothing to lessen his intense attraction for her.

'You are taking us away,' she murmured, for something to say.

'Not far . . . some fourteen miles to Caerwedros – a commote where the Penteulu is my especial friend. We shall be there within three hours. Your children shall be sleeping safely again before dawn.'

She nodded, then shivered again within the circle of his leather-clad arm. 'I must get warm clothing – for them and myself.'

Gently, she pulled herself away and moved towards the curtained doorway where the bed-chamber lay.

Like steel following a lodestone, Owain followed her. Once through the door, he took one look around the dim chamber, then pulled the door shut and dropped the bar into its sockets.

The sound made Nest turn round quickly. They stood staring at each other in the flickering red light, almost like opponents ready for combat.

'What is this, Owain?' she asked in a low voice.

He knew that her words held no fear, only awareness. Two steps brought him to her and then his arms were around her again and his lips were on hers.

Bernard Knight, *Lion Rampant*

4. *The Death of Owain Cadwgan*

And Owain was gladdened by the promises, and he gathered a host, and Llywarch along with him. And together they went to Ystrad Tywi, where they thought Gruffudd ap Rhys was staying; for it was a wild wooded land both difficult to traverse and easy to rush upon enemies in it. And then they came to the bonds of the land, all Owain's host and the king's son and their supporters, they sent their forces into the woods, every man in his own area, on this condition: that he was not to spare the sword against man or woman, boy or girl, and whomsoever they caught they were not to let him go without killing him or hanging him or cutting off his members. And when the common folk of the land heard that, they sought how they could find protection for them-selves. And so they were dispersed, some lurking in the woods, others fleeing to other lands, others seeking protection from the nearest castles from which they had come; – as is said in a Britannic proverb, 'The dog licks the spear with which he is wounded'. And after the host had been dispersed into the woods, it chanced that Owain and with him a small troop, about ninety men, made for the wood and were looking whether they might see the tracks of people fleeing. Lo, they could see the tracks of people leading to Carmarthen castle, where they had made their peace. And he pursued them right up to the castle. And after seizing them there, he returned to his comrades.

In the meantime a host of the Flemings from Rhos chanced to come to Carmarthen to meet the king's son, and Gerald the steward along with them. Lo, those who had escaped coming with a cry towards the castle and making it known that they had been plundered and pillaged by Owain ap Cadwgan. And when the Flemings heard that, they were fired with hateful envy towards Owain because of the frequent injuries that Owain's comrades had previously inflicted upon them. And at the instigation of Gerald the steward, the man whose castle Owain had burned and whose wife Nest together with his booty and spoils he had carried off by force, they pursued him. But Owain, not thinking that there was opposition to him, went on his way calmly. They, however, in pursuit of him quickly came to the place where he was, and the spoil with him. And when Owain's comrades saw a huge multitude pursuing them, they said to him, 'Behold a huge multitude pursuing us, with none able to resist them.' And he gave them answer, 'Be not afraid,' said he, 'for they are the forces of the Flemings.' And having said that, he fell upon them in an attack. And they bore his attack manfully. After arrows had been shot on either side, Owain fell wounded. And after he had fallen, his comrades turned to flight. And when Llywarch ap Trahaearn heard that, he returned, he and his men, to his land.

The Chronicle of the Princes, † 1116

5. *Ystrad Rwnws*

'Your father,' she interrupted quietly, 'did he meet his death in arms?' And again, an odd look passed between William and Maurice.

'Not directly,' Maurice said.

'How then?'

'He – he was leading a Flemish company in pursuit of some rebels. William and I were riding with him. We had crossed the bridge over the Towy near Ystrad Rwnws when we saw a party of about ninety men approaching from the north. They were moving without haste, and were laden with booty. They were laughing, and shouting in Welsh.'

'*Welsh?*'

'Yes, my mother. The King has persuaded many native leaders to take the field against Gruffydd ap Rhys.'

'I see. So these were on the Norman side?'

'They were: their lance-pennants were decorated with the golden leopard of the King . . . We rode forward to join them and to ask their news. Then, without warning, our father ordered us to halt. Thinking that he jested, I looked at him and found his face all ridged, as it were by iron sinews underneath. His eyes were fixed on one man in the company, and his hand was on his sword.'

Maurice put his head down on her knee, signing to his brother to continue for him.

'I was on the opposite flank,' William said reluctantly, 'and could not see my father. But I heard his order to the Flemings who now crowded up behind him in a tight rank: "There are William of Brabant's murderers; attack the bodyguard, leaving the leader to me." Then he spurred his horse into a great charge and unsaddled Owain ap Cadogan, Prince of Powys –'

'*Owain* . . . ?'

'It was he, my mother, newly knighted by the King in Normandy, and armed so splendidly that none of us, except our sire, had recognized him.'

'They fought – these two?' she asked slowly.

'There was no fight; no mercy. Owain lay upon the ground and our father bent over him while the Flemings held the Welsh at bay. He leaned down, his sword-point at the Prince's throat, and slit the lacings of the helm. I know not whether he asked absolution for what he was about to do – it was all too quick, too sudden . . . Next moment, he had pressed upon the sword until it clove the turf beneath.'

Her shuddering was so violent that Maurice pressed his hands upon her knees to quiet her. She did not weep then – not for a long time afterwards – but the cold that had gripped her in that moment was yet unthawed, as though the breath of winter had blown across her life, freezing down through every level of consciousness.

She could not remember when the end of the story was told to her, or by whom, but the pageant of death passed clearly before her eyes and it seemed to her that she watched her husband – no, more than that: she looked out from his eyes, felt her heart beating as one with his – from the instant in which he killed the Prince of Powys until his own body ceased to breathe . . .

With his enemy's blood still unwiped from his sword, Gerald de Windsor had galloped back over the Towy bridge at such speed that the timbers parted, and he had to urge his mount into a desperate leap to reach the other bank. All the while, he was shouting like a madman: 'Defend Pembroke! Defend Pembroke from the men of Powys!' – but his escort dared not follow him across the bridge. By the time they had forded the river at another place, their commander was many miles ahead and still travelling at a furious pace.

After a long while, he looked back and could see nothing but the ruin of Carmarthen castle, which Gruffydd ap Rhys had burnt . . . Twenty miles to Pembroke! He had to organize his garrison there against a siege, for undoubtedly the men of Powys would seek to avenge their Prince's death.

De Windsor was not afraid; neither had he any sense of remorse for the killing; but the jubilation which he might have felt, six, or even five years previously, was absent. Owain ap Cadogan was dead: Gerald de Windsor's honour was satisfied, his unsleeping vengeance finally at rest. But now, there was a curious lack of purpose about everything else – even the defence of Pembroke, to which he had given his life.

Eleanor Fairburn, *The Golden Hive*

6. *Rhys ap Gruffudd sends the Normans packing*

The following year the Lord Rhys ap Gruffudd subdued the castles which the French had built all over Dyfed and he burned them. In the meantime he led his army to Carmarthen and laid siege to it. And then Reginald, son of king Henry, came against him, and along with him a mighty host of French and Normans and Flemings and Saxons and Welsh. And Rhys left the castle and gathered his men together on the mountain of Cefn Rhestr. And then the earl Reginald and the earl of Bristol and the earl of Clare and two other earls and Cadwaladr ap Gruffudd and Hywel and Cynan, sons of Owain Gwynedd, and a mighty multitude of horsemen and foot-soldiers along with them, encamped at the castle of Dinwileir.[1] And without having dared to attack the place where Rhys was, they returned home empty-handed. Thereupon they offered Rhys a truce. And he accepted it, and gave his men permission to return to their land.

The Chronicle of the Princes, † 1157-1159

---

[1] Dinefwr.

7. *The Lamentation for Rhys ap Gruffudd*

The following year there was a mighty pestilence of mortality through-out the whole island of Britain and the bonds of France, so that an untold number of the common people and gentlefolk and princes beyond number died. And in that pestilential year Atropos and her sisters, who were formerly called the Goddesses of Fates, showed their envious, venomous powers against such an eminent prince that neither the histories of Statius the historian nor the songs of Virgil the poet could tell how great a lamentation and grief and misery came to the whole race of the Britons when Death, in that accursed year, broke the wheel of Fate to snatch the Lord Rhys ap Gruffudd on its wings under the subduing power of Death; – the man who was the head and the shield and the strength of the South and of all Wales and the hope and the defence of all the race of the Britons. That man was sprung from a most noble line of kings. He was conspicuous for the numbers of his kindred; and the force of his mind compared with his kindred; counsellor of the magnates, warlike against the strong, protection of the vanquished, assaulter of fortresses, attacker in battles, arrayer and ruler of armies, overthrower of hosts; and like to a boar growling or to a lion attacking, so raged his ferocity against his foes. Alas for the glory of battles, the shield of knights, the defence of his land, the splendour of arms, the arm of prowess, the hand of generosity, the eye of reason, the light of worthiness, the height of magnanimity, the substance of might! A second Achilles for the might of his breast-bone, a Nestor for gentle-ness, a Tydeus for doughtiness, a Samson for strength, a Hector for prudence, a Hercules for excellence, a Paris for beauty, a Ulysses for speech, a Solomon for wisdom, an Ajax for mind, and the foundation of all accomplishments!

The Chronicle of the Princes, † 1196-1197

8. *The Funeral of Sir Rhys ap Gruffudd*

I saw him, noble peerless ruler, on a day of destruction, in a chancel, my stag, under cover, hidden in Carmarthen, a great body before me on the floor, and all his people mourning him, and his spear in its fastening, woe to those who see him, and his stallion by his side, and his keen sword with jagged blade, and his shield, they all went to the ground, and his shining black mantle, lord, and his banner upraised, and his funeral rites, and his brilliant shroud, and his cuirass and his bright grey helmet, and his trappings like stars, and his azure armour with no one to wear it; and his soul, he was a lord, let that go to the fair country of the Lord of Heaven.

Iolo Goch †

9. Dynevor Castle under Siege

And after Rhys Gryg had been summoned to answer to the king's command, he said in answer that he would not share a single acre with Rhys Ieuanc. And Rhys Ieuanc was enraged. And he gathered a mighty host from Brycheiniog and came by force to Ystrad Tywi, and he encamped in the place called Trallwng Elgan on the Thursday after the eighth day from the feast of St Hillary. And on the following day, Friday, there came to him Owain, his brother, and Falkes, seneschal of Cardiff, and their hosts. And on the following day they made for the territory of Rhys Gryg and they arrayed their troops and placed Rhys Ieuanc and his troop in the van and Falkes and his troop in the centre and Owain ap Gruffudd and his troop in the rear. And it was not long till Rhys Gryg and his host met with them. And in the battle with the first troop Rhys Gryg and his men were defeated, and he retreated in flight, after some of his men had been slain and others had been captured. And then Rhys Ieuanc went with the intention of laying siege to the castle of Dinefwr. But nevertheless Rhys Gryg forestalled him and fortified the castle with men and arms. And after having burnt Llandeilo he retreated thence. But nevertheless Rhys Ieuanc made for the castle. And on the following day he placed engines and contrivances to lay siege to the castle, and made ladders against the walls for his men to climb over the walls. And thus he gained possession of the whole castle except for one tower. And in that the garrison undertook to fight and put up a defence with missiles and other engines; and outside there were archers and crossbow-men and sappers and knights besieging them. And thus they were forced before afternoon to surrender the castle. And they gave three hostages against surrendering the castle unless they received help by noon the following day, on condition that they should have their raiment and their arms and their members safe. And so it was done. And after the castle had been taken Rhys Gryg and his wife and his sons and his war-band fled to Maelgwn, his brother, after the castle of Llandovery had been fortified with men and arms and food and engines and other necessities.

And a second time Rhys Ieuanc went to Brycheiniog. And then he gathered a mighty host of Welsh and French and made for Llandovery. And before they encamped, the garrison surrendered the castle to him on condition that they should have their lives and their members safe.

The Chronicle of the Princes † 1213

10. ELEGY FOR RHYS GRYG

Many freely-flowing tears course down
about the fortress-tomb of Rhys,
ruler of Dinefwr, a man of splendid children,
lion of battle, and its privileged king.

Privileged Rhys, a powerful king,
battle-companion, one who feeds ravens
the chosen hawk among mighty hawks,
we are lost because of the dragon who has departed.

I am lost in my grief, enslaved to lamentation,
we are lost without the chieftain, a red-speared lion,
Rhys son of Rhys, despoiler of Rhos,
has met his end in a stone tomb at St David's.

Near St David's I saw Rhys the attacker of Rhos,
the chieftain, lion of Haverford,
heroic prince, in a battle of ten thousand men,
handsome, iron-clad prince.

Rhys of the splendid court, captor of Rhos,
ruler of a host while he lived,
proud, of stammering speech, and gapped sword,
deep his wrath, ferocious in battle.

Attacker in battle, lion with dripping blade
was Rhys, red-speared, prompt to anger on the slope
a stammering prince, lord of shining (drinking) horns,
his hand was a safeguard to his armies.

Hendregadredd MS †

11. DAFYDD AP GWILYM AT TALLEY

Dafydd who made a wealth of poetry
by his quick inspiration,
he has gone to our last home in the grave,
great is our anguish for our brother's death.

We cry and we lament – alas, how sad –
dead is the artificer of song;
no further rebirth of the muse can come
again to work upon our language.

Concerning gifted Dafydd of trusty speech,
Taliesin, a powerful poet prophesied:
there would be born in Brogynin
a poet whose *cywydd* is like wine.

In one thousand, 300 and 68 the year
in sad grief the noble poet died
the son of Gwilym of fine animated song.

In the grave he rests beneath this stone
– a grievous loss, his shining verse –
There in a meadow lapped by waves,
Place above water, Talley lakes fair.

attrib. Hopcyn ap Tomos ab Einion † 1380

12. *'Over My Bellie'*

Sir Rhys ap Thomas had nineteen hundred tenants bound by their
leases to attend him on horseback at the shortest call; and a poet of
those days wrote –

Y brenin bia'r Ynys,	The King owns the island,
Ond sy o ran i Syr Rhys:	Save what pertains to Sir Rhys.

The couplet was considered to impeach Rhys's loyalty, and led to his
arraignment.

After the defection of the Duke of Buckingham from Richard III, and when a marriage was being concerted between the Lady Elizabeth, eldest daughter of Edward IV, and the Earl of Richmond, Rhys ab Thomas's assistance was regarded as of great consequence; and Milford Haven was the safest, if not the only place at which the earl could land; but here Rhys was completely master; his friendship was therefore essential, and consequently a reconciliation was effected between him and the Duke of Buckingham. Enmity having existed between the families since the time of Gruffydd ab Nicholas, about this period, Buckingham had sent Rhys a message to say that unless he gave him satisfaction for a certain injury, he would come shortly and cudgel him out of his castle of Carmarthen. Rhys coolly answered that the roads being hilly and rough, his highness might spare himself the trouble of the journey, for he intended waiting upon him shortly at Brecknock, to receive his commands.

The mission from the Lancastrians to Rhys was entrusted to Dr Lewis, a former tutor of Rhys, and now physician to the Countess of Richmond. Dr Lewis found Rhys at Abermarlais, preparing for the expedition to Breconshire, and succeeded in obtaining Rhys's consent to make up his difference with Buckingham. Rhys and Buckingham, soon after this, met at Trecastle, where they agreed to bury all past animosities in oblivion; but Rhys's views on the main question – Red or White Rose – were not then ascertained. Richard being apprised that a plot was hatching, demanded distinct assurances and hostages from those whose fidelity he doubted. Among others, commissioners were sent to Rhys ab Thomas at Carmarthen, to administer to him the oaths of fidelity, and to require his only son, Gruffydd, five years of age, as an hostage. Rhys took the oath without hesitation, but wrote a letter to the king, praying to be excused from parting with his son, on account of his tender age. He expressed indignation at the suspicion of his loyalty, observing that such suspicion might read to some of fickle minds and unstable thoughts evil lessons against themselves. He made, however, the following 'voluntary protestation':

> 'Whoever, ill-affected to the State, shall dare to land in those ports of Wales where I have anie employments under your Majestie, must resolve with himself to make his entrance and irruption over my bellie.'

The general opinion is that Rhys was perfectly sincere in his declarations in this celebrated letter which is a very able composition, drawn up by the Abbot of Talley, a zealous – though, to Rhys, concealed – Lancastrian. It is filled with such expressions of loyalty as were likely to satisfy Richard, but, at the same time, couched in such equivocal terms, as might leave Rhys (under the guidance of his spiritual counsellors, the Abbot of Talley and the Bishop of St David's) at liberty to break with the king, with what he might deem a safe conscience, should he afterwards see cause.

Richard was satisfied, and sent Rhys instructions in the commands he held. Rhys, however, was uneasy in his mind. At this juncture, the abbot and bishop declared openly to Rhys their real views, and urged him to break with the king. 'The conversation at their interview exhibits a most curious specimen of casuistical reasoning on the part of the pious churchmen, to silence Rhys's scruples as to his oath, and the declaration of loyalty contained in this letter. They succeeded in shaking his resolution, and in a short time afterwards he gave them his explicit assurances of support; and in due time preparations were made to receive Richmond at Milford Haven. When the appearance of the French fleet was announced, Rhys was at his castle of Carew, whence he advanced with a noble band of chosen followers, well-mounted and armed to meet Richmond at Dale. On the earl coming ashore, it is stated that Rhys in order to make good his word to the king, lay on his back on the ground so that Richmond might pass over him; but a popular tradition in the neighbourhood asserts that Rhys satisfied his conscience by remaining under a small bridge while the Earl of Richmond passed over. The combined forces were now ordered to march for Shrewsbury in two divisions – one under Richmond through Cardiganshire, the other under Rhys through Carmarthenshire. The beacons were lighted, and the whole country was immediately under arms. 'By the time Rhys had reached Brecon, his followers had swelled to an incredible multitude', out of which he selected a body of two thousand horsemen; and afterwards a body of infantry of five hundred men, which he entrusted to the command of his younger brothers, David and John. They were left as a guard in the Principality; the remainder were discharged with proper acknowledgements for their readiness to serve him. Rhys then joined Richmond at Shrewsbury. It was not until just before this event that Richard was informed of his danger; he lost not a moment in preparing himself for the contest. The two armies encountered at Bosworth, where a hard and sanguinary conflict ensued. In the heat of the battle, Richard made a bold effort to attack Richmond personally in the midst of his guards. Being strongly supported, and having overthrown Sir

William Brandon, the Earl's standard bearer, the situation of Richmond became highly critical. Rhys ab Thomas, perceiving the state of the contest, sent to inform Sir William Stanley of the Earl's danger, and to implore his instant aid. Stanley, who had thus far kept aloof, instantly advanced, and being joined by Rhys, the two commanders bore down on the king's troops with irresistible impetuosity, and put them to the rout. The Welsh tradition asserts that Rhys ab Thomas slew King Richard in this encounter, fighting with him hand to hand. But whatever foundation there may be for this story, the conduct of Rhys on this memorable day was so distinguished, that Richmond ascribed to it the issue of the battle, and ever afterward in testimony of his gratitude applied to the Welsh hero the title of Father Rhys. The spoils of King Richard's tent were shared between Rhys and Sir William Stanley, the earl's father-in-law. Then, after the latter had placed the crown on Richmond's head, and the army had saluted him King Henry VII, as the first act of his reign, he conferred on Rhys ab Thomas the honour of knighthood.

William Samuel. *Llandilo and its Neighbourhood* 1868

13. SYR RHYS AP THOMAS

Beat the English with force, you with the grip of a giant,
wolf-like, sound the alarm with lamentation on stretchers
the seventh planet is disturbed,
the whole earth trembles with the horns of the army of the South,
the entire world trembles with the blows of the Raven,
air and fire, the sea with its waves.

The prognostications of Anglesey will be fulfilled
(when) the first of May is on a Thursday,
the giant of the Island of Britain will be found at the
time of the prophecies,
the whelp of strong Efrog will be had to make war,
friend of great Caesar will be had to give chase.
March – conquer the fortresses – (like) Beli Mawr,
brave giant of conquests and of good qualities.

Tudur Aled, from *Cywydd i Syr Rhys ap Thomas* †

14. *The Dynevor Line*

The Dynevor estates were given by Henry the seventh to Sir Rhys ab Thomas, and descended with his other possessions to his grandson Rhys ab Gruffydd, from whom, through an act of the most cruel injustice, they again reverted to the crown, in the reign of Henry the eighth. Rhys's ancestors had been in the habit of occasionally adding Ab Urien, or Fitz Urien, to their names, in conformity to the general Welsh practice, in order to shew their descent. This designation, after being disused for some time, was again adopted, probably in a vain frolic, by young Rhys. The circumstance being reported to the king, and being associated with the immense possessions and unbounded popularity of the family, was construed into a design to assert the independence of the principality, and to dissever it from the English government. It was also supposed, without the shadow of proof, that this was part of a concerted plan to depose King Henry, and bring to the English throne James the fifth of Scotland. To increase the absurdity of the whole business, the plot was said to be founded on an old prophecy, that James of Scotland with the bloody hand, and the Raven, which was Rhys's crest, should conquer England. On such frivolous grounds was this young chieftain, himself one of the first commoners in the realm, and connected by marriage with the family of Howard, arraigned for high treason, found guilty, and beheaded.

On the accession of Queen Mary, his son, Gruffydd ab Rhys, had his blood restored, and received back part of the estates; and Charles the first relinquished to Sir Henry Rice all that were at that time of them in the hands of the crown. The estates thus restored to the family were valued at about three hundred pounds a year; these constitute their present Welsh territories, and are all that remain to them of the princely possessions of their ancestors.

The house of Dynevor has always held considerable influence in the county, and has in several instances furnished its parliamentary representatives. George Rice, who died in 1779, married in 1756 Lady Cecil Talbot, only child of William, Earl Talbot. This nobleman was afterwards created Baron Dynevor, with remainder to his daughter, who, on his death in 1782, became Baroness Dynevor. On the death of her mother in 1787, she took the name and arms of De Cardonel, which are still borne by the family. Her ladyship died on the 14th of March 1793, and was succeeded by her eldest son George Talbot Rice, the present Baron Dynevor.

Thomas Rees. *The Beauties of England and Wales* 1815

15. *Lewis Glyn Cothi*

This is the country which produced the 'Immortal Lewis, the greatest poet, after ap Gwilym, in all Welsh literature . . .' His period of vigour and song seems to have been from about 1460 to 1490. He was both poet and soldier, for he fought much in the Wars of the Roses, was an enthusiastic Lancastrian, a follower of Jasper, Earl of Pembroke, and a sufferer in his cause. When Jasper had to fly the country, Lewis remained and was hard put to it in avoiding capture. He hid in Chester in disguise, but was eventually found and deprived of everything he possessed, a proceeding which accounts for his loathing of the men of Chester, and his complimentary poems to any leader who made havoc among them. Then or at another time he got into trouble in the same city for marrying a widow without the leave of the magistrates – a serious offence for a Welshman in the century following Glyndŵr's war. One of his best known poems in fact is a most virulent satire on an English wedding in Flint, to which he had been invited. He would doubtless have abstained from criticising the meat and drink as he did, but for the dire offence of slighting his performances in favour of a piper, the player too of an instrument despised by the Welsh. The brutal Saxons apparently would have none of Lewis, but 'bawled for Will the piper, lowborn wretch', and this is the poet's picture of poor Will, or rather a sample from it:

> The churl did blow a grating shriek,
> The bag did swell and harshly squeak,
> As does a goose from nightmare crying,
> Or dog, crushed by a chest, when dying
> This whistling box's changeless note
> Is forced from turgid veins and throat.
> The sound is like a crane's harsh moan,
> Or like a gosling's latest groan,
> Just such a noise a wounded goat
> Sends from her hoarse and gurgling throat.

Whether on account of his sufferings or his talents as a poet, he had most certainly a rooted notion that his friends and patrons ought to be generous to him, and the number of poems he addressed to donors, or potential donors, on this supposition is quite remarkable. One would gather from these metrical petitions that the writer was being continually unhorsed. To John Phillip of St Clears he prays for a horse, because the other bards get to musical and literary competitions ahead of him, and so gain undue advantage. To Howel ab Evan of Radnor he writes for a saddle, the Earl of Pembroke having promised him a horse. Of the men of Elvael in Radnor he not only begs a horse, but describes the points he would like it to possess. In a poem to a Rhayader friend, again, he condoles with him on a bad sabre cut on the face, but thinks that the crucifix shape he bears it has assumed should be accounted a vast consolation. Of one David Lloyd he begs a bow and arrows since those already given him were stolen. To Gutyn of Oswestry he writes for a new rapier to teach the accursed men of Chester better manners. In poems to other people who have befriended him, he writes in lavish praise of their horses and hospitalities. To 'Gwenllian of the golden locks and the skin like drifted snow', Glyndŵr's illegitimate daughter, who married Rhys of Cenarth in Cardiganshire, he indites a well known ode. He was naturally enthusiastic on the accession of Henry VII, for every reason, and spent his last years, let us hope, in comfort on the banks of the Cothi with a good horse to ride and no lack of hospitable friends.

A. G. Bradley. *Highways & Byways in South Wales* 1905

16. *The Death of Picton*

The French columns were marching close up to the hedge; the English advanced to meet them, and the muzzles of their muskets were almost touching. Picton ordered Sir James Kempt's brigade forward: they bounded over the hedge, and were received with a murderous volley. A frightful struggle then ensued: the English rushed with fury upon their opponents, not stopping to load, but trusting solely to the bayonet to do their deadly work. The French fire had, however, fearfully thinned this first line, and they were fighting at least six to one. Picton, therefore, ordered General Pack's brigade to advance. With the exhilarating cry of 'Charge! Hurra! hurra!' he placed himself at their head, and led them forward. They returned his cheer as they followed him with a cool determination, which, in the words of the Spanish chief Alava, 'appalled the enemy'.

The general kept at the head of their line, stimulating them by his own example. According to the Duke of Wellington's despatch, 'This was one of the most serious attacks made by the enemy on our position.' To defeat it was therefore of vital importance to the success of the day. Picton knew this, and doubtless felt that his own presence would tend greatly to inspire his men with confidence. He was looking along his gallant line, waving them on with his sword, when a ball struck him on the temple, and he fell back upon his horse – dead. Captain Tyler, seeing him fall, immediately dismounted and ran to his assistance: with the aid of a soldier he lifted him off his horse; but all assistance was vain – the noble spirit was fled.

The rush of war had passed on, the contending hosts had met, and none could be idle at such a moment. Tyler, therefore, placed the body of his lamented friend and general beneath a tree, by which he could readily find it when the fight was done; and he rode forward to report to Sir James Kempt the loss which the army had sustained. That general, as senior officer, immediately assumed the command of the division: but 'Picton's intrepid example had done its work. Animated by their gallant chief, the men fought with a degree of fury which nothing could appal or resist: at one moment formed into squares, they received and repulsed the dreadful assaults of the lancers and cuirassiers; at another deploying into lines, their vigorous arm and undaunted courage drove back the enemy's masses at the point of the bayonet.'

How the British fought, and how they conquered upon this day, is already fully recorded upon the pages of many a history. As long as the name of Waterloo shall be repeated with national exultation, so long will Picton's death be remembered as one of the noblest of the sacrifices by which that victory was purchased.

When the sanguinary struggle had ceased, and the victorious English were called back to the field of battle, leaving the Prussians to pursue the enemy, Captain Tyler went in search of the body of his old general, with feelings which even the events of the day and its surrounding horrors could scarcely moderate. He found it easily. Upon examination, the ball was discovered to have entered near the left temple and passed through the brain, which must have produced instant dissolution: after this, meeting with some resistance, it glanced downwards, and was found just under the skin near the articulation of the lower jaw.

Upon looking at the dress of Sir Thomas Picton in the evening of the 18th, a few hours after his fall, it was observed that his coat was torn on one side. This led to a further examination, and then the truth became apparent – on the 16th he had been wounded at Quatre Bras; a musket-ball had struck him and broken two of his ribs, besides producing some further bodily, and it was supposed internal, injuries: but, expecting that a severe battle would be fought within a short time, he kept this wound secret, lest he should be solicited to absent himself upon the occasion. Regardless of every selfish consideration, he only divulged this secret to an old servant, with whose assistance he bound up the wound; and then, with a command over his feelings almost incredible, he continued to perform his arduous duties. The night of the 16th and the whole of the following day he was in constant activity. By the morning of the 18th the wound had assumed a serious aspect; but the assurance that the French were about to attack the British position roused every energy of his almost exhausted frame; he subdued his bodily anguish; and when the moment came which called for his great example, the hand of death, which it is supposed was even then upon him from the wound alluded to, could not, while sufficient life yet remained, check for a moment his zeal and courage.

H. B. Robinson, *The Life of Sir Thomas Picton*

17. *Cilycwm's Roll of Honour*

The River Towy comes down as a mountain brook from one of the loneliest regions of South Wales, or anywhere south of the far Highlands of Scotland, covering some 500 square miles, and for the first few miles of its journey forms the boundary between Cardiganshire and Brecknockshire, only entering Carmarthenshire at Ystradffin, so that the greater part of this wild region is outside the scope of this book; but if anyone wants to know what real loneliness is like, let him explore this great region of the 'everlasting hills', and learn that even in this crowded island of ours it is still possible to get very far indeed from the 'madding crowd'.

Returning down the west bank of the river to Cilycwm, the wild scenery mellows to a gracious beauty, but this is still a lonely region, and it comes to many as a surprise to find the active part played by the people of the district in wider affairs. Not only does Cilycwm claim, with much show of reason, to have the first Methodist meeting-house in Wales – which only two other places can hope to dispute – but it has played a leading part in the history of Welsh Methodism, whilst one of the most noticeable features of the mural tablets in the parish church is the number of people from this remote parish who have known the distant places of the earth. Walter Price, Bwlchtrebanau, was for many years Vice-Consul at Tangier; Anne Jeffreys was the daughter of Daniel Price, 'Provost Martial' of Monserrat, and later domiciled in Demerara; David Powell Price, who was a Rear Admiral of the White Knight of the Redeemer in Greece, began his naval career at the bombardment of Copenhagen in 1801, and ended it with his death when in command of the combined English and French squadron before Petropolovsci in 1851; Daniel Saunders, surgeon of HMS *Conqueror*, who received the thanks of the Government for his bravery in the Burmese War, died on his return from Japan in 1852, and was buried at sea in the Bay of Bengal; and the Rev. William Bowen was for many years chaplain on board HMS *Dreadnought*. The church dates from the fourteenth century, with a slightly later tower and an early fifteenth-century aisle. During the restoration two mural paintings were discovered and preserved.

Another distinguished native of the district was Morgan Rhŷs, the son of Rhŷs Lewis of Efail Fach, who was born there in 1716. He was one of the itinerant teachers employed by Griffith Jones in his Circulating Schools, and taught at various places, chiefly in West Wales, including the Cilycwm school. He was an original thinker, and his hymns, though limited in number, show such a broad outlook and adventurous imagination that they are second only to those of the great Pantycelyn, and are better known to modern congregations than those of any other hymn-writer.

Maxwell Frazer, *Introducing West Wales*

18. GOD BLESS THE PRINCE OF WALES

Among our ancient mountains
And from our lovely vales,
Oh! let the pray'r re-echo,
'God Bless the Prince of Wales!'
With heart and voice awaken
Those minstrel strains of yore,
Till Britain's name and glory
Resound from shore to shore.

Should hostile bands or danger
E'er threaten our fair Isle,
May God's strong arm protect us,
May Heav'n still on us smile!
Above the throne of England,
May fortune's star long shine!
And around its sacred bulwarks,
The olive branches twine.

Chorus – Among our ancient mountains, &c.

Brinley Richards

19. PARRY THOMAS AT PENDINE

So down to the runway of that beach you drove again,
Over the streaming sands
Towards that distant horizon . . .
Head in brown leather helmet,
Clenched like a boxing glove,
Knuckling down behind the weaving wheel;
Gears punched into place, first, second,
The zipped crescendo to each cogged change,
Third, then into the infinity of top.
Straight through the marker flags you sped
Onward as the revolutions climbed
Each soaring pinnacle of power
Fuelled infinitude, the live sands
Rushing to meet the flared nacelle,
The echoes of the sea drowned
In the fury of the hot exhaust
As the broad bombarded beach exploded and became
A shell of sound.

Into the measured mile you stamped,
Under the heralding banner, holding course,
Fighting the juddering wheel, reverberation
Of disaster, vibration
Of sprocket, chain and wheel.
Into your own world you hurtled,
Far away the caves sang,
Flung behind the tracks retreated;
In slow gyration
The world turned,
But you still sped
In split-second eternity.

As a tidal wave, gathering force over oceans, breaks,
The chain, stretched beyond all previous pace,
Snapped
And lashed like an iron whip
Across your skull.

As the bulbed glove bursts
On a jaw, and the tight skin
Splits like a grape
The helmet ripped,
The glove's stuffing spilled,
And your face was a hollow cup
Of air.
Ignition of nerve and brain.
When your mechanic reached you
He wept.

Douglas Phillips, from *In Memory of J. G. Parry Thomas*

20. *Plaid Carries Carmarthen*

By the late 1950s even its opponents could see that *Plaid Cymru* was developing into an organisation of substance, offering an increasing threat to the status quo. It was chronically short of money – membership was five shillings a year and the fund was swelled by raffles. But in 1962 the party's ailing finances were given a lift when the writer and patriot D. J. Williams sold his family farmhouse, which he had immortalized in a book, and gave the proceeds of £2,000 to his party. *Plaid Cymru's* president, Gwynfor Evans, wrote: '. . . he gave every penny to the party, although he had little but his pension to live on. This handsome act did the party a power of good and can be seen now as a turning point in its fortunes.'

At each general election the party fielded more candidates. In 1955 it put up eleven and won 45,000 votes, in 1959 it fielded twenty and polled 77,000. In 1966 it again put up twenty, but received 16,000 votes fewer than in 1959. The other parties took comfort from this: it looked as if some of the steam had gone from nationalism. But fifteen weeks later came the rude shock of the by-election of Carmarthen.

This constituency was a fickle one and had pendulum'd between Liberals and Labour since the war. Lady Megan Lloyd George, a former Liberal, won the seat for Labour in 1957 and held it at the next three elections. In 1966, when she was seriously ill and could not go out campaigning, she had forty-six per cent of the poll. Gwynfor Evans, the nationalists' president since 1945, came second with sixteen per cent of the poll, more than seven thousand votes. Lady Megan died shortly after the election.

In the by-election campaigning, *Plaid Cymru* pulled out the stops. Also, it had as much television exposure as the other parties, something it does not get in general elections. Even so, on polling day a distinguished political journalist felt able, just before boarding his train to London, and before the count had taken place, to telephone his office with the opinion that 'Labour have it in the bag'.

The result, with Gwynfor Evans taking thirty-nine per cent of the poll, and Labour coming second with thirty-three per cent, was a traumatic blow for Labour and for the Liberals. And, possibly, for the distinguished political journalist.

As Gwynfor Evans, first Welsh Nationalist MP, toured his constituency in the role of conquering hero, and was then welcomed by an ecstatic crowd and flapping Red Dragons as he reached Paddington on the way to the House of Commons, the Labour Party was dismissing the result as a freak, a protest vote and not a positive one, an electoral indulgence.

There can be no single explanation for the *Plaid Cymru* success at Carmarthen. The party put it down to its great growth during the sixties, to a steadily growing feeling in Wales of rejection of London government policies. The element of the protest vote was certainly there, although in the fifteen weeks since the General Election little had happened that was of electoral significance. The severe economic measures and the collapse of the national plan were then in the future. I think that the electors of Carmarthen were annoyed with the Labour Party for allowing Lady Megan, a very seriously ill candidate, to stand in the General Election. There was, in any case, a flood tide of nationalist feeling as well as the solid core of traditional nationalist voters. Television was clearly an important factor; Gwynfor Evans emerged as the most outstanding candidate and, on polling day, there was a mood of 'Let's vote for good old Gwynfor'.

Trevor Fishlock, *Wales*

21. AFTER THE ELECTION

Llanglydwen, Henllan Amgoed, Pant-y-caws,
Have you ever heard their names before?
Hardly, it seems, it's easier far
To follow the main road than turn to the woods
And twist around corners of the narrow lane.
But venture on it sometime, not because
Flowers fill the hedgerows, and sounds
Of curlew and the skylark glory there,
But because Huw amidst the harvest hay,
And Jac before he drove his load of milk,
And William on his way with pigs to mart,
And Llinos before her bus-trip to the sands
Believed, this Thursday morn, this was the day
To determine that their Wales be a Wales that's free.

Margaret Bowen Rees † 1966

22. *Grand Slam*

It was during one of these tackles that my nose was broken. Benoit
Dauga, the big second row forward, fought his way almost to the try
line but was stopped close to the corner flag. He was upright, but sway-
ing, as I jumped at him. Had he fallen to his left he would have scored
a try; to his right he would be in touch. I leaped to push him into
touch and as we both fell I got underneath him and his elbow accidentally crashed on to my nose.

I went off the field for attention. On the touchline a French doctor
looked at my nose, which was bent down over my face, and suddenly
pulled it hard. There was a click and a burst of pain. But it was straight.
Cotton wool was pushed into my nostrils to staunch the flow of blood
and I went back to the game.

I was feeling hazy and for a few minutes played by instinct. Our
incessant tackling and undermining of the French defence began to pay
off. They felt penned and began to be rattled. Gareth scored a try and I
kicked a penalty to give Wales a six points to five lead.

And then came my great chance. There was a set-piece scrum, with
the backs marking each other carefully, and Jeff Young got the ball

against the head. Gareth shot it out to me. I saw that Berot, the fly-half, was slightly out of position and as I accelerated I saw the others bearing down on me. I ran straight at Bertranne, the inside-centre, but he started to move across and I deduced that he was anticipating I would pass to John Dawes. Berot was within feet of me now, moving very fast, but I sensed that we already had the try – it would be me or John. In an instant I changed the course of my sweeping run and beat Berot: I felt his outstretched fingers running down my back as I went over for the try. For me it crowned a good personal performance, a complete performance in terms of attacking and covering.

Well, the French are most difficult to beat in Paris and this was clearly a glorious way to achieve the Grand Slam for the sixth time. The champagne and the celebration dinner helped to relieve the discomfort I felt from my aching and throbbing nose. We had that sense of fulfilment that comes from completing a mission successfully.

What made the celebration even more enjoyable was the sportsmanship of the French players and their officials. They love winning, of course, but if they have played well and are beaten in a great game they are just as happy.

Barry John, *The Barry John Story*

V

Bits of
Characters

1. *Tom the Waggoner*

I remember as if it were yesterday the first time I saw Gwilym and Benny Bach, even though it is many years ago now. Three years of age Gwilym was at the time, and Benny Bach was a year younger. I was walking, on a fine day in summer, from Llanelwid station to the 'New Mansion', where my sister was living. I knew that Henry, my brother-in-law, was in the middle of hay harvest, and I did not want him to send a horse to meet the train at such a stressful time. And so, I had not uttered a word to him about what hour of the day I would arrive at Llanelwid; except that I would be at Plas Newydd sometime on Saturday. Easy enough to find one's directions to the Plas. There was a main road running past the house, and there was no alternative but to follow it, and, though I wasn't very familiar with the area, I arrived at the junction of the little roadway that leads to the farmyard of Plas Newydd without one mishap or mistake.

At the bottom of the road stood two children. I didn't know for sure whether they were little girls or boys, because the two of them had long curly hair, and they were dressed in a frock and little petticoat. The elder of the two was holding onto the other's hand, and showing clearly that he was ready to defend him from any harm. Though I had never seen them in my life before, I knew at once they were my sister's children, Gwilym and Benny Bach. Their whisps of curly locks shone golden like flowers of the broom; but whilst Gwilym had his father's darting dark eyes, Benny had his mother's two eyes, blue-green as leeks, and depth in them as if you looked into high heaven.

I stood a moment without saying a word, looking at the two tots standing hand-in-hand in the middle of the road. They were eyeing me, the stranger, and visibly enough doubting what to do. But after a second here was Gwilym giving Benny Bach a pluck and asking, looking straight up into my face:

'Uncle Swansea you are, is it?'

'Well,' I said, laughing, 'I must know first who you two are.'

'Plas Newydd children we are,' said Gwilym, 'and mammy has told us to stay here to tell uncle to go up to the house through the small road.'

'Oh dear,' I said, 'and what makes you think that I am your uncle?'

'Mammy said that uncle would be sure to stop and look at us, 'cause he was always fond of children,' said Gwilym.

I hurried to change the subject.

'And what's your name, then?' I said.

'Gwilym is my right name, but dad sometimes calls me Wil,' said the little man.

The smaller little one had stood mute, up until this, without taking his eyes off me, but on hearing his brother talking so readily, here he began to take heart.

'A-a-a-a–' he said, failing in his eagerness to speak, to bring out the words 'a-a-a-and Benny Bach is my name.'

'Well, well, is there a kiss for uncle?' stooping and bending my head.

The two were expecting the question. On cue Gwilym pulls a hanky out of his pocket and wipes Benny Bach's lips, and says to him exactly as, I'm sure, he had heard his mother say many times before.

'Now, Benny Bach, a nice kiss for uncle.'

'A nice kiss for uncle,' Benny Bach echoed, turning his face up.

And there I lifted the two up into my arms, and in carrying them towards the house, I got to know the whole history of the entire farm – the way the calves were all in the Small Field, and the foals in the Boundary Big Field, and the cattle in the Dale-under-the-house, that daddy was with the servantmen carting hay from the Centre Marsh, and that two hay byres were full and that the harvest would be finished with nightfall. I got to know, too, the names of all the horses namely, *Duchess* and *Lester*, and *Jolly*, and *Ventin*, and *Black*, and the two ponies, *Bess* and *Silver*; and the names of the servingmen. But we spent most of the time talking about Tom the waggoner, because never was there ever such a hero as he, so I should have thought. He could drive the waggon to fetch lime with four horses in it.

'And he comes down the Black Mountain like the fire,' says Gwilym.

'Aye,' says Benny Bach, 'he goes like red-hot fire.'

'And he beats Cwm-brân's waggoner right off the road,' says Gwilym.

'Aye, right off the road,' says Benny Bach.

'And he got the prize in the ploughing match,' says Gwilym, 'and he's got a slash in his whip as long as that' – stretching his arm out full length.

'And he makes the slash go gric-grack,' says Benny Bach.

'And he's got a peacock feather in the side of his hat,' says Gwilym, – and, beyond all argument, Tom the waggoner was the greatest man in the world.

W. Llewelyn Williams. *Gwilym a Benni Bach* † 1897

2. *Lunchtime Legend*

The Second World War victory party continued well into the sixties. Sexual intercourse began about then with the Beatles first LP, as Philip Larkin quite rightly said. The Pill permitted people to think about other things, ending the big party – though we all know it still went on in some places. No where more so than in the great pubs of the Towy valley: The White Horse, the 'Refresh' and The King's Head, Llandilo, prominent among them.

Out of the babble and guffaw of tap-room and saloon, astonishing how war-time folk tales grew, and men became legends even in their own lunchtime. One July day in 1959, Hardy McHardy of Taliaris was proof of this. It so happened, that morning, the legendary Hurricane and Spitfire combat pilot 'Bob' Stanford Tuck, DSO, DFC and two bars, chauffeur-driven by his friend and Stalag Luft 3 fellow-intern, 'Paddy' Byrne, stopped for petrol at the Esso service station, Llandilo *en route* for Ireland. Both had family there. In conversation with the proprietor, Mr Ray England, they learnt that there were no Monday mid-day crossings from Fishguard and that the next sailing would be at midnight. This left the Wing Commanders with a whole day to kill in rainy west Wales.

On learning that he was in Llandilo, Tuck inquired grandly whether the name 'McHardy' meant anything. Pretty soon, they found themselves at a country house on the Talley road where even at ten in the morning the curtains remained drawn and the world stood still in slumber. But the day sprang alive. When old comrades meet, long-term residents of Stalagluft 3 in particular, who have not seen one another in a long time, it is occasion for celebration. On a large scale.

'Slap-up', rather than *cordon bleu* was parlance then for an exceptionally fine meal, and George Wheeler's hospitality at the King's Head was, in those post-rationing days, deserving of blue ribbons, even Michelin stars. To suit the occasion he produced for the war heroes his very finest. Chateaubriands with mossy clarets were followed by sylla-bubs and crusty ports. Late into the afternoon, the table on a roar, old friends were well met. A famous lunch encroached upon dinner time: came the hour for departure.

Breathalysers were unheard-of in those innocent days, but drunken drivers ran the gauntlet all the same. DBH McHardy directed RRS Tuck, DFC (and many bars), navigating VGLD Byrne at the controls, to the ferryboat by a minor road, to avoid the police. Or so he thought. On arrival home, Hardy was summoned to the telephone. 'Squadron

Leader McHardy?' The Ammanford constabulary. 'Have WinCos Tuck and Byrne in custody. Erratic driving, seemingly lost'. Hardy furious. 'Outrageous way to treat visiting friends . . . Distinguished war aviator. Top Gun. Shot down 29 Huns. Will arrange bail immediately'. Local solicitor, Glasbrook, summoned to accompany forthwith, and together they motor down to Ammanford 'to sort out misunderstanding'.

But, when relief arrived at Ammanford police station, there was confusion – and embarrassment. The birds had flown! 'Paddy' Byrne had winged it through the lavatory window. And was never seen again, that night. 'Bob' Tuck was absent in pursuit. The moral of the story being that you dare not presume to detain men involved in the Wooden Horse and the Great Escapes for more than minutes in a Welsh town jail!

The tale, as happens, varied with the telling, as befits an Englishman, an Irishman and a Welshman (by adoption). Vincent George Lowther Davy Byrne was, nevertheless, granted £500 bail in the surety of Donald Balentine Hardy McHardy and summoned to appear before the magistrates at Ammanford on September 25th, at 10.30 o'clock. This, and other stories about Hardy McHardy's exploits, entered post-war Towy valley folklore, and are still re-run, miles from any truth. Did he fly a Tiger Moth under Llandilo Bridge? A risky undertaking. He certainly 'dropped' a bag of layers' pellets in on Mr Reynolds, a Milo farmer, who had long been promised them. Hardy was a Bibby's farm-food rep at the time, whose usual mode of transport, a fold-up Corgi scooter, was not the best for hill-farm deliveries. So he kept his promise to Reynolds at barn-roof level from a Swansea Flying Club Auster.

He may well have landed aircraft on hayfields, paying visits to his mother, family or friends. Many remember his spectacular aerobatics over the town and valley, and he would frequently 'buzz' friends' houses to test the fortitude of their chimney stacks. A cheque for two hundred guineas in payment for graphic work done for the Steel Company of Wales was used to establish a useful line of credit at the White Horse Inn, his bankers. He requested money there late one evening with a personal cheque 'To Cash' in the curious amount, £3.7.5d. The explanation to 'Jumbo' Lewis, proprietor: '7/5d for a round owing across the road – and a few quid in me pocket for tomorrow, dear boy, if you please!' When he borrowed Stan-the-Maerdy's new Triumph TR2 sports, and tried her out on the switchback Talley road, Hardy was able to advise the proud owner that 'she took off at 100mph on the brow of the dip beyond The Hope'.

Lynn Hughes. *Carmarthenshire Life*, November 2002

3. *Y Gwter Fawr – Brynaman*
(*The Big Gutter*)

'I have not eaten anything since I left Llandovery. What can I have?'

'We have veal and bacon,' said she.

'That will do,' said I; 'fry me some veal and bacon, and I shan't complain. But pray tell me what prodigious noise is that which I hear on the other side of the passage?'

'It is only the miners and the carters in the kitchen making merry,' said one of the girls.

'Is there a good fire there?' said I.

'O yes,' said the girl, 'we have always a good fire in the kitchen.'

'Well then,' said I, 'I shall go there till supper is ready, for I am wet to the skin, and this fire casts very little heat.'

'You will find them a rough set in the kitchen,' said the girl.

'I don't care if I do,' said I; 'when people are rough I am civil, and I have always found that civility beats roughness in the long run.' Then going out I crossed the passage and entered the kitchen.

It was nearly filled with rough unkempt fellows smoking, drinking, whistling, singing, shouting or jabbering, some in a standing, some in a sitting posture. My entrance seemed at once to bring everything to a dead stop; the smokers ceased to smoke, the hand that was conveying the glass or the mug to the mouth was arrested in air, the hurly-burly ceased and every eye was turned upon me with a strange inquiring stare. Without allowing myself to be disconcerted I advanced to the fire, spread out my hands before it for a minute, gave two or three deep ahs of comfort, and then turning round said: 'Rather a damp night, gentlemen – fire cheering to one who has come the whole way from Llandovery – Taking a bit of a walk in Wales, to see the scenery and to observe the manners and customs of the inhabitants – Fine country, gentlemen, noble prospects, hill and dale – Fine people too – open-hearted and generous; no wonder! descendants of the Ancient Britons – Hope I don't intrude – other room rather cold and smoking – If I do will retire at once – don't wish to interrupt any gentlemen in their avocations or deliberations – scorn to do anything ungenteel or calculated to give offence – hope I know how to behave myself – ought to do so – learnt grammar at the High School at Edinburgh.'

'Offence, intrusion!' cried twenty voices. 'God bless your honour! no intrusion and no offence at all – sit down – sit here – won't you drink?'

'Please to sit here, sir,' said an old grimy-looking man, getting up from a seat in the chimney-corner – 'this is no seat for me whilst you are here, it belongs to you – sit down in it,' and laying hold of me he compelled me to sit down in the chair of dignity, whilst half-a-dozen hands pushed mugs of beer towards my face; these, however, I declined to partake of on the very satisfactory ground that I had not taken supper, and that it was a bad thing to drink before eating, more especially after coming out of a mist.

'Have you any news to tell of the war, sir?' said a large rough fellow, who was smoking a pipe.

'The last news that I heard of the war,' said I, 'was that the snow was two feet deep at Sebastopol.'

'I heard three,' said the man; 'however, if there be but two it must be bad work for the poor soldiers. I suppose you think that we shall beat the Russians in the end.'

'No, I don't,' said I; 'the Russians are a young nation and we are an old; they are coming on and we are going off; every dog has its day.'

'That's true,' said the man, 'but I am sorry that you think we shall not beat the Russians, for the Russians are a bad set.'

'Can you speak Welsh?' said a darkish man with black bristly hair and a small inquisitive eye.

'O, I know two words in Welsh,' said I, 'bara y caws.'

'That's bread and cheese,' said the man, then turning to a neighbour of his he said in Welsh: 'He knows nothing of Cymraeg, only two words; we may say anything we please; he can't understand us. What a long nose he has!'

'Mind that he ain't nosing us,' said his neighbour. 'I should be loth to wager that he doesn't understand Welsh; and after all he didn't say that he did not, but got off by saying he understood those two words.'

'No, he doesn't understand Welsh,' said the other; 'no Sais under-stands Welsh, and this is a Sais. Now with regard to that piece of job-work which you and I undertook.' And forthwith he and the other entered into a disquisition about the job-work.

The company soon got into its old train, drinking and smoking and making a most terrific hullabaloo. Nobody took any farther notice of me. I sat snug in the chimney-corner, trying to dry my wet things, and as the heat was very great partially succeeded. In about half-an-hour one of the girls came to tell me that my supper was ready, whereupon I got up and said: 'Gentlemen, I thank you for your civility; I am now going to supper; perhaps before I turn in for the night I may look in upon you again.' Then without waiting for an answer I left the kitchen and went into the other room, where I found a large dish of veal cutlets and fried bacon awaiting me, and also a smoking bowl of potatoes. Ordering a jug of ale I sat down, and what with hunger and the goodness of the fare, for everything was first-rate, made one of the best suppers I ever made in my life.

Supper over, I called for a glass of whiskey-and-water, over which I trifled for about half-an-hour and then betook myself again to the kitchen. Almost as soon as I entered, the company, who seemed to be discussing some point, and were not making much hurly-burly, became silent and looked at me in a suspicious and uneasy manner. I advanced towards the fire. The old man who had occupied the seat in the chimney-corner and had resigned it to me, had again taken possession of it. As I drew near to the fire he looked upon the ground, and seemed by no means disposed to vacate the place of honour; after a few moments, however, he got up and offered me the seat with a slight motion of his hand and without saying a word. I did not decline it, but sat down, and the old gentleman took a chair near. Universal silence now prevailed; sullen looks were cast at me; and I saw clearly enough that I was not welcome. Frankness was now my only resource. 'What's the matter, gentlemen?' said I; 'you are silent and don't greet me kindly; have I given you any cause of offence?' No one uttered a word in reply for nearly a minute, when the old man said slowly and deliberately: 'Why, sir, the long and short of it is this: we have got it into our heads that you understand every word of our discourse; now, do you or do you not?'

'Understand every word of your discourse,' said I; 'I wish I did; I would give five pounds to understand every word of your discourse.'

'That's a clever attempt to get off, sir,' said the old man, 'but it won't exactly do. Tell us whether you know more Welsh than bara y caws; or to speak more plainly, whether you understand a good deal of what we say.'

'Well,' said I, 'I do understand more Welsh than bara y caws – I do understand a considerable part of a Welsh conversation – moreover, I can read Welsh, and have the life of Tom o'r Nant at my fingers' ends.'

'Well, sir, that is speaking plain, and I will tell you plainly that we don't like to have strangers among us who understand our discourse, more especially if they be gentlefolks.'

'That's strange,' said I, 'a Welshman or foreigner, gentle or simple, may go into a public-house in England, and nobody cares a straw whether he understands the discourse of the company or not.'

'That may be the custom in England,' said the old man; 'but it is not so in Wales.'

'What have you got to conceal?' said I. 'I suppose you are honest men.'

'I hope we are, sir,' said the old man; 'but I must tell you, once for all, that we don't like strangers to listen to our discourse.'

'Come,' said I, 'I will not listen to your discourse, but you shall listen to mine. I have a wonderful deal to say if I once begin; I have been everywhere.'

'Well, sir,' said the old man, 'if you have anything to tell us about where you have been and what you have seen we shall be glad to hear you.

'Have you ever been in Russia?' shouted a voice.

George Borrow. *Wild Wales* 1862

4. *Englyn English*

A wily cat in holy kit,
A robot in the pulpit:
Ever fat, never fit –
A bolshi and a bullshit.

Anonymous graffiti, *A Vicar of Llandybïe*

5. *The Personality of Kilsby Jones*

Altogether he was startlingly unconventional; but his powerful personality commanded respect in spite of all, I have elsewhere stated that[1] 'nothing could be less ministerial' than his appearance. He wore a wide-brimmed slouching hat, oftenest of straw, and a large loose collar, revealing (after he, in later years, had cropped his long beard) the foundations of the neck and its sinewy strength. His countenance was stern and tender, serious and comic, in its rapid alterations. His eye darted light with every piercing look; yet it was tremulous with merry glances that played 'hide and seek' in every corner. The central ornament – the nose – which gave character and individuality to the whole, was long, straight, and firmly fixed; and by an occasional dilation of the

[1] *Echoes from the Welsh Hills.*

nostrils asserted supremacy in royal fashion, and shot upward a three-fold furrow, dividing into two counterparts the towering forehead above, that had braved many a storm, and thought many a noble thought. A fine mouth, powerfully set, but indulging occasionally in a playful pout, completed the picture of forehead and face. It presented an index of the man, who was as stern as a judge, yet frolicsome as a schoolboy. The transitional expressions of righteous indignation, withering contempt, and melting tenderness, and especially the relaxation of that face in the presence of woman, child, or congenial spirit were a study. The head and neck were upheld by a large expanded chest, and a pair of shoulders, which in the days of physical prowess would have alone asserted his pre-eminence among his fellows. Had he not feared God he would have been terrible, for he never feared man in his life.

As an illustration of his bold defiance of the conventional and customary, and of his striking independence of judgement and utterance, I give an instance told me many years ago by Sir William Davies, solicitor, Haverfordwest, of what occurred when Kilsby was walking arm in arm with Mr Rees, Sir William's predecessor – a local magnate to whom the residents, as a rule, entrusted their souls, and the farmers of the district *even their money*! As the two friends proceeded along the leading street, a poor man, recognising Mr Rees, took off his hat repeatedly and bowed and cringed slavishly as he passed by. To Kilsby the sight was abhorrent. At last straightening himself to his full height, he turned to the man and said to him, 'Put on your hat, my man, and stand on your feet; worship God – and not Rees, the lawyer!'

He not only had little or no regard for the conventional, but also had even an obsession for the unconventional. He shocked people in those days (when so much attention was paid to a suitable, and, at least, a decorous garb for the pulpit) by appearing there in a velvet coat, or shooting jacket, with bulging knicker-bockers and striped Welsh stockings. Indeed, at Tonbridge Chapel, London, his persistence in shocking people's sensibilities with regard to the conventionalities of pulpit dress, seriously damaged his usefulness; but he gave up the church, rather than submit to be dictated to as to the cut of his coat, or the style of his trousers, in the pulpit or out of it.

He could not be any other than unconventional. I remember his being called upon in 1884, to say grace before dinner at the Rock Hotel, Llandrindod, at the height of the season, and his getting up and repeating, as he frequently did on such occasions, the words of Robert Burns:

> Some hae meat, and canna eat,
>   And some wad eat that want it;
> But we hae meat, and we can eat,
>   An sae the Lord be thankit!

I remember the amazement on the faces of some English visitors, who had never before heard such a daring departure from, 'What we are about to receive'. And yet, when dinner was over, they admitted the wonderful appropriateness of that Grace to the occasion. Kilsby was vindicated; and the Scotchmen present were not a little elated.

David Davies, *Reminiscences*

6. *Kilsby at Carmarthen Races*

Dr Rowe, of Haverfordwest, had a habit of staring at people through his eye-glasses as they passed; but one day the doctor met his match. Kilsby was coming along on horseback, and the doctor, in a most conceited fashion, looked at Kilsby through his eye-glass. Then Kilsby, always ready and quick as lightning, took his foot out of the stirrup, raised the stirrup to his eye, and looked and stared at the doctor.

Kilsby was very fond of describing the eloquence of his old tutor, Dr Phillips, of Neuaddlwyd. He did so, because it was different from that of many that he knew. 'His tone was as natural when preaching, or lecturing, as in asking for an ounce of tobacco. He had not a voice for Sunday, and a voice for week-days – one for the kitchen and one for the sanctuary.'

A truer description than the above could never be given of Kilsby himself, for the glory of Kilsby was the glory of *naturalness*.

When a student at Carmarthen, he went to the races. Among Nonconformists then, as well as now, it was looked upon as an unpardonable sin to attend races, for the racecourse was regarded as the hunting ground for thieves, debauchers, and gamblers. But Kilsby went, and took his seat outside on the top of the coach, and paid for a place on the grand-stand, among the gentry, from where he could see everything that was going on. The news soon spread through the College among the students; and it got to the ears of the professors that Kilsby had been to the races. A committee was appointed to sit on his case. It was a rule in Carmarthen town to expel all members who patronised the race-course; and it was confidently expected that the same fate awaited Kilsby.

He was called in before the committee, and the president asked him if he had any explanation to make.

'I went,' said Kilsby, 'in obedience to the command of the apostle.' 'Dear me,' answered the president, 'what do you mean?' 'Well,' continued Kilsby, 'the apostle said, "Prove all things, hold fast to that which is good." I have done that,' said Kilsby, 'and found it bad, and I am not going to the races any more'.

Kilsby was not expelled.

Vyrnwy Morgan.
The Life and Sayings of Rev. Kilsby Jones 1896

7. *Twm Siôn Cati's Cave*

A violent rush upon our hero, by the whole party, now ensued; but Twm eluded their eager attempts to grasp him, sprung upon the table before the bench, and drawing a couple of pistols from his coat pockets, held one in each hand, and kept them all at bay, protesting that he would shoot the first who would advance an inch towards him.

By this time Evans of Tregaron, with some of his followers, got behind him, and clung to his right arm, but with one violent effort Twm shook them away, as the mighty bull throws off the yelping curs that dare attack him. Then, with a single leap, he sprung from the table into the crowded court, where a lane was formed for him, and rushed out at the door unimpeded, and pursued by his accusers. They soon lost sight of him among the moving multitude, some of whom dispersed from fear of accidents, while others followed him as spectators. To the great astonishment of his pursuers, they next caught a view of him mounted on that grand subject of contention, the grey horse. He took the route to Ystrad Feen, followed by them all, including several constables in the employ of Evans of Tregaron, and many disinterested people from the fair. Loud were the shouts of the numerous riders; loud the tramp of galloping horses; and wild the disorder and terror created, as Twm at different intervals turned on his pursuers, and fired his pistols. This caused a powerful retrograde movement among them, by which the foremost horses fell back on those behind them, unhorsing some, who lay groaning and crying with fright on the ground, and frightening others altogether from the pursuit. It was on this occasion that a bard of that day wrote the stanza which appears in the title page, thus translated by the late Iolo Morganwg:

> 'In Ystrad Feen a doleful sound
> Pervades the hollow hills around;
> The very stones with terror melt,
> Such fear of Twm Shôn Catty's felt.'

Twm at length, although closely followed, reached the foot of Dinas, where he dismounted, sprung from stone to stone, that formed the ford of the Towey, and climbed the steep side of that majestic mount, with the utmost agility and ease. Like a prudent sea-captain chased in his small boat by a fleet of rovers, till he reaches his own war-ship, and springs up her fort-like side, and treads his deck in the ecstasy of sur-mounted peril, conscious strength, and superiority. Thus Twm now attained the summit of a prominent knoll, and waved his hand tri-umphantly, in defiance of his foes below. Evans of Tregaron, with his crew of catchpoles, made an attempt to climb also; Twm permitted them to advance about twenty yards above the river, when he com-menced, and at the same time ended his warfare, by rolling down several huge stones, that swept them in a mass into the bed of the river Towey, sadly bruised, but more frightened, from whence they were extricated by the amazed and terrific spectators.

The Tregaron magistrate met a woeful disaster on this occasion; starting aside, to avoid the dreadful leaping crags that threatened to crush him, his pistols went off in his pockets, and carried away, besides his coat-skirts and the rear of his black breeches, a large portion of postern flesh, that deprived him forever after of an easy seat, on that agree-able cushion which nature had provided. Amusing to the population of

Tregaron was the singular sight of their crestfallen magistrate and his hated gang, brought home in woeful plight, as inside passengers of a dung-cart, which had been hired for the purpose; and more than all, that their discomfiture should have been caused by their long-lost countryman, Twm Shôn Catty.

Our hero, in the mean time, like a princely chieftain of the days of old, enthroned upon his native tower of strength, marking in his soul's high pride the awkward predicament of his baffled foes, perceiving them all depart; leaving him the undisputed lord of his alpine territory, the glorious height of Dinas. After witnessing, with his limbs stretched upon his mountain couch, the glorious beauty of the setting sun, he entered the cave, tore from its top a sufficiency of fern and heather to form his bed, threw on it his fatigued, over-exerted frame, and soundly slept till morning.

T. Llewelyn Pritchard,
The Adventures and Vagaries of Twm Shôn Catty,
A Wild Wag of Wales

8. *Jane the Gardenwoman*

But of all our *famiglia* (the charming Italian word used to express the indoor and outdoor staff of a large establishment) at Bryn Myrddin, the figure I most like to recall is that of old Jane, the garden woman. She was a fine example of a type of Welshwoman that has now wholly vanished. For her working-day dress she always wore a short russet skirt, buckled shoes and a blue-and-white check apron; whilst her head-gear consisted of a peaked black felt hat with ear lappets of coarse white lace. With her bent back, her peaked hat, her wizened face and with her besom in her hands, she looked exactly like one of those pictures of witches in old books, and one almost expected to see her sail away one day on her broomstick to keep a tryst on Frennifawr or the Van Mountain, or wherever the local hags held their festival. For some reason old Jane always had her mid-day dinner by herself at a side-table in the kitchen; and I remember her on one occasion remonstrating with one of my uncles for keeping on his hat whilst in the kitchen, for the old lady was a great stickler for the proprieties, and was evidently not afraid to speak out boldly if ever she considered that these were being violated.

She died when I was a boy, and in her last illness I used to visit her with my mother in her tiny cottage at Abergwili, and I have often reflected since on the true piety and contented humility of this grand type of a past age.

Herbert M. Vaughan. *The South Wales Squires* 1926

9. A Visit to Grandpa's

In the middle of the night I woke from a dream full of whips and lariats as long as serpents, and runaway coaches on mountain passes, and wide, windy gallops over cactus fields, and I heard the old man in the next room crying, 'Gee-up!' and 'Whoa!' and trotting his tongue on the roof of his mouth.

It was the first time I had stayed in grandpa's house. The floorboards had squeaked like mice as I climbed into bed, and the mice between the walls had creaked like wood as though another visitor was walking on them. It was a mild summer night, but curtains had flapped and branches beaten against the window. I had pulled the sheets over my head, and soon was roaring and riding in a book.

'Whoa there, my beauties,' cried grandpa. His voice sounded very young and loud, and his tongue had powerful hooves, and he made his bedroom into a great meadow. I thought I would see if he was ill, or had set his bedclothes on fire, for my mother had said that he lit his pipe under the blankets, and had warned me to run to his help if I smelt smoke in the night. I went on tiptoe through the darkness to his bedroom door, brushing against the furniture and upsetting a candle-stick with a thump. When I saw there was a light in the room I felt frightened, and as I opened the door I heard grandpa shout, 'Gee-up!' as loudly as a bull with a megaphone.

He was sitting straight up in bed and rocking from side to side as though the bed were on a rough road; the knotted edges of the counter-pane were his reins; his invisible horses stood in a shadow beyond the bedside candle. Over a white flannel nightshirt he was wearing a red waistcoat with walnut-sized brass buttons. The overfilled bowl of his pipe smouldered among his whiskers like a little, burning hayrick on a stick. At the sight of me, his hands dropped from the reins and lay blue and quiet, the bed stopped still on a level road, he muffled his tongue into silence, and the horses drew softly up.

'Is there anything the matter, grandpa?' I asked, though the clothes were not on fire. His face in the candlelight looked like a ragged quilt pinned upright on the black air and patched all over with goatbeards.

He stared at me mildly. Then he blew down his pipe, scattering the sparks and making a high, wet dog-whistle of the stem, and shouted: 'Ask no questions.'

After a pause, he said slyly: 'Do you ever have nightmares, boy?'

I said: 'No.'

'Oh, yes, you do,' he said.

I said I was woken by a voice that was shouting to horses.

'What did I tell you?' he said. 'You eat too much. Who ever heard of horses in a bedroom?'

He fumbled under his pillow, brought out a small, tinkling bag, and carefully untied its strings. He put a sovereign in my hand, and said: 'Buy a cake.' I thanked him and wished him good night.

As I closed my bedroom door, I heard his voice crying loudly and gaily, 'Gee-up! gee-up!' and the rocking of the travelling bed.

In the morning I woke from a dream of fiery horses on a plain that was littered with furniture, and of large, cloudy men who rode six horses at a time and whipped them with burning bed-clothes. Grandpa was at breakfast, dressed in deep black. After breakfast he said, 'There was a terrible loud wind last night,' and sat in his armchair by the hearth to make clay balls for the fire. Later in the morning he took me for a walk, through Johnstown village and into the fields on the Llanstephan road.

A man with a whippet said, 'There's a nice morning, Mr Thomas,' and when he had gone, leanly as his dog, into the short-treed green wood he should not have entered because of the notices, grandpa said: 'There, do you hear what he called you? Mister!'

We passed by small cottages, and all the men who leant on the gates congratulated grandpa on the fine morning. We passed through the wood full of pigeons, and their wings broke the branches as they rushed to the tops of the trees. Among the soft, contented voices and the loud, timid flying, grandpa said, like a man calling across a field: 'If you heard those old birds in the night, you'd wake me up and say there were horses in the trees.'

We walked back slowly, for he was tired, and the lean man stalked out of the forbidden wood with a rabbit held as gently over his arm as a girl's arm in a warm sleeve.

On the last day but one of my visit I was taken to Llanstephan in a governess cart pulled by a short, weak pony. Grandpa might have been driving a bison, so tightly he held the reins, so ferociously cracked the long whip, so blasphemously shouted warning to boys who played in the road, so stoutly stood with his gaitered legs apart and cursed the demon strength and wilfulness of his tottering pony.

'Look out, boy!' he cried when we came to each corner, and pulled and tugged and jerked and sweated and waved his whip like a rubber sword. And when the pony had crept miserably round each corner, grandpa turned to me with a sighing smile: 'We weathered that one, boy.'

When we came to Llanstephan village at the top of the hill, he left the cart by the 'Edwinsford Arms' and patted the pony's muzzle and gave it sugar, saying: 'You're a weak little pony, Jim, to pull big men like us.'

He had strong beer and I had lemonade, and he paid Mrs Edwinsford with a sovereign out of the tinkling bag; she inquired after his health, and he said that Llangadock was better for the tubes. We went to look at the churchyard and the sea, and sat in the wood called the Sticks, and stood on the concert platform in the middle of the wood where visitors sang on midsummer nights and, year by year, the innocent of the village was elected mayor. Grandpa paused at the churchyard and pointed over the iron gate at the angelic headstones and the poor wooden crosses. 'There's no sense in lying there,' he said.

We journeyed back furiously: Jim was a bison again.

I woke late on my last morning, out of dreams where the Llanstephan sea carried bright sailing-boats as long as liners; and heavenly choirs in the Sticks, dressed in bards' robes and brass-buttoned waistcoats, sang in a strange Welsh to the departing sailors. Grandpa was not at breakfast; he rose early. I walked in the fields with a new sling, and shot at the Towy gulls and the rooks in the parsonage trees. A warm wind blew from the summer points of the weather; a morning mist climbed from the ground and floated among the trees and hid the noisy birds; in the mist and the wind my pebbles flew lightly up like hailstones in a world on its head. The morning passed without a bird falling.

I broke my sling and returned for the midday meal through the parson's orchard. Once, grandpa told me, the parson had bought three ducks at Carmarthen Fair and made a pond for them in the centre of the garden; but they waddled to the gutter under the crumbling door-steps of the house, and swam and quacked there. When I reached the end of the orchard path, I looked through a hole in the hedge and saw that the parson had made a tunnel through the rockery that was between the gutter and the pond and had set up a notice in plain writing: 'This way to the new pond'.

The ducks were still swimming under the steps.

Grandpa was not in the cottage. I went into the garden, but grandpa was not staring at the fruit-trees. I called across to a man who leant on a spade in the field beyond the garden hedge: 'have you seen my grandpa this morning?'

He did not stop digging, and answered over his shoulder: 'I seen him in his fancy waistcoat.'

Griff, the barber, lived in the next cottage. I called to him through the open door: 'Mr Griff, have you seen my grandpa?'

The barber came out in his shirtsleeves.

I said: 'He's wearing his best waistcoat.' I did not know if it was important, but grandpa wore his waistcoat only in the night.

'Has grandpa been to Llanstephan?' asked Mr Griff anxiously.

'We went there yesterday in a little trap,' I said.

He hurried indoors and I heard him talking in Welsh, and he came out again with his white coat on, and he carried a striped and coloured walking-stick. He strode down the village street and I ran by his side.

When we stopped at the tailor's shop, he cried out, 'Dan!' and Dan Tailor stepped from his window where he sat like an Indian priest but wearing a derby hat. 'Dai Thomas has got his waistcoat on,' said Mr Griff, 'and he's been to Llanstephan.'

As Dan Tailor searched for his overcoat, Mr Griff was striding on. 'Wil Evans,' he called outside the carpenter's shop, 'Dai Thomas has been to Llanstephan, and he's got his waistcoat on.'

'I'll tell Morgan now,' said the carpenter's wife out of the hammering, sawing darkness of the shop.

We called at the butcher's shop and Mr Price's house, and Mr Griff repeated his message like a town crier.

We gathered together in Johnstown square. Dan Tailor had his bicycle, Mr Price his pony trap. Mr Griff, the butcher, Morgan Carpenter, and I climbed into the shaking trap, and we trotted off towards Carmarthen town. The tailor led the way, ringing his bell as though there were a fire or a robbery, and an old woman by the gate of a cottage at the end of the street ran inside like a pelted hen. Another woman waved a bright handkerchief.

'Where are we going?' I asked.

Grandpa's neighbours were as solemn as old men with black hats and jackets on the outskirts of a fair. Mr Griff shook his head and mourned: 'I didn't expect this again from Dai Thomas.'

'Not after last time,' said Mr Price sadly.

We trotted on, we crept up Constitution Hill, we rattled down into Lammas Street, and the tailor still rang his bell and a dog ran, squealing, in front of his wheels. As we clip-clopped over the cobbles that led down to the Towy bridge, I remembered grandpa's nightly noisy journeys that rocked the bed and shook the walls, and I saw his gay waistcoat in a vision and his patchwork head tufted and smiling in the candlelight. The tailor before us turned round on his saddle, his bicycle wobbled and skidded. 'I see Dai Thomas!' he cried.

The trap rattled on to the bridge, and I saw grandpa there; the buttons of his waistcoat shone in the sun, he wore his tight, black Sunday trousers and a tall, dusty hat I had seen in a cupboard in the attic, and he carried an ancient bag. He bowed to us. 'Good morning, Mr Price,' he said, 'and Mr Griff and Mr Morgan and Mr Evans.' To me, he said: 'Good morning, boy.'

Mr Griff pointed his coloured stick at him.

'And what to you think you are doing on Carmarthen bridge in the middle of the afternoon,' he said sternly, 'with your best waistcoat and your old hat?'

Grandpa did not answer, but inclined his face to the river wind, so that his beard was set dancing and wagging as though he talked, and watched the coracle men move, like turtles, on the shore.

Mr Griff raised his stunted barber's pole. 'And where to you think you are going,' he said, 'with your old black bag?'

Grandpa said: 'I am going to Llangadock to be buried.' And he watched the coracle shells slip into the water lightly, and the gulls complain over the fish-filled water as bitterly as Mr Price complained:

'But you aren't dead yet, Dai Thomas.'

For a moment grandpa reflected, then: 'There's no sense in lying dead in Llanstephan,' he said. 'The ground is comfy in Llangadock; you can twitch your legs without putting them in the sea.'

His neighbours moved close to him. They said: 'You aren't dead, Mr Thomas.'

'How can you be buried, then?'

'Nobody's going to bury you in Llanstephan.'

'Come on home, Mr Thomas.'

'There's strong beer for tea.'

'And cake.'

But grandpa stood firmly on the bridge, and clutched his bag to his side, and stared at the flowing river and the sky, like a prophet who has no doubt.

Dylan Thomas,
A Portrait of the Artist as a Young Dog

10. *Uncle Jâms and the Squirrel*

I was very fond of Uncle Jâms in this early period, and I followed him everywhere. Like draws to like, they say. His name for me before he had heirs of his own was 'little heir'. And my name for him at that time, they say again, was Uncle Bow Down', because he was so fond of singing that noted piece 'We Never Never Will Bow Down', which he had learnt, I dare say, in Price Bach's choir. On market-days or fair-days, when my father and mother were out and Uncle Jâms was the one-day king, were the occasions when some of the big things that have remained in my mind in a special way usually occurred. Here, for example, is one incident that I remember to-day as clearly as when it had just taken place.

It was one morning straight after breakfast, a glorious morning in the middle of May to go by the impression I have of the colour of the foliage and the freshness of the fields, and it seemed as if there had been some rain during the night. My parents were already well on their way to Llandeilo or to Lampeter, perhaps. I don't know how it began, but there was a small group of us, the maids and the men, Uncle Jâms and Pegi and myself and the dogs, you bet, gathered together for some reason or other at the lower end of the whitewashed dwelling-house opposite Cwm Bach. We were watching a sprightly squirrel jumping from bough to bough on the ashes and sycamores and tall larches that shelter the fold. Seeing so many of those queer and noisy beings on the ground beneath watching intently, the little creature began to get excited. For safety, I suppose, it jumped to a higher branch and then to still higher ones, until it found itself on the highest top branch that it could risk its light body upon. Whether fairly or not, squirrels were blamed for harming the pine-tree shoots and so spoiling the freshness and straightness of their growth. Some one suggested to Uncle Jâms that he fetch the gun to it – Mari Fiddle-Faddle possibly. My uncle had an aptitude for inventing facetious nicknames, and Mari Fiddle-Faddle was his name for our second maid, a plump, red-faced bundle of a girl who ran trot-trot the livelong day without being by the evening much nearer catching what she was after. His name, by the way, for the first maid was 'The Buck', a strong, healthy woman with wondering brown eyes; a hefty one for getting the work through her hands, but rather abrupt and graceless in her manner of speech. By to-day I think that Uncle Jâms was a bit afraid of 'The Buck'. She hadn't much patience with anyone who dilly-dallied with work. And sometimes when he had been more of a hindrance than a help, as he frequently could be, he was allowed to know her opinion of him in pretty plain terms. That is what inspired the name 'The Buck', I dare say. But Fiddle-Faddle was just to his liking. With her, as with himself, work and time did not count much in life. 'A *diawth'i*, Mari fach, you're quite right – that my lady wantth to be brought down,' I imagine my uncle saying. 'She hath left too much of her mark on the woodth already. Fetch the gun, Harrith bach.'

As I said a while back, Uncle Jâms was no shot at all, he was so short-sighted. But he had a good gun, a double-barrelled one with a dark mahogany stock, but it hadn't enough bow to give it an easy aim. Every one knew when this gun came out that it was going to be 'a day for the king', and Mari Fiddle-Faddle was, like Mac the sheepdog, giving little squeals and wagging her tail. There hadn't been such a day since she came there to service last All-Hallows.

'Jâms bach, you'll never shoot her,' said the first maid, seeing everybody's time being wasted like this with work on their hands.

'A *diawth'i*, it ith you 'the Buck' thpeaking? Go to the houthe and put the broth on the fire, that'th a good girl.' My uncle knew how to make her hopping mad at any moment by calling her this name. She left, fuming. Fiddle-Faddle had too much entered the spirit of the occasion to hear her command to follow her.

The preparations for the Bisley went forward, my uncle being the hero of the hour. At last, after taking a long aim, during which all held their breath, two shots *Powns*! *Powns*! following each other like that echoed through the woods. The squirrel jumped one or two holds further up, but she saw that this wouldn't do. They swayed under her too much, and back she went to the same place as before, up in a fork, and this time on the far side to the spectators. The company moved a little to the left to get a better view of her.

'*A diawrht'i*, ith that how it ith, mith? Well, we'll try another little pipeful.' And so he did. Two more shots. But it was of no avail. The little squirrel rode the fiery storm without being one hair the worse for it as far as one could judge.

Some of the enthusiastic spectators blamed the stock of the gun. The powder had got a bit damp, others suggested, or perhaps the shot was too small. No one suspected the shooter. Through the perforated zinc window of the dairy where the first maid was now at work she secretly watched it all, and in her sullen temper she rejoiced over each failure. As Uncle Jâms was not used to loading a gun, the preparation for each new broadside was protracted. After the fifth or sixth bombardment a white spot could be seen a good yard below the target where the tree had been barked.

'*Diawl*, Jâms Williams, keep at it. You're on the right tree anyway,' said Dai the head man. Dai had been charged strictly by my mother not to use bad language in my presence, and I was to tell her if he happened to fall. 'You didn't hear me, now, did you, boy?' asked Dai with a smile at the corners of his eyes. 'No, Bafydd,' said I innocently. This 'Bafydd's' father was the incomparable Benni Bwlch y Mynydd, and he was his father's son. '*Dee-ary*, Jâms, she won't come down today, you shall see; the little squirrel's enjoying herself fine up there,' said Dafydd Trefenty, the old worker, so taciturn and conscientious, turning to leave the merry company. 'Perhaps she'll come down to dinner,' said Harris Bach sweetly.

While this facetiousness was afoot and the lull between the firing rather longer than usual, there's the little red squirrel taking the leap of no return, and in a twinkling she was on the next tree and the next and next, and twigs of the tall trees were dancing all the way under her from the roadside into the security of the middle of Cwm Bach wood, where she would find leisure in due course to tell her partner about the warmest morning of her life.

'Dinner,' said the Buck from the corner of the house.

'*Diawtht'i, she* won't come back here in a hurry to plague uth around the fold,' said Uncle Jâms, going to dinner along with the others in the mood of a man who had accomplished a precious morning's work.

D. J. Williams. *The Old Farmhouse* † 1953

11. *Old 'Lias*

In former times there was a tradition in Llansadwrn of paying five pounds to make a child of the poor 'a parish apprentice'. The last of the apprentices was 'the old 'Lias', as he was called when I first remember him. Elias was apprenticed as a boy of ten as a servant lad or a page to Admiral Sir Thomas Foley, at Abermarlais mansion. The Admiral was married to Lady Lucy Fitzgerald, daughter of the Duke of Leinster, and sister of Lord Edward Fitzgerald, husband of Pamela, and hero of the 1798 revolt. He was the first, in his battle-ship *Goliath*, to engage the French forces in the battle of the Nile, and Nelson was on his ship, the *Elephant*, in the battle of Copenhagen, and that same hero was at his side when he raised his telescope to his blind eye. He died as Admiral of the Fleet in Portsmouth in 1833, in the arms of 'Lias, parish apprentice from Llansadwrn mountain. His widow, Lady Lucy, went to live in France where she spent her remaining days, and 'Lias with her. When the old Lady died around 1850, she left Two thousand pounds in the *Three per cents* to 'Lias for him to live on the interest, and Llettyrywen Farm, adjacent to my old home, for him as long as he lived.

When 'Lias went to Abermarlais as a boy, he knew not a word of English. After living with the old Admiral in England for years, he also lost close on every word of the old language. Having remained in France for ten years and more, he became more familiar with French than English. And from there, when he was almost fifty years of age, he came back to live in the old parish, where only an occasional one was in the least familiar with any 'thin' language . . .

But to come back to 'Lias. After his return to Llansadwrn, he married a girl from the village, and he did his best to become a farmer. But despite his best endeavours, fortune did not smile on his efforts. A valet was 'Lias, and it's hard to make a farmer out of an old valet. He endeavoured to re-learn Welsh, but he spoke some extraordinary mixture of Welsh and English, and many an oath and expletive in French. There was no scarcity of stories about the old Admiral and Lady Lucy – especially Lady Lucy. Her name was so readily on his tongue that old Griffith the blacksmith christened old 'Lias 'Lady Lucy', and he was stuck with the nickname as long as he lived. Until I reached an age when I could understand what 'Lias was talking about, people of the district had wearied of his old yarns. The old man had become hard of hearing, and would take an hour over a tale that a skilled raconteur could tell in a tenth fraction of the time. In his old-age, therefore, 'Lias happened upon weary days. Nobody was willing to while away an hour listening to the *laudator temporis acti* boasting about the fortitude of the old Admiral and the purity of Lady Lucy, with her quaint sayings and her incomparable deeds.

Although Llettyrywen was only a meadowsbreadth from my old home, I didn't know much about old 'Lias until I was about twelve. A wart started to grow on 'Lias's nose; the doctor told him that it was cancer, and couldn't be cured. But in those early days there were many 'hedgebottom doctors' in the district. In Llansawel there was a bone doctor; in Llangadog lived a man who had an extraordinary salve for fire-burns; in Talley there was a blacksmith who had an excellent ointment for ringworm and erysipelas; and in the Plough Inn in the village of Caio, Morgans the innkeeper had an incomparable balm for curing cancer. 'Lias, determined to try the innkeeper's medicine, and since he didn't have a car, the responsibility of transporting 'Lias to Caio once a week to have the cancer ointment put on his nose fell upon me. That's how I came to know and to love his countless stories. Old 'Lias's memoirs were as good as viol and harp to me, since I had never read any fiction except *The Pilgrim's Progress* and *Uncle Tom's Cabin*. Never before had old 'Lias had such an audience, and from that time till the day of his death he looked upon me as his 'silly bucket' (as Coleridge said) into which he poured his memories.

'Do you know why your homestead house is called Brownhill?' he said one time. 'No? *Mon Dieu*, what ignorance! Well, when the prize-money after the Battle of Copenhagen was paid to the old Admiral thousands and thousands of pounds – he decided to buy an estate: *cette va sans dire*, that's what all the Admirals did! He was the son of the Squire of Ridgeway in Pembroke, only a small estate was that one – not big enough, *comprenez vous*, for a great man like Sir Thomas. Abermarlais estate was up for sale – it had been in Chancery for 60 years and more – and the Admiral bought his half, and Williams the A'Bishop, your ancestor, *mon ami* – a quarter of it. The old mansion had gone a hopeless ruin – no one living there for 60 years – the Admiral pulled it down, and from the stones he built the new mansion of Abermarlais and Brownhill farmhouse. He built also the little house where Isaac Nathan lives, and he called that Copenhagen after the battle, you see. He wanted to call your house Copenhagen Farm, but my lady would not have it. Lady Lucy was a great admirer of Bobby Burns – all the Whigs loved Burns and hated William Pitt – and because Bobby had once lived in a place called Brownhill, Brownhill they called the new house.'

I do not know till this day present whether the old 'Lias was right or not in his explanation of the name: but I believe him to be correct by his saying that it is from the old stones of the famous Abermarlais mansion that Brownhill was constructed in 1801. In the old mansion Dr Lewis, physician to the Duchess Richmond, and Rhys ap Thomas plotted together to make it possible for Henry Tudor to land at Dale and conquer Wales and England. There, too, Vicar Pritchard was signatory to his will. Well, well, the fact that I drew my first breath between the stones of the old mansion brings Wales Past somewhat nearer to me.

'We always loved to have the Napier boys staying with us,' said he another time. 'Lady Lucy was closely related to them. *Eh bien* – those were great days. The lads were every time full of fun and frolic. I remember once Lady Lucy heard that Charlie was killed in the Peninsula. Every servant-man had a suit of mourning, but, *ma foi*! The first day we wore them, who should turn up but Charlie himself. And what a feast we had!'

But perhaps the best story in my estimation at the time was the live description of the *guillotine* at work in Paris in 1848, with the heads severed and the corspes dancing in the basket! I never tired of hearing the history, and after I had recounted it to the children of the area, they would crowd round old 'Lias on the highroad, shouting 'Tell us, 'Lias Lewis, the way they cut the heads off in France.'

W. Llewelyn Williams, *'S Lawer Dydd* †

12. Ford Hughes, Night-rider

Perhaps the most eccentric of Welsh squires in recent years was Ford Hughes of Aberceri. He was the only son of another freak, old Davies of Nantgwylan, near Newcastle Emlyn. Although his father was rather an odd fish, he was conventional in comparison with his son. Why the latter assumed the name of Hughes I never knew for his only sister (whom I remember well) was always called Miss Lloyd-Davies. Although a wealthy landowner with one or two places of his own, Ford Hughes had a perfect mania for both buying and renting vacant country houses. For years he was a perfect godsend to the impoverished gentry of the

Tivyside, for he would apply for the refusal of any house that that happened to be for sale or to let.

After spending his early life in London and Paris, when he must have mixed in very queer company, Ford Hughes finally settled, not in one of his many mansions but in a mean house in Union Street, Carmarthen. Here he lived alone, though a few relatives or friends occasionally visited him in his squalid solitude. His unfortunate sister who was an ardent Roman Catholic and keen supporter of St Mary's Mission Church in Carmarthen had lodgings near her brother, and used to be admitted from time to time to see him. Otherwise Ford Hughes was never seen by daylight, but occasionally he would hire a fly at nightfall and drive long distances through the darkness to visit one or other of his country seats, arriving at some unearthly hour and only staying a few minutes, in order to reach his Carmarthen house again before daylight.

And such a house as he owned! From the street the passer-by could note the filthy windows that were heaped inside with masses of dirty rags, ashes and old newspapers. His meals were brought in by a boy from an inn in Lammas Street and deposited outside his locked door. The sanitary conditions of the house were indescribable, especially after his water-supply was cut off by the authorities. And yet the Corporation of Carmarthen allowed this poor crazy eremite to exist thus for years! At length when the food was found untouched outside the locked door, someone or other thought it time to interfere, so officials broke open the doors and invaded the house. The unhappy man, then helpless with his last illness, was taken to the workhouse sanatorium, and I do not know how many layers of underclothing were removed or scraped from his body. The stench in the house was such that some of the rescuing-party were made sick on the spot.

Herbert M. Vaughan, *The South Wales Squires*

13. THE TALCEN SLIP

He died on March the 31st,
His only trouble was his thirst.
He spent his life in drinking beer
And drink it now if he was here!

Benjamin Hughes, *Hen Rhysin Pembanc*

14. *Rowland the Outlaw and Sackville Gwynne*

A less generous fate befell Howell's eldest son, however, for Rowland Gwynne of Glanbran (d. 1675), who became High Sheriff of Carmarthenshire in 1660, was ousted from office on the return of Charles Stuart and even outlawed, but too much should not be read into this latter punishment, which at that time could be pronounced for relatively minor transgressions of the law. In his will, Rowland, a graduate of Oxford, where he had matriculated from Merton College, referred to his lands in the counties of Carmarthen and Brecon, and among properties devised by him was the house called Whitehall in Llandovery, which he left to his wife.

The three sons of outlaw Rowland left no issue, the last surviving being the youngest, Sackville Gwynne (1670-1734), who received his first name after a close friend of his father, Sir Sackville Crow, Bart. This, the first Sackville Gwynne, who became High Sheriff of Breconshire in 1701, died a bachelor and was buried in the little church of Tirabad at Llandulas, which he had rebuilt. By will he left Glanbran to his kinsman Roderick Gwynne of Garth, Breconshire, and it was this Roderick who built the eighteenth century mansion, the ruins of which are all that now remain. After matriculating from Jesus College, Oxford, Roderick was admitted to Lincoln's Inn and called to the bar in 1719. He married, in 1748, Anne Howe, daughter of the first Lord Chedworth by Dorothy, eldest daughter of Henry Frederick Thynne, ancestor of the Marquis of Bath, and died in 1777 aged eighty-one.

The son of this union was the notable Sackville Gwynne who was born about 1751. Without his father's knowledge, he fell in love with the daughter of a Glanbran tenant and a runaway marriage was solemnised at Dublin in 1772. A story is told that he took flight with a very large sum of money and during the journey lost one of his money-bags containing £6,000 without realising it. The lost bag, it has been recorded, was found by a Carmarthenshire farmer, who is supposed to have bought an estate as a result, a story which may or may not be true. Sackville's bride is sometimes said to be Catherine, daughter of one Prydderch (or Prytherch), but according to the marriage certificate her name was Catherine Thomas.

The runaway bridegroom may not have rued the day, but five years later he paid the price of his unsanctioned adventure into matrimony by forfeiting part of his inheritance, for Roderick Gwynne made a new will by which Sackville received only Glanbran, the Buckland estate (which Roderick had purchased) and other property being passed to the younger brother, Thynne Howe Gwynne. A quarrel between the two brothers ensued and never did they speak to each other afterwards.

Sackville Gwynne is remembered as a patron of music, particularly of the harp, and he himself was reputed to have been one of the finest exponents of the triple harp in his day. He received many of the best harpists at his home, a patronage which continued at Glanbran well into the nineteenth century, long after his death. John Richards of Llanrwst (1711-1789), a famous harp maker, died at Glanbran and was buried at Llanfair-ar-y-bryn.

E. Vernon Jones. *Fingers of Forsaken Stone.*
The Carmarthenshire Historian, Vol. IX, 1972

15. *Howel y Pedoulau*

Till very lately another curious monument was preserved in the chancel* near that above-mentioned, which, according to the vulgar opinion, was intended to commemorate *Owen* y Pedoulau. This also was of the altar kind, with the figure of a warrior, having his arms placed in a supplicating posture, as usual, on his breast, but holding in both his clenched hands a large horse shoe, as if in the act of breaking it asunder in the middle. This is supposed, with a great degree of probability, to have been intended for Howel ap Pedoulau, than for Owen; the former of whom, we are told by the Welsh records, was foster brother to king Edward the second, Sir Howel's mother having been the young prince's nurse, and that he was so strong as to be able to break, or straighten horse-shoes with his bare hands. We may easily perceive in what manner he came in after-times to be called Owen instead of Howel; his posterity assumed the surname of Owen, and being recognized as the great ancestor of that family, the transition is readily accounted for. The whole of this monument, which was of fine gypsum, was destroyed fourteen years ago by the workmen employed to repair the church. According to the condition of their engagement, they were to provide materials for the cornice work, and finding the stone of this monument reduced to plaister, would perfectly well suit the purpose, the villains actually broke it up to save themselves expense.

E. Donovan. *Descriptive Excursion Thro' South Wales* 1805

* St Peter's Church, Carmarthen.

16. *John Harries, Cwrtycadno*

John Harries, Pantcoy, Cwrtycadno, better known as 'Doctor Harries', was an Astrologer, and a Wizard, and these qualifications he made great use of in dispensing medicine to a large practice. He was very popular in his day. The sick and sorrowful came to enquire of his oracles from all parts of Wales, and from the testimony of the oldest people in the district, he was eminently successful in his cures. Lunatics were brought to him from parts of Pembrokeshire and Radnorshire, and he had a wonderful power over them. The course of treatment would include what he would term the water treatment, the herbs treatment, and the bleeding treatment. One of his chief methods was, he would take the afflicted to the brink of the river, and fire an old Flint revolver; this would frighten his patient to such a degree, that he would fall into the pool. He assumed the power of charming away pain, and was so successful, that people believed thoroughly that he was in league with the evil one. Patients went to him from all parts, some would tramp, and others on horseback over 40 miles to see the 'Doctor'. The following is a copy of one of his Printed bills:

. . . . 182 . .

Pant-teg

Mr . . . .

       To John Harries.

   To Medicine and Medical attendance as per account rendered

£   :   :

Sir,

    Unless the above amount is paid to me, on or before the . . . day of . . . next, adverse means will be resorted to, for the recovery.

                    Your Humble Servant,

          . . . .

Hundreds of tales are told of him, and are believed zealously to the present day. One originated from the fact or rumour that a young girl in the district was lost, and could not be found high or low; so the friends at last went to Cwrtycadno and consulted Doctor Harries. He informed them that she had been murdered by her sweetheart, and that he had hid the body. Her body was hid in the earth, under the shades of a tree, in the hollow of which they would find a Bee's nest. The tree stood alone near a brook. The searching party at last came across the spot indicated by Harries, and here they found the body buried. The young man was found, and confessed the crime. The authorities of the law became aware of these facts. Harries was brought before the Magistrates at Llandovery, when Lloyd, Glansevin, and Gwyn, Glanbran, sat on the Bench. Harries was charged with knowing and abetting of murder, otherwise he could not have known she was murdered, and where she was buried. He was however discharged. He told the Magistrates that if they would tell him the hour they were born, he could tell them the hour they would cease to exist.

Another tale relates to a married woman who lost her wedding ring. So one day she walked 15 miles up to Cwrtycadno to see the Doctor, in order to consult him as to the missing ring. As soon as she went into the house, the Doctor told her she was a married woman, and that she had come to see him respecting a wedding ring lost. He then told her that the ring was with some relation of hers, and that the ring would be returned in the course of a few days. She went home satisfied. The ring was taken away by her son, who returned it a few days afterwards. When he returned it to her, he said he could now die in peace, as he had returned the ring. Two days afterwards the son died.

Another tale is, that the Doctor always said that he would not die a natural death, as his planet showed him this distinctly. So that after dinner on the day his planet became due to be fulfilled, in order as he said to cross his planet, he went to bed, so that no harm should befall him. However, he was awakened from his slumberings, by someone crying that the house was on fire. This soon roused him, down he came to assist to put out the fire. He went up a ladder, which leaned against the roof, in order to throw water on, when the ladder slipped, and down he went and was killed. So after all he failed to cross his planet.

Fred S. Price, *History of Caio*

17. *The Wizard of Caio*

We have heard of countless numbers of impostors in every age, who were effective and successful securing credibility for their enchantments from the populace; but there is some impudence and deviltry in Mr Henry Harries's card, far above anything ever on offer before, particularly

in the Principality of Wales. We have heard of the old 'Red Doctor' –
Roland Jones from Pistyll, Abraham Wood, Bela from Denbigh, etc.
besides Jannes and Jambres from Egypt, together with the prophets
from Caldea; but Mr Henry Harries, Cwrtycadno has thrown them all
in the shade and has cast himself for all time as the Prince of the
Fortunetellers of the Earth. There is nothing concerning which people
are more anxious than to receive information and knowlege in relation
to the time that is to come. But the wisest and most knowledgeable
people of the ages have abandoned the matter as unattainable and allow
the great providence of heaven to give birth to those happenings which
are to meet the sons of Adam in this life. But it now seems that an
amazing turn of events has come about, mysteries which are not mysteries
any longer, darkness which is no longer darkness, and omniscience which
is no longer God's prerogative, because Mr Henry Harries Cwrtycadno
also is all-knowing. Spolasco is but a midget beside Henry Harries and
he is like some tower a hundred miles high on the shoulders of the
Lilians, the Agrippians and the Baretts together with the great and the
minor conjurors and the circle-speckled conjurors of the world at large.

Now, according to the card Mr Henry Harries has issued he professes
knowledge of things to come and takes upon himself knowledge of an
art through which he can give information for almost every accident
and occurrence together with all man's adventures in this life. He can
foretell, he says, all the ordinary happenings of a man throughout his
life, he can predict his success or lack of it, a man's honour, his wealth,
his travels, his voyages, together with everything else in the World
pertaining to him throughout his life. In fact, here is a Prophet risen in
the Principality of Wales, and more than a prophet; and he can properly
proclaim: With me is the Wisdom. I myself possess knowledge, and there
is nobody besides me.

David Owen ('Brutus'). *Yr Haul* † 1839

18. BACHELOR

'I can't, I can't,' cried bachelor Tom
who farmed where the river met sea,
where shelduck came
and heron flew
and blackthorn grew.

'I can't, I can't,' the old man sighed.
'I can't go to a stiff white bed
in that city place for the sick and dead,'
said this deacon of Zion,
where the bible was iron,
where the floor heard his knees
and the rafters his prayers
and the minister keened
on wheat and tares.

'I can't, I can't,' he moaned to the cow.
'I'd rather make an end of it now.
I can't, I can't,' he called to his flock,
'I'd rather drown, weighed down by a rock.
I can't, I can't,' he told the hen.
'How could I go to be nursed by women,
to have their young hands touch me *there*
and lay my trouser secrets bare?
I can't, I can't,' he cried to the cocks,
'I'd rather be screw'd in my wooden box.'

For women's hands pry deeper
than the claws of Mark the Lion,
thought the deacon of Zion.
And women's eyes burn tender skin
fiercer than the frown of Him
who reigns in Zion.

He took the rope for leading the horse,
– not too fine nor yet too coarse –
and looped a noose from the truss of the barn
and stopped the breath of Tom Pensarn.

So by his prostate gland he died,
on a day in June
when the sea was blue
and curlew cried
where campion grew.

Kusha Petts

19. *Meeting a Miser*

Monday [May 17th, 1819]. Got up at 6 o'clock and at ½ past 6 as on my way to Lampeter, past Lord Robt. Seymour's estate of Taliaris, the name brought poor Julia's fate fresh to my recollection. I was seated on an old bridge close to the estate, of Lord Robt., and as I thought contemplating the beauties of his estate when a singular looking figure mounted on a dirty half-starved Welch pony with a piece of cord round its nose by way of bridle, issued from the wood close by me. The man was about 5 feet 2 inches high, looked about 70, his beard full 6 months growth, his skin the collor of excrement, an old patched drab-colored coat, no shirt, a ragged handkerchief round his neck, a pair of greasy leather breeches, patch'd with sheep's skin with the wool on, and large jack boots, with a cole-heaver's hat on. He rode direct to me and said 'were do you come from?' A little surprised at the abbruptness of the question and appearance of the questioner, I replied, 'pray what is that to you.' He begged my pardon, but added, 'that he thought I was a fisherman and intended to direct me to a better part of the river, than that I was by.' This assured me of the civility of his intention, and fancying there was something in such a determined character, I continued the conversation by asking, 'Whoe's beautiful grounds those were?' Mine, was his answer, and they extend for 300 acres. I could hardly believe my ears. We found we were going for about 3 miles on the same road, and he very good naturedly offered to dismount and let me ride. This I declined with many thanks. Our conversation was too continued to enter it here, more particularly as I cannot forget it, but he seemed to take vast fancy to me asked me if I would give him my name in writing, on which I gave him my card. He told me to write down that I had met J— N— of Llatharmawr, in the Parish of Llandilo, that his attorney was a Mr Williams of Aberistwyth and that his brother, the only relation he had, was drowned about 2 years before. We went into a little hedge ale-house at Talia, and he wanted to treat me with a pint of ale. However, I drank a little with him, and had a quart of boiled milk for breakfast. He asked me if I had seen any of the new gold coin, I told him yes, I had one about me; on which he asked to see it, and expressed a great desire to have it, but offered me such a torn dirty note in exchange that I would not take it. After I left him I learnt from many that he is one of the richest men in Carmarthenshire – without a relation and a horrid miser. He in general carries brown sugar about him to satisfy his hunger when travelling, and that he was never known to offer to treat anyone to anything. The road from Llandilo to Sir James Hamlyn's estate about a mile and a half from the village I breakfasted at, is very pretty, but from there to Lampeter is very hilly and stony, walked over Sir James's estate (an old fashioned mansion), got a drink of milk from the dairy. At 1.40 arrived quite exhausted by the heat of the weather and weight of my jacket at Pumpsaint, where I had fried eggs and bacon and a jug of ale at the Pumpsaint Arms. At 3.30 set off, felt a good deal exhilirated on entring Cardiganshire as the county of my forefathers.

Captain Jenkin Jones. *Diary* from *The Transactions of the West Wales Historical Society*, Vol. I

20. *Farewell to Shanco*

His first notion that something was wrong was when Twm arrived on foot at Ystradffin. It was the deep middle of the night. Some honeycomb cloud had hidden the moon, and the earth was held in monumental stillness. Woodlarks held their tongues and the shivering owls blinked silently from their hollow oaks. Twm saw the hulk of Ystradffin dark against the ravine. This was the very lunacy of love; for what, now that he asked himself, could be gained by his being at Johane's house in the middle of the night? He knew then that some impulse beyond reason had drawn him there just to be near, to look at the house which now stared hollow-eyed back at him, to breathe the same air and to hear the same sounds as his sleeping love. It was the middle of the night. Who knew at that time that he was alive? None but a few. Hush! He was a spirit.

There were lights leaking from every room behind drawn curtains. There were horses, many horses, carts and carriages drawn up in the yard. It was the hour before dawn. There was something seriously amiss. Twm felt panic, light-headed panic. He thought, thought hard. There was one explanation: Tom Williams might be ill. Either that or Johane. He would have to find out! His heart began to race. He prayed to God that no harm had come to her. The desperation he felt was overwhelming. It took his breath away.

The servants here would not know him. He knocked on a cottage door. A cowman or a shepherd came sleepily out of the dark. His voice was as gruff as his dog's.

'I have been sent for,' said Twm in a deep voice. 'Is it your master, or is the mistress sick?'

'Oh! Are you the physician? Doctor Williams from Myddfai? You have come very quickly.'

'Who has the sickness?' Twm had to restrain himself from shouting at him.

'Not sickness, sir. Wounded he is. Fell in battle on the mountain.'

'Who were they fighting?'

'Twm Siôn Cati's men.'

Twm forgot his deep voice. He stepped forward.

'Any taken? Any taken on their side? Any casualties?'

The cowman turned his head on one side to look at him.

'What's it to you?'

Twm realized he had slipped. He took out a pistol and held it to the man's face. Cold metal against Adam's apple. The whites of the man's eyes grew large.

'Tell me!'

The man swallowed hard. The dog began to bark.

'I don't know. Who are you?'

'Never mind who I am. What happened?' Twm pushed him into the dark kitchen. The man fell over a stool. Someone stirred in a bed in the corner.

'Don't move or say a word!' Twm warned. He brought the second pistol into play. 'I mean you no harm. But, so help me, I must know what's happened.'

'It's Twm Siôn Cati, drop dead,' said a woman's voice. 'I know you. Rhys is married to my cousin, Harrieta. They said you were hanged in Brecon!' Twm put away his pistols. 'Is it true that you are my lady's sweetheart?' she said sitting on the edge of the bed. Twm saw the gossip's smile in the firelight.

'What happened up there?' Twm insisted. They told him all they knew. Sir Tom was near dying. Twm reckoned with dread that either Rhys or Shanco had gone. A bad business. He was too late.

'I must see her,' said Twm, 'Can I trust you?' He knew that by noon she would be as tonguetied as a jay at an owl roost. A risk he would have to take. That there were ways of ensuring loyalty and buying time he knew, but they deserted him. He would have to trust to love, and the world loving lovers. The woman put on her shawl, her bonnet and her wooden clogs. She could hardly contain her excitement.

'Remember,' Twm warned, '*he* stays here with me.' He flashed a pistol. 'No meddling. No tricks.' He referred to her husband, who had become struck dumb once she started.

'Oh no, sir. Don't you worry.'

But Twm was very worried as she clopped off towards the house. Now the man talked a little again. It appeared that Stedman had arrived with a priest. He and several neighbours were keeping the vigil with poor Johane. Twm felt suddenly very cold. He was sitting in a nest of marten cats. One slip and they'd drink his blood. The cowman sat on his haunches, his arms loose over his knees. He sighed to himself.

'You can trust us,' he said kindly.

Cocks were shouting now from the barns and larks could be heard winding towards heaven. She would have need to hurry or it would be daylight and all would be lost. The clogs came back across the slates. Alone. The woman stood at the doorway of the cottage, looking defeated and much older. She also sighed.

'It is very bad in there, sir. Very bad indeed. My lady is too much in distress. I hadn't the heart to disturb her sorrow. She cries all the time like a child.' Twm understood; of course he understood. There was nothing anyone could do. The woman's account was genuine. Twm wanted then to be there with Johane, to hold her in his arms, to give her strength. And he too felt a chill of sorrow for one he supposed had been his enemy. There had to have been good in Tom for Johane to have loved him so dearly. Poor old man to die victim to greedy ambition.

'How is he?' Twm asked quietly.

'Poorly, poorly,' she said, shaking her head. 'Death would be a mercy, he is in such pain. But I doubt he will be spared the suffering. They say the arrow came from young Stedman's bow.'

Twm had heard enough. Green was filtering into the leaves which shook in the near-dawn breeze.

'Well, fancy,' he heard her say.

With dry mouth and aching breast Twm made his way up through scree slopes, among the boulders of the ravine. The Towy rushed below him. The clamour of birdsong hung like a mist in the green leaves; with every step he knew it was about to break his heart. He thought of Rhys's little children and Harrieta, and begged it was not him. He thought of Shanco. And could think no further. '. . . as for a soldier, boys. Look out!' he heard. And the tears at last came. He sat, looking down at the unspeakable beauty of the summer dawn, and he knew it was Shanco.

*   *   *

They had found Shanco's chalk-white body drifting idly round and round in the backwash of a pool below Pwll Uffern. They carried his great body up onto the heather and closed his eyes. One of his boots was near by and Wil searched desperately, tears welling out of him, till he found the other, lodged in under a root. He dived in fully clothed to fetch it. But they could not get them on him. It seemed more terrible than the fact of death. They carried him in silence to a headland which commanded views over landscapes that denied the existence of man. The Van Mountains of Carmarthenshire abutted defiantly the wastes below, touched by the evening sun. The Brecon Beacons saluted them through the purple haze and all the acres and miles of Cardiganshire and Carmarthenshire stood firmly to attention while they put Shanco finally to rest.

They took the stones out of a cairn that the ancient people had put there. They took them all out till they found the stone slabs deep in the ground. It was too small a place for great Shanco, so they made it bigger with their hands. There they laid him: Shanco with the chieftain, his ancestor. They said some words, the words Shanco had used in Brecon burying the money: 'In the midst of life we are in death.' And they remained there and watched over him all night.

There Twm found them the following morning. They had not seen him coming towards them out of the heather until a grouse had burst out underfoot, frightening him: 'Go back! Go back! Go back!' she had warned. But Twm Siôn Cati did not heed her warning. There was no question of retreat.

When he reached the cairn, he put his arms round them all in tribute to their grief. He kneeled at the grave and prayed. No one spoke.

They all left him then, without once looking back.

Lynn Hughes, *Hawkmoor/Twm Siôn Cati's Men*

21. AFTER THE FUNERAL
    (In memory of Ann Jones)

In a room with a stuffed fox and a stale fern,
I stand, for this memorial's sake, alone
In the snivelling hours with dead, humped Ann
Whose hooded, fountain heart once fell in puddles
Round the parched worlds of Wales and drowned each sun.
(Though this for her is a monstrous image blindly

Magnified out of praise; her death was a still drop;
She would not have me sinking in the holy
Flood of her heart's fame; she would lie dumb and deep
And need no druid of her broken body).
But I, Ann's bard on a raised hearth, call all
The seas to service that her wood-tongued virtue
Babble like a bellbuoy over the hymning heads,
Bow down the walls of the ferned and foxy woods
That her love sing and swing though a brown chapel,
Bless her bent spirit with four, crossing birds.
Her flesh was meek as milk, but this skyward statue
With the wild breast and blessed and giant skull
Is carved from her in a room with a wet window
In a fiercely mourning house in a crooked year.
I know her scrubbed and sour humble hands
Lie with religion in their cramp, her threadbare
Whisper in a damp word, her wits drilled hollow,
Her fist of a face died clenched on a round pain;
And sculptured Ann is seventy years of stone.
These cloud-sopped, marble hands, this monumental
Argument of the hewn voice, gesture and psalm,
Storm me forever over her grave until
The stuffed lung of the fox twitch and cry Love
And the strutting fern lay seeds on the black sill.

Dylan Thomas, from *After the funeral*

22. *Bestial People*

Not far to the north of Carmarthen lies Pencader, which means the head of the chair. When, in our own days, Rhys ap Gruffydd was forced to surrender, more by a trick than by force of arms, and was carried off to England, Henry II, King of the English, sent a knight from Brittany, in whose prudence and fidelity he could trust, with Guaidan, the Dean of Cantref Mawr, to conduct him, with orders to examine the site of Dinevor Castle and to report back on how strongly the terrain was fortified. This priest was told to lead the knight to the castle by the easiest route and to make his journey as pleasant as possible. Instead he made a point of taking him along the most difficult and inaccessible trackways. Whenever they passed through lush woodlands, to the great astonishment of all present, he plucked a handful of grass and ate it, thus giving the impression that in time of need the local inhabitants lived on roots and grasses. The knight went back to the King and reported everything worth mentioning that he had seen and heard. The district was quite uninhabitable, he said, inaccessible and virtually without roads, providing sustenance only for a bestial race of people, who were content to live there like animals. Thereupon the King made Rhys swear an oath of fealty and hand over hostages. Then he sent him back to his own affairs.

Giraldus Cambrensis, *The Itinerary Through Wales*

23. *John Waunfawr*
The Man who went back to the Neolithic Age

John, as the only son, lived and worked with his parents on a moorland farm, Waunfawr (literally, the big moor), high up out of sight of us who lived in the cultivated farms on the slopes and in the vales below. Up there, too, rolled the mists to rest, and interpose a screen between it and the more restless world lower down. It was a bleak, tree-less, upland stretch of heather and hill grass, with here and there a scrubby bush of gorse and other shrubs indigenous to high altitudes, behind which a small mountain sheep might find shelter as it isolated itself for its labour and to be its own mid-wife and doctor as well as the mother. No road led to the homestead, but through a dilapidated gate, opening from a broken, pit-infested track, which served rather to mark the once high-water mark of declining cultivation than as a means of facilitating transport, there ran a grass-grown, unfenced cart-way, threading its way over the higher and drier patches. It is true that round the home there were a few cultivated fields bounded by peat hedges, along which ran one strand of barbed wire. Here, in suitable years, quite good crops of oats, potatoes and coarse hay were harvested. The home itself was of the primitive long-house type, universal at one time in moorland areas, with a passage from the kitchen to the byre, all under the same roof. The advantage of this arrangement will be immediately apparent to anyone who can visualise the conditions on the moor in stormy weather, or in periods of deep snow, as it enabled the farmer to attend to the needs of his cattle without exposing himself to the elements.

John's parents were very old-fashioned people, who led a hard and primitive existence, but were reputed to be quite comfortable in their material circumstances. They burnt peat instead of coal and followed, generally, old, forgotten ways, so much so that their dress and mode of life was sufficiently unique to be a matter of talk and wonder to their neighbours. Still, they went on in their own way – a 'mountain way' the people called it (ffordd fynyddig). How could it be otherwise? For on this moorland plateau that stretched for miles and miles across Wales, dividing the watersheds, sending half its streams down to the Bristol Channel and the other half away north to Cardigan Bay, they were surrounded by numerous remains of primitive man – barrows, menhirs, cromlechs, cairns, crugs, hearths, circles and forgotten meeting-places where man dwelt long before he moved down to clear and inhabit the 'cwms'. Up in the silences of these upland stretches, hemmed in by the mists, lived on, from the age of the barrows, old thoughts and ways, old ghosts and superstitions, old remedies and old beliefs.

When I think of John, I am led to believe that these ancient remains possess some mysterious power to grip, in a way unperceived and un-suspected, the minds of those who live amongst them, and hold them to old ways and thoughts and levels. John, whom the spirits of the barrows and cromlechs had pulled back much further, and held far more completely, than they had his father and mother, was in his 'teens and twenties an active and loyal member of his chapel and Sunday school. He was extraordinarily well-versed in the Bible and could recite long passages by heart. Gradually, so gradually that it evoked no comment at first, he began to slacken in his attendance at both, his clothes became shabbier, his face remained unwashed and unshaved, his unkempt appearance became a matter of comment and disgust. Finally he left the chapel altogether. Soon after his father's death the old house was blown down, but John built a primitive shack in a field near-by, dis-pensing with the horses, the implements and the cows, retaining only the sheep and a few chickens. Women avoided him on the roads; the men, especially those who knew him well, spoke sharply to him about his appearance and his mode of life, and told him to pull himself together, but John beamed innocently on them and protested that he was quite warm and healthy and very happy. Some said he was lazy, others that he was mad. But he was not mad except in the sense that to cling to the philosophy of life of the Stone Age man, and retain his simple ways, is madness in our own. He could be seen against the sky-line from earliest dawn to dusk, indeed, he was often met walking about at dead of night, living now without clock or calendar, without count of days, festivals or months, noting only the seasons.

Now, what gripped him and pulled him back so far and so completely? Back from the twentieth century, from civilization, even from the pursuit of agriculture, yes, back beyond the Iron Age to that of the barrows and cairns, amongst the inhabitants of which his appearance would have excited no comment!

He had become acquainted in some curious way with the fabled history of the Ancient Britons. It was from him that I first heard of the mythical heroes, Gog and Magog; of Gomer; of Brutus leaving Troy with his followers to conquer this island and name it after himself, Brutania! It was such a curious mixture as might have been derived from Geoffrey of Monmouth. But back, back, John was drawn all the time. He abandoned trousers in favour of the kilt, declaring it to have been the dress of the Ancient Briton. He armed himself with the bow and arrow. Now, of course, the curious came in their crowds to see this strange figure; representatives of the daily papers came; the photographers came – not one understood John, for no one noticed the cairns and the barrows.

Strangely enough he did not resent the presence of these crowds at all; eventually, however, they ceased to come and John was allowed to live on in his own way. Four years ago he was found dead in his shack. And then the most stupid crime of all was committed, which showed so little understanding of this son of the moors and of the forces that lived on there. John, the last of the Stone Age men, was put in a coffin and carried down to the parish church, the church of the sixth-century martyr, Celer, old enough in all conscience, but not as old as John . . .

If ghosts and spirits weep, many tears of bitter anguish were shed round the cairns, cromlechs, crugs and circles the night their last child was taken away from them. They wept not for themselves but for John, for he was taken to sojourn for ever in an alien land where speed and progress, toil and iron, ruled supreme. In him they had found a new lease of life, and while he roamed the heath their age was not over. But now it was gone for ever and they returned to the everlasting silences of the deep, dark passages underneath the barrows. I shall not see or hear them again, but I shall ever believe now that I know them, for I knew John, and love them, too, for I loved John the last representative of the simple, innocent, care-free children of the moorland.

D. Parry-Jones, *Welsh Country Upbringing*

VI

Some
Blaggards

1. *Trial by Joust*

At Carmarthen on New Year's Day 1448, Owain ab Philip accused Ieuan ap Gruffydd Gogh of felony. No ordinary trial followed, for the deputy-justicar of South Wales, Gruffydd ap Nicholas, showed an unusual interest in the case. Ieuan's suspicions and Owain's bewilderment were intensified when the former [Ieuan] saw his accuser [Owain] taken into Gruffydd's house and maintained there in unaccustomed comfort for eight weeks, for three days of which he was entertained at Gruffydd's own table. When the day appointed for the settlement of the business arrived, Gruffydd produced white leather jackets and other clothing for them, and his men proceeded to decorate a place chosen for battle in the true style of the medieval joust. In the ensuing fracas Ieuan was slain, and Owain's charges, therefore, were apparently justified, for although the procedure of the judicial duel was well-nigh obsolete in fifteenth century England, recourse to it was still valid. What made the episode a travesty of even antiquated justice was the order by the deputy-justicar that Owain be promptly beheaded. The head was sold to his friends for £40 and the bill for preparations, amounting to 24s, was met out of royal revenue. Gruffydd's contempt for justice, for the Crown, and for human sympathy was boundless, for the spectacle was nothing more than a morbid entertainment for the court of a powerful gentleman.

Ralph Griffiths. 'Gruffydd ap Nicholas and the fall of the House of Lancaster'. *Welsh History Review,* Vol. 13, 1965

2. *Rhys ap Griffith*

(Sir Rhys ap Thomas's) son Griffith had predeceased him in 1521, and he had married his young grandson and heir, Rhys ap Griffith, to Katherine Howard, sister of the third duke of Norfolk.

Partly on account of his youth, the young Rhys did not succeed to his grandfather's offices of Justice and Chamberlain at Carmarthen; They were given to Lord Ferrers of Chartley. For a generation the most powerful man territorially in Carmarthenshire had also been in full command of the administration, judicial and financial, in the county: it was not surprising that his officers and tenants under their new lord should resent the activities of the bailiffs of the new Justice. In March, 1529, Rhys wrote to Cardinal Wolsey, reminding him that he had encouraged Rhys to declare any grievance of himself and his tenants; he complains that his servants and tenants are being 'put to vexacion by the lyght and malicious myndes of suche lyghte persons that be deputies under my Lord Ferrers': and requests the Cardinal to arrange with Ferrers for Rhys's appointment as his deputy at Carmarthen. Rhys was, of course, prepared to pay for this arrangement, but nothing came of it, and during Ferrers' visit to Carmarthen in June, to hold the Sessions, matters came to a head. A quarrel about billets between their retainers was followed by a violent scene between the two protagonists on account of the arrest of one of Rhys's men, and Rhys was taken into custody. A demonstration in Carmarthen by his retainers and friends from Cantref-mawr, Emlyn, and Kidwelly followed his arrest but did not effect his release. He was tried in the Michaelmas term before the Star Chamber, and it was due to Wolsey's interest that he regained his freedom. The Cardinal fell before the end of 1529, and within a year Rhys, who had in the interval dwelt not in Carmarthenshire but in London, where he had a house at Islington, was lodged in the Tower on some unspecified charge. Released on bail in the following June on account of ill-health, he was again taken there, was tried before the King's Bench in November, and executed in December, 1531; and in the Parliament of the following year he was attainted. The charge was that he had conspired with two of his countrymen to procure the help of King James of Scotland to make Rhys prince of Wales: according to the indictment, 'they had often repeated that there was in Wales an ancient prophecy that King James, with the Red Hand and the Ravens, should conquer all England.'

The true explanation of Rhys ap Griffith's tragic fate is to be found in the general political situation. Henry VIII was breaking with Rome and about to marry Norfolk's niece, Anne Boleyn. Rhys shared his fellow countrymen's hesitation to follow the Tudor king in his estrange-ment from Rome; and we are told that 'there is a rumour about town that, had it not been for the ladey (la Dame [Anne Boleyn]), who hated him because he and his wife [Norfolk's sister] had spoken disparagingly of her, he would have been pardoned and escaped his miserable fate.' The unfortunate clash with Ferrers, the unguarded utterance of prophecies, the indiscretions of a high-spirited wife, attachment to the old religion, all these contributed to the early downfall of the disgruntled young Rhys, whose large possessions of lands and goods were not unwelcome to the crown when the king was short of funds.

Sir J. E. Lloyd, *A History of Carmarthenshire*

3. Rhys ap Griffith before Wolsey

And it chanced that I was present on that day, with many others from all parts of the kingdom, when and where I heard the ugliest accusations and charges that two gentlemen could bring each against the other – charges and accusations which thousands of poor men would not for any amount of wealth have had brought against them by word of mouth, much less in writing . . . And notwithstanding the numerous threats of the Cardinal against them, I never once heard a word from him in defence of the poor, whom both had grievously wronged, according to the written statement of each about the other. At the court (of King's Bench in Westminster) each of them made the most serious complaints and allegations against the other that was possible, not only about the affray (ffrae) that had been between them, but in respect of the oppression of the people and the bribery of which each said the other was guilty. And when the Court had listened to their mutual accusations for some time, the Cardinal summoned the case before him into the Star Chamber.

*Elis Griffith, 'A Soldier of Calais', *Mostyn MS*

4. Footsteps in the Snow

William Powell's chief enemy was William Williams, a tradesman in the town of Llandovery. There had been some litigious disputes between them. But the most bitter cause of enmity between them was the fact that Williams had disturbed Powell's domestic peace. In August, 1768, Williams ran away with Powell's wife, and took her, and her children from the boarding school, to London. Mr Powell was obliged to apply to the Court of the King's Bench for a Habeas Corpus to get at his children, and, by the recommendation of the Court, he allowed his wife £100 a year for a separate maintenance.

---

* Elis Griffith felt no love for Rhys. He records that his death was generally looked upon as the visitation of God, for the many deeds of injustice and spoliation done by his father, grandfather, and great grandfather – a statement which is hard to reconcile with the known facts of young Rhys's career and his great popularity in South Wales.

Note by W. Llewelyn Williams from
'A Welsh Insurrection', in *Y Cymmrodor* XVI

Soon after Williams set about accomplishing Powell's death. He hired a person to murder him when returning from Swansea, but this assassin returned without doing so, having failed to meet Powell. Then Williams formed a conspiracy to take away Powell's life. Two motives instigated him to commit this heinous act; he wished to revenge himself for some unsuccessful lawsuits he had brought against Powell, and he also desired to remove every obstacle to make Mrs Powell his own lawful wife. Such was the excess of immorality and irreligion in those days, that he found many desperate characters willing to join in the conspiracy. Five of his accomplices were his fellow townsmen at Llandovery – William Thomas, a constable; William Morris, a saddler; David Morgan, and Walter Evan, tinkers; and David Llewelyn, of the adjacent village of Mothvey, farmer, and a tenant of Williams. These five made their way on Sunday evening, the 7th January, 1770, to a small public-house called Cwmdu, near a farmhouse still existing, and called Gwlyndu. This public-house has since disappeared. When it existed it was about a mile and a half distant from Glanareth, where Powell was then living. It was kept by a person called Charles David Morgan, who was one of the conspirators. In the course of that night others joined those who had already arrived – John Isaac, William Spiggot, William Charles, and some whose names have not been preserved. They all remained there throughout that night, and the following Monday evening, after carefully disguising them-selves, started for Glanareth about six o'clock armed with guns, swords, and daggers. On their way they met John Spiggot, the servant of Glan-towy Farm, whom they compelled, so he stated afterwards, to accom-pany them. There was a crisp snow on the ground, which enabled their footsteps to be followed, both going and returning, and some of their footprints to be sworn to. When they reached the house William Powell was sitting in the parlour, and three men with him for the sake of company and protection. In the kitchen there were some half a dozen persons, including two servants of the house – John Morgan and Margaret Jones. The conspirators approached the house through the back entrance in the garden. A knock was heard at that door, and a little girl opened it, when a rush was made into the house; two persons stopped at the door leading from the passage to the kitchen with a sword and a gun, to prevent anyone from coming out to give assistance or raise an alarm. Some of the others forced their way to the parlour. The three persons that sat with Mr Powell were not assaulted, but allowed to escape, which they did as quickly as they could. Powell was struck and stabbed by more than one of his assassins, his chief enemy running him through with his sword. He fell, covered with wounds, seven of which were afterwards pronounced to be of a fatal character.

The deed was done! Now the authors must flee from the Nemesis that would soon be on their heels. But it was very loth to move after them, and unusually slow to overtake them. They returned to the small inn on the hillside, and, having changed their disguising dress, and removed every trace of disfigurement, they left the house, and each went his own way, never all to meet again, or to derive the benefit they had promised themselves from the commission of such an atrocious deed. Williams had promised £100 to each of them if they succeeded in accomplishing his purpose. The promise was never fulfilled, nor did any of his accomplices claim the reward, and but few of them lived to require it.

There was a mixed feeling in the country when the crime became known. There was a feeling of gladness that such a desperate character was removed from the world, and of conviction that he had undoubtedly merited his fate, inasmuch as he had frequently committed deeds deserving death, but on each occasion he had wrested himself from the clutches of the law and disappointed the public executioner. His own brother-in-law, Marmaduke Bowen, of Cefentrenfa, when he heard of his murder, said 'Praise be to God! The villain is gone at last. He troubled many people in his lifetime.' Yet a great horror spread over the principality when it was seen that it was possible to secure the services of such a gang of desperadoes do to the bidding of a malicious person. The authorities were very slow in endeavouring to bring the criminals to justice. The night the murder was committed nothing was done. All seemed paralysed. The neighbours fled from the house, and left the servants in charge of it with their master's corpse weltering in blood on the parlour floor. There is strong authority to the oral tradition that the two chief servants already named took advantage of that awful lonely night to take quiet possession of a good sum of money hoarded by their master in the house. It was missed afterwards, and never discovered by its rightful owners. But John Morgan and Margaret Jones became soon afterwards man and wife, and removed to a distant part in an adjoining county, and took a large farm there beyond the capability of ordinary farm labourers to stock, and brought with them to their new neighbourhood a firkinful of guineas.

When the magistrates did bestir themselves in the affair several of

An Exact REPRESENTATION *of the* CRUEL MURDER *of* WILLIAM POWELL, *Esq;*

the conspirators had disappeared from their homes. It was reported that one of them had gone to North Wales. Two constables were sent after him. They discovered his hiding place, but failed to take him into custody. He had once a very narrow escape. He was going along a road on foot, and they were riding after him. It seemed all over with him, when there happened to be near him a person driving a cart laden with brushwood. He asked the driver to throw the load upon him by the roadside, to hide him from the two persons riding after him. He said that they were constables coming after him to take him to prison for some debt he owed in South Wales. The kind North Walian at once complied. The fugitive lay down in the ditch and the brushwood was thrown upon him. Soon the mounted constables overtook the empty cart and asked the driver if he had seen a person pass that way. He said that he had gone just a few minutes before them. They followed his direction with all speed. They soon disappeared, and the driver then removed the brushwood and liberated the quick-witted fugitive, who rose unhurt from the ditch and finally escaped.

William Williams also went to North Wales; his horse was found near Newtown, in Montgomeryshire, but he himself managed to escape out of the country. A reward of £100 was offered for his apprehension, and he was described as 'slender, straight, and well-made, and about five feet nine and a half inches high, and 28 years of age; a small scar upon his upper lip, a long visage, and pale complexion; large and hard hands, and 'tis supposed one hand is larger than the other, as he was a great ball player.' It was said that he made good his escape over the sea to the Continent. When the French soldiers that landed at Fishguard in February, 1797, passed in custody through Llandovery, some said that Williams was among them, and that some of his fellow townsmen recognised him. This is hardly credible, as his age would then be at least fifty-five, much too great an age for him to be in the ranks; and it is highly improbable that he should have been made an officer, or would have volunteered to act as guide to a hostile force invading his native country. Besides, it is not likely he would have risked the chance of being known and captured. Those of his accomplices that fell into the hands of the authorities were tried in the ensuing Spring Assizes at Hereford. The trial, according to an old Act made in the reign of Henry VIII, relating to the Counties of the Lordships' Marchers of Wales, moved to that town. For the prosecution was fully aware that no Caermarthenshire jury would convict the murderers of the notorious Squire of Glanareth; they would have much preferred to acquit them, and given them a grand ovation for ridding society of such a pest. Three of the accused were acquitted, and six found guilty, and executed on March the 30th. Two bodies were hung in chains on Hardwick Common, near Hay, and the four others were delivered to the surgeons. An account of the trial, with a verbatim report of the evidence, was published in a pamphlet in that year. A short history of the tragedy appears in the 'Gentleman's Magazine' for the same year. Of course contemporaneous personal evidence has long since disappeared; the last survivor of that age was probably one Jemima, a centenarian, who died in 1858 at a farm house, in the parish of Llandilofawr, called Craig y Moch. She was eleven years of age when the murder was committed, and a nurse at Glantowy in 1770, and, therefore, a fellow-servant of John Spiggot, who was forced to be present at the murder, though he was acquitted at the trial of being accessory to it. Old Jemima's eyesight had long failed her before her decease, but her memory was clear to the end, and she was fond of giving the details of the great murder to the close of her long life. Several particulars in the foregoing narrative are due to her relation of them when she was in her hundredth year.

J. Bowen Jones. *The Red Dragon* (Vol. 1) 1882

5. *Meet the Family*

This happened. Christopher Challener, a chef, started in retirement to research his family tree. As far as possible this story, as bizarre and perfect as you can imagine, is told in his own words.

My father rarely talked about his family. He never talked about anything much, having been on the Death Railway in Burma. But he told me that my grandfather had died in 1913 installing electric circuits when he, my father, was a baby.

And that, if you'll excuse me was the first shock.

It wasn't difficult, tracing the family back. It's an odd name, ours, particularly the way we spell it, so when I read in a family history magazine that someone was trying to trace the Challeners I got in touch. That was how I met a distant cousin, who told me that my father hadn't died in 1913, but had run off to Liverpool with a woman, abandoning his family, and had died there in 1945.

I couldn't confront my father for he had died in 1988, and, quite possibly, it was the story he had been told. I can just see his mother, as in a Victorian melodrama, saying 'He's dead to me'. Still, my cousin and I, we traced the family back to 1756, and we were very happy trawling through the Challeners.

But something had always troubled me. I had this vague, insistent memory that I once had a little sister, only, my mother having died and my father having married again, whenever I asked, I was told to be quiet. Yet suddenly my research came up with a death certificate for a baby who had died in 1951, when I was two and three-quarters, and my step-mother admitted, yes, this was so. So not only had I acquired an absconding grandfather, I now had a sister. I was beginning to wonder what I would acquire next. A slaver?

My father had told me his mother's name was Tremble and that her family came from Ireland. But when I traced them on the 1881 Census I found she and some of her brothers and sisters had been born in Wales, in a pub called the Sexton Arms in the village of Caeo in Carmarthenshire, though by then they were living in Clapton. What was even more puzzling, there was no mention of a father. At 38, my great-grand-mother was a widow with six children.

Anyway, time passed and, intent on moving to Wales, I was looking at houses there, when my partner and I, trying to work out a route back to Gloucestershire, noticed how close on the map we were to Caeo. It was 5pm on a Friday evening.

When we got there, to a village in the hills, near no main road, there was no Sexton Arms, but there was a pub, and a barman, a young chap, said, yes, there was a house called the Sexton just three doors away. This was opposite the graveyard, but it seemed so small, just two up two down, I couldn't see how it could ever have housed six children and two adults. It was then the barman introduced me to a chap he said was the church-warden.

I told him I was looking for my great-grandfather, and when he asked me his name I said 'Henry Tremble'. Until then we'd just been chatting, but when I said that everything stopped. His eyes bulged and he just sat there, as though all the lights had gone out in his head. I got a bit worried and bought him a pint, at which the lights began to come on again. Very slowly he said, 'That name is very well known around here'.

To the lost grandfather and the lost sister there was now added a lost murderer. In 1876 Tremble, the butler at nearby Dolaucothi House, one August morning, having made his will four days earlier, shot the squire, wounded his daughter, then shot all the dogs. His motive was that his employer, having promised him the tenancy of the Dolaucothi Arms, had gone back on his word. But it was what happened next that made this the crime of the century. Christopher Challener takes up the tale.

The man told me the story and this time *my* eyes were bulging. He then took me across the road to the church where he un-locked this chest with a huge key. Among the details of burials we came upon something scratched out, across which someone had written, 'This space reserved for Tremble', which puzzled me. I thought murderers were buried in the gaol in quick lime after being hanged.

The church-warden couldn't explain this, but he took me to see a woman living in the house called Sexton, whose mother might have the answer. But the old lady was so ill we returned to the pub. It was about 9 by this time. Anyway the woman suddenly appeared in the doorway, beckoning. Her mother, she said, had had got up just to see me.

Even the sick were rising.

I remember she didn't ask me in. Well you wouldn't, would you, faced with the great grandson of a murderer? She peered out at me, the door between us, as she told me what happened *after* the murder. Tremble, besieged in his house at Caeo, shot himself and was buried in the churchyard just across the road. But the villagers dug him up, and took the coffin by night across the county boundary to a waiting grave, from which, three months later, the people of Llandulas in Breconshire, having found out who he was, dug him up again. This time, the driver, having lost his way in the dark, the cart arrived in Caeo with the dawn, so the villagers woke to find a coffin dumped at the church gate. And that was the end of his travels, for he lies in an unmarked grave, not far from his victim.

One hundred and twenty five years later, on a May night, the police near Llandovery stopped a car that was being driven so slowly that it had aroused their suspicions. When questioned, the driver said this was because he had just found out that his great-grandfather was a murderer, which cleared everything up wonderfully.

Byron Rogers. *Saga*, October, 2002

6. *The mystery of St Clears*

One fine day in the spring of 1816 or 1817, a chaise stopped at the White Lion Inn at St Clears with a lady of superior appearance, but infirm, accompanied by her son. They were followed on horseback by two gentlemen and a young lady of extraordinary beauty and elegance. This was the daughter of the lady. The gentlemen were her nephews. The party excited considerable attention and interest. They took up their residence at the White Cottage. All the gentry of the place called upon the newcomers. The remarkable talents, elegant accomplishments, and fascinating manners of the daughter took everyone captive. Miss Burnes – for that was her name – entered into all the society of the place, always attended by her cousins, while Mrs Burnes and her son remained at home. The melancholy, abstracted air of the latter was no less remarkable than his habits. It was reported that he was passionately fond of chemical experiments, to which a small darkened room was devoted, close to the sitting-room which his mother always occupied. No one ever entered this dark room, and, when he left it, it was always locked up. Here he spent the day and the midnight hour, never appearing to any visitor, nor being seen out in broad daylight. A walk by moonlight or twilight was all the recreation he had. The large orders they gave the tradespeople were remarkable. They often sent into a neighbour's house to ask if they would take a saddle of mutton or a piece of beef or a turkey, for they always had more than they needed. The offer was generally accepted and money returned for what was taken.

> 'Found, on the evening of the 22nd, in the vicinity of St Clears, a pocket book, containing a large sum in Bank of England and local notes. By describing the same and paying for the advertisement, the owner may receive it on application to A. Thompson, St Clears.'

Miss Burnes and her cousins, whose names were Thompson, had been spending the evening with one of the neighbouring families, with whom she remained for the night, while her cousins returned home with the vicar of St Clears. In their path they saw a pocket-book on the ground. One of the Thompsons picked it up and examined it by moonlight. The vicar caught sight of some bank-notes in it. No reply was ever received to the advertisement, and curiosity regarding it flagged before the mystery was unravelled. At this time an old established bank at Carmarthen was suffering from a forgery committed upon it. Its notes were so well imitated that the spurious could scarcely be detected from the real, and the casual presentation of two notes of the same fraud. The partners of the Carmarthen Bank were informed that strong suspicion attached to a family at St Clears, so they paid a visit to the latter place; and as they drove past the White Cottage, they involuntarily looked towards it. Miss Burnes and her cousin were seated in the porch before the door, and the visitors thought they saw a kind of movement that indicated alarm or confusion in them.

Soon after this it was rumoured that the mysterious room was now left open, that everything in it had been taken away, and that the family were busy in the garden all night. Mrs Burnes explained that she had induced her son to give up his pursuits as they injured his health, and that he had gone to Bath to procure medical advice, and that they intended to join him. They left in November to meet the mail in Carmarthen. Here one of those curious coincidences happened, which cannot be foreseen, and which the most adroit management could not frustrate. One of the partners of the bank was in the coach office when the waiter of the inn came to secure two places in the Bath coach for two ladies, and presented a £10 note in payment. The partner just glanced at the note and thought he saw something peculiar in it. He examined it and declared it a forgery. He made enquiries and found that the young lady at the inn had made purchases at various shops in the town and paid in notes. It was in notes that Burnes had paid for everything at St Clears. The partner at once sent after the son, whom they found in a lodginghouse at Bristol, with all the implements of forgery and the die of the Bank of England, that plate and many beautifully executed notes. There were all placed in gaol.

I must pass over the imprisonment before the trial, which took place at Carmarthen. The two ladies were found guilty and sentenced to death. The son on his trial requested that no witnesses might be called, that he alone was guilty, and he trusted he should be the only sufferer. This confession had the effect of commuting the sentence passed on the ladies to a year's imprisonment, and gaining a free pardon for the Thompsons.

As no notes of the Carmarthen Bank, nor implements of forgery connected with them were found upon the son, the bank could not make a charge to affect his life. His counsel begged him not to accuse himself. When in prison a plan was laid for his escape, but his abstracted habits prevented its success. He seemed to have suffered from the beginning for the sake of his mother and sister, who, in return for his generosity, displayed a selfishness, want of affection, and common feeling of a shocking kind, even at the hour of his execution. He wrote a touching letter to his mother and sister just before his death. It afterwards turned out that the crutches used by Mrs Burnes were a deception. After the lapse of several years might be seen, on the stage of the Adelphi Theatre, London, a very beautiful actress, who was no other than Miss Burnes. This profession injured her health, and she went with a family to Switzerland as governess. At the end of a year or two she became companion to the Dowager Duchess of Riversdales, at Florence; and, finally, she obtained a coronet for herself. Conway Lascelles, the very 'soul of honour', who dreaded 'collision with inferior minds,' who had to the age of forty-five resisted the efforts of every mother and of all the lovely and elegant women by whom he was surrounded to draw him into marriage, and who had publicly declared his intention 'to remain sole sovereign of his heart,' united himself to a former inmate of the Carmarthen prison!

J. Phillips, *The Red Dragon*

7. *Tremble's Will*

15th August, 1876,

I Henry Tremble Butler at Dolecothy in the County of Carmarthen do hear by authorise the Revr. Charles Chidlow Cayo Viceage To take up my Money that is now in the Nationel Provential Bank Carmarthen and to pay the said Moiney quarterley at the reat of from £30 to £40 per year to my Dauter Elizebeth Susan Tremble for the mintanins of hus selfe and hur Sisters and Brothers Namely, Susan Louisa Tremble, Charles Henry Tremble, Alice Jane Tremble, John Tremble, Frances Sarah Tremble

I will leave all the Mony that I can in a little Box, & the Bank Recipt also, the key of which I will inclose to you that you will be able to judge how long that Money will last before you draw on the Bank

Sir I hope you will ecuse me taking this liberty as I have no Friends in this Country or do I know any one that would be likely to take any interest in thy child except you as a Christan Clergey Man. hopeing at some future time that you will be found amongst the Good Shepards is the ernest wish of your obedient servent

Henry Tremble

To the Revd. Charles Chidlow
Cayo Vicarage
There will be about £8 in My pocket

H.T.

Carmarthen Record Office

8. *The crime of Henry Tremble*

Dolau Cothi – Friday December 29, 1876.

Here is a long and terrible interval – on the morning of the 19th August last, I went after breakfast to the library to see dear Papa as usual, talked to him for a few minutes chiefly about the Aneroid which he had just bought and the difference between it and the Barometer . . . then I went out to the kitchen to order dinner – in passing the Dining-room door saw Henry Tremble the Butler standing reaching across as if to remove the Silver Tray, (the one presented to Papa on his resigning the County Court Judgeship in 1861) he was to leave his service on that day by his own desire and I had told him to put the Plate on the Diningroom table for me to count over – This man or rather fiend had been a trusted servant in this house for seventeen years and had lived besides with my Husband from the time he was a boy helping with the stables, (his Father a man from Liverpool having rented a cottage on the Monart (?) estate from Mr Cookman) – except for a short interval and had never received anything but the utmost kindness from us all throughout – I went to the Kitchen found Margaret Davies the Cook was not there, turned back as far as the passage door to the yard, when I saw Margaret coming in from the Larder with three jugs in her hand from which she had been bottling Rasberry Vinegar. I spoke to her for a minute then walked with her into the Kitchen, as I got just to the middle of it, at the end of the long table opposite the window I heard a hurried step which made me turn round facing the door when I saw Henry Tremble with a large breech loading gun in his hand, take up his stand on the mat at the passage door, opposite the Kitchen door. He raised the gun to his shoulder, took deliberate aim said 'Take that for your persecution of me and fired at me. I *saw* the fire come out of the muzzle of the gun I turned suddenly round and the whole charge entered my back and down the thigh, I fell on my face towards the scullery door, fortunately escaping the fire and cock of the boiler, the muzzle of the gun must have been about 7 or 9 feet from me I think. How long I lay insensible I know not, but I was lifted up, laid on a mattress on the Kitchen floor where I fainted several times, and after the Doctor came I was about 3 o'c carried upstairs to the Colton room, where the dreadful wound was poulticed. Our kind friends rich and poor within reach collected round us in an incredible short space of time . . . it was a cowardly deed, but far worse than this deed was done before he came to shoot me the murderer went into the Library and deliberately shot to death our beloved Father, the fiend fired two shots, the first not taking effect, into his body. Cottie (Lady Wilkinson) and Jane Jenkins the housemaid, hearing the shots, rushed in, darling Papa said 'I am dying, Henry Tremble shot me, mind he is taken.' He was sensible and very calm he never uttered a harsh word even against his brutal murderer, he did not pass away for about an hour, and he died as he had lived all his life, a Saint, with a blessing on his lips, his last words were 'God bless my children and I know He will bless them.' He asked for me and said I must be wounded as I was not with him. His cowardly murderer must have told him he was going to shoot me or would never have imagined I was shot.

Hearing a shot apparently so near the house my maid Anna Dixon ran down the stairs from the East room into the passage leading from the North room to Kitchen, and saw the murderer standing on the mat at the kitchen door reloading his gun and looking at his murderous work, saying, 'I do not care for God, man or the devil' then moving off to the back door he said, 'If I thought she was not dead, I would beat her brains out with the butt of the gun,' or words to that effect – Anna would have been his next victim he did begin his way to the room she was working in, but she saved her life, (not then having an idea that I was shot) by running away. He told her the night before at supper that she should not be here after him, the meaning of which she did not understand of course and replied, it was no reason because he was going that she should go too. He then went up to the Kennel called out the poor dogs one by one (Jacky saw this) and shot them, he beckoned to Thomas the Waggoner and Benny the gardener, who through some providence did not answer the summonses or they too would have been murdered, he then went to Caio, it is said levelled the gun at his wife but it was struck down, and threatened to shoot anyone who came near him, pointing the gun at the Policeman and those who attempted to seize him, asked for John Davies at Caio Inn with the intention of murdering him, as he had an idea that he would be let the Dolau Cothy Arms being an applicant among many others – He said he was sorry that he had not made certain that I was dead and sent his daughter here to find out – When driven to bay he went upstairs to Myrtle Cottage at Caio and shot himself, thus cheating Justice of her due – It was found that besides the gun and cartridges he had in his pocket a pistol and a bag of bullets, so determined was he not to be taken and he said of his crime at Caio when charged with them 'Yes I *thought* of it and I *planned* it all before hand' which indeed is proved by a Will he wrote himself about three weeks before he did the foul deed. Take note that the murderer was perfectly sane and not drunk or an habitual drunkard – The sole reason for the diabolical crimes was that Papa had (for *many* just and cogent reasons) refused to let him the Dolau Cothy Arms Inn at Pumpsaint whereupon he gave warning and from that moment must have meditated the hideous crime of murder.

Charlotte Johnes, *Journal*

9. *Interment of Henry Tremble*

Henry Tremble, was duly buried, in accordance with the Coroner's warrant, in solemn silence about eleven, on Monday night, 21st August. Although there had been a large fair in the village that day, and a considerable number of people were about, everything was done in good order at dead of night in the Caio Churchyard. It was believed by many that the bodies of the murdered man and of his murderer could not rest peacefully, even in death, within the same burial ground, so arrangements were made to exhume Tremble's body, and to convey it elsewhere for burial. The place chosen was Llandulas, Breconshire, and thither it was conveyed during the night. The inquisitive grave-digger had to be content with knowing that it was the body of a foreigner, – 'Dyn o wlad bell,' and was handed a letter which he took to be the customary certificate, but on its being opened all it proved to be was blank paper. This aroused suspicion, and in about three months the people of Llandulas learned that the 'foreigner' came from Caio; they determined he should return there, they planned a night descent, but lost their way, and arrived with the dawn at Caio Churchyard, so they hurriedly left the coffin on the pathway leading through the Churchyard, placing a sheet of paper (kept in place by four stones), containing the reasons for their action, upon the lid. They then journeyed homewards, throwing out the straw which had covered the coffin in the 'gambo' into the ditch near Aberbowlan, where it remained for years a 'Bwgan' to frighten timid persons and children.

The coffin was found in the morning, and the officials had it buried near its previous resting place. These repeated burials show better than anything the attitude of the inhabitants towards a murderer.

Fred S. Price, *History of Caio*

10. *Dafen Murder*

On Saturday November 12th, a man named Thos Davies, employed as a messenger of the Dafen Tin works, Llanelli, was found in a dying condition, brutally battered about the head, in the corner of a field on Bryngwyn Hill. A hanger, or instrument used in the Tinworks, was found near the body, covered with blood and hair. A bag which Davies had been carrying, with £390 in gold and silver, wages for the men of Dafen, was found at some little distance from the body. £300 was missing of its contents. Later in the day, David Rees was arrested on suspicion, a perfect web of circumstantial evidence was subsequently obtained against him, together with a crowning statement of an eye witness to the crime, a lad named W. J. Lewis, was concealed in a hedge overlooking the place where the deed was committed. The lad spoke of a second man being engaged in it, assisting Rees, but that man has not yet been found.

It was well known that Davies was in the habit on the weekly or monthly pay day, of carrying a large sum of money in his bag from Llanelli to Dafen. Rees was in want of money because he tried to borrow from a number of people who refused him.

Frederick Hopkins, who lived in the same row as Rees met him at the top of the road to Dafen at about 10 in the morning on the 12th, November. Rees went down through the fields to Box Cemetery, because, he said, he wanted to meet the Postboy. He did meet the Postboy, and then walked with Hopkins as far as Cae Cotton, where the road forked and Rees left Hopkins at about a ¼ past 10, saying he wanted to get his shoes nailed, and a shave. P.C. Daniel saw Rees near the slaughter-house at about a ¼ past 10, and then Rees was met by Ann Williams by about 20 past ten, crossing the Box Tramway. P.C. McCoy saw Davies walking towards the Dafen tin works shortly before 11. Then a woman, Elizabeth Sampson, met both Rees and Davies going towards Dafen at between ½ past ten and 11. She met Rees first, and Davies afterwards.

Next came the evidence of the boy. W. J. Lewis, who said that when he was in the field, next to that in which the murder took place, he saw a man walk back and fore from the Dafen way. The great difficulty about the boy's evidence was that he fixed no part of the time satisfactorily. However, there were three independent witnesses who brought Rees to the spot where the murder was committed, within a very short time of the murder.

Carmarthen Journal, March 18th, 1888

11. *Tearful Sentence*

The jury brought in their verdict in 32 minutes, and Rees having given no audible answer to the usual question of whether he had anything to say, sentence of death was passed, with great solemnity. Then followed a circumstance which we believe is unprecedented in the annals of such events. After the prisoner went below he professed not to have understood the sentence or that he was condemned to death. The governor of the Gaol (Mr O. Thomas) sent a message to the Judge, who returned to the Bench, and the prisoner was brought up and placed at the bar. The Judge, without again assuming the black cap, repeated the sentence, and the interpreter (Mr Long Price) repeated it in Welsh to the prisoner. In doing so Mr Long Price broke down completely, and everybody was very much affected by the repetition of the solemn scene. The prisoner also gave way to weeping, and again retired in charge of the warders. This closed a most remarkable trial, lasting from the Wednesday midday till 8.20 on Friday night, the actual sittings of the Court being about 23 hours altogether.

Amongst the visitors who called upon Rees on Saturday last were two Independent ministers – Rev. D. S. Davies, Carmarthen, and Rev. D. Wynne Evans, Llanelly. On their entering the cell they observed that Rees had been weeping very much, and was then in tears. His eye had lost its old fire, and his hair was dishevelled. In reply to a question of how he was, Rees said he was very well, and then added in Welsh something to the effect that he was in a 'sad pickle'. In further conversation Rees went on to say that he was an innocent man, that he was wrongly convicted, but that he would rather be there in those circumstances than have that crime on his conscience. His words are: 'Ond mae'n well gen i fod yma ar gam na bod yma yn euog.'* His visitors reminded Rees of the admission he had already made, and he again replied emphatically that he was not guilty of the murder, and had nothing further to say about it. He had said all he had got to say on the matter, and added he was glad he did not kill Davies, laying emphasis on the word 'kill', Being asked who did kill him, Rees replied: 'Dyna beth sy yn dywyll i fi, sir.' [That is what puzzles me, sir.] He was asked if he had anything he would like to say, and, mistaking the question, Rees replied that he would like them to read and pray. His visitors explained that they could not do so without the leave of the chaplain, and that they had not obtained. The question as to whether he had

---

* 'But I'd rather be here under false pretences than be here guilty.'

anything to say was repeated, and Rees replied that his brother and other friends had been to see him and he had said to them all he had to say. One of the rev. gentlemen then suggested to the prisoner that his time was very short, that he should repent and seek forgiveness, and in order for that should make a full confession and reveal his accomplice. To this appeal, repeated more than once, Rees replied with a doubtful 'hum', as though considering the matter. Beyond this, and the protestation of innocence did he not go; and the benevolent effort of the visitors was apparently without result. In parting, Rees, said to Mr Evans, 'They all know me at Llanelly. Remember me to them all.' The strong impression left upon the minds of the rev. gentlemen was that Rees was bent upon screening someone; while Mr Evans concluded that his protestations of innocence were an attempt to adhere to what Rees had said to him when the case was before the magistrates, namely, 'I am as innocent of the murder as the dead.' Mr Evans further expressed the opinion that Rees was in a confused or muddled state, and did not understand his position at all.

Carmarthen Journal Special Edition, March 13, 1888

12. *Memorandum of David Rees your son March 11th, 1888*

My dear Father and Mother and Brothers Sister and relations all at penygar yspitty Llwynhendy Pontarddulais Abervon and everybody at Llanelly and all my friends.

I do wish you all goodby goodby for ever and ever may the Lord be with you Amen.

Dear Father a(nd) Mother Hant Nance Unkle David at Penygar I am very sorry about you because they are trying to put the fault on you they are nothing but wicked men the same as those men that sead what as been sead about me and against me.

But I hope you will forgive them the same as I do forgive those men that as sead those wicked things against me. And I hope you will pray and ask the Lord to strengthen you to forgive them the same as I have done.

May the Lord be with you
Amen

Dear Father a Mother Brothers Sister relations all I do hope you will never forget me as long as you live.

And I hope you will do your very best to prepare yourselfs to meat your God. Father a Mother thats the best friends we can ever think of and I am very glad to have the strength to right you these few lines to tell you that I do pray and trust on him.

Father a Mother I do pray on the Lord, day and night and every hour and asking him to forgive all my sins and I do hope that you are doing the same or that you will do it for us to try to meat one another in a better land that is in heaven above. May the Lord be with you all and I do hope that to myself.

May the Lord be with you namely Perants a Brothers Sister and relations all Amen.

Please show this to all the relations

Father a Mother
From
David Rees Your Son

Miss Sarah a Davies. I do right to you these few lines and the tears on cheaks to, I am verry sorry for you but I do hope that you will trust in the Lord to strengthen you and healp you in every thing but I must tell you this that I must wish you farewell farewell for ever and ever Amen I hope you will never forget me as long as you live and I do ask you to tell your relations the same, Sarah I never thought I should meat my Death in such way as it as pasted for me and against me Sarah may the Lord be with you and your relations all, but you namely, Sarah I never thought that we should have to part with oneanother in cause of such a thing and in such a way but Sarah I hope that we will meat one another again in a better land that is in heaven above.

May the Lord be with you and that you will do your best with him. Amen.

(David Rees was executed in Carmarthen gaol at 8.00 a.m. on March 12, 1888.)

Carmarthen Record Office

13. *Cadno Murderer*

Men in Welsh coracles, such as the ancient Britons used, searched rivers with long ash paddles. Hillside and field and vale were beaten by coveys of searchers. For two or three days the grim beaters roamed the district, but found nothing. Bogs, ditches and woods were beaten and scoured by a growing army of searchers. By the Sunday some six hundred volunteer searchers were spread over the grim Marros mountain. Troops were brought in to comb the sand-dunes of Carmarthen Bay. The district was covered by farmers on horseback. Others with sheepdogs tramped uplands and thick stretches of wild undergrowth. The great hunt converged on the village of Marros.

'Never in our history,' said the Chief Constable, 'has such a large gathering of men met for such a purpose. Do not overlook any trifle you may find,' he cautioned the searchers.

But as the short day waned the hundreds came back without finding the missing pair. The Sunday's great search had been directed by loudspeaker set up at the village war memorial. A mobile canteen arrived and more than a thousand cups of hot tea were prepared for the bitterly cold searchers.

When the police were at a complete loss for the next move to make in the search Sergeant Phillips of Carmarthen (Llandilo) remembered something that had little significance at the time he heard it.

He recalled someone saying Ronald Harries had been digging a pit for a new well in one of the fields at Cadno Farm on Friday, October 16th. The significance of the remark had been lost at the time, and afterwards he had forgotten it.

But his memory suddenly recalled what he had overheard.

It was enough for Capstick to check a possible time sequence. The Yard man found that there was a sufficient interval of time for a killer to have carried the bodies of John Harries and Phoebe in the Land Rover to Cadno Farm and buried them in the pit, covered the remains, and then been at Pendine to give John Lloyd Harries and his wife a lift back home. No one would have known of the burial and the covering of the bodies.

Sergeant Phillips had started something. He went to Cadno to finish it.

He arrived at Cadno and began inspecting some of the fields. In one in which a fine crop of kale was growing he observed that some of the roots had the appearance of being displaced. He examined them, and came to the conclusion that a portion of the field had been dug up and filled in again. The kale had the look of having been replanted and its growth interrupted.

Sergeant Phillips pulled up the recovering roots of kale and began clearing away the earth with his bare hands, for it was not his intention to warn Ronald Harries of what he was about by going to collect a spade.

He had to scratch more than eighteen inches of soil from the suspect piece of field before his groping fingers encountered cloth.

It had been little more than a hunch but it had paid off. It explained, too, why Ronald Harries had been so cocksure of himself. He must have been enjoying a rare and bizarre joke at the thought of hundreds of local people searching mountains and moors for his missing uncle and aunt. They were under the kale, where he could keep a watchful eye on their last resting-place.

He had been very clever, but, like a good many clever persons and would-be clever persons, he had talked too much, and his tongue had betrayed him.

Sergeant Phillips reported his find to Inspector Fred Fox. Police went to the field of kale and began digging. It did not take them long to remove earth and kale roots and to uncover the bodies of John and Phoebe Harries. The diggers uncovered the woman first. Apparently John Harries had been buried before his wife. The skulls of both victims had been smashed with heavy blows, as though from a hammer.

Capstick and Heddon had found the bodies they had left London to discover. One part of their job was finished. The second part remained to be completed. They had to find and arrest the murderer.

There was no doubt in Capstick's mind as to the identity of the killer. Indeed, his opinion was shared by the local police and a good many people in the neighbourhood of Pendine and Llanginning. But proof had to be established. As Capstick judged Ronald Harries' character, he would have kept the murder weapon available. He would not have buried that, too.

Bruce Sanders. *Murder in Lonely Places* 1960

14. *Capstick at Cadno Farm*

While the great mass-search of the Carmarthenshire farms and beaches was proceeding Ronnie Harries sent messages several times to see me, saying that he was willing to come in and make a voluntary statement; but each time I sent word back: 'Tell him he can come in when I am good and ready. Until then I don't want to hear from him.' I knew the only way of beating this confident young man was to break him psychologically, or in plain coppers' parlance, keep him sweating.

Meanwhile I had to find the mortal remains of John and Phoebe Harries. I no longer had any doubt that Ronnie had murdered them; but the thought that was making *me* sweat was that he might have had the intelligence to sink their bodies somewhere in the long sweep of Pendine Sands. Sometimes I would walk along that golden shore and catch him watching me, and cold beads of moisture would run down my backbone. If he had been clever enough to use the sands as his graveyard, my chances of recovering the bodies of his victims were remote. Yet somehow I felt that he had not been cunning enough for that, and I was staking my reputation – and the Yard's – on being right. That is why I was so ostentatiously keeping away from Cadno Farm.

Jack Thomas, one of the old hands of the *Empire News* crime team, was covering the case for his paper. Relaxing over a drink in the Boar's Head, where Bill Heddon and I were staying, he said to me: 'You know, Mr Capstick, I'm darned sure the missing couple are buried up in Cadno. I'm a Welshman, and I know how Welshmen tick. Young Harries wouldn't be so sure of himself if the bodies weren't right under his nose – in a place you haven't searched. I'd make a bet that's where you'll find them.'

I made some non-committal acknowledgement and promptly changed the subject. Not one of the horde of reporters in town realized that late at night, when we were supposed to be safely asleep, Bill Heddon and I used to climb out of our hotel window and hot-foot it up the Red Roses Road to Cadno, where Ronnie Harries was living with his mother and father. We would prowl the farmyard and the outbuildings, flashing our torches and making quite considerable noise as we wandered about. After a while we would hear Ronnie's bedroom window open. Sometimes the white beam of his flashlight would dart in the direction where we stood safely hidden, but he never called out, as you would expect an honest man to do when he heard trespassers in the middle of the night. There would be just the sound of the window opening and shutting; but we knew what he must be feeling. It was brutal nerve-warfare, maybe; but the man we were after was a brutal killer, too, and I had no compunction about my tactics.

When I felt that the time was ripe I brought into play the old trick which I had learned with Alf Dance on the Flying Squad. Night after night Bill Heddon and I went to Cadno armed with reels of green and black thread. Patiently we tied strands across every exit from the farm-yard and every entry to the surrounding fields; and regularly, when we made a round of inspection later, we found some broken. We were not the farm's only night prowlers. And at last our efforts were rewarded, although not quite in the way I had expected.

The cattle from Derlwyn, the cattle which Ronnie claimed his uncle had given to him, were kept in a field adjoining the Pendine-Red Roses road. Known as the Top Field, it was on the Red Roses side of the gate of the track leading from the main road to Cadno farmhouse. Two of the hedges met at a point by the gate: the main road hedge, high above the road, and a low hedge with a lane on the farm side of it. The lane ran parallel to the hedge, and some distance along the latter there was a gap partly closed by four wooden upright posts fitted loosely into the ground. There was plenty of room for a Land Rover to be driven into the field through that gap, and the field itself was invisible from the main road and practically invisible from the farm side. Just made, in fact, for secret villainy.

During the night of Sunday, November 15, Heddon and I ran our thread across the gap in the hedge and along the four upright posts. When we looked next the cotton was intact but certain signs on the muddy ground called for thorough examination. I felt that at last our long search was over.

Early on Monday morning, acting on my instructions, Inspector Fred Fox and other officers of the Carmarthenshire County Constabulary went into the triangular Top Field and made their way to the narrow point ending in the farm road gateway. The first thirteen yards of this corner were thickly overgrown with bracken and brambles, bounded by a surface drain. The rest of the field was planted with kale.

John Capstick. *Given in evidence* 1960

15. *Murder, but no body*

Finally, Mr Davies dealt with the bloodstains found in the farmhouse kitchen, Cwmdu. 'About forty miles of the country around the farm was searched by the police and farmers, but no trace of the body was discovered – that is outside the farmhouse.' Inside the farm kitchen on three of the four walls, and particularly in the region of the fireplace, were found thousands of small splashes of blood. They were also found on the ceiling 7ft. 7in. above ground level. 'On the dresser was found the imprint of a bloodstained hand; on a plasterboard beside the fireplace were found 2,728 stains. They were found to be human bloodstains.'

Mr Davies said that in two places on the plasterboard some writing was found and it was the handwriting of Sykut. It would appear he had written a document and while it was still wet applied it to the plasterboard, acting as blotting paper. Bloodstains were superimposed upon the ink impression. A pathologist had expressed the view that the blood must have come from a subject which was either still alive or was only shortly dead and while the body was still being struck.

'The case for the prosecution,' said Mr Davies, 'is that that kitchen was the scene of a vicious struggle between these two men which ended only in the death of one of them.'

The prosecution's accusations were supported by many witnesses. Two friends of Sykut's had questioned Onufrejczyk about his disappearance. 'Sykut went to London like the Harrieses went to Carmarthen,' one of them told him . . .

Expert opinion was given as to the bloodstains found in the farmhouse kitchen. Chief Detective-Inspector Foster said that on the dresser there appeared to be a handmark in blood. From the distribution of blood in the room he formed the opinion there had been a fight there with the blood 'spurting about the place'. Cross-examined by Mr Elwyn Jones, he said the great majority of the bloodstains were extremely minute. He would not like to give the amount of blood that would cause them, but it was probably very small. He said he searched the floor for any sign of blood, but found none.

Emlyn Glyndwr Davies, principal officer at the Home Office Forensic Science Laboratory, Cardiff, said he found bloodstains on three of four walls and the ceiling of the kitchen. On a plasterboard alongside the fireplace he counted 2,728 stains. At random he selected 100 of these stains, which proved to be blood. He then selected 36 of these 100, which proved on test to be human blood. The stains on the plasterboard, on the whole, seemed to have been made on one occasion. He could not say whether the bloodstains in the room generally were caused on the same occasion.

Mr Justice Oliver: 'Is this splashing of blood common in cases of heavy violence?' Mr Davies: 'Splashing may accompany heavy violence, particularly to the skull. I have never before met with a case of much splashing without finding an accumulation of blood on the floor.' The Judge: 'Someone who is found to be attacked on the head generally falls down.'

Rupert Furneaux. *Famous Criminal Cases* 1955

VII

Ancient Monuments & Holy Places

1. TOWY VALLEY

Now, I gain the mountain's brow,
What a landskip lies below!
No clouds, no vapours intervene,
But the gay, the open scene
Does the face of nature show,
In all the hues of heaven's bow!
And, swelling to embrace the light,
Spreads around beneath the sight.
Old castles on the cliffs arise,
Proudly tow'ring in the skies!
Rushing from the woods, the spires
Seem from hence ascending fires!
Half his beams Apollo sheds
On the yellow mountain-heads!
Gilds the fleeces of the flocks:
And glitters on the broken rocks!

John Dyer, from *Grongar Hill*

2. *Excavating Twlc y Filiast*

The chief discovery made in the area of the chamber was the existence
of an outer compartment separated from the inner one by a low sill and
formerly enclosed by three small uprights of which only the sockets
remained. These features had been hidden below a shallow deposit consisting, in the chamber, of charcoal from fires lit within in recent times,
brown earth, fragments of pottery and glass vessels and other rubbish
of sixteenth- to nineteenth-century date, and numerous small pieces of
quartzite like those found in various parts of the cairn. The lower part
of this deposit was sealed, against the uprights inside the chamber and
just outside it on the south, by a sort of paving of small flags which had
been disturbed towards the centre of the chamber. As many fragments
of post-medieval pottery were found sealed by this paving it was evidently
not contemporary with the cromlech, but rather connected with the
use of the cromlech as a shelter for fires in comparatively recent times.

It was not until this paving had been removed that the sill came to light. This consists of five small slab-like stones placed on edge end to end and bedded into the yellow clay subsoil, with the easternmost resting against a comparatively large block which acts as a sort of jamb backing on to the packing stones of the eastern upright, while the westernmost rests against the stones which shore up the western upright. The sill only rises about 4 in. above the yellow clay surface, but the 'jamb' stone is about 9 in. high. On clearing the cairn material from the interior of the chamber a small oval hollow filled with dark earth was found dug in the yellow clay, about 1 ft. from north to south and 8 in. from east to west and 6 in. deep. The charcoal flecks, which occurred on the surface of the yellow clay throughout the chamber and immediately outside it, were also found on the sides and bottom of this hollow.

South of the sill removal of the paving slabs revealed three small roughly oval sockets, each about 6 in. deep, but ranging from 1 ft. 4 in. to 2 ft. in maximum width and filled with brown earth, into which quartzite fragments and modern potsherds had penetrated, and with charcoal flecks on the surface of the yellow clay at the bottom. These are interpreted as sockets for the pointed bases of uprights smaller than those remaining in position. Immediately north of socket No. 3, south of the eastern upright, was a recumbent slab of conglomerate sandstone 2 ft. 7 in. long, rounded at the western end and flat at the eastern end, with a hollow beneath its centre which may have been a socket. This slab may have been one of four small uprights forming an antechamber. If so, the uprights would have carried a separate, lower, capstone which has disappeared. Two unusually shaped stones, elongated with rectangular sections, lying near the eastern sockets, may in this case have been corbel stones. That there was, in fact, some form of antechamber at Twlc-y-filiast was suggested by the discovery of a second, larger, hollow in the yellow clay immediately south of the sill, oval, 2 ft. from east to west and 1 ft. from north to south, and 6 in. deep. Not only were flecks of charcoal found at the bottom and on the sides of this hollow, but minute fragments of burnt bone. More fragments of burnt bone were found in crevices of the cairn material immediately south of the west end of the sill. Unfortunately none of the fragments were large enough to establish their human character, but there does not seem to be reasonable doubt that they represent the remains of a cremated burial, possibly only of part of the burnt bones, deposited in the antechamber at the time of construction of the monument; no doubt much of the deposit had already been scattered as a result of the post-medieval activity on the site. The charcoal flecks which occur on the yellow clay surface under cairn material both within and without the chamber may have been derived from the pyre; if so, the cremation and the pits with which it was associated would belong to the period of construction of the cromlech and its surrounding cairn.

H. N. Savory.
Bulletin of the Board of Celtic Studies 1956

3. *The Welsh Defence*

During the four centuries before the Romans came, the laborious and skilful work of the Welsh in building hilltop forts is remarkable. Lasting down to our own time, they are more numerous in Wales than in any other part of Britain, the most important remains we have of pre-Roman Welsh life. By 1960 five hundred and eighty of them had been discovered; of these three hundred and forty are more than an acre in area, and sixteen are over twenty acres. Long before it was the land of the castles Wales was the land of hill forts. Since so little archaeological work was done in Wales in the past, they are still coming to light. For example, in the west and south-west of Carmarthenshire, in a region which makes up one-fifth of the county, 74 hill forts and enclosures have already been found. It can be gathered from this that the population of Wales was probably larger in pre-Roman times than in the Middle Ages, and probably heavier than the population of mid and east England – where there were more bogs and forests – an important factor to remember when considering the fate of the Brythonic language in England. Some of them show extraordinary building ability. The small forts, mainly in the west, have been compared with castles; and the bigger ones with fortified towns or villages. Where there are remains of circular stone houses, the number of people living in them can be estimated. Only a very few of these great monuments of the Iron Age have been excavated yet, but enough has been done to show that there was trade between these pre-Roman Welsh and people living around the Mediterranean.

Gwynfor Evans, *Land of My Fathers*

4. *Garn Goch and its Satellites*

Actually the term Garn Goch covers a large camp, locally known as Y Gaer Fawr (or the Upper Camp), and a smaller satellite fort known as 'the Lower Camp'. In addition, there is a third fort above Coed Llwyn Maendy, which is not usually recognized, and may be called the Llwyn du Fort. The upper camp, which is the largest, occupies the summit of one of the spurs of the Black Mountain on the south side of the Towy. This spur is overlooked by higher ground, but is isolated therefrom, and from the valley in front, by two small streams that almost surround the camp. The summit of the hill is no more than 400 feet above the banks of the Towy, and about 700 feet above ordnance datum, but its sharp precipitous slopes made the hill top well-nigh impregnable under the conditions of primitive warfare. The defences of the camp are formed of ramparts of dry stone walling, much of which is now disintegrated. The enclosure is an irregular parallelogram, the two longer sides being very nearly the same length, namely, 2,000 feet on the south and 2,200 feet on the north. The breadth varies from 500 feet at the west to 400 feet at the east end. The line of the enceinte is planned to enclose the largest possible area of fairly flat ground, but the interior presents a much diversified surface with considerable outcrop of natural rock. Near the centre of the camp is a small pond, which is, however, usually dry in summer time. The stone walling surrounding the enclosure varies in height and width in different parts; every advantage was taken of the outcrops of natural rock along its course, and above precipitous slopes the rampart was less massively built. On the western side the wall still averages twenty feet in height, and is nearly the same thickness. The walls increase slightly in thickness on either side of the main entrance in the south-western corner. The opening is now about thirty feet wide; it is probable that its original width was less and that stone has been removed from time to time. There appear to have been secondary entrances to the fort, one in the eastern, and the other in the south-eastern wall. All the ramparts are built of local stone (from scree on the hillside); nowhere is there any trace of a ditch. On the northern side the ground outside the ramparts extends at a slightly lower level as a fairly flat platform for some distance; then it falls precipitously to the river valley below. This platform is partly enclosed by a wall of the same character and apparently of the same construction as the surrounding wall of the camp proper, and thus forms a kind of annexe to the main enclosure. This annexe wall is about 1,300 feet long. The surface of the land everywhere around the camp is strewn with loose stones, many of which have doubtless come from the ramparts. The eastern slopes show in addition a large number of mounds of unusual shapes; these may conceal both graves and dwelling sites. Terraces and undoubted pit-dwellings occur to the north-east of the camp. It may be noted that there are similar collections of mounds below the two large hill forts on the Presely hills of Pembrokeshire. Inside the camp, near the north wall, is a great cairn of stones – elongated in plan – the significance of which is not known. Of the satellite camps the largest is on a hillock to the west of the great camp. This oval enclosure measures about 550 feet by 400 feet, and is built of dry stone walling. There is a double line of defences on the north-west side – the inner wall ending abruptly. There are traces of a hut circle within the camp. The main approach seems to have been from the south-east. The other fort, Llwyn du, has no stone walling, and is pear-shaped in outline with an entrance through the south-eastern rampart; adjacent to the entrance is an outer bank. The fort is divided into two parts by a low bank ditched on its south-western side. At the south-western extremity of the fort there are other outer banks, and a causeway with a ditch, or possibly a terrace, below. No surface finds from any of these fortresses have been recorded, but the structural detail of the main fort bears a close similarity to some of the North Wales forts, especially Tre'r Ceiri in Lleyn and Dinas Penmaenmawr in North Caernarvonshire. These appear to have been constructed in the late first or early second century A.D.

Sir J. E. Lloyd (ed.), *A History of Carmarthenshire*

5. *Garn Goch*

At Duffryn Ceidrych Mill, the carriages were left behind, and in a quarter of an hour all had reached the house of Carn Goch, and prepared for the stiff climb necessary to reach the upper camp. The place is enclosed by great walls of cyclopean masonry. The camp has already been described in the *Archaeologia Cambrensis*, when the researches of Mr Longueville Jones and others were explained. In extent, it takes in about fifteen acres, being in length nearly 3,000 ft, and in breadth 560 ft. The walls of dry masonry are about 16 ft high, and are excellently preserved. They are of enormous thickness, and have a number of small chambers, which were evidently used as habitations and storehouses. Nearly in the centre of the camp is a fine pool – an exceptional circumstance that must have made Carn Goch a fortress of great importance, as the supply of water in these pre-historic camps is frequently defective. The entrances were arranged in the same manner as at the similar fortress of Tre'r Ceiri, in Carnarvonshire, by long avenues of walling thrown out so as to prevent the enemy from approaching in large numbers.

The company having assembled, Mr Edward Laws, Tenby, the author of 'Little England beyond Wales', read the following paper: He had, he said, undertaken to describe a city, for such Carn Goch must have been, but he had had no archives to refer to, nor had its secrets ever been laid bare with pickaxe and shovel. We were quite safe in calling these encampments pre-historic, for history they have none. We were also quite safe in declaring that at some period a people using stone cutlery sheltered within these walls, for he had found lying on the surface of the stones a flint chip (which he now exhibited), showing undoubted evidence of human manipulation, and which might either have been a point for a javelin or have been used for scraping purposes. Stone implements were naturally connected with the very ancient people whom ethnologists have christened Neolithic or new stone folks, in contradistinction to the Palæolithic, or old stone men, with the latter of whom they had now nothing to do. The new stone people were a small race with a narrow head, absolutely ignorant of metals, using sharpened stone and bone for the purpose of cutting, boring, and scraping. They had no wheel turned pottery, but were clever in making it by hand. They buried their dead, putting with them such articles as were dear to the deceased. He had had some experience in exploring the camps of this people. He found that usually (in West Wales at all events) they selected a site already fortified by Nature, and supplemented its natural strength by a simple but effective arrangement of bank and ditch where there was a depth of soil, or of loose stone walls where they would answer the purpose better. These enclosures were generally very small, exposed to all the winds of heaven, and scarcely ever supplied with water. The conclusion he drew was that they were not dwelling-places, but refuges for a sparse population who lived in the valleys below, and that when danger appeared the braves of the tribe hurried their women, children, long-faced oxen, hairy little sheep, and great long-legged pigs into these little camps, where they made a stand until relieved by their neighbours. These circumstances were all opposed to the arrangements on Carnedd Coch. There they had an excellent water supply, gigantic works, which proved the co-operation of a very considerable population, and engineering of a very different order from the little cliff castles. The inhabitants probably lived with their flocks and herds within the walls. Notwithstanding the finding of the little flint chip, he thought they must give up the Neolithic people. Next on the *role* of time came a big, sturdy, round-headed folk, differing very much from the Neolithics, carrying in hand a bronze tomahawk for fighting purposes, but still using stone for common implements. They burned their dead and smashed such chattels as they placed by the ashes, apparently with the notion that they thus made ghosts of them and enabled them to go to ghostland with their spectral owner. They also invented, or at all events introduced, the potter's wheel. Now, the pottery which usually went by the name Bronze Age ware, consisted of badly burned decorated urns, which were apparently actually baked in the funeral pyre. Besides these, he had also found a common rough potsherd, wheel turned and fairly well baked in association with bronze remains, and a fragment which he had picked up between the camps seemed to be of that nature. Taking into consideration the flint chip and this bit of rough pottery, he was inclined to say that the walls of Carn Goch were put together by the people who used bronze axes, and afterwards bronze swords, spears, &c. The Neolithic people might have had a settlement here also, but he did not think the existing walls were constructed by them. Still, the whole erection might be later, for periods overlapped each other; for instance, the last use of stones for warlike purposes in Wales, of which he had found record, took place only 244 years ago, when Oliver Cromwell was beleaguering Pembroke Castle in 1648. The ship carrying his cannon balls sank at Sharpness Point, so masons were set to make him limestone cannon balls, with which he bombarded the town. Succeeding generations had dwelt on Carn Goch, and he should not be at all surprised, if they dug within its walls, to find Roman remains turned up, seeing the many relics of that people which still exist in the neighbourhood. The fortification closely resembled certain camps in North Wales, and was exceeded in size by some of them, but it was the largest in the Southern counties. One like it existed on Strumble Head, in Pembrokeshire, but that was inferior to the Carmarthenshire Camp. Were he to dig within the walls of Carn Goch he would clean out the pond that was within them and the interior of the oval inclosure, the curious circular spaces in the walls, and examine the cairn. But all this should be done most carefully by skilled hands, for the man who destroyed relics of the past to gratify a senseless curiosity was guilty of a crime little short of sacrilege.

Edward Laws,
The Caermarthenshire Miscellany, Ed. Arthur Mee

6. *Straight Roads*

The almost proverbial straightness attributed to the Roman roads does not seem to hold good in Wales. The hilly nature of the country accounts for this in some degree, but one may be sure that where possible they took the bee-line towards their objective and this usually being the next hill top, if they found themselves a little out they would make a slight bend in the right direction. Hence bends in the roads are to be found or looked for on the hill tops. However crooked the tracks may now seem it does not follow that they were originally so, since these lines must have been liable to constant alteration during the succeeding sixteen hundred years.

Where the surmised track is now only represented by crooked lanes one must look for the original one at either one side or the other. Most of the early coach roads of the country followed the Roman lines as being the only available routes, and it was not until the advent of that great road engineer, Telford, that the first properly metalled roads since Roman times were made in Wales, at the beginning of the nineteenth century.

In describing the Roman roads it is found most convenient to take Carmarthen as a centre or starting point, though of course, those which touched the town reached it from various directions, passing on to other centres or forts.

For purposes of reference the different routes are numbered. The existence of the first four of these is not disputed, but even these do not all appear to have been hitherto traced throughout.

I. This is the western branch of the main military road leading right away to Caerhun (Kanovium) on the Conway river. From Carmarthen its course is by way of Abergwili, Sarnau, Allt Wallis, Gwyrgrug, Spital (New Inn), Maes Nonni farm (inscribed stone), Pencarreg (gold coin), passing Pen-y-Gaer and crossing the river Teifi at (approximately) a ford marked in the 6-ins. O.S. as Pont Hamilton into Cardiganshire. Although the modern high road is fairly straight as regards general direction it has evidently not been superimposed exactly on the Roman way.

II. This is the so-called Via Julia, passing along the north side of the Towi and not too close to the river. Leaving the northern road at Abergwili it goes by Pont Dulas, Pen-y-banc, Dynevor Castle (Temple and remains), Abermarlais Park (ring found),

Llanwrda, crossing the river at Llandovery (fort at Llanfair-ar-y-bryn) and proceeding along Cefn Llwydlo over the border (close to Sarnau Cwrtau) making for the fort at Castell Collen.

III.   This communicates with south east Wales, evidently going due south from Carmarthen to join another route near Kidwelly, otherwise it would probably have chosen a more direct way by Pont Antwn and Pont Yates. It proceeds through Pensarn, Croes-y-ceiliog, Pen-yr-heol, Broadway, Portway and over Mynydd Penbre, to Llanelly and Loughor (fort).

IV.   This is a branch of the Sarn Helen which does not go near Carmarthen, crossing the north eastern portion of the county. It branches off the other road near Llanfair Clydogau proceeding due south by Farmers to Pumpsaint (Villa and Ogofau Gold Mines), Caio, Porth-y-rhyd, Ffynnon Gwenno, Aber Bowlan, Llwyn-velyn farm, Cwm-sarn-ddu, Ddalfa, Heol Rhos to Llandovery, entering Brecknock near the fort 'Y Pigwn'. The portion between Caio and Llandovery has hitherto been untraced, and the crooked lanes obviously cannot have represented the exact route. The significant place names quoted give sufficient clue as to the approximate course, and here is one of the portions which call for and might repay local exploration. A few Roman coins have only just recently been found near Porth-y-rhyd.

V.   It is highly probable that the Romans would want a more direct way to the big fort 'Y Gaer' near Brecon than that afforded by going on the north side of the Towi round by Llandovery. Although not represented by modern lanes, there are numerous place-names which support the route surmised. These, starting across the river at Penysarn are Tafarn Trap, Logyn-dwr, Pont-Pibwr, Lletty, Llanddarog, Porth-y-rhyd, Pen-rhiw-goch, Windsor Gate, Berach fortress; the river Cennen would be crossed at Meusyddhirion and the ridge road taken by way of Storm Hill Lodge (Coed-cae-Helen), Dafadfa-isaf, Neuadd, Morgan-ddu, Capel Gwynfe, Henbont, Bailiglas, Cilmaen, Talsarn (Bryn Helen) and over Mynydd Wysg to Trecastle and Brecon.

S. O'Dwyer, *The Roman Roads of Wales*

7. Roman Mines of Gogo-fau

About ten miles west of Llandovery, on the right of the road to Lampeter, occurs one of those elliptical, quartzose masses, so frequent in the 'Cambrian System', of nearly half a mile in length, trending from north-east to south-west like all the associated strata. It is called Gogo-fau, or '*the Caves*', the hill being perforated in many directions by horizontal galleries, considered to have been the work of the Romans. That these galleries were mines, there can be no doubt, since they follow precisely the course of the veins. That they were the work of the Romans is certain; for they have not been used during the period of modern history, and the galleries are much too long, wide, high and deep, to have been the work of the ancient Britons. This opinion has been recently confirmed by Mr Jones of Dolecothi, who has discovered the remains of baths, medals, gold ornaments, implements, inscriptions, Roman tiles, &c., thus proving that there was a considerable Roman station at the western foot of this hill. The antiquary may decipher these inscriptions, and attempt to inform us which of the Caii left his patronymic to the adjacent village of Cynfil '*Cayo*', whilst the geologist and miner are left to speculate on the probable cause, which led these adventurous and indefatigable conquerors to perforate hills with magnificent galleries, some of which are eight feet high.

The rock of Gogo-fau is a quartzose grit and sandstone, with very slight appearances of slatey cleavage, and in parts exhibiting the rippled surfaces of bedding. The strike is from north-east to south-west, and the beds dip for the most part to the north-west, as seen in the chief building stone quarries of Clochty. Numerous veins of white crystallized quartz, containing abundantly crystallized iron pyrites, traverse the beds both at right angles and obliquely to the strike, as represented in this wood-cut.

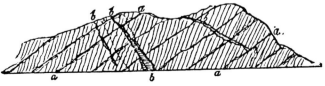

a. a. Laminæ of deposit. *b. b.* Quartz veins.
The highly inclined lines mark the planes of slaty cleavage.

The largest of these veins have been followed, in some instances, to their termination. To these galleries the Welsh assign various names, such as Ogor-hwch, or the Hog's cave; Ogof-fawr, (large cave); Gogor-gowge, &c. The great extent of these excavations is attested by the enormous mounds of white quartz or vein stone debris.

For what purpose these mines were wrought by so sagacious a people as the Romans remains un unsolved problem. As no particles of lead or copper ore can be detected in the mounds of refuse, and as the pyrites seemed to have been occasionally separated from the quartz, it occurred to me that if in any degree auriferous, it might have been quarried for the gold which it contained. On subjecting, however, some of this pyrites to the examination of that excellent chemist, my lamented friend Dr Turner, he was not able to detect any trace of gold worthy of notice.

R. I. Murchison, The Silurian System

8. *Roman Gold Mines*

While in this area of central south Wales there is one recently excavated site, unique in Britain, that can be visited at Dolaucothi, located three-quarters of a mile south-east of the village of Pumpsaint, halfway between Llandovery and Lampeter. Gold was mined at Dolaucothi during the Roman period, and remains of the opencast and tunnel workings are still to be seen. The mining methods in use here were up to the most advanced technological standards of the time and made use of two aqueducts that supplied water to the site for washing ore and perhaps for powering stone crushing mills. One of the aqueducts, traversing a distance of seven miles, was capable of supplying some three million gallons of water per day to the mines and the water from both aqueduct channels was controlled by a series of massively con-structed reservoirs and sluices that directed the water to the various areas along the mine workings. In the National Museum of Wales is one of the large wooden water-wheels used at the mines for baling out water from the underground workings. Such wheels were worked by slave labour and are a harsh reminder of the darker side of life in Roman Britain. The complexity of the mining techniques in use at Dolaucothi can be paralleled, on a much larger scale, from the rich gold mines worked by the Romans in Spain. It is significant that the auxiliary unit stationed in the nearby fort of Llanio was from Asturia, in north-west Spain, where some of the largest of these gold mines were located. It seems likely that it was engineers from this garrison who were responsible initially for developing the Dolaucothi mines.

Jacquetta Hawkes, *A Guide to the Prehistoric and Roman Monuments in England and Wales*

9. *Aqueducts or Corrugi*

I cannot well say that here is all; for there is another labor behind, as painfull every way as the other, and withall of greater cost and charges than the rest, namely, to wash the breach of this mountaine (that is thus cloven, rent, and laid open) with a currant: for which purpose they are driven many times to seek for water a hundred miles off, from the crests of some other hills, and to bring the same in a continued channel and stream all the way along unto it. These Rivers or furrows thus devised and conveyed, the Latines expresse by the name of *Corrugi*, a word as I take it derived *à Corrivando*, of drawing many Springs and rils together into one head & chanel. And herein consisteth a new piece of worke as laborious as any that belongs to mines. For the level of the ground must be so taken aforehand, that the water may have the due descent & currant when it is to run: and therefore it ought to be drawn from the sources springing out of the highest mountains; in which conveiance regard would be had as well of the vallies as the rising of the ground between, which requireth otherwhiles, that the waters be commanded by chanels and pipes to ascent, that the carriage thereof be not interrupted, but one piece of the work answer to another. Otherwhiles it falleth out, that they met with hard rockes and crags by the way, which do impeach the course of the water; and those are hewed through, and forced by strength of man's hand to make room for the hollow troughs of wood to lie in, that carrie the foresaid water. But a strange sight it is to see the fellow that hath the cutting of these rockes, how he hangeth by cables and ropes between heauen and earth; a man that beheld him afar off would say it were some flying spirit or winged divell of the aire. These that thus hang for the most part take the level forward, and set out by lines the way by which they would have the water to passe; for no treading out is there of the ground, nor so much as a place for a man's foot to rest upon. Thus you see what ado there is.

Pliny, *Natural History*, Book XIII †

10. *Roman Llandovery*

A fort may have been built at Llandovery in the late A.D. 50s or early 60s. Pottery of that period was found in excavations and may be linked to the earliest of four phases of fort building.

Llandovery holds the key to the upper Tywi valley, and is in the area considered to be part of the territory of the *Demetae*. Because Tacitus, the Roman historian, only mentions the *Silures*, it has been assumed that the *Demetae* were a more peaceful people who readily accepted the Roman conquerors, perhaps even preferring them to their neighbours, the *Silures*.

The strategy behind the disposition of forts and their interconnecting supply roads is clear: the forts control the river crossings and valley junctions; blocks of upland are cut off from each other and movement of native people, if not restricted, was at least put under surveillance. Actual campaign routes can only be guessed. It may be that a sea-borne force secured control of the western coasts and estuaries with forts at Carmarthen and Loughor, while other detachments advanced overland from the east.

Heather James, *Roman West Wales*

11. *Cilyrychen Caves*

Mr Stepney-Gulston afterwards read a most able and interesting paper on the 'Bone Caves at Craig Derwyddon', near Derwydd, Llandebie, of which we subjoin a short resumé: These famous bone caves were discovered in 1813 by lime-burners working down upon them from above. The natural entry had been stopped up and was unknown to them. A great 'fault' in the lime-stone formation having taken place at this point, the cave passed under the outer fold of the great wall of this 'fault', and so on from the south in a northerly direction until it plunged again under the great mass of the Craig Derwyddon. Through the kindness of my neighbour, Mr Southern, of Pantyrodyn (said Mr Stepney-Gulston) I have been able to examine all the correspondence and papers compiled by the late Professor Rolleston, who in 1878 visited these caves, and he thus speaks of these prehistoric remains: 'Ten or eleven skeletons were found in a cave near Llandebie in 1813. One skull from the 'find' we have in the Oxford University Museum. It is filled with crystalline loaf-sugar-like stalagmite, which has of course preserved its original outlines.' Here Mr Stepney-Gulston went on to say: I have during the last year been able to learn full particulars of this interesting cave. It was of an ovate form, with a lateral opening some thirty feet in length. The vault itself was 16 or 17 feet long by 12 or 13 feet wide, and about 4 feet high. Twelve skeletons in all were found; seven lying with their feet towards the entrance, and their heads, therefore, towards the west. In juxtaposition were three others lying transversely; and about ten yards further in to the southern arm of the cave, two other skeletons of great size were found. All the skeletons were fully extended, with the faces upwards. Unfortunately, with the exception of one skull, above mentioned, none of the bones have been preserved, or if any are preserved, they lie buried under a great heap of the 'Talus', or spoil of the quarry. All the skulls were described as exceedingly large, and there was still a tradition in the locality that the hat of the largest-headed man about proved too small for the smallest of the skulls. As Professor Rolleston has said, 'it is a question with regard to the digging away of this 'Talus', whether anyone could be found sufficiently enthusiastic to risk some £500 in a doubtful scientific investigation.' We may add that Mr Stepney-Gulston, in the course of his very instructive paper, gave full particulars of all that is known about these now celebrated bone-caves, and we understand that the paper will shortly be published at length in the Society's Journal, the *Archæologia Cambrensis*.

Mr Edward Laws thought they ought to be very grateful to Mr Gulston, who, if he had not succeeded in digging out the remainder of the bones, had at any rate succeeded in digging out some of the old papers connected with the discovery. It was from his (the speaker's) house that Professor Rolleston started in quest of the bones, and the latter thought it was a most important discovery, and his old friend, Professor Rolleston, would, at the time, talk of nothing else.

Mr Gulston pointed out that on the opposite side of the gap in the ridge the noted cave of Owain Law Goch was to be found. Near the Pantyllyn bone caves is a place called Craig Derwyddon, and close by is the scene of the exploits of Owain Law Goch, a character who appears to have absorbed some of the features of Arthurian romance. A cave in the locality bears Owain's name. At Llwyn Beddau was seen a stone cist, in very good preservation, said to be the sole survivor of a row of 70. Mr Gulston observed that he could remember the graves to the number of seventeen.

Arthur Mee, *The Caermarthenshire Miscellany*

12. *The Great Stone: Maen Cilan*

Monday, 31st July [1809] – Reflecting that we had imperfectly examined the great Stone, and that we had pushed the work of the Pickaxe so far as to ascertain the nature of the grounds exactly under its centre, attended by my Friend Doctor Symmons, I attacked it again with his Labourers, who dug fairly under it till we saw light through, and dug so low that we came to the natural soil, a loose rab mixed with clay. Nothing turned up to indicate its having been sepulchral, neither charcoal, bone, or relicks. The Stone is of a truncated Pyramidal shape, a mass about 20 or 25 Ton weight, in height [c. 8 ft.]. If it had been an object of idolatrous worship, it probably would have borne a more grotesque appearance, or supposing it might from its stability conveyed a symbol of the Deity, yet we should as in general is the case, find it accompanied with circles or some other Druidical relicks. It may then be more properly considered to be some trophy or memorial of a battle or a federal compact.

Richard Fenton, *Tours in Wales*

13. *Carreg Fawr, Abermarlais*

The above remarkable stone is doubtless known to many of your readers, standing as it does close to the high road on the western side of the Towy between Llandilo and Llandovery. Not long ago Mr Robert Etheridge, now at the head of the Geological Department of the noble Natural History Museum, South Kensington, was kind enough to point out to me where it had come from. He said that it had been ice-borne from Mynydd Bwlchygroes, from a point on that mountain. I presume about five miles beyond Llandovery. I consider that having been so brought in the line of the river it must in prehistoric time have been set on end, where it now stands, in commemoration of some notable event of days long past, when the beautiful valley now well cultivated was mainly an extensive forest.

Christopher James Thomas, *Carmarthenshire Notes*

14. *Crannog, lake-dwelling at Talley*

The party then went to the pre-historic lake dwelling, discovered by the Rev. Charles Chidlow in the neighbouring lakes. Some have erroneously described this as a crannog, but there appears to be no evidence that it was built on piles, or that it shows the usual features of that kind of dwelling. The two lakes at Talley seem originally to have been one, somewhat contracted at the centre, like the figure 8, where they are now divided by about three acres of marshy land. On this exposed surface is a mound of the diameter of one hundred feet, and a height of from ten to twelve feet, and having a well-defined, though shallow, trench about ten feet wide running around the base. On the exterior side, this trench is continued for some distance in every direction, forming a kind of platform, with a drop at its outer edge of one or two feet. On the north and south sides, facing the present lakes, a small channel has been cut through the platform, as though to reach the central mound. The communication with the shore was probably at the east side, where wood was, perhaps, used to form a causeway. When the level of the lakes was a few feet higher than at present, the water covered the intervening ground, leaving the mound, with its platform, standing out as an island. No systematic investigation has been made of the interior of the structure, as it is considered undesirable to disturb it, except under the guidance of a competent scientist.

Arthur Mee. *The Caermarthenshire Miscellany* 1892

15. *Paxton's Tower*

The traveller will see at Llanarthney one of the most robust and most beautifully located follies of all, the odd triangular one, most of its cement coating fallen away, which Sir William Paxton of Middleton Hall raised as a tribute to Lord Nelson.

It is not much more than a shell now, roofless, with blunted castellations, but it has about it the stout defiance which characterized both Paxton and the 'invincible commander Viscount Nelson' commemorated in his inscriptions. A former vicar, the Reverend J. Jenkins, wrote in his 'Llanarthney' that from the tower it was possible to follow the course of the Towy from Ystrad-y-ffin to Myrddin Hill, and to see the haunts of 'the Robin Hood of Wales' (Twm Shôn Catti) and rivers full of trout and salmon.

However, there is another tale to complicate this simple explanation: a tale so thickly strewn with statistics, lying about like stones from a dismantled cairn, that it is hard to dismiss. It seems that the 1802 county election, during which polling went on for two weeks, found Sir William Paxton (Whig) at loggerheads with Sir J. Hamlyn Williams (Tory). Paxton lost the election by 107 votes, in spite of spending £15,690.4.2d on such items as 11,070 breakfasts, 684 suppers, 8,879 bottles of porter and nearly 37,000 dinners. Ale, sherry, cider, ribbons, whisky, it all mounted up, yet 107 men, or, to be on the safe side, 108, still held out. Paxton then built his monument to Nelson (there's a *non sequitur* somewhere, but there's also something unhinging about that odd tuppence).

A tamer account relates that Paxton's proposal to build a bridge over the Towy was turned down, and that he consoled himself by commissioning an eminent architect to design his tower, and just show them!

All the narratives may be partly true; yet there is no real reason why a well-to-do banker of that date should not sincerely admire Nelson, and wish to be seen to admire him.

Sir Hugh Casson, Follies

16. *The View from Nelson's Monument*

We made our carriage wait while we scrambled up a very steep ascent leading to a prospect-house built by Sir William Paxton in memory of Lord Nelson. This distinguished hero has been rather unlucky in his monuments, they are all so remarkably ugly. Those at Dublin, Edinburgh, and Glasgow are complete failures.

> But his bright laurels ne'er shall fade with years,
> Whose leaves were watered with a nation's tears.

From this temple of Fame that whole country may be overlooked at one single glance, which we had taken an entire day to drive through. What can be compared to the wide and rapid grasp of sight! We travelled with our eyes over fifty miles in one fleeting moment. A man born blind would be as unable to imagine the possibility of such a fact, as we are fully to comprehend the greatest wonders recorded in revelation. Here we gained a distant view of Middleton Hall, one of the finest mansions in Wales belonging to the Paxton family; and we also saw Lord Cawdor's park, where he has built a new house, the grounds about which well deserve their name of 'Golden Grove', on account of the glowing fertility they display. This Thane of Cawdor is better off than his predecessor on the Highland moor; for the witches themselves would have stopped dancing to admire the view of his seat, which we enjoyed from that elegant summer-house. The Welsh monument to Lord Nelson does not supply pilgrims with ices and pastry like its colleague in Edinburgh, for a due consideration, but it left open constantly for the benefit of visitors gratis; so that if any one be ever at a loss to find a night's lodging in Wales, he may know where to go, and place himself on an altitude whence the plain beneath seems spread out like a map for inspection. Here tourists may feel themselves raised for a time above the anxious cares, and the much-ado-about-nothingness of their busy lives, while, if the mind could be elevated like the body, they might

'View the distant tops of thoughts,
Which men of common stature never know.'

Miss Catherine Sinclair.
Sketches and Stories of Wales and the Welsh 1860

17. Dynevor Castles, Old and New

The apparent remains of *Dynevor Castle* are at the s.w. extremity of Newton Park, and seem to indicate that it is a place of small importance; but the vestiges of a wall and ditch at some distance from the conspicuous ruin may be traced, which prove it has been of considerable dimensions. It was built by Rhŷs ap Tewdwr, in the time of William the Conqueror. Its original form was circular, fortified by a double moat and rampart. The most prominent parts are the apartment already mentioned, a massive round tower, the ancient keep, and a subterraneous passage. Giraldus saw a castle here which was destroyed in the year 1194, about six years after he wrote his Itinerary; it was, however, soon rebuilt, and became the royal seat of the princes of S. Wales; but frequently changed its proprietors, until it fell to the crown of England. Henry VII made a grant of it to Sir Rhys ap Thomas, K.G., a lineal descendant of the Welsh princes, and ancestor to the present proprietor.

It was inhabited till about 1760, when the combustible part of it was destroyed by fire.

The modern mansion of Lord Dynevor, situated on a level about ½ m. from the castle, is a large quadrangular structure, having turrets at each corner, crowned with domes. An avenue of trees extends thence to the castle, which is broken into clumps, harmonising with the general style of the park, which is of considerable extent, and includes the greatest possible variety of picturesque beauties. The upper part has a fine undulating surface, and displays considerable taste in its plantations; while on the other side rises a steep lofty hill, whose declivities are clothed with rich wood, and on whose brow are seen the venerable walls and towers of Dynevor Castle. The beauty of this scene is considerably heightened by the rolling of the Towy, whose waters here wanton in endless variety, amidst the most delightful verdant meadows and rich plantations. In this vale there is a fine development of the lower formation of the Silurian rocks, composed of dark-coloured flags, mostly calcareous (Llandeilo flag), with some sandstone and schist.

Newton park contains the delightful modern residence of Lord Dynevor, and affords the most extensive and picturesque view of this vale. Under the keeper's attendance pass through waving lawns and woody knolls to a bold hill where, embosomed in tufted trees, appears the picturesque remains of *Dynevor castle*. A winding path, cut through the leafy honours of this eminence, conducts the tourist beneath their dark umbrage to the summit. Climbing a massive fragment of the ruin, and reaching an apartment called 'Ladies' Dressing-room', a prospect teeming with the most fascinating natural charms, may be examined from a Gothic window overhung with ivy. It has been described as a galaxy of picturesque beauty, at which remembrance becomes entranced, while description falters. Immediately beneath the expansive Vale of Towy appears in full display; a hue of the richest green marking the luxuriance of the soil. The translucid stream here wantons in perpetual variety among gay meadows and embowering plantations, till it disappears behind projecting groves. The rich wood which surrounds the castellated eminence clothes a precipitate descent to the water's edge, and with the sylvan decorations of the park, forms the near boundary of the vale. On the opposite side, a lofty and dreary mountain rears its desolate summit to the clouds.

Emilius Nicholson.
The Cambrian Traveller's Guide 1840

18. *The Old Spring at Llandyfân*

When I was young I loved to walk, or go 'on the bike' in the direction of Llandyfân and Trap. My great grandmother on my mother's side was a native of the area, namely Sarah, daughter of Job Roberts ('Job the Limer', as he was called) of Cefnblewyn. It was to the Llandyfân area as well that we would go to fetch that sand which couldn't be bettered to put on the *sharpener* for whetting scythes. Mindful of the old rhyme:

> Kidwelly pig lard
> And sand from Llandyfân
> By sharpening often, often,
> It'll cut very clean.

Going by way of Gelliwastad and Garnbica (where we used to lift turnips in the winter months when I was a boy, and the hoar-frost gnawing at my fingers, in Elfed's phrase) and turning (right) by Blaengweche one comes directly to the Anglican chapel of ease at Llandyfân.

Gwilym Teilo held that the name commemorates Dyfan, a saint who came to Wales in the second century with Fagan, Meudwy and Elfan to proclaim the Christian faith to the Welsh. A saint whose name is linked with Merthyr Dyfan in Glamorgan, and perhaps, also, he says the name recalls Dyfnan, one of the sons of Brychan Brycheiniog (Breconshire). Evidently the church authorities must associate the chapel with Dyfan as 'St Dyfan's Church' appears on ordnance survey maps. But this is conjecture and pretence, because the place was ever Llandyfân with the accent on the last syllable.

But it is the big spring that spouts a mighty stream nearby the chapel that is the main attraction in Llandyfân, and it was there before the chapel was built beside it. Edward Lhuyd, the Antiquary, makes reference to it around the year 1696 'the name of a medicinal spring' in the parish of Llandybïe, and he notes also that the river Gwyddfân springs from it too. Is it this river – *guid maun* ('gwydd mawn') – noted within the bounds of Maenor Myddynfych in the Book of St Chad, recorded and written towards the end of the eighth century? Incidentally, Llandyfân is in the parish of Llandeilo Fawr, on the boundary with the parish of Llandybïe.

Richard Fenton was on tour in the area at the beginning of the last century and he saw the spring, enclosed in a square building without a roof, and steps leading down to it. There was a 'waddyish, unctuous' look to the water he said – did he mean dark and soapy? He also saw a small chapel connected to Llandeilo Fawr whose services were held once a month. Many resorted to the spring in olden times, he says, and many medicinal virtues were attributed to it. According to Thomas Rees's *Topographical and Historical Dictionary of South Wales* (1815) the spring had a reputation as a medicine for curing paralysis and similar ailments. In some old maps it is ascribed 'The Welsh Bath at Llanduvaen' and that would seem to suggest that the sick would be immersed in the water, as they did formerly in the Lake of Siloam. But no doubt the water was also drunk.

Some years ago I was informed by Mr D. L. Davies of 'The Bon' shop in Swansea (who was brought up at Glyn Hir Mill nearby) that, as he had heard his father relate, whosoever went to the spring and drank of its waters from a human skull, (as at Llandeilo Llwydarth, in Pembrokeshire) would be cured of his ills. But only an ordinary cup was used by Mr Walters who lived in the farmhouse beside the chapel. Was the family of this farmhouse the guardian of Llandyfân Spring? The skull of St Teilo was used, according to a tradition of the Melchior family, at Llandeilo Llwydarth: and it mustn't escape our notice that Llandyfân lies within the bounds of Teilo's monastic at Llandeilo Fawr.

It is not known exactly when the first chapel was raised by the spring, but according to David Jones's *History of the Baptists* (1839) the land surrounding the spring was in the possession of the Dynevor family and he maintains that the local gentry erected the chapel as a charitable gesture to the sick who visited the spring from all over. But we cannot accept that 'the spring was inside the building'. David Jones said also that some corpses were buried in Llandyfân – poor devils who had come to Llandyfân for a cure but died of their ailment.

By the eighteenth century the spring had lost its distinction as a curative medicine, but the place continued to be a spot where the local country people would come and play diverting games, such as dancing and playing ball, especially on Sundays. That is the reason perhaps why Howel Harris of Trefecca came there in 1740, 1750 and 1751. He had a congregation there and an opportunity to evangelise and preach to the worldly. Things went from bad to worse there and one of the Mansels of Margam had to put an end to the sports and games on Sundays. In the year 1748 Peter Williams, the (Bible) commentator, came there and was given permission by the local people to preach in the chapel of ease. Money was collected to buy a Bible, and to raise a pulpit in the chapel, and Peter Williams visited the area for the rest of his life. A school grew up there too – and we know that one of Gruffydd Jones' circulating schools was there in the winter of 1766-67.

The Baptists themselves had a mission at Llandyfân, and David Jones believed that the ritual of baptism through immersion was performed as long ago as 1771. Nearer 1785, perhaps, is accurate. It caused a bit of a stir in the area when the first baptism took place in the spring. The Methodists objected to what they called 'this new religion' (their term) and there was much fuss as a result. In the meantime some Independents, such as Evan Griffith from Gwynfe, and Thomas Coslett, preacher and manager of the Forge ironworks nearby, got permission to preach in the chapel. A mixed congregation, thus, were here, Methodists, Baptists and Independents and 'the Chapel of Mixtures' (oats and barley) they called the place as a result. To muddle the situation further, the Baptists divided into two camps, Calvinists and Arminians: and through those the Unitarians got the chance to stick their heads in. By 1808 there were three ministers and three denominations competing with each other at Llandyfân. But before long deliverance was at hand. The Independents went to Tabernacle Ffairfach, the Baptists to the new chapel in Soar, a mile or so away leaving Llandyfân to the Unitarians. And so the Unitarians built Onnen-fawr chapel near Trap and in 1838 the old chapel of ease at Llandyfân returned to the care of the Established Church.

In time the old chapel was pulled down and a new one raised at the expense of Lady Dynevor and Mrs Dubuisson of Glyn-hir. The spring was also renovated and in 1897 Llandeilo Town Council was given permission to pipe water from it to quench the thirst of the inhabitants of the town, for a payment of £10 a year to the parish church for the privilege.

There is very little to add. I remember enthusiastic eisteddfodau being held in Llandyfân's barn in the twenties of this century. During my first ministry at Clydach in the thirties one of the Walterses of Llandyfân was a faithful member of my church. He kept a 'Welsh Produce' shop in the village selling goods which he procured weekly from his family in Llandyfân. For years we obtained eggs, butter and buttermilk fresh from Llandyfân. Those three delicacies, and the loveliest of the three – tastiness of the kind we loved specially – was the buttermilk.

Gomer M. Roberts. † *South Wales Guardian* 1976

19. *Nantrhibo Spring*

Near Dinevor, on the other side of the River Tywi, in Cantref Bychan, that is the Little Cantref, there is a spring which, like the fitful tide, ebbs and flows twice each twenty-four hours.

Giraldus Cambrensis. *The Itinerary Through Wales* 1187

20. *The Parish Church of Llandeilo Fawr*

Llandeilo-Fawr is a market-town of Carmarthenshire, beautifully situated on a descent to the justly famous *Vale of Towy*, in the hundreds of Caeo, Perfedd, and Is Cenen. The church, situated near the centre of the town, is very ancient, and consists of two aisles, so low, that the pillars which support the arches upon which the roof rests are not more than 5 ft. high. The ancestors of Lord Dynevor are interred at the E. end of the N. aisle, under the pew belonging to the family. The living is a vicarage, and the structure is dedicated to the British saint Teilo. Three sacred edifices attached to this parish are extinct, Llandyfaen, Capel-yr-

Ywen, and a chapel in Carreg Cennen Castle. Lord Dynevor has presented the site of a new church, and his lordship's son, the Hon. George Rice Trevor, M.P., has announced his intention of endowing it with 25*l* annually. His lordship's eldest daughter, the Hon. Frances Rice Rice, laid the first stone, April 2, 1839; the Bishop of St David's patron. Previous to his elevation to the see of Gloucester, Bishop Nicholson had the spiritual charge of this parish. He was the author of a valuable Exposition of the Church Catechism, which he dedicated 'to all his loving parishioners of Llandeilo-fawr,' in the year 1661. When archdeacon of Brecon, he wrote 'An Apology for the Discipline of the Church of England'. He had the reputation of a learned divine. and was a man of great prudence, charity, and moderation.

Emilius Nicholson.
The Cambrian Traveller's Guide 1840

21. *Llandeilo no longer*

A goodly number of Teilo foundations have become extinct. There was formerly a Llandeilo 'in the same cemetery' as Hentland, in Herefordshire. In Bishopston a chapel at Caswell, possibly Llandeilo Porth Tulon, formerly existed. Several have disappeared in Carmarthenshire; such as Llandeilo Nant Serw; Llandeilo Garthdefir, in the parish of Talley, on a farm called Brondeilo, where, from under the hill hard by, gushes out Pistyll Teilo; in the parish of Caio, Capel Pumsaint, called in the *Book of Llan Dâv* Lann Teliau Pimp Seint; in the parish of Llanegwad, Llandeilo Rwnws (= Brunus), its materials having been used up in building the farm-house of the name. There is a Holy Well and farm, called Ffynnon Deilo, near the village of Nantgaredig. In Llandeilo Fawr and neighbourhood his name is, or was, perpetuated by Ffynnon Deilo, in the churchyard, near the east end of the church, but now covered over, and the water conveyed into Church Street, for general use; Carreg or Sedd Deilo, now destroyed, at Glynmeirch, on the boundary between Llandeilo and Llandebie parishes; Ynys Deilo, and Maenor Deilo. Capel Teilo, in the parish of Kidwelly, has its south wall still remaining. Llandeilo Brechfa in Ceredigion was probably the Brechfa near Tregaron; Ystrad Teilo, a farm near Llanrhystyd, in the same county. Llandeilo Llwyn Gwaddan and Henllan, in Llanddewi Velfre parish,

Pembrokeshire, are extinct. Stepsau Teilo, his Stepping Stones, across the river Ogmore, near the church of Merthyr Mawr, no longer remain; Westwood confounded them with the still existing Stepping Stones, fifty-two in number, set in the Ewenny, near the ruins of Ogmore Castle. At Llandaff are Croes Deilo, a Celtic cross about three feet high, at Llandaff Court, and Ffynnon Deilo, on the steep hill near the Cathedral. In the Old Welsh *Privilegium* of S. Teilo is mentioned Gundy Teliau, his Gwyndy, but what is the exact ecclesiastical import of the name is not clear. It probably meant originally a stone house, like Candida Casa, now Whithern, in Galloway; but in the Latin paraphrase of the Welsh the name is rendered 'Curia Llandaviæ'. In the Demetian Code of the Laws of Hywel Dda 'Llann Teilaw' (near Maenclochog) is given as one of 'the seven Bishop-houses (Escobty) in Dyfed,' and it is stated that 'the abbot of Teilo should be graduated in literary degrees'. It is not exactly known what these houses were, but it is evident that they were some kind of monastic houses ruled by abbot-bishops.

S. Baring-Gould & J. Fisher.
Lives of the British Saints, Vol. IV 1913

22. TALLEY ABBEY

Here above the scattered stones of Talley Abbey, a bird bullets
Down the sky, drops down to die and stuns the clear air,
To where the lake lies dreaming in the still winter's day.

The eye, caught in the dark valley's timeless clutch,
Sees the twin worlds of air and water work once more –
A finned and diving bird below the water's floor!

Talley, one great rising arch of forgotten faith,
Remains in mind, cross-nailed by time, in the years
That wheel from childhood to the final darkness of our fears.

Five centuries away from sainthood, God's one boxed room
Of blind prayer stands, stone on stone, under the blasphemy of birds,
By the waiting water where no faith will ever burn again!

A sadness slumbers here in lake and dumb gray wall –
All signs of sanctity gone in the work of weather, man and bird –
Challenged only by the cry of creatures feathered, finned, and furred.

The lake remains, stones winter crack and fall, and Wales
Lives on in the stunted men who walk her lanes and lonely hills . . .
The memoried nets sieve still and only the dogma kills.

The old land creaks on in heave of mountain, crack of furrow,
Where this race and their speech stubborn the tide of history
As the nightwind cries along the lakeside and stirs the water's face.

And now, here above lake and abbey, another, soaring, bird
Spins in the trawled sky over Talley; and only a dog's distant bark
Disturbs the valley's silence and the slow dusk of Mabinogion dark.

Bryn Griffiths

23. *Præmonstratensians*

Of none of the Welsh religious foundations of the Middle Ages has
there been preserved a clear and connected history, or the graphic
chronicles that imparted human interest to the story of several English
houses. Talley was more than usually unfortunate, the only published
documents relating to it being those contained in the last edition of
Dugdale's 'Monasticon'. Even the religious Order to which it belonged
had been a subject of dispute. Dugdale thought it had been a Benedic-
tion house, and his latest editors had not troubled to inquire into the
point for themselves. A Cambridge MS. styled it Cistercian. Leland
thought it had belonged to the Præmonstratensian Order, an opinion
in which Bishop Tanner concurred; while the latest historian of the
diocese, Canon Bevan, doubted the correctness of Tanner. It would
now be settled for good that Talley was Præmonstratensian from its
foundation (with a slight intermission) to its fall. Of its founder, of the
date at which its inmates were introduced into Carmarthenshire, or the
abbey buildings commenced, no fresh documentary evidence could be
adduced. It had been conjectured, and, no doubt, rightly, that it was
founded by Prince Rhys ab Gruffudd, who received the title of justiciar
of South Wales from Henry II, and who died in 1196 or 1197. He was

the founder of Strata Florida and a large benefactor to Whitland, both Cistercian abbeys. This was the popular monastic Order in Wales, and they might have been recommended to the Princess of Wales, not alone because of their religious austerity, but also for their devotion to agricultural pursuits. The Præmonstratensian Order, an offshoot from that of Augustinian Canons, was introduced into England in 1143. The Austin Canons were distinguished from the monks in being in Holy Orders and in being attached to particular churches. The naves of all their churches were parochial, and it was, no doubt, owing to this circumstance that the fine church of the priory of St John at Carmarthen was spared at the dissolution, when the other monastic churches of Wales were dismantled or destroyed. The monks were originally no more than laymen, bound by vows spontaneously assumed, but when the appropriation of parochial churches commenced it became customary for some of them to take priest's orders, and at a still later period it was usual for all monks to become priests. The Præmonstratensians resembled the Cistericans in their love for solitary places and in their attention to agriculture. Talley occupied a typical Cistercian site, the arrangement of its buildings being more after the regular Cistercian plan than was usual with Præmonstratensian houses. Their early foundations always comprised separate houses for men and women, and, though it was not possible to show that canonesses had ever lived at Talley, the likelihood of such a thing was greatly strengthened by the reference in Welsh genealogies to an Abbess of Talley. It was unfortunate that Giraldus Cambrensis did not mention Talley in his account of his journey through Wales with Archbishop Baldwin in 1187, and he (the speaker) thought it showed that Talley was not then in existence. It must, however, have been established before Giraldus' death, which took place in 1223, because in his last written work, called 'Speculum Ecclesiæ', he gave an interesting account of the high-handed proceedings of the Abbot of Whitland against a 'poor house of canons of the Præmonstatensian Order', culminating in their forcible ejection and the seizure of their houses by the Cistercians. The Canons appealed to Hubert, Archbishop of Canterbury, and afterwards to the Pope, and eventually regained their possessions. Now, Hubert died in 1205, and, as he (the speaker) considered the house could not have been founded before 1190, it brought the exact date of that foundation within narrow limits, and also showed that the Cistercians had not remained long in possession. In 1208 they came upon the first express mention of Talley, in which year King John confirmed to it a grant of lands in the modern parish of Llanegwad. In 1215 the Abbot Gervase, or Iorwerth, was elected Bishop of St David's; he was probably the abbot during the troubles with the Cistericans, and his success in that affair might have led to his promotion to the bishopric. In 1291 the income of the house was £8 16s 6d per annum, about £230 of our money, compared with over £2,600 for Strata Florida and nearly £1,200 for Whitland. Much of the wealth of the Cistercian monasteries proceeded from their cattle and sheep, but the canons of Talley did not appear to have engaged in that profitable branch of agricultural industry. The abbey fared badly during the struggles that terminated with the complete conquest of Wales in 1282, and in the thirteenth year of Edward. It was placed under the 'paternal jurisdiction' of Welbeck, the chief of the English Præmonstratensian houses. If history had been made within its walls it had found no chronicler, and only one person of importance was recorded as buried within its church. After this the abbey throve, and its reputation must have been good, for in 1332 it obtained several important gifts in the parishes of Llansadwrn, Llan-sawyl, and Cynwil Cayo, and the grange of Carreg Cennen. But its chief wealth lay in the tithes or in the sums produced by their ferm [sic] of the many churches which had been appropriated to the abbey. Of these the Church of Llandeilo was the most important, and several small chapels were also mentioned in the inspeximus charter published by Dugdale, Long Price, and Alcuin Evans, which seemed to have been abandoned before the abbey itself was dissolved. There was at the Record Office a petition of Rhys ab Meredydd ap Rhys Gryg, who was executed in 1291 as a rebel, asserting that his father, the founder of the Abbey of Talley, had always received the homage of the abbot, but that the King's bailiffs of Dynevor had diverted the suit done by the abbot from the said Rhys, for which he prayed justice. This claim of founder could only have meant that Meredydd ab Rhys was of the founder's family, and was the patron of the house, just as in various unpublished documents the Abbots of Whitland, Strata Florida, and St Dogmael's called the Kings of England 'founders' of those houses. By the middle of the fourteenth century monasticism had greatly declined in useful-ness and public favour. The Canons of Talley, no doubt, suffered from the economic disturbances produced by the Black Death. In 1382 Richard II issued a commission to inquire into the losses sustained by the abbey, the restoration of its property, and the repair of its buildings. This commission was renewed in 1392. Notwithstanding the law-lessness of the times, the canons clung to their property, and in 1429 obtained a confirmation of the charter of Edward II. It had been stated that the Abbot of Talley was the chief instrument in determining Sir Rhys ap Thomas's adherence to the cause of Henry of Richmond, afterwards Henry VII. This was quite probable. But it was a curious fact that the abbey, though situated close to the residence of Sir Rhys, was not mentioned in his will, though there were bequests to the Priory of St John at Carmarthen, to St David's Cathedral, and to a number of churches. At the dissolution, in 1535, its income was £136 9s 7d., Whitland being valued at £135 3s 6d, and Strata Florida at £118 7s 3d. The lands were for the most part retained in the hands of the Crown, and formed the present Manor of Talley. The first minister's account showed that the abbots, with a premonition of coming trouble, had followed the example of many English houses, and granted lengthened leases of portions of the abbey property. In a case such as this, where the old tenants were not dispossessed or the lands divided amongst a number of new proprietors, it was probable that some of the farms were still held by the descendants of the abbey tenants, and a local genealogist, working from the documents that would soon be available and from the parish registers, should be able to establish the continuity of Carmarthenshire history, and to link their own days with those in which the White Monks of Talley had exercised a beneficent influence over the district in which they were then assembled.

Edward Owen. *A Contribution to the History of Talley Abbey*
from *The Caermarthenshire Miscellany* 1892

24. *The Skeletons of Llangendeirne*

At Llangendeirne, a church on the Gwendraeth creek that flows into the Towy at Kidwelly, a curious discovery was made a few years ago when the church was being restored. It was discovered that beneath the floor were the skeletons of 497 men laid in layers five deep closely packed; all had apparently been thus buried in tiers simultaneously. There were no women's or children's bodies among them, and no signs of wounds on the skulls or limbs. All were full-grown men. They had been laid without any covering save a few box-leaves scattered over them. Nothing whatever is known on the subject of the burial of nearly five hundred bodies at one time together.

The church is dedicated to S. Kentigern, the apostle of Glasgow, who spent some years in Wales when driven away from his church in Scotland. It is possible that there was an early monastery here founded by Kentigern, and that the bodies are those of monks swept off by the Yellow Plague in 547.

S. Baring-Gould. *A Book of South Wales* 1905

25. *The Bishop's Palace*

Many distinguished churchmen have played the host in this charming and old-world spot by the Towy's banks, the name of Thirlwall coming, perhaps, most readily to the mind. In the eighteenth century, and later, the Welsh bishoprics were regarded either as mere steps in the ladder of promotion, or as valuable sinecures for aged persons who had achieved distinction or good fortune elsewhere. In earlier times, their poverty put them in the first category. Later on, when the industrious attachment of livings to the Episcopal endowments, by acquisitive prelates, had made the Welsh sees valuable, meritorious or well-connected veterans were sent there to spend the evening of their days, in leisurely indifference to their uncongenial surroundings. But neither veterans nor ambitious juniors, as we all know, troubled Wales greatly with their actual presence between the reigns of Anne and Victoria, nor was any Welshman during that time elected to the Episcopate of his own church. The Bishop, with the *coterie* he introduced, parasitical, more or less, was regarded as a useful agent in the crusade against the Welsh tongue. Still more, political interest counted for almost everything, and Welshmen were not rich in this. It is indeed surprising that any church at all was left in Wales to start afresh upon. It would be a moot question which type of bishop was the most mischievous: the one who lived in residence and used the church revenues as a milch cow for himself and his relations, or the other sort, who seldom or never came into the country at all. It is needless to say that there were exceptions, and St David's had more than its share of them, as is only fitting for the largest and most important of the four sees.

Whether the Bishop of St David's was a good man or not, he was always a very great one, and there must ever be a certain glamour about a diocese of such cast and varied character, such turbulent and romantic history, to say nothing of its superior antiquity to all others, save its less striking Welsh neighbours. There was a collegiate church founded here at the Edwardian conquest, so that, in the words of its charter, 'Ystrad Towy hitherto places of misery should be changed into places of spiritual joy.'

A. G. Bradley. *Highways & Byways in South Wales* 1905

26. *The Pilgrims' Graves*

The eminent Cambrian, Professor Westwood, referring to the graves (at Llandeilo Abercywyn) wrote that they were 'affirmed to be the sepulchres of certain holy Palmers who wandered thither in poverty and distress, and, about to perish for want, slew each other, the last survivor burying himself in one of the graves which they had prepared and pulling the stone over, left it ill-adjusted in an oblique posture. One of these stones is said to be the grave of a mason, the stone being perforated with a hole; the upper part contains the figure of the head, neck, and crossed arms of a man, having a cross sculptured on his breast, and with the feet visible at the bottom of the stone. The second has an upper part similar, but the part below the crossed hands is covered with a lattice-like ornament, and the feet are not represented. This is said to cover a glazier; and the third, which is covered, has merely cord-like mouldings with a cross at the head, and refers to a rope-maker. The sanctity of these pilgrims, the natives affirm, keeps the peninsula and Llanfihangel free from serpents, toads, or venomous reptiles, the exception being when the tomb-stones are overgrown with weeds. Two similar memorials, the one coffin shaped and other bearing a head, cross, etc., lie a few yards further to the south. On opening the middle grave there was found, at a depth of four feet, a sort of cist-faen, composed of six slabs of stone arranged in the shape of an ordinary coffin, two more slabs formed the top and bottom for the sepulchral chest. In it were some small bones of a youth or female, and half-a-dozen shells each about the size of a palm of he hand, by description previously corresponding to the cockle-shells of the pilgrims; thus evidently proving the graves to be those of persons under a vow of pilgrimage performed by or attributed to them. I apprehend these graves may be attributed to the fifteenth century.' Professor Westwood wrote those words in 1847. In *Archaeologia Cambrensis* for 1900 there is the following comment on them: 'There is a similar story to this told in *Black's Guide to South Wales* and other references of no particular authority; and evidently Professor Westwood told it as he had read it or heard it simply setting down the legend as a legend and nothing more. The suggestion that a mason, a glazier and a ropemaker were buried there is evidently the invention of simple peasants, anxious to find a meaning for symbolisms which had become unfamiliar in their day. The one element of truth in the story, the learned man seems to tell us, is that these graves are really and truly the graves of some noted pilgrims. Who the original wanderers were who found rest here, and what class of pilgrims or palmers they were, we shall probably never know; but there must have been something in their history which impressed the popular mind with a profound idea of their sanctity . . . Most British pilgrims had their halting-places at Strata Florida and Whitland, but those arriving from the west on landing at, say, Kidwelly which was once the best port in South Wales, would cross the Llan-stephan ferry, and make a convenient pause for bodily and spiritual refreshment at the Pilgrims' Church.' According to Benjamin Thomas, a local character, there was a Pilgrim's Lodge attached to the church at one time, but it has long since disappeared.

Conway Evans, *The Story of a Parish*

VIII

Houses
Great & Small

1. CARMARTHENSHIRE CALENNIG SONG

Happy New Year to you all
In this house so big and small.
Can't you hear us when we call?
Happy New Year to you all!

Traditional

2. IN PRAISE OF RHYDDERCH AP RHYS OF CATHEINIOG

Never was found in the lands of Cadell's son
a better host than his father.
To Rhys ap Griffith there were
many glass-windowed courts:
in Llandecwyn in Gwynedd
There was a court that gave a feast,
a fair court in Llangathen that
was seen after that.
And in a grove in yonder Dryslwyn
he had the third.
A hall of dressed stone in one
for Rhydderch is their sister.
His houses after his father
rank equal to Caistor
the men made out of the fortress
houses into a splendid city on an ox-hide.

Howell Dda ap Cadell made a better
sanctuary above a forest.
Men here designed by his teaching
a law that was good . . .

Since Adam was the like of Rhydderch;
in husbandry no one did
what he has done in wisdom.
He has a superb hall
and a citadel sparkling with lime-wash,
and all around it

nine gardens in greenery,
orchard trees, and drooping vines,
young oak-trees to the sky.

Lewys Glyn Cothi †

3. *Hirlas Horn at Golden Grove*

Among other remarkes at Golden Grove are seen a drinking Horn
above exhibited beautified with silver artifice being the first vessell
Henry Tudor Earl of Richmond afterwards made King of England by
the name of Henry VII drank out of after his landing at Milford Haven
in Pembrokeshire in order to the marrying the Lady Elizabeth and
deposing Richard III.

This Horn was presented by himself to the noble Earls of Carbery
where it hath remained ever since, and is kept among the noble Earles
choicest Raritys. The Foot is of silver in the form of a mount upon
which stands a Dragon and a Greyhound of the same imitation of the
supporters of the Royal Armes of Henry VII which follow on the other
side the leaf shervington the dexter side a Red Dragon (the Engsigne of
Cadwalader the last king of the BRITAINS from whom by his male
line he derives his pedigree according to Sandford's Genealog of Kings
P434, and on the sinister side a Greyhound argent collar'd Gules, which
he gave in right of his wife the Queen, Elizabeth of York descended
from the Nevills by Anne her Grandmother the daughter of Ralph
Nevill Earl of Westmoreland and wife of Richard Duke of York.

The Portcullis upon the kipping or rim of the mouth is in token of
his descent by his mother from the noble family of the Beauforts, to
this device on his, Mansole or Royale Sepulture at Westminster is added
this motto:

ALTERA SECURITAS

as who should say As a Portcullis is a further security to a gate, so his
mother corroborated his on her Titles from this Device he instituted a
Pursuivant at Armes and named him Portcullis as from the leading
supporter y Red Dragon had been instituted by him also y Pursivant
called Rono Dragon.

The Roses on the rim I suppose to speak the Union of the two houses of Lancaster and York by his marriage. Those among other devises are often repeated in and about Hen VII's Chappell Westminster as a Crown in a Hawthorn bush to commemorate his being with Richard's formerly usurp'd Diade in Bosworth Field which was said to be found there after the victory in a bush bearing Haws. This is seen also painted on the Glass on the Stone Gallery of the ancient Abby of Lacock in the county of Wilts. The Red Dragon also is again seen on a banner in the hand of an angell on ye south east of the foot of this monument at West-Standard at Bosworth and afterwards offered up amongst other Trophyes of his Victory at ye Cathedral of St PAULS LONDON.

Bosworth field Battle was Aug 22 1485.

Thomas Dinley. The Account of the Official Progress of His Grace Henry the First Duke of Beaufort through Wales 1684

4. *Abermarlais House*

Nothing is known of the original house of Abermarlais; however, in the reign of Henry VIII we are fortunate in possessing a fairly detailed account of the house which had been 'new mendid and augmentid' by Sir Rhys ap Thomas. On the attainder of his grandson in 1531, Abermarlais passed to the king who caused a survey to be made of the property.

From 'The View of the Manor place of Abbotmarles' made in that year we learn that within a park stood the house, moated and encompassed 'w't water round aboute'. The building was of one storey, 116 ft. long and 23 ft. broad, within which were a hall, two low chambers over them, a study or closet nigh to the hall with a little chamber over it, buttery, pantry, and larder, with a chamber over them, kitchen, and bakehouse. This building, containing the above thirteen rooms, stood on the east side of the site.

On the south side was the entrance gate, on the west side of which stood a low chamber with a chamber over it, being 30 ft. long and 22 ft. broad; and on the east side of the gate stood a little tower which contained a low prison house with a chamber over it.

On the west side was a stable, 100 ft. long and 24 ft. broad, with five chambers over it.

On the north side stood a chapel with a cellar (? crypt, vault) beneath it, 36 ft. long and 23 ft. broad. At the west end of the chapel was a stable, 51 ft. long and 19½ ft. broad. At the north end of the first storey was a brewhouse with a chamber above, 30 ft. long 'p'telie in dekay for lack of sklatyng'.

All the above buildings were 'of late buylded', the walls of stone, the roofs slated, and the timber everywhere 'good & substanciall'. The survey ends with this summary: 'The contents of the buyldyngs w't'in Aberm'les aforesaid. First: a haull, a chapell, a buttre, a pantr', a seller, a kechyn, a larder, xii chambers, a closet, a prison-house, ii stables, a brue house w't a corn chamber ov'. The p'ke there is paled & in cu'mpas ii miles & a half & well wooded. It'm, a wo'd nigh to the seid manor called the Nether Forest, well replenished w't wood.'

From this description it is clear that Abermarlais was roughly rectangular in form, built around a courtyard, and no great effort of the imagination is required to form a picture of it in one's mind's eye. Fortunately another mansion that belonged to Sir Rhys ap Thomas, dating from the late fifteenth century, has survived, its essentials unchanged thanks to the interest taken by its successive owners. This is Bryn y Beirdd on the slope opposite Castell Carreg Cennen, built around a courtyard entered through a gateway, the main residence on one side, the chapel on another, with outbuildings completing the other sides. Bryn y Beirdd conforms very closely to the layout of the Abermarlais of 1531.

Francis Jones. *Welsh Interiors, Arch. Camb.* 1967

5. *Privet Garden of Eden*

Of all the gardener's arts, that of topiary must be the most painstaking to create and the quickest, if neglected, to be lost. Highly popular in Victorian and Edwardian days, it was one of those manifestations that transcended class, being as popular in the stately demesne as in the front garden of a terraced house.

Not much remains today. Old photographs, however, preserve memories of some wonderful creations, but not many places in Britain can rival the fantastic display once found at an unpretentious house in the village of Abergwili, a mile east of Carmarthen – The Garden of Eden.

This was the vision and achievement of a certain Mr D. Davies of Glyn Aur (Golden Vale), Abergwili, who was justifiably proud enough to publish a set of six postcards depicting it in the 1920s. It is fortunate he did, as nothing of it now remains, and nothing seems to be remembered about him. He died before the last war, leaving a son who was blind, the local piano tuner. The garden is now partly built over.

Facing the road were two tableaux, one of animals, one of birds. There was another of Adam and Eve, plus serpent and angel approaching to boot them out! The back garden was New Testament: the flight into Egypt, with a splendid donkey carrying Jesus; a huge Last Supper in the style of Leonardo, all suitably labelled; and a detailed Crucifixion, so faithful as even to have Christ's head leaning to one side. The last scene is a huge crowd on both sides of a path. Davies gave us no

name to this. It is unlikely to be, for instance, the Sermon on the Mount, as there is a large cat toward the rear and something resembling a boot on the right! A nursery rhyme intrusion, perhaps: though, oddly, my father remembered as a boy Mr Davies shouting at him to clear off, on the basis that topiary and small boys do not mix!

Such extraordinary Bible scenes – panoramas – required a long life of devotion, both physical and spiritual. Someone must know more of Mr Davies. Was his topiary vision ever equalled?

Thomas Lloyd, *Historic Gardens Trust Newsletter No. 8*

6. *The Old House of Stradey*

The name Stradey is derived from the Welsh *ystrad*, plural *ystradau*, meaning a level area, a vale. It occurs fairly frequently in Carmarthenshire, such as Ystrad near Carmarthen, Ystrad near Llanwrda, Ystrad Corrwg in Llanllawddog, Ystrad Edryd in Llanfihangel Rhos-y-Corn, Ystrad Ferthyr in Llangyndeyrn, Ystrad Wallter in Llanfairarybryn, Yatrad-wrallt near Nantgaredig and Ystradffin in Llanfairarybryn.

Certain remains and place-names suggest early settlement in the area. To the north of the mansion is a four-acre field marked as 'Cae Caerau' in a terrier of 1805, while on the wooded slope now called Stradey Hill, to the west of the river Dulais, an enclosure called Gaer Fach is shown in the same terrier and still marked as an earthwork on O.S. maps.

No reference has been found to a mansion at Stradey until the Mansels came there during the first half of the seventeenth century. The earliest references to the name occur in the Muddlescomb archives, now preserved in the National Library of Wales, which show that the lands there were owned by yeomen. Deeds of the period 1552-1610 refer to lands at 'Straddy', 'Parke Estrade' and 'Park Ystradey'. It is significant that during the Elizabethan period the word 'park' was used to denote an enclosed field or area, and this may well have been the enclosed meadowland which later became part of the demesne around the residence of the Mansels.

Stradey constituted an estate in the first half of the seventeenth century when the Mansels settled there, and in all probability the original mansion was built by John Mansel who died before 1675. It stood on low ground near the banks of the Dulais, about 350 yds. to the south-west of the present residence, but what it looked like is impossible to say, and doubtless many changes were made to the structure during succeeding years. The detailed map prepared in 1805 by the surveyor Mathew Williams, shows the house to have been L-shaped, with outhouses and a yard on the northern side, lawns and ornamental gardens around its eastern and southern sides, and separated from the parkland by a ha-ha, part of which remains fairly intact to this day.

When Thomas Lewis inherited Stradey in 1808, he was living in a large comfortable house in the town of Llandeilo. There he continued to live, but made visits to Stradey where he stayed from time to time. His daughter Catherine also stayed there, probably for longer periods. The Mansel Lewis muniments show that the mansion needed repair, and in 1820 Mr Lewis took steps to deal with dilapidations and to improve the interior arrangements, but before embarking on the programme he ordered a complete inventory to be taken of the contents.

Francis Jones. *Stradey*, from *Arch. Camb.* 1976

7. *Ugliness and Laissez-faire*

The only flaw visible in the beautiful landscape at Dynevor, consists of a plain, ugly, oblong-square house, at present the family residence. The venerable old trees did their best to hide it from us, evidently ashamed to be seen in such companionship; for certainly the finger of taste has never been there. Children every day cut out precisely such houses on white paper perfectly square, with small square apertures at the upper story for bed-room windows, a row rather larger below, for the drawing-room ones, and a wide square door. The only attempt at ornament consisted of four very thin turrets, placed one at each corner, looking like rushlights surmounted by extinguishers; and the whole seemed newly dressed in a coat of white-wash. Where nature had done so much, art might surely show herself to more advantage. We strolled round the house and offices during nearly an hour, wishing to discover someone who might conduct us over the place; but not a living creature became visible, except a furious little dog, which barked as if we had been robbing the house; and certainly evil disposed persons might have done so with impunity, if there had been anything that they happened to fancy.

Next morning, having been more successful in catching a cicerone, he told us that the proprietor here felt so much satisfaction in the anti-

quity of his beautiful place, that no alterations, however trifling, are permitted, and no changes are considered improvements. When an old fence, or a mildewed wall, gives way, our informant assured us, it must always be rebuilt precisely on the original pattern, and the aged moss or weeds are carefully readjusted in their places; so that, if any previous lord of Dynevor returned, he would find these grounds in the same dishabille in which they were left on his decease. Peculiarities are always entertaining, and from the moment we were initiated into this trait, so like Mrs Edgeworth's Goodenough, it became amusing to observe all the old unreformed abuses.

Miss Catherine Sinclair.
Sketches and Stories of Wales and the Welsh 1860

8. *A View of Laugharne & Castle*

The descent to Laugharne is highly romantic; the town is built on the edge of a marsh, in a very low situation, open to the sea, and backed by very high grounds. It is one of the most sequestered places that can be conceived; and is much inhabited by half-pay officers, and families which seek an economical retirement. It is by far the best built little town in Caermarthenshire, and very well supplied with provisions; but its heat in summer is intolerably oppressive. The church is large, hand-some, and in good condition; with some respectable monuments. The churchyard is remarkable for occupying the side of a rather steep declivity. The view from the upper part of it is very rich; it is well planted with some large yew as well as other trees. The church and churchyard are more than usually ornamental to the place. The castle is a picturesque subject, in the point of view at which it is taken in the annexed plate; but the proprietor has laid out the inner court as a modern garden, and in every respect done his utmost to destroy the character of the ruin towards the water. Not only the area, but even one of the towers, is converted to the purposes of horticulture, and filled with the incongruous ornaments of evergreens and flowering shrubs.

Benjamin Heath Malkin,
The Scenery, Antiquities and Biography of Wales

9. *Dylan's Laugharne*

I expect that Laugharne will be Dylan's town henceforth. To come to the Boat House, where Dylan lived, it is necessary to walk from the centre of the town along a narrow lane which leads you along the edge of the cliff above the sea.

> In my seashaken house
> On a breakneck of rocks . . .
> At poor peace I sing
> To you strangers . . .
> Out of these seathumbed leaves . . .

Near the house you will see an unadorned wooden shed. There is a lock on the door now, but by looking through a fissure in the wall you will see a plain wooden table, and on it an ink bottle and writing pen. Here is the poet's workshop, and there is nothing improper in calling it that for Dylan above everything was a conscientious craftsman. Because he was known as a man with a wonderful voice and an unequalled talent for talk, many were deceived into thinking that he was a careless craftsman, tumbling wasteful words without paying much attention to form or sense. But there has never been a poet who paid more attention to the craft, nor ever an English poet who placed so many shackles on his writing. In this respect his poetic art belongs in the line of poets Cerdd Dafod, and many a page could be used to show the similarity between him and poets such as Dafydd ap Gwilym or Dafydd ab Edmund. But this is a travel book, and yet it need not solely belong to travel in itself, at least for me anyway, any virtue apart from the thrill that comes from time to time, of connecting a place or a piece of land, or a view, or some building with a certain person it is man, after all, who gives meaning to a place. Laugharne would be, without Dylan, without Peter Williams, without Bridget Bevan, only a name on a map. And through

Dylan's eyes mainly, can we gain the spirit of the town. I went out at dawn one morning to try and capture that rapture that he felt for this sleepy, out-of-the-way little town. There was mist, or drizzle coming in from the sea exactly as the poet saw it;

> Pale rain over the dwindling harbour
> And over the sea wet church the size of a snail
>   With its horns through mist and the castle
>   Brown as owls . . .

In the shadow of the castle with its round towers under a thickness of ivy, the early smoke of the hearths rose in streaks from the chimneys of the houses around the square of the harbour. There is no port here by now just a refuge for an occasional boat lying on its side on the pale sand. On the quay there is a large old building, a cockle factory. This is where the cockles that are collected on the beaches of the bay are bottled and sent to the shops of Wales and England.

The towers are all that's left of the old castle that Sir Guido de Brian built about the end of the thirteenth century, but the hand of the proud Norman still presses hard on Laugharne, and you cannot avoid his influence whichever way you turn. From the point of view of language, atmosphere and culture the town belongs more to Pembrokeshire than to Carmarthenshire, and the inhabitants' English sounds strange to the ears of the visitor. Towns such as Newcastle Emlyn, and Llandeilo are English enough, more's the pity, but English in a very different sense to Laugharne. A sort of shallow snobbery without character is the Englishness of these towns, but for Laugharne it is as if it is rooted in the soil, and this is what gives one the feeling of being in a foreign and strange country. A lost town, says Dylan Thomas of her – 'this unique, this waylaying, old lost Laugharne' . . . a night in one of the taverns is enough to prove that there is more than a thimbleful of truth in his description. Perhaps the characters of *Under Milk Wood* are strange creations of his huge imagination, but I would not be surprised if I came face to face with some of them whilst walking the streets of the town.

Aneirin Talfan Davies, † *Crwydro Sir Gâr*

10. *Two Poor Dabs in a Stained Box*

16th May 1938   Gosport Street, Laugharne

Dear Henry Treece,
　　I've been moving house. That is, I've left, with trunks and disappointment, one charitable institution after another and have found and am now occupying, to the peril of my inside and out, my rheumatic joints, my fallen chest, my modern nerves, my fluttering knutted pocket, a small, damp fisherman's furnished cottage – green rot sprouts through the florid scarlet forests of the wallpaper, sneeze and the chairs crack, the double-bed is a swing-band with coffin, oompah, slush-pump, gob-stick and almost wakes the deaf, syphilitic neighbours – by the side of an estuary in a remote village. The village also contains bearded Richard High-Wind Hughes, but we move, in five hundred yards, in two or more different worlds: he owns the local castle, no roof and all, and lives in a grand mansion by its side and has a palace in Morocco . . .

16th June 1938   Gosport Street, Laugharne

Dear Henry Treece,
　　I'm very glad indeed that you both will come and spend some time with us in the summer; any time, for any time. I warn you that our cottage is pokey and ugly, four rooms like stained boxes in a workman's and fisherman's row, with a garden leading down to mud and sea, that

our living and cooking is rough, that you bathe or go dirty. You will find my wife extremely nice; me small, argumentative, good-tempered, lazy, fumbling, boozy as possible, 'lower middle class' in attitude and reaction, a dirty tongue, a silly young man. I hope you like drinking, because I do very much and when I have money I don't stop. There are three good pubs here, the best bottled mild in England, and no prohibitive drinking hours. There are walks, and boats, and nets to pull, and colossal liars to listen to. There is a double bed in one room, two single beds in the other; you can sleep in the double bed, or in the two beds, or sandwiched in a single one. There is an earth lavatory and it smells like a shit-house. Welcome; and let me know when. (By the way, what do I call you? Throw your Treece away.)

This is a bad time for me again, and I can't buy a stamp for you. I haven't a single penny, or half-penny, or filed French slot-coin. Smoke-less and breadless, we face a bad weekend. We wait for shillings which we have no right to expect. Bitter, cruel Laugharne; my pipe is full of butt-ends from the grate, my table crowded with the dead ends of poems, my head full of nonsense. The sun is shining on the mud; my wife is out cockling. I am writing to a critic in Northumberland. A little girl has called with buns; I say, 'no buns', though all my ever-lasting soul shouts for them and my belly is turned by the sight in the kitchen of two poor dabs we caught, two out of all the breeding monsters in the sea, with a broken net yesterday. Last week I finished a long story about my true childhood, and here's a letter from *Life & Letters* saying they will print it and pay for it in September.

Dylan Thomas, *Letters*

11. YESTERDAY AND TODAY

Here's Y Llain. Can this be the place
Where I spent my early days?
The garden paths, where once there was joy,
These, those same dear walks
Under this thick-cropping bramble
Choking all the old loveliness.
Sister and brother? A cold trench of earth
Is their resting place.
Gone are father and mother
With their eloquence. A place of no return

Is the lip of the grave; once there
Not one comes away.

The wooden cowshed like a closed world,
Stall-less, without three-legged stools;
Go to the sty – no butting there
Nor ringed nose; the memory's regret
Is that my world that was so innocent,
Has vanished from me.

They raped, through brambled lust,
Language's root, in our garden
Weeds will grow (a dreaded chord)
Blind to our own old cultivation.
Sad homestead, downtrodden by a miscreant!
Though the place, this is not Y Llain.

Eirian Davies †

12. *Llandawke Lane; the Rectory*

The approaches to it from Laugharne are very pretty. The lower road
winds between hills which slope gracefully to the level ground; near its
end a large cluster of trees cast a grateful shade on a sunny day; they
have disappeared. Some people here have an unfortunate propensity for
cutting trees down. The upper road is its rival in beauty; it is but a narrow
lane, just wide enough for two abreast, shut in with high banks; it is
called Llandawke Lane, and the Bromwast Road. Its banks are enamel-
led with spring flowers in the season, often entirely covered with primroses, and luxuriant with ferns. This lane rises and declines at intervals;
about the middle it makes a deep descent, and gives one of those pretty
and sudden turns that conceals its further progress. Near here is a lovely
peep of the sea, and a bit of the coast with a headland; now and then
you get through a break in the bank a passing view of the undulating
hills, or of a field where cattle are grazing, or an accumulation of hills
of varied height sloping to the plain each after its own fashion. One
bears a solitary tree, another small patches of wood, and if it be harvest
time, mows will be scattered about waiting for the farmer to gather the
corn in. Now you approach a pretty scene – a curious old church with
the Rectory at its side, lying in a dell. You look down on them. A hill

on the left rises far above the Rectory thickly set with trees to its base, where an ancient well of good water lies. Behind the Rectory, and on its right, numerous fir-trees shelter it, towering above. Within the Rectory garden blossoms a fine laburnum; in the season it is a mass of yellow flower, and when the sun casts on it its brightest gleam, verily it is all aglow. There is something indescribably sweet and quiet in the scene here.

Mary Curtis, Antiquities of Laugharne,
Pendine, and their Neighbourhoods

13. Cennen Tower, Pridham's Folly

There is a shire in South Wales that has a soft, peculiar beauty. Its wildness is not quite that of the North, though it has its desolate places too. But its ruggedness is chastened, and through its meadows for miles fair rivers flow, until suddenly they meet a crag upon which stands an ancient castle, its walls full of history.

They seem to encircle it lovingly, then wander on, adding brightness to little grey market towns, until they reach the sea.

But the hills are its real glory, the long ranges of mountains that enfold it – and I am thinking of the Red Garn, Three Hills, and the Black Mount.

These three stand one behind the other. The Red Garn with its wealth of bracken is the baby, Three Hills, with its strange heaps of loose stones at irregular intervals all along its top, is the second sentinel, the seasoned soldier, with the white snow of age oftener on its peaks; but behind them, and towering many hundred feet above them is the Black Mount – their common mother.

Strangely enough, though she is far higher, snow quits her more rapidly than it does Three Hills. I have often looked at the three ranges in the sunset of an autumn day. There is a knoll near Bethlehem Village, from which, during the five minutes of the last gleam, I have seen the Red Garn a mass of fire, the bracken showing here and there queer work of marquetry. Above the fantastic play of light on Three Hills is marked by a desolate tower, built two hundred years ago, in a wild spot. Yearly it falls into deeper ruin, but an ogive window on the south-west side still remains intact. Through the orifice of that window a white bird sometimes flies.

The Tower is called Cennen Tower, or Pridham's Folly. Little is known of the builder, save that he was connected with the East India company, and had his reasons for living retired from the world. In 18 – the Tower, and the small estate around, descended to a great nephew, Charles Pridham, who entered with no little trepidation upon his new inheritance.

But his fears fled, and a great joy overtook him. He was a scholar and a poet. He was sensitive, with a rare refinement, and the weather beaten mountains around became the temples of his daily worship. He drank in the glorious air, and took the wind and rain as it came. Better than the sheep he knew their folding places; all the tracks were familiar to him.

J. W. Nicholas, *The White Bird*

14. *Taliaris Park*

The Road about a Mile or a Mile and a half farther on takes its course on the declivity of the Hill through fine woods belonging to one Nicholas, and Taliaris. Enter, after passing a small neat chapel in a sequestered situation belonging to Taliaris. Enter the Grounds by a handsome Gate through a winding Avenue, well wooded by thriving plantations of the present owner, interspersed with some few venerable Foresters. The Mansion on two sides presents rather magnificent fronts, and was certainly meant for a cube, the most prevailing figure then followed, but the plan being contracted, the capacity of the House falls very short of its imposing appearance in the fronts seen [sic]. It has a large Walled Garden, and is surrounded on all sides by rich woods, and backed by a ridge of high and parkish ground, ending in a mountainous summit, with a broken outline.

Ascend the Hill, and find on the other side a Lake about three quarters of a Mile round, stocked with Perch and Eels. Near its edge, on a rough piece of ground, is the circle mentioned by Ed. Lhwyd. The Lake seems to have been one of those Craters, where the fountains of the great deep were broken up, out of which, with the water, were vomited forth the lava of stones on its banks. The Hill to the North was occupied by a sort of Encampment with an Agger of the loose stones everywhere covering it, called the Gaer Vawr. Under the Camp, on the side of the Hill, issues a Spring, to which the common people ascribe many medical, almost miraculous, powers, and it acts sometimes as an Emetick; and a little lower down a Water used in Complaints of the Eye. On a little rising to the left there were small Cannon found.

Richard Fenton, *Tours in Wales*

15. *Vicar Pritchard's House*

The old vicarage of Llandovery is a very large mansion of dark red brick, fronting the principal street or market-place, and with its back to a green meadow bounded by the river Bran. It is in a very dilapidated condition, and is inhabited at present by various poor families. The principal room, which is said to have been the old vicar's library, and the place where he composed his undying Candle, is in many respects a remarkable apartment. It is of large dimensions. The roof is curiously inlaid with stucco or mortar, and is traversed from east to west by an immense black beam. The fire-place, which is at the south, is very large and seemingly of high antiquity. The windows, which are two in number and look westward into the street, have a quaint and singular appearance. Of all the houses in Llandovery the old vicarage is by far the most worthy of attention, irrespective of the wonderful monument of God's providence and grace who once inhabited it.

The reverence in which the memory of Rees Pritchard is still held in Llandovery the following anecdote will show. As I was standing in the principal street staring intently at the antique vicarage, a respectable-looking farmer came up and was about to pass, but observing how I was employed he stopped, and looked now at me and now at the antique house. Presently he said:

'A fine old place, is it not, sir? but do you know who lived there?'

Wishing to know what the man would say provided he thought I was ignorant as to the ancient inmate, I turned a face of inquiry upon

him; whereupon he advanced towards me two or three steps, and placing his face so close to mine that his nose nearly touched my cheek, he said in a kind of piercing whisper –

'The Vicar.'

Then drawing his face back he looked me full in the eyes as if to observe the effect of his intelligence, gave me two nods as if to say, 'He did, indeed,' and departed.

The Vicar of Llandovery had then been dead nearly two hundred years. Truly the man in whom piety and genius are blended is immortal upon earth.

George Borrow, *Wild Wales*

16. *Neuadd Newydd, Llandovery*

When it was built, the High Street wing of Neuadd Newydd must have been the best house in the town although, by modern standards, the accommodation on the two main floors was limited. The addition of the larger wing at the rear turned the house into a mansion such as few gentlemen of Wales could boast at that time. It was clearly intended as a display of wealth but certain details – such as the absence of stone carving and the use of oak instead of stone for the mullioned windows – suggest that the Vicar aspired to more than local craftsmanship could provide.

The dates at which the two wings of the house were built is a matter of guesswork but the building periods must have corresponded to stages in the Vicar's rise to fortune. The earlier High Street wing may have been erected at the beginning of his ministry in Llandovery, 1602, or perhaps c.1615, after he had become Rector of Llanedi and a Prebendary of Brecon. The rear wing almost certainly came into existence much later, when he had been for some time in receipt of the revenues of the Chancellorship of St David's and the Vicarage of Llawhaden, both of which he began to enjoy in 1626. The building must have been completed before the beginning of the Civil War, which, from Vicar Pritchard's letter of complaint to Dr Oliver Lloyd, appears to have cramped his style of living.

A. T. Arber-Cooke,
Pages from the History of Llandovery

17. *Wretched Dwellings*

Llandilo – three o'clock, afternoon

The inn at Llandovery is a bad one, but the people are very civil. The road from thence hither is good, and very beautiful . . . I thought the town of Llandovery a miserable one, but that of Llandilo is much worse. I never saw any place that had a more deplorable appearance. The streets, if so they may be called, are narrow, dirty, and half paved with stones the sharp ends upwards. The houses are built with a kind of stone; but it is of so crumbling a nature, that they appear to be all falling to decay. The inhabitants are very decent in their manners, and in their outward semblance: they do not seem fit tenants for such wretched dwellings.

Mrs Mary Morgan. *Tour to Milford Haven in the year 1791*

18. *Three-Arch Bridge, The Bear*

The bridge over the Towy [at Llandilo] consists of three very light and elegant arches, built by David Edwards, of Beaupré, in Glamorganshire.

The Bear *Inn* at this place, mentioned by Sir Richard Hoare, as 'the worst in S. Wales', and by Miss Spence, as 'very uncomfortable and exorbitant' has assumed a new character. The editor has been assured that under subsequent management it deserves as much commendation as it formerly merited censure. In 1831 the population of this town amounted to 1258 inhabitants. The *market* is held on Saturday, and is well supplied with corn; the *fairs* are held Feb. 20. Palm Monday, and June 4; that of *Fair Fach*, distant from Llandeilo-fawr 1m., is on Nov. 22.

Emilius Nicholson.

The Cambrian Traveller's Guide 1840

19. Glynhir

Glynhir, on high ground east of the village [Llandybïe], Jacobean with an indifferent Georgian front, has an interesting octagonal stone-built dovecote. Inside, a ladder revolves on a wooden central shaft around the serried nest-holes. The story that a pigeon bringing the first news of the battle of Waterloo homed here cannot be proved. In the grounds, rhododendrons impede access to the *Loughor* river waterfall, which provided Hugh Hughes (c.1815) with one of his most beautiful wood engravings in the *Beauties of Cambria*.

Vyvian Rees, *Shell Guide to South West Wales*

20. Glynhir Falls

Hence to Clynhir the Seat of Mr Du Buisson, who came into this country concerned in an Iron Work, which was carried on by the River Lochor, which passes through the farm of Clynhir, now made by great perseverance and profound agricultural knowledge, from cold mountain ground, as good land as any in the County. Here the Gardens, by being well sheltered, are productive of most excellent fruit. To the South of the House, passing the Gardens, you descend into a deep and beautifully wooded Valley, at least a Mile in length, and crossing a wooden bridge over a deep rocky channel, through which the River takes its course, you turn to the left on the other side, and after crossing a little gulley in the Hill, down which a most picturesque torrent constantly pours, as may be seen by the attrition of the rocky channel it frets its way through, you walk down by the margin of the whole River, which, just above you, is precipitated down a steep – [*sic*] high, forming the most graceful and elegant fall I ever saw, with the finest possible accompaniment of Wood.

Richard Fenton, *Tours in Wales*

21. *Richard Steel at the Ivy Bush*

There are some very good houses, but they are not in general advantageously placed. The situation of the principal inn, the Ivy Bush, removed to what was lately a gentleman's seat on the banks of the river, is one of the best in the town. The rooms command a charming reach of the river up to Abergwilly Palace. The late Ivy Bush was the house of Sir Richard Steele, who obtained it and his property in this neighbourhood by marriage with the only child and heiress of Jonathan Scurlock, Esq. He died here on the 1st of September, 1729; and there are two or three very old people still living in the town who recollect his person. Sir Richard, in the course of this theatrical career, has introduced many a magician to the public; I shall therefore avail myself of his example and authority, while I state the pretensions of mine.

Benjamin Heath Malkin,
The Scenery, Antiquities and Biography of Wales

22. *Edwinsford*

Hence to Llansawel, a small Village with 2 or 3 publick Houses. The Church has a tower, but is a poor miserable building without and within. No Monument. Pass Edwinsford, an old Mansion, pretty large, lying low on the banks of the Cothy, which winds under the beautifully wooded Hills near it. There is a large walled Garden, a great part of which is of mud, said to be the best for fruit. To characterize the different farm Offices, there occur several well executed figures in lead painted, such as a large Pig near the Piggery, Hay makers near the Haggard, and at the Stables or Kennel an admirable fowler. Near the House are shewn 13 large Trees planted the year Thos Williams Esq. of this House was Sheriff, by him and his 12 Javelin Men after their return from the Spring Assizes – a central tree with 12 others round it.

A little farther on opens the Vale of Talley or Tal y Llychau, taking its name from its situation near two Lakes, the largest near a Mile and a Quarter round, and the lesser about a Mile. The Water Lily adorn the sides. They abound with Eels, Perch and Pike. The water belongs to Edwinsford, and Fish for their own consumption, but the property besides in the Fishing is in Admiral Foley as Lord of Llansadwrn.

Richard Fenton, *Tours in Wales*

23. *Mushrooms of Edwinsford*

A man emerged from the darkness of one of the rooms – I understood before I left the reason for the darkness – and I greeted him. He did not have enough English to converse with me, but he turned to call on someone in his own language, and presently behold a young woman with a worried look came towards me.

'Good afternoon.'

I explained my errand, and immediately she offered to take me around the house. She explained that there were three families living there at the time, and led me from one room to another. Here we are in a spacious room with windows opening on to the lawn, and two enormous mirrors facing each other from two parallel walls. The gilt on the frames had long since lost its freshness, with many flaws on the mirror itself because of the dampness, I suppose. The plaster of the beautiful ceiling, also, was in no better condition. *Ichabod.* The glory has departed. But, standing there, it was not difficult to recreate and re-populate the room with the glory of the days of its prime, and to see the floor full of happy couples in their gorgeous dresses dancing the minuet to the sound of the harpsichord and fiddles. The Edwinsford family takes us back over many centuries in the history of our nation; whatever out attitude may be to that history, or our opinion of the value of the contribution of these families to society and the life of the nation, we cannot but feel some little pang of sadness to see the ball winding to its end and the last inch of wool disappearing into the un-concerned cloth of time. The family lived in this place from the twelfth century up to the beginning of the last war, when the last baronet (the fifth) of the family moved to live in England.

Later in the afternoon in Talley Abbey I saw a tombstone inscribed:

IN MEMORY OF THE MEMBERS OF THE EDWINSFORD
(RHYD EDWIN)
FAMILY BURIED (OR NEAR) THIS VAULT FROM THE TWELFTH CENTURY
(OR EARLIER) TO THE NINETEENTH CENTURY.
THIS MONUMENT IS INSCRIBED BY THEIR DESCENDANT
JAMES WILLIAMS DRUMMOND 5TH BARONET, 1931.
REQUIESCENT IN PACE.

And this is their end! A little earlier I mentioned a man emerging from the darkness of one of the rooms; the darkness was explained to me when the woman led me into another room. This one was dark, almost pitch-black, until my eyes grew accustomed to the darkness. In it I saw row upon row of oblong boxes, some foot in depth and about two and a half yards long and a yard wide. They were full of soil, but on the soil hundreds of mushrooms were beginning to appear. And that was the secret!

How are the mighty fallen!

Out we went from the darkness into the sunlight, and I turned the conversation between me and the Polish woman, from the history of the Edwinsford family to a tragedy of another kind – refugees trying to recreate and rekindle the flame of life in a strange and inaccessible spot. Her story was the same as that of the soldier in the stables. A little child played at her feet, and every now and then she would turn and greet him in her own tongue – Polish.

'You still keep your language?'

'Why yes.'

'Does he speak any other languages?'

'No, not yet.'

'Where will he go to school?'

'Talley.'

'But that is a Welsh school.'

'Yes.'

'Will he learn Welsh?'

'Of course, he will.'

'What about English?'

'He'll learn that too, if need be.'

'You don't think that is too much?'

'Why should I? I speak four languages, and so can he.'

And formulating the servile question heard on the tongues of so many people in Wales, I said,

'But what use will Polish be for him?'

'What use?' she said astounded, 'What use? That, surely is a silly question. One day he'll return, perhaps, to Poland and see his grandfather and grandmother, and I would be ashamed if he could not speak to them in their own language – and his.'

Aneirin Talfan Davies, † *Crwydro Sir Gâr*

24. *Sir Rhys ap Thomas's Four-Poster*

The bedstead is immensely interesting, a truly fine example of what a late fifteenth-century craftsman could achieve. Knights and their chargers, standard-bearers and bowmen are depicted on the frieze, all telling their own tale to knowledgeable students of history and heraldry. In particular, I remember one bold little man with a homely whiskered face who appears mounted on a curiously shaped Welsh cob, the animal having a remarkably large head and very short legs. I imagined that this mounted knight was Sir Rhys ap Thomas himself.

Lewis Glyn Cothi, more than all other Welsh poets, delighted in describing the possessions of his patrons, and indeed from his descriptions of bed-curtains and bed-coverlets it is easy to form a mental picture of the famous bedstead at Derwydd gorgeously decked out for the repose of some distinguished personage. Probably the curtains drawn between the carved posts would have been much like the famous Arras curtains which the bard – always an archbeggar – asked Annes of Caerleon to bestow upon himself, he having suffered at Chester the theft of all his household goods. It was embroidered with beasts, birds, and trees, trefoil and French gardens. But the Holy Cross was there also, and our Lord, His mother, and His saints and the twelve apostles, and we are told that

> Each corner holds an angel bright;
> The centre shows the God of Light,
> And symbols too are found thereon
> Of Matthew, Mark and Luke and John.

And decidedly the bed of Sir Rhys must have had a coverlet of the same variety as one the poet coveted, which was made of wide tapestry with willow leaves upon it, and trees, with nine figures, nine birds, nine stags, and nine deer, and twelve blue leaves and ten leaves green and black in hue, a hundred green and a thousand crimson and yellow. There were oak-trees on it also and a grove of birds and images, the whole of the fine work of maidens' hands. Some of the old coffers at Derwydd were no doubt once filled with such treasures as Lewis Glyn Cothi writes of in connection with the bride, Alice of Herast, or such rich materials as were stored by the careful Jonet Lewis, who according to the poet not only provided liberally for the poor, but also provided herself with fine ornaments and costly attire.

Some day I hope I may be allowed to look at the treasures of that famous old mansion again, and I think I should like to go there with my volumes of Lewis Glyn Cothi under my arm, for no writer can help us to see a Welsh home of the fifteenth century in the same light as the adventurous bard, who, being forced to exist to a great extent on the bounty of his wealthy friends, had naturally a detailed knowledge of their possessions.

Evelyn Lewes. *Out with the Cambrians* 1934

25. *Mayhew's Mayhem*

Bishop Rudd's son, Sir Rice Rudd, involved himself in long and unsuccessful electioneering, as a result of which he became so financially burdened that he was obliged to mortgage Aberglasney, 'In vain ye search the Domes of care./In vain ye search, she is not there.' The mortgager was the Hon. Thomas Watson-Wentworth who appointed Robert Dyer, a local solicitor living in the Llanfynydd area, to foreclose on the defaulting Rice Rudd around the year 1700. The poet Dyer was then a one-year-old baby. Dyer senior found the £2,201 deposit through property dealing, to raise a mortgage to live in Aberglasney himself. ''Tis thus the busy beat the air/And misers gather wealth and care.' There was, understandably, resistance from Rudd when Dyer moved in to take possession as tenant himself.

Fighting took place between Rudd's and Dyer's men. 'Open wide the lofty doors./Seek (him) on the marble floors.' In a matter of years, the astute Robert Dyer sold off parcels of land, to clear the mortgaged purchase price of £8,601. But in 1720 he died, before completion. 'Never covet what you see.' His sons were only able to clear up matters after a protracted action in the Chancery Division, 'yet time has seen, that lifts the low./And level lays the lofty brow . . .'

Another ambitious father who troubled his sons was Col. Mayhew who married into Aberglasney in the mid-19th century. He set about exorcising a curse. The drink. He closed down the village pub and founded a Temperance Hall in Llangathen. The motto which stood emblazoned on it until recently – Watch and be Sober – has considerably been stolen.

His eldest son who was at Oxford watched soberly long enough for the opportunity to return his many friends' hospitality and show them the splendours of Aberglasney. He learned that his father had business that would detain him in London long enough for him, with the connivance of the servants, to hold a party. Now, here's where Oliver Goldsmith takes over. Mayhew, on the road to London, stopped the night at an inn where he met a company of young people travelling west to . . . Aberglasney. The following evening at the height of the celebrations, the old man appeared. Mayhem. He ordered the servants to pour the intoxicating liquors into the ornamental lake. Not all the corks were drawn first. Napoleon brandies and vintage ports were found by workmen digging a drain in the 1930s.

Lynn Hughes. *The Curse of Grongar Hill,*
Western Mail Weekend Magazine 1977

26. ABERGLASNEY

Up Grongar Hill I labour now,
And catch at last his Bushy Brow.
Oh! how fresh, how pure the Air!
Let me breathe a little here.
Where am I, Nature? I descry
Thy Magazine before me lie!
Temples! – and Towns! – and Tow'rs! – and Woods!
And Hills! – and Vales! – and Fields! – and Floods!
Crowding before me edg'd around
With naked Wilds, and barren Ground.
See below the pleasant Dome,
The Poet's Pride, the Poet's Home,
Which the Sun-Beams shine upon,
To the Even, from the Dawn.
See her Woods where *Eccho* talks,
Her Gardens trim, her Terras Walks,
Her Wildernesses, fragrant Brakes,
Her gloomy Bowers, and shining Lakes.
Keep, ye Gods, this humble seat
For ever pleasant, private, neat.

John Dyer, from *The Country Walk*

IX

War & Strife

* 1. *The Battle of Mynydd Carn*

And in the meantime, after Gruffudd had been in Ireland for years as a guest with king Diarmait and with the other nobles, at last he assembled a royal fleet from Waterford which the king had given him, full of Scandinavians, Irish and Welsh. After setting sail on sea, with the wind favourable behind them, and the sea calm, he came to Porth Clais beside the archbishop's house of Mynyw.

And then Rhys, son of Tewdwr, king of the Deheubarth of Wales, and the bishop and his learned men and the whole community of the Lord Dewi and the one church of Mynyw, proceeded as far as the harbour. And Rhys first conversed thus with the lord Gruffudd: 'Hail Gruffudd, king of the kings of Wales. Unto to thee am I fleeing. Before thee do I fall on my knees to seek thy help and strength.' 'Who art thou?' said Gruffudd, 'and for what hast thou come here?' 'I am Rhys,' said he, 'the son of Tewdwr, the lord of this land a little while before now. And now beaten and in flight and almost vanished, I am in hiding in this sanctuary.' 'Who put thee to flight?' said Gruffudd. 'Lord,' said he, 'three kings from the chief kingdoms of Wales and their forces attacked my kingdom of late, and they are ravaging it every day.' 'Who,' said Gruffudd, 'are the kings who march through thy men and lands with forces in this way?' 'Caradog, son of Gruffudd,' said he, 'from Gwent Uch Coed and Is Coed, and his men of Gwent, and the men of Morgannwg, and many Norman cross-bowmen with him; Meilir, son of Rhiwallon and his men of Powys with him, king Trahaearn and the men of Arwystli.'

And when Gruffudd heard the name of his oppressors, he snorted in anger, and asked him what he would give for fighting on his behalf against those men. 'In truth,' said Rhys, 'I will give thee half my territory, and along with that I will be thy vassal.' And Gruffudd agreed with that. And after that meeting, they proceeded together to the church of Dewi in prayer. And there they became faithful allies by swearing on his relics.

---

* The Life of Gruffud ap Cynan, prince of Gwynedd (d. 1137) was written probably in the 1160s. It was first written in Latin, and later translated into Welsh, in the first half of the thirteenth century as is most likely.

Here we have related the events leading up to the battle of Mynydd Carn, somewhere in north Pembrokeshire. This battle was fought between Gruffudd and Rhys ap Tewdwr of Deheubarth and other Welsh princes. The battle is also recorded in the Chronicle of the Princes (*Brut y Tywysogion*) under the year 1081. (D. S. Evans).

And after they had entered into an agreement in that place and had received the bishop's blessing, Gruffudd marched forward on that same day, with his Scandinavians and Irish and many men of Gwynedd to the number of one hundred and sixty, with Cynddelw, son of Conus of Môn, leading them. Rhys also and a few men of the South marched with them, joyous in his heart because of the help he had received.

And after he had marched a long day's journey, around eventide they came to a mountain, where there were the encampments of the kings spoken of above. And then spoke Rhys to king Gruffudd, 'Lord,' said he, 'let us delay the battle till tomorrow, for it is now eventide, and the day is fading.' 'Delay thou,' said Gruffudd with a sigh, 'if thou dost wish it. I and my army will make for them.' And so it happened. And the kings, however, took fright as they saw the various mighty hosts and the armies of king Gruffudd and their ensigns opposing them, and the Scandinavians with their two-edged battle-axes, and the Irish with spears and their iron balls fitted with knives, and the men of Gwynedd with spears and shields. Gruffudd, the foremost fighter, made for the battle like unto a giant and a lion, and did not cease from scattering his adversaries with a flashing sword. He instilled vigour into his men to repel their enemies bravely, so that they would not flee from them in any way. And then there was a battle greatly to be remembered by descendants after their forbears. The shouts of the fighters were raised to the sky: the earth echoed to the tumult of the horses and foot-soldiers, the warlike sound was heard from afar: the commotion of the arms sounded often: the men of Gruffudd intensifying their ferocity, and their enemies submitting to them: the sweat of toil and the blood forming running streams. And in the meantime, Trahaearn was pierced in his bowels, until he fell to the ground dead, nibbling with his teeth the fresh grass and groping on top of the arms; and Guckharki the Irishman made bacon of him as of a pig. And in that one place there fell around him of his own guard twenty-five horsemen. Some of them were killed in the first contingent. Many thousands of them were killed, and the others showed their backs to the men of Gruffudd and turned to flight. Gruffudd for his part, as was his custom, victoriously pursued them with his retinue through the bushes, the valleys, the swamps, the mountains, throughout that night by moonlight, and throughout the following day. And hardly did any one of them escape from the battle to their own land.

Historia Gruffud vab Kenan †

2. *Norman Conquest*

(1090-1093). One thousand and ninety was the year of Christ when Rhys ap Tewdwr, King of Deheubarth, was slain by the French who were inhabiting Brycheiniog. And then fell the kingdom of the Britons. And then Cadwgan ap Bleddyn ravaged Dyfed on the second day from May. And then, two months after that, about the Calends of July, the French came to Dyfed and Ceredigion, which they have held to this day, and they fortified them with castles; and they seized all the land of the Britons.

The Chronicle of the Princes †

3. A STANZA FROM THE *OIANAU*

O little pig, it will not be hidden
When a battle-host sets forth from Caerfyrddin,
And leading them, skilfully, two youths
Of the offspring of Rhys, the stay of combat, battle-charger of an army.
When the English shall be slain in the confluences of war,
Blessed will be the Welsh, an estimable people.

From *The Black Book of Carmarthen** †

4. *Hardy McHardy, Battle of Britain Pilot*

Squadron Leader Hardy McHardy was a very remarkable character. Somewhat frail as a child and bullied at school, he came to Carmarthenshire from London, to Taliaris Park, Llandilo, when his mother, a First World War widow, married Humphrey Peel. He was brought up in style, albeit somewhat genteel down-at-heel, but he loved the Welsh countryside and soon had a half-brother, Robin, as playmate and companion. Despite a nervous and artistic temperament, he found his place

---

* This stanza is from the *Oianau*, a prophetic poem found in the Black Book of Carmarthen (*c.* 1250) and ascribed to Myrddin, a poet who was reputed to have prophesied in the sixth century. It probably describes the campaigns of Maredudd and Rhys (later the Lord Rhys of Deheubarth) who were in possession of Carmarthen from 1151 until 1155. They were the grandsons of Rhys ap Tewdwr (*ob.* 1093), mentioned in the fourth line. The word translated 'confluences' (*cymerau*) may possibly be a place-name. (A. O. H. Jarman).

in the RAF where he took a commission after flying training at Tern Hill, in 1938.

40928 Pilot Officer Donald Ballentine Hardy McHardy was posted to RAF Carew Cheriton – between Tenby and Pembroke – where he flew Gloster-built Hawker Henlys as a member of B-Flight IAA Co-op Unit. Their (dangerous) role was to tug drones as practice targets for trainee Royal Artillery air defence Anti-Aircraft gunners, based at Manorbier, Aberporth and Towyn. The standard of airmanship demanded was exacting. His commanding officer, Group Captain Ken Bachelor, retained the very highest regard for McHardy's flying ability. In many hundreds of sorties with B-Flight he recorded only one single mishap – a forced landing due to engine failure.

In June, 1940, Hardy was posted to an elite squadron, 229, equipped with Hawker Hurricane Mk Is, who were moved from Wittering, Northamptonshire, to Northolt, Middlesex, in defence of London. Pilot Officer McHardy flew over a hundred patrol and raid interceptions before and during the Battle of Britain. His section (Blue) of F Squadron, led by Pilot Officer Simpson, supported by Flight Sergeant Ommanny were frequently in the thick of it, Simpson being credited with six enemy casualties, McHardy none.

The flamboyant, gladiatorial streak that singled him out for the grim ritual of hand-to-hand fighting – stock-in-trade of the fighter pilot – was countered by a rare gift for clowning that came close to what in actors and public figures is termed 'star quality'. Known as 'Fou' (French: 'Mad') Hardy was early spotted by the cartoonist, Giles, of Express Newspapers, and his tall, gaunt, slightly stooping frame, wispy hair and the boyish grin through handlebar moustaches was to provide the model for Giles's famous 'Flying Officer Kite' series. Somewhere in the Beaverbrook files there may still exist a cartoon depicting many dozens of Hardy McHardys, aka 'F/O Kites', crowded into a wartime Officers' Mess bar.

In sheepskin flying-jacket, Service Dress hat askew, obligatory light blue silk scarf, cigarette-holder clamped in a stained grin, he was always a joy to meet: 'Dear Boy! How the Devil are you? How *good* to see you!' Everybody knew Hardy as he'd pass, hooting, folded up in his battered Austin Seven, waving a skeletal arm. He was a celebrity; yet treated you as one. This unfailing cheerfulness, his nobility of bearing and fierce courage was his shield against the world. Hardy was complex – extrovertism concealed a shy sensibility. He had visited the extreme and come back from it.

In the Public Record Office, Heathrow, the 229 Squadron Diary records Hardy becoming separated from his section on September 18, 1940. He landed safely at Lymne. A week later, he force-landed his Merlin-engined Hurricane at Biggin Hill with engine failure. On the morning of October 26, 1940, the Squadron was scrambled for a false alarm. Before they had time to refuel they were called up a second time. The Permanent Historical Record reads:

> Patrol took off again at 10.55 to patrol Croydon in conjunction with a number of Polish squadrons. A number of ME 109s were seen and these were chased by No. 302 Squadron (Polish). No. 229 Squadron following. This was subsequently proved to be a trap and the two squadrons found themselves over the French coast and returned to base without engaging the enemy. F/O Simpson, Leader of the Blue Section, emerged from cloud at 4,000 feet and saw an HE 59 [a mine-laying sea-plane] about half-a-mile from the shore and detached himself from the Squadron, followed by Sgt Ommanny and P/O McHardy of his section. They went down to attack and Sgt Ommanny fired two bursts at the enemy aircraft which alighted on the water. This pilot, then being hotly engaged by ME 109s from the rear and gunfire from the shore, made off flying low across the Channel to reach Home Base. F/O Simpson and F/O Hardy were last seen heavily engaged by ME 109s and did not return.

McHardy was reported 'missing, flying battle casualty' at 11.45 a.m. on October 26, 1940. The next day a report reached England that he was 'safe, injured'. He had brought his aircraft, his favourite Hurricane, V6704, to a forced landing in a field, 3 miles north of Boulogne. He always maintained that he had passed the point of no return on fuel, and would not have made it home. Simpson was never found.

Somewhere extant there is a photograph of Hardy being visited in hospital by his Luftwaffe assailant, a young pilot officer who was to go on to a distinguished flying career, none other than (Capt) Hauptmann Phillipe. That he claimed McHardy as his 'first blood' could not have assisted the interview, especially as McHardy lay there with a broken upper jaw from collision with the gunsight in the crash, and smashed front teeth. What it proves, though, is a certain chivalry from the First World War and earlier times that still obtained in the early weeks of the Battle of Britain. It did not endure to 1942.

When he was sufficiently mended, Hardy was slammed up in Dulag Luft, an initial interrogation centre for RAF prisoners-of-war, in a leafy suburb near Oberursel station, where he was, by all accounts, a trouble-some customer, and subjected to severe beatings from the Gestapo. He was then transferred to the notorious Stalagluft 3, at Sagan and then Belario. During his long four-years of detention, there is little doubt that he played a major role in prisoner morale. Letters that he wrote to his mother, the Hon Valentia Peel, and brother Robin, at Taliaris are on deposit in the County Archive at Carmarthen. They are well-written accounts of daily life in Stalagluft 3, revealing a studious person and a devoted son.

He gives news, between the lines, of fellow-prisoners Bader, Blount, Hoare, Trench and Stanford Tuck. 'Stanford Tuck is in the room at the moment, chasing one hand round with the other, demonstrating some air battle or other.' He reports that he won the camp art prize in 1942. He designs scenery for the camp theatre and plays in *The Importance of Being Ernest, Blythe Spirit, Rookery Nook, Night Must Fall* and *Treasure Island*, the pantomime.

Hardy's hour-long lecture on even higher mathematics, 'The relative merits of the Prelate system of Calculus', was acclaimed a *tour de force* for a man not well-known for his inability to stumble in a count to ten. The meat of the thesis had been prepared by Tony Trench, a boffin who shared rooms with the tyro lecturer. Stooges, loaded with marvel-lous questions, were posted among the hundred-strong audience settled between the cookhouse and Hut 120.

Fou makes his entrance with a sheaf of papers under his arm, resplen-dent in officer's peaked cap, a very off-white handkerchief knotted around his throat, open-necked shirt revealing a hairless chest. He is sporting home-made shorts and flying boots. McHardy introduces his audience to the progenitor of his subject, the Prelate, an apparent Belgian Abbé, then dives straight into a surreal and mesmerising pre-sentation, illustrated with swift equations and solutions that are wiped off the blackboard no sooner than written.

The planted questions are expertly fielded. Brilliant nonsense from start to finish puzzles equally the guards and those infuriated, with genuine queries. The whole show ends in uproar and is quickly, and luckily, disbanded by a pervading thunderstorm. Rain empties down. Sweeping up his papers, Fou makes a dramatic, Mephistophelian, exit to the shelter of his room.

McHardy loves and plays classical music on an old gramophone. Welsh history interests him, but his attempts to learn Welsh are the cause of much merriment. Among his Welsh tutors were Rupert ('Maigret') Davies, 'the preacher's son from Carmarthen' and Gwyn Martin.

In *Up and Under*, his autobiographical account of wartime experiences as a Wellington bomber navigator and prisoner of the Nazis, Gwyn Martin vividly recalls his first encounter with McHardy:

> I read a notice asking for someone with a knowledge of Welsh to contact a Flt/Lt McHardy in Block 62. I went along to this room of very senior Kreigies [PoWs], feeling a complete sprog. From a top bunk, from under a pile of bedclothes, came a most English public school voice.
>
> 'It's me you require, dear boy. I'm F/Lt Donald Balentine McHardy.'
>
> The owner of the voice disentangled itself from the bedclothes and slithered from the bunk to the floor, he was fully dressed in uniform, peaked cap and flying boots but unwashed and unshaven, the gaps in his teeth were many and filled with breadcrumbs. He was about six feet tall, stooping like a Mantis, in profile resembling a question mark. I wondered if it was the start of a leg-pull and was about to ask when he said, 'Let's do a circuit, old boy. All will be revealed.'
>
> His proposition was that I should teach him conversational Welsh with the help of *Welsh Made Easy*, by Caradar. The terms agreed upon were two hours per day at ten Players cigarettes per hour. He explained that he lived at Taliaris Park near Llandilo and his mother and he were acutely conscious of their inability to converse with their tenants in their native tongue, nor could they understand when they being talked about.

It becomes clear that Martin, though he recognises the comic element in Hardy's character 'straight from the pages of PG Wodehouse', is judgmental and betrays a Valleys-boy 'chip' in matters of rank and class. In the book, his portrait of a delightful, original and most genteel character is not affectionate. Hardy was teaching himself to be a painter, and had sent via the Red Cross a portfolio of sketches and water-colours, including 'View from the Terrace at Taliaris' (where he and Robin had often fired off an ancient canon) to his mother. Valentia had them exhibited at her club, 'The Sesame', in London, to raise money for the Red Cross. But Gwyn Martin's take on it is that:

> The result was disastrous, DBH was proclaimed an Artist; prior to this he had merely looked like one, now he started to live the role, doing everything short of cutting off his ear. I laboured

hard to teach Hardy conversational Welsh, but without success; at the end of a year all he could say was 'Good morning, Gwyn. It's a beautiful day. The sun is shining.' In his Cheltenham College accent.

All these activities mask the serious underlying purpose of escape. There were several tunnels being excavated beneath different blocks, masterminded by 'Wings' Day, and several attempted escapes. Of the major breakouts, first there was the so-called 'Wooden Horse' and then the notorious 'Great Escape' where 47 or 50 (the record is unclear) defecting officers were shot by the Germans in June, 1944, including Hardy's friend Roger Bushell.

Perhaps he drew a long straw, or just not being a Key Person, Hardy luckily, did not qualify for any escape party. His morale-boosting genius was better employed within the camp — where, poor soul, he remained until released in May, 1945. He walked home across Europe, playing his old wind-up gramophone.

His dreams had been of becoming a painter and of 'living in a cottage with a studio in the Tregaron hills, surrounded by trees'. It was not to be quite like that. He continued in the RAF for a while, flying Tempests in Silt, north Germany, and in Scotland. But his health was affected. He became ill, underwent major surgery and was invalided out. He nevertheless joined the RAF Voluntary Reserve and was promoted Squadron Leader.

Hardy McHardy died in 1962, aged 44, leaving a widow, Nobby, and son, Graham. He is buried in the little churchyard of the Holy Trinity, near his family homes of Maerdy House and Taliaris Park.

His talent for graphic design and painting, allied to his sociable habits, combined to earn him a casual living in later life designing and painting inn signs. The cortège bringing his body back home from Bath for the funeral halted to rest awhile and refresh the undertakers at a public house outside Brecon, the Old Ford Inn. The hearse stood under the sign for an hour. It had been, ironically, his first commission in that craft.

Squadron Leader DB Hardy McHardy was one of 'the Few'. A casualty of war, not killed in action like his father and their comrades, but sacrificed; not a hero for the number of enemy casualties he inflicted but a hero for the way in which he 'did his bit' and with admirable modesty.

Lynn Hughes. Adapted from *Life and Times of a Modest Hero*,
Carmarthen Journal, January 1991

5. RHYS GRYG

Firstly I will make for the court of Deheubarth,
towards the true chief of princes.
I will go, in my glory, to Rhys son of Rhys,[1]
attacker in battle, heir of Cadell.
Itinerant bards make for his court,
a much-frequented place, to seek generosity.
You have attacked Rhos – devastation of (their) shelter
and Pembroke with the greatest triumph.
You have overcome the French – the troops of Carmarthen.[2]
many a Frenchman in flight;
and made Abertawe a township in tumult,
shattered towers – and today there is peace.
and Sanclêr on shining white lands,
the English are not the people who rule it.
In Abertawe – savage key to England –
its women are completely widowed.

From *Hendregadredd ms*, † early 14th century

6. *Rhys ap Gruffydd*

We crossed the River Tywi in a boat and travelled on to Carmarthen, leaving Llanstephan and Laugharne on the rocks by the seashore on our left. These were the two castles which Rhys ap Gruffydd took by assault after the death of Henry II, King of the English, the garrisons being forced to capitulate. Rhys then ravaged the provinces of Pembroke and Rhos with fire and sword, completely devastating the whole neighbourhood and besieged Carmarthen, but failed to take it. Carmarthen means the town of Merlin, because, according to the *Historia Regum Britanniae*, Merlin was discovered there as the offspring of an incubus.

This ancient town is enclosed by brick walls, parts of which still stand. It is situated on the noble River Tywi, and surrounded by woods and meadowlands. To the east lies Cantref Mawr, that is the Great Cantref, a safe refuge for the inhabitants of South Wales, because of its impene-

---

1. Son of Rhodri Mawr and ancestor of the Deheubarth rulers.
2. In 1215 Llywelyn Fawr and Rhys Gryg and others took Carmarthen and razed it to the ground. (*Brut y Tywysogion*) Afterwards did the same to St. Clears.

trable forests. There, too, is Dinevor Castle, built on the top of a high hill which overlooks the River Tywi and which is held to be the royal seat of the princes of South Wales. In ancient times there were three royal castles in Wales: Dinevor in South Wales, Aberffraw in North Wales, on the island of Anglesey, and Pengwern in Powys, now known as Shrewsbury. Pengwern means the head of the alder-grove. My pen quivers in my hand as I think of the terrible vengeance exacted in our own times by the King's troops on the subject people of the commote of Caeo in Cantref Mawr.

Giraldus Cambrensis, *The Itinerary Through Wales*

7. WAR OF THE CHILDREN

For their army a field was set
like the field that was for the host of Moses,
and eight banners in the shape of gloves
with three ravens at the very top,
sixty and more helmets,
nine guns as in the great Guisnes.
There were nine wards besides the vanguard
and nine armies unarrayed –
they had long bows
crossbows were bickering,
lions with a host of lances,
and a field host of large battleaxes.
And when the army formed three crescents
on Glasfryn, the father's homestead,
the Duke on the morrow came thither
from the border of Gwent and his host with him,
and the Duke when he heard that the place beyond
was guarded by their armies
sent, of his own accord,
two men to treat with them.
They made the king's brother captain
and dispensed wine to his men,
white wine, gifts all round,
wine there in plenty too,
osey for the Welsh upon the hill,
osey down below for the English.

The grandson of Nicholas saw
the backs of many in fear of their chase.
It is unlikely that an Englishman
will approach Abermarlais from his lair any more.
Merlin the paragon foretold
that in two summers would come about,
and that the ravens of Owen that was
would perform a great work by the seas.
They made battle in every gap,
they would make the battle ever better.
May there be 'Hwi' on the seven peaks of Pembroke,
it has become 'Hey' by now.
The country has come to Elidir's tribe,
may all Rhos join the three shires.
And the heavy hammer of the sons of Thomas
gave their enemies a wonderful tumble,
and perchance they will again
throw down some who may be heavy.

Lewys Glyn Cothi,
The War of the Children of Thomas ap Griffith ap Nicholas

8. *The Collapse of Dryslwyn Castle*

From Grongar Hill on the crest of which, perhaps unknown to Dyer,
stood a Roman legionary marching camp it is only a mile to another
place he knew: Dryslwyn. This tiny hamlet looks upwards at the castle,
which set its deepest mark on history only after the conquest by
Edward I. Its earliest record, wholly Welsh, is of a castle commanding
the Towy from its hill and built to serve the purposes of the Princes of
the South, which were mainly to confirm their power over their rival
Welsh lords. In the 13th cent., it was held by Rhys son of Maredudd,
and this Lord Rhys extended the tradition of Welsh feuding into a
determined effort to overthrow at last the Princedom of the North. He
allied himself with Edward against Llywelyn the Last. What part he
played in the tragedy at Cilmery is doubtful; what ambition he hoped
to serve by his allegiance to Edward can only be guessed – perhaps he
thought he could play a role of allied but independent sovereign such
as had been the good fortune of the Lord Rhys of the days of Henry II.
But he found himself put under the jurisdiction of Edward's Justiciar,

Robert of Tibetot, and everything taken from him but this one castle of Dryslwyn. He refused such an indignity, raised his men, and in 1287 rallied them to the cause of Welsh independence he had three years before betrayed. He captured both Dynevor and Llandovery, avoided an English force, and besieged Emlyn. Driven from this, he escaped to Ireland, returned in 1290, and headed a great army of revolt. But his Welsh peasants were untrained, and he was taken, carried to the King at York, dragged at the tail of a horse, and beheaded. Dryslwyn Castle made his effort possible. It was too strong to be taken by the Earl of Cornwall who beset it, and, when one of its towers was mined, it fell expertly on Lord Stafford and his staff, putting them forever out of action. It stands now, rather like Castell-y-Bere over the Mawddach valley, a melancholy monument to the loss Wales suffered through its internal factions.

Wynford Vaughan-Thomas & Alun Llewelyn.
The Shell Guide to Wales 1969

9. LAMB OF PEACE

On Dryslwyn hill its mighty days
  Remain in ruins like a ghost,
    The hill where clashed the Baron's host
A little lamb has climbed to graze.

J. T. Job

10. *To Agincourt*

It is a Thursday morning, June 20, 1415. In the Great Hall of the King's castle at Carmarthen a priest is writing names on a parchment as they are called out. The hall is filled with men: as the names are called each acknowledges his presence. It has been going on like this since dawn, and one man moves impatiently in his seat. It is nearing 10 a.m. and that is dinner time.

This man is the King's Chamberlain, Thomas Merbury. He has been entrusted with the recruitment of archers for the coming French war. Five thousand archers will fight at Agincourt. Of these 240 will be from the county of Carmarthenshire. Merbury knows these men: 12 years earlier some of them, in Owen Glyndŵr's uprising, would have tried to kill him. Nothing sharpens an appreciation of skill so much.

They had taken this very castle in 1403 and, again, with French help, in 1405. The uprising petered out, though it devastated Wales. This is one of the reasons why so many men wait patiently in the hall, that and the fact that Henry V is paying foot archers four pence a day for the campaign. The Statute of Labourers in 1351 fixed ploughmen's wages at *seven shillings a year*.

The men in the hall are being contracted, with that legalistic obsession of the Middle Ages, to go 'God willing, with our most excellent lord the King in his journey into France' for a period of 45½ days.

In the history of archery there can never have been men so highly trained. Archery was the sporting obsession of the day, and these were its finest exponents. In 1346 their fathers had brought down the chivalry of France at Crécy (1,200 men had gone from the county, one of the heartlands of the bow), and again in 1356 at Poitiers. They can shoot bows with draw-weights of between 80 and 120 pounds (the modern composite bow is between 30 and 40), and release 15 aimed arrows a minute so that the sky turns black. They can wound at 150 yards, their long bodkin spikes brushing mail aside as though it were paper. At 50 they can send their great clothyard shafts up to the flights in a charging horse.

As they stand in the hall they look ready for anything. Some lean on their bows as they wait. One or two are in mail, many in brigandines, quilted jackets with iron plates sewn into them. They wear stockings of wool and long hooded cloaks. Their belts bulge with daggers and swords.

Since Crécy these men have walked through Europe, awestruck by its cities and great cathedrals, sleeping as rough as tramps, boozing, living off nuts and berries; and the heavy armoured cavalry that has dominated European history for a thousand years, since the Goths rode down the Roman legions at Adrianople in 378, has melted before them.

In Europe no knight in the early 15th century goes to war as an archer. It has never happened before in the technology of war that its most devastating weaponry is in the hands of the most deprived elements of its population. A moment like this will never come again.

The strange thing is that the names of the men in the hall stand out from the anonymous poverty of the Middle Ages. In the Public Records office in Chancery Lane there is a document heavy with seals and covered with the spiky brown hand of mediaeval bureaucracy which lists them. You look on something that the man wrote down one July

morning in Carmarthen five and half centuries before. The parchment
has survived.

Most names and patronyms (surnames were not common in Wales
until the middle of the 16th century) Richard ap Gruffydd of Caeo;
Little Evan of Iscennen; Jenkyn ap Henry and David Thomas of Llanstephan; Philip Bennett of St Clears; Thomas Cooke and Philip ap Adda
of Laugharne. The surnames are those of English colonials in the boroughs.

None of the heralds, those sportswriters of the Middle Ages, will
record these names. They are outside the rules of chivalry. No one would
have bothered to take these prisoner, for such men have no money for
ransoms. They would have been ridden down like chickens by proud
French lords like the Dukes of Alençon and Bar who did not ride home
from Agincourt.

Byron Rogers,
from *The Telegraph Sunday Magazine*

11. TO AN OLD REBEL

What would they make of you,
Henry Gwynn, this St David's Day,
the stalls an upturned blur
of middle-aged applause
for the English Royal Box?
What *would* they make of you?
Five hundred and seventy years ago
you fell at Agincourt.
No great death, nothing
to nudge the chroniclers and leave
you rampant in eternity.
The Towy estuary was far
from that damp field, and your
high castle of Llanstephan.
It is only a lawyer's hand,
a spiky brown, commends you
to our notice, confiscating
your estate because you died,
trampled with the thousands in the mud,
at Agincourt, on the French side.

Byron Rogers

12. *Glyndŵr Excitement*

'For as much as I say I may not spare any man from this place away from me to certify neither my king nor the lord my prince in the mischief of the countryside about, nor no man pass by anyway, hence I pray you and require you that you certify them how all Carmarthenshire, Kidwelly, Carnwaltham and Yskenyed were sworn to Owain yesterday. And he lay tonight in the castle of Drosselan with Rhys ap Griffith and there I was on truce and prayed for a safe conduct under his seal to send home my wife and her mother and her train but he would not grant me. This day he is about Carmarthen and thinks to abide there until he may have town and castle; and his purpose then is to go into Pembrokeshire for he holds sure all the castles and towns in Kidwelly, Gowersland and Glamorgan for the same counties have undertaken the siege of them until they be won.

'Excite the king's advisors that they should excite the king here in all haste to avenge himself on some of his false traitors he has cherished overmuch and to rescue the towns and castles in these countries for I dread full sore there be few true to maintain them.'

John Skydmore, *Letter* to Lord Faireford
from Carreg Cennen Castle

13. HENRY AP THOMAS AP NICHOLAS

They invite Englishmen every January,
to the south across the sea
and woe to them who accept the invitation.
I do not know that one will be protected.
Merlions of Abermarlais
will plant two seals on an Englishman's skull.
No man will come to the Black Mountain alive
from England without being maimed.
Harry will allow no adventurers
nor a York churl nearer than Leicester,
nor England nearer than Lugg,
nor the men of the March to Carmarthen again.
Harry has a thousand soldiers
like the grey sons of Lear,

a thousand bows, a thousand steels,
thousands and more of swans,
a thousand guns, six thousand men,
ten thousand more of lancers
three positions, three banners of three armies
press in the face of Jesus.

Three armies would go to the old earl,
three wards to the bull from Urien,
three languages will be the rescue of our language
May God give Harry three lives.

Lewys Glyn Cothi,
from *In Praise of Henry ap Thomas ap Nicholas*

14. *Cromwell at Golden Grove?*

A popular tradition, which personally I very much doubt, relates that
Cromwell went out of his direct route to spend a night at Golden Grove
near Llandilo, the seat of the leading Royalist in South Wales, Richard
Vaughan, second Earl of Carbery, celebrated as the patron of Jeremy
Taylor. This legend further relates that Lord Carbery, who was then
living quietly in retirement, on learning of Oliver's approach, fled to a
neighbouring farm-house, where he remained in hiding until his unwelcome visitor had departed. Still further the story proceeds to add
that a year or two later Cromwell sent his unwilling host a present
of some deer from the royal parks, but with what object he did so is
not clear, unless it were to be considered as a belated return for Lord
Carbery's involuntary hospitality.

Herbert M. Vaughan.
Trans. Hon. Soc. Cymmrodorion 1937

15. *New Cambriol*

In 1616 Sir William (Vaughan) obtained a sub-grant of land from the
'Company of Adventurers to Newfoundland'. This was a commercial
enterprise headed by Sir Francis Bacon, to whom James I had granted
authority to colonise the island. Vaughan's territory lay on the south

coast of the curiously-shaped eastern part of Newfoundland. It included Cape Race. Naming this area Cambriol as a compliment to his native land, he felt certain that here was the new country 'reserved by God for us Britons'. John Guy of Bristol, himself a Newfoundland pioneer, had hailed the venture in verse:

> New Cambriol's planter, sprung from Golden Grove,
> Old Cambria's soil up to the skies doth raise,
> For which let Fame crown him with sacred bays

In 1617 Sir William sent a number of Welsh colonists of both sexes to Cambriol, at his own expense. He had intended to sail with them to settle permanently there. But ill-health prevented him from leaving Wales. During 1617 he met Sir Richard Whitbourne, a man of considerable experience in colonisation, and offered him the governorship of Cambriol. Whitbourne accepted, and in 1618 he departed to Newfoundland with another group of emigrants. Two ships undertook the voyage, one carrying the settlers, the other engaged on a fishing expedition, but also conveying stores and equipment needed by the colonists. Unfortunately the fishing vessel was waylaid by one of Raleigh's captains who had turned pirate. The loss of this ship and its cargo was a severe blow.

When Sir Richard and his newcomers arrived, they found that the original settlers had made very poor progress. Little had been achieved in any direction. The new Governor, in fact, decided that the earlier emigrants had been thoroughly lazy and shown much lack of pioneering initiative. So he sent all but six of them home again.

This loss of manpower compelled Vaughan to hand over the northern part of Cambriol to Lords Falkland and Baltimore, two other pioneers, who agreed to look after it until things improved. In 1622 Vaughan himself sailed to the colony with more settlers and supplies. During the three or four years he stayed there it appears that he spent more time in writing *The Golden Fleece* and other works than in galvanising his colonists into hard work. He returned to England to arrange for the publication of these books, and went back again to Cambriol in 1628.

In fairness to the colonists, it must be said that they had to face persistent enemies who wantonly destroyed much of their property, and so wrecked their chances of prosperity. These were pirates, corsairs and privateers who preyed on the islanders. Perhaps worst of all were the ruthless French and other fishermen of the Grand Banks, who hated the settlers because of their encroachment upon their waters. Canada was in the hands of the French. Crops and buildings were set on fire, trees mutilated, havens blocked and fish-drying sheds broken up.

In 1626 Sir William reported that the damage done in pillage and destruction amounted to £40,000 and that, in addition, his colonists had lost a hundred pieces of cannon.

A further blow was the Arctic winter of 1628, though the Cambriol people did not suffer as severely from cold and scurvy as Lord Baltimore's settlers further north. But Sir William was still undaunted. He returned to England in 1630 to settle his own financial affairs. He wrote, that for all he could see, he would have to rely upon his own resources to support Cambriol until the colony 'be better strengthened'. At the same time he made great efforts to persuade his brother-in-law, Sir Henry Salusbury of Denbigh, with 'some gentlemen of North Wales' to join him in Newfoundland where, he said, they would be greeted with open arms. But though he made them grants of land there, not one Squire responded to his call.

A further instance of Sir William's far-sightedness is to be found in the medical handbook which he published in 1630. This was entitled *Newlander's Cure*. It contained information and advice designed for colonists on the preservation of health, with curious prescriptions for sea-sickness, scurvy and numerous other ailments. This book makes him a pioneer also in the adaptation of medical knowledge, such as it was then, to the special needs of emigrants.

The Welsh atmosphere of Cambriol is clearly indicated in its title, together with other place names like Vaughan's Cove, Golden Grove, Cardiff, Pembroke, Cardigan, Carmarthen and Brecon. These names appear on John Mason's map of Newfoundland published about 1622.

It is uncertain whether Sir William returned to the colony after 1630. In view of the persistent depredations of pirates and the fierce antagonism of the men of the French fishing fleets, it was becoming more and more difficult to establish Cambriol as a self-supporting concern. The founder's resources no doubt were becoming severely strained, and he appears to have had no financial backing from any of his fellow countrymen. Finally, the gallant pioneer, now approaching sixty years of age, had to abandon his cherished dream of a prosperous New Wales some time between 1630 and 1637.

In 1637 the Privy Council was officially informed that the efforts of pioneers like Sir William, Lord Baltimore and other 'men, ingenious and of excellent parts', had failed. A new monopoly over the whole island was granted to another Newfoundland adventurer, Sir David Kirke, though trouble with the fishermen and the pirates continued throughout the 17th century.

It would be difficult to find a nobler tribute to Sir William Vaughan than that written by Dr E. Roland Williams: 'Whatever Vaughan's shortcomings – and they were many – at least the crime of the unlit lamp and the ungirt loin is not to be laid to his charge. He spared no pains or sacrifices in his attempt to realise his ambition, and his devotion to his ideal burns with a clear light through the mists and fumes of those eccentricities and absurdities which were also part of his character . . . Before Vaughan had been laid to rest in the little church in the valley of Llangyndeyrn in August, 1641, the silent, primaeval wilderness was already erasing, slowly, but relentlessly, all the signs of his strivings and sacrifices.'

On the island itself, the Welsh place-names have long disappeared, and apart from the name 'Newfoundland', which, some years ago, at any rate, denoted a farm or two in the mid Tywi Valley, there is no memorial left of this courageous pioneer. He was a man whom Carmarthenshire should be proud to honour.

A. G. Prys-Jones, *The Story of Carmarthenshire*

16. *Jac Tŷ Isha: Rebecca*

John Hughes was the twenty-four years old son of farmer Morgan Hughes of Tŷ Isha farm near the mining village of Tumble. His two brothers and five sisters were aged between five and fifteen and the family was one of the most respected of the district. It was no secret among his neighbours, though, that this strong and intelligent young man was very active in the Rebecca movement, for who was not among the struggling farmers of the Gwendraeth Valley? And he took it seriously, even to the extent of training his horse to remain steady under fire, with the enthusiastic help of his mother Mary, who held the bridle while John fired his shotgun. Morgan Hughes, on the other hand, was rather less happy about his son's involvement.

Riot by proxy was by now well established in the Gwendraeth Valley, for when the farmers did not wish to go gate-breaking themselves – after all there was the corn harvest to be gathered now – they would employ their labourers and servants and local colliers to do it for them.

The going rate for riot by proxy was also well established: half a crown a man, and provide your own powder and shot. At more than a quarter of a collier's weekly pay of nine shillings, a few night's work for Rebecca could be quite profitable, even allowing for the expense of powder and shot, so there was no shortage of takers. In fact the colliers soon had the measure of the farmers' dependence on them and began making demands of their own. At one of their night meetings for instance (at Llangyndeyrn, two or three miles from Pontyberem) on Monday, 14 August, the 'Colliery Rebeccaites':

> . . . came to resolutions that inasmuch as they had assisted the farmers in the reduction of rents and turnpike tolls, they should now call upon them to reduce the price of butter and other agricultural produce and insist upon the publicans reducing the price of beer.*

But for the night of Wednesday, 6 September it was a farmers' Rebecca, John Hughes (or Jac Tŷ Isha as he was better known) who donned his mother's copious nightgown and straw bonnet, blacked his face, loaded his brace of pistols and, at about ten o'clock, mounted his horse (the only white one in the party) and led the ride to Pontarddulais and Hendy.

The group swelled as mounted men rode in from side roads and wayside farms and as others were brought from their beds – some at gunpoint – and forced to disguise, arm, and saddle their horses. But however they came – whether for their half crowns or forced along, or simply because they were true God-fearing, justice-seeking devotees of Rebecca's cause – all were soon infected with the thrill of the march as horns blew, rockets streaked into the sky and men talked excitedly of past exploits. And spirits *were* high because they had become used to riding without serious challenge, except, as some laughingly recalled, by the Lion of Porthyrhyd on being roused by his sixtieth lash!

It was a clear night, brightly illuminated by a full moon, and Chambers, Scott and the soldiers of the 76th, walking in single file behind the roadside hedgerows towards Hendy, had their first intimation that Rebecca was out when they saw the trail and starburst of a rocket above the hills towards Llanon. As they drew near to Hendy Bridge the sounds of horns drifted over the night air, and assuming that the Rebeccaites were riding straight for Hendy, Chambers split his force, leaving Payne and six soldiers to block the Llanelli road and taking Captain Scott and fourteen other soldiers on to the bridge, where they lay in the hedge-row, guns loaded and primed, and waited.

On the far side of the river, Captain Napier, his seven policemen and the three magistrates, were nearing the end of a wearying ten or eleven mile, two and a half hour trek, walking their horses across the fields from Penllergaer, during which they had seen the rockets and heard distant gunfire over in Carmarthenshire. It was about ten minutes to one when they arrived in the field four or five hundred yards on the Swansea side of the toll gate, from which Napier planned to launch his attack, and it was there that they heard voices and the sound of many horses' hooves. The police and magistrates could only guess what was happening, but what they were hearing were the sounds of a hundred and fifty men, nearly all on horseback, riding past the Red Lion Inn, the home of Griffith Vaughan still on bail for gun-running for the Bolgoed rioters, and crossing the Loughor Bridge.

Suddenly Rebecca shouted 'Come, come, come' and there was a great fusillade of shots as her daughters buried their felling axes in the spars of the gate and applied their crowbars, hatchets, pickaxes and sledgehammers to the toll house. Napier ordered his men to secure their mounts in the field and waited for a few minutes until he judged that the Rebeccaites were fully occupied with their work of destruction. And then he led his party on foot from the field, and, giving the order 'Fall in', placed them in line abreast across the road.

So preoccupied were the Rebeccaites (some of whom were also on the Swansea side of the gate) that they did not know the policemen were there until Captain Napier cried 'Stop!' At once, three of the mounted men who seemed to be the leaders wheeled their horses and galloped full tilt at the police. One, whose white horse distinguished him from the crowd, aimed his pistol at Napier and fired. He missed, and Napier, pointing to him and calling to his men 'Mark that man', shot his horse and at the same time shouted 'Fire!' The shot horse reared up, spun around three or four times and threw its rider, while the line of police and magistrates, firing as one, sent a volley of shot whistling across the gate and into the crowd. The Rebeccaites fired a massive volley in return – but immediately broke in panic amid the frightened rearing and neighing of horses flailing about in all directions, the yells of equally frightened men, the ragged crackle of unaimed gunfire and one more crashing volley from the police and magistrates.

But with a hundred and fifty men and nearly as many horses pressing back onto the bridge in total confusion there was panic and chaos for some ten minutes before defeat turned into rout. Captain Napier was still struggling with the dismounted Rebecca leader who had shot at him. He was just gaining the upper hand when he was struck over the head from behind and rendered momentarily unconscious, but Sergeant Jenkins, turning around and seeing his chief fall, fired his pistol at a yard's range and shattered his opponent's arm. The sergeant was too busy disarming another horseman to chase the wounded man as he headed back to the bridge on foot, but Constable John Price saw him running by and seized him. 'Let me go, let me go my good fellow,' he cried, holding his bleeding arm in evident pain. 'You have broken my arm already.' 'Where did you get it broke?' asked the officer. 'Over yonder, at the gate,' said Rebecca. Price arrested him and he gave the officer his name – John Hughes of Tŷ Isha.

Two men had thus been secured, and a third (later identified as John Hugh) was captured by Constable Thomas Jones who saw him fire his shotgun in the volley fired by the massed horsemen when challenged by Captain Napier. The officer saw him throw down his gun, wheel his horse and join in the great press of men and horses heading for the bridge, and he pulled him from his horse and arrested him.

Eventually the jam on the bridge began to clear, and the fugitives galloped and ran back into their native Carmarthenshire, scattering in all directions, heedless of the cries of the wounded and spurred mindlessly on by the homing instinct of the panic-stricken. They galloped and they ran back into those hills until breath could carry them no further.

William Chambers and his infantrymen listened with some apprehension as the sound of volleys and fusillades of gunfire carried clearly over the half mile from Pontarddulais for a good ten minutes. Having no idea that there was anyone at Pontarddulais to oppose the Rebeccaites and that the gunfire signified a battle, Chambers thought it was merely the sound of an unopposed attack and that when it ceased it would very soon be Hendy's turn.

All this was only the work of a few minutes and since the main body of the Rebeccaites had still not appeared Chambers gathered his troops and marched them along the road towards Pontarddulais in order to intercept them and keep them well away from Hendy gate. It was then that they heard the thunder of hooves. They fixed bayonets, spread out across the road and in the light of the moon they could just distinguish the horsemen only yards away as they reined and formed into line abreast. The foot soldiers' fingers tightened around their musket triggers.

For their part, the mounted men saw a line of figures armed with guns barring the road ahead and, to a smart order, they drew their swords, pointed them to the front and spurred their horses. But the order 'Charge!' froze on the lips of their leader as he suddenly recognised the line of men facing him as red-coated infantrymen. And in the same instant, William Chambers, Junior recognised his opponents as cavalrymen.

Thus did Her Majesty's 4th Light Dragoons and 76th Regiment of Foot come within an ace of setting a bloody seal on that night of confusion by fighting the first battle between British soldiers on British soil in two hundred years!

When the combined force of cavalry and infantry reached Pontarddulais it was all over. They found the gate reduced to matchwood, the tollhouse gutted and partly demolished and Captain Napier and his men in possession of a large collection of tools and weapons and several wounded and abandoned horses. They also had three black-faced, dejected and bloodstained prisoners – Jac Tŷ Isha, David Jones and John Hugh – sitting manacled on the ground by the ruined and shot-peppered tollhouse, still wearing their Rebecca disguises.

Jac Tŷ Isha was in considerable pain with a pistol ball lodged in his upper arm, to where it had travelled from his shattered elbow, while David Jones seemed to be in danger of dying from three sword cuts on his head and a number of pistol balls and shot pellets in his back. All three were taken to Swansea by an escort of dragoons and Jac Tŷ Isha and David Jones were put into the prison infirmary. John Hugh's less severe injuries were attended to by the prison doctor before he was put into a cell.

It was at the prison that Jac Tŷ Isha was searched and what was found on him identified him beyond doubt as Rebecca, the leader of the attack. He had powder and ammunition on him of course, but he also had two incriminating pieces of paper bearing handwriting in Welsh. One, a note signed 'Becca', was addressed to Daniel Jones, Brynhir (in Llanon), telling him to 'Come with all to assist to Jac Tŷ Isha Wednesday night next, or you will have no further notice.' The other, addressed to 'Mrs Becca', was wrapped around five shillings in coin and, though its message was garbled, later events would show that it contained a threat to the gatekeeper at Hendy.

Pat Molloy, *And They Blessed Rebecca*

17. *An Encounter with Rebecca*

The locality we were now traversing is one of the most untamed and desolate in either Division of the Principality; it has indeed with perfect truth been called the 'great desert of Wales'. Vast sweeping ranges of hills with rounded tops, add to the dreary aspect of this nearly un-peopled region; and the cottages or 'shielings' you very rarely fall in with, are wretched and primitive in the extreme, scarcely affording shelter to the rude but hardy peasantry from the inclemency of the weather. If human habitations are scarce, churches are few and far between, the parishes being of considerable extent; and it is, we believe, a fact that in some parts the inhabitants have to travel from eight to ten miles to church or chapel.

The portentous stillness that prevailed around was unbroken by the slightest sound; not a living creature was visible, except a few scared sheep, which, unused to the sight of the stranger, scampered off, utter-ing that peculiar shrill bleat or whistle which *Welsh* sheep always emit when suddenly disturbed. It is the signal of danger amongst them; and it is amusing to observe when the note is sounded by some patriarch of the flock, how they start, and dart away at the top of their speed. Our guide, after proceeding apparently almost at random for several miles, brought us at last to the edge of a hill, at the foot of which we observed a thin blue column of peat smoke proceeding from the rude chimney of a solitary farmhouse; and we at once joyfully hastened to make acquaintance with its interior, for by this time the heat and fatigue we had endured during the day rendered it necessary to obtain, if possible, some refreshment. The exterior of the dwelling was miserable and primitive enough, but quite in keeping with the desolate appearance of the surrounding scenery. Amidst the barking and yelping of curs, that evinced a great desire to be more familiar than agreeable, we entered a dark smoky apartment with a great turf fire blazing on the rude hearth, over which a huge iron cauldron was suspended, the contents of which were to form the evening supper for the family. It consisted of what appeared to be a mess of flour and milk, resembling what is called 'furmenty'. The farmer rose at our appearance, and, in the language of the country, bade us welcome. He was a tall, hard-featured man, with the true Celtic cast of countenance, clad in a threadbare, blue, home-spun coat, corduroy continuations, and dark blue woollen hose – the usual costume of the Welsh peasantry. Our stock of Welsh being limited, we were obliged to have recourse to the 'Saxon' dialect, which we found our host understood sufficiently well to comprehend our wants. *Bara a caws*, bread and cheese, *ymenyn*, butter of excellent quality, and some home-brewed *cwrw*, were speedily produced; and the appetizing effect of a long walk through the 'incense-breathing' air of the mountains added not a little to the zest of the repast. Our wants being satisfied, we produced a case of cigars, and handing one to the farmer, we were highly amused at his awkward attempts to smoke it; after which we asked him the news of the country. 'Deed to goodness,' said he, 'these be strange times; yes, indeed, we have lately had several "Rebecca" riots; and it was only this morning that a large party of "Rebecca's" men had been chased from the vicinity of Llandovery by a troop of dragoons hastily sent for from Brecon. The soldiers did not arrive, however, until one of the toll-gates had been destroyed.' We had before heard of the exploits of 'Rebecca' and her followers; but we were not aware at the time that the insurrection had extended so far to the eastward. This news, therefore, rather damped our ardour, as a rencontre with a band of these lawless desperadoes would be far from agreeable; and there was every reason to believe, from the farmer's account, that several of these bands were outlying in this neighbourhood. When, therefore, we expressed our intention of proceeding to Llandovery that evening, our host earnestly endeavoured to dissuade us, as several travellers, he said, had recently been attacked, robbed, and in some cases ill-treated. However, we determined to proceed at all hazards; and trusted to get to our quarters at the 'Castle Hotel' without molestation. It was also probable that the reports which had reached the farmer's ears might have been much exaggerated . . .

After partaking of a parting glass with our host, and dispensing with the further services of the guide, we prepared to resume our journey. The evening was exceedingly fine and serene, although from the heat of the day, the far-folded mist began to envelope the mountain-tops, and as it might possibly descend and spread over the lowlands, we deemed it a matter of precaution to obtain the services of one of the farmer's sons to guide us to the head of the dingle, which we understood led down to the river Towy: once there, there would be no further difficulty in finding our way, as the path runs through the gorge until it reaches the Llandovery road.

After heartily shaking hands with the farmer, and wishing him '*Nos da i chwi*' Anglicè, 'good night to you,' with many thanks for his kindness and hospitality, as we were passing out of the house, one of the sons came to us and made a demand of 'one shilling and a half,' in

Welsh, '*un swllt a chwe cheiniog*,' in payment of the bill. The charge was moderate enough, but we felt hurt and surprised at the demand, so contrary to the time-honoured observance of Cambrian hospitality; however, we pocketed the affront without any observation. The name of this vupary habitation is Blaen-Twrch-Uchaf; it stands in one of the most naked, desolate situations we had ever seen. With the assistance of the farmer's son, we now made tolerable progress across a wild bog, which in winter must be almost impassable. It was nearly eight p.m., and the twilight was rapidly approaching. Our companion, a raw, ignorant lad, was shy and taciturn, partly arising, perhaps, from his entire ignorance of English, and all attempts to draw him into conversation were of course useless. Before our departure, we had foolishly paid his father in advance for his services, and the young rascal, aware of this, after proceeding for about two miles, suddenly left us in the lurch, pointing in 'dumb show' with his hand something after the fashion of the countryman and the fox the direction we were to take. Although we shouted and halooed to urge him to return, he was deaf to entreaty, and bounded away with the speed of a roebuck. We were now left in a pretty 'fix'; the more so, as the fog was rapidly increasing in density, and began to enfold us in its chilly embrace. There was now no time to be lost, every minute was of consequence, as the increasing gloom would soon prevent any trace of the route from being seen. The moon, we knew, would rise in an hour or two, and, at the worst, we must endure for a time exposure to the raw chilly fog, which increased in density every moment. Thanks, however, to the invigorating effects of the *cwrw*, we felt tolerably fresh, and pushed on at our best pace. After walking for nearly an hour, we at length perceived, to our great delight, the opening of what appeared a woody dingle or gorge, this we were certain must be the one we were in search of. Previously, we had certainly felt rather nervous at the prospect of a night's lodging on the wild hilly waste a not very enviable position to be placed in. We now hastened on, and soon came to the head of the gorge, and got into a precipitous path leading down it, well clothed with coppice wood. Presently we heard the rippling of water, at the bottom of the dingle, and we knew we were safe: soon afterwards, the distant barking of a dog assured us we were again in the vicinity of a human dwelling. How cheering is such a sound to the solitary wayfarer! It absolutely revels in his ears like distant music, and dispels in a moment the gloom and depression which had previously come over him. As near as we could guess, we had still six or seven miles to walk before we could reach our destination. The stream we were following, we had reason to believe, was the Dothie, one of the tributaries to the Towy. To the left of us lay Capel Ystrad Ffyn, and we were in the immediate vicinity of 'Twm Sion Cati's Cave'. The wild country we had left behind is called the 'Forest of Esgob', and on referring to a map, it will be seen there is not the name of a place laid down for eight or nine miles. This region, from its name, was probably covered with wood in ancient times.

Soon after we resumed our march, we got clear of the mist; the moon had risen, and by the light of her silvery rays we were now enabled to follow the path with ease and safety. We were much impressed with the magnificent scene before us, and the fragrant odour of the honeysuckle and sweetbriar, covered with bright dewdrops, sweetly perfumed the air, as we leisurely surveyed the exquisitely beautiful glen through which we were silently wandering. Well may the 'land of the gorges' be called one of the *gems* of Wales. At length we got into a road, and commenced anew to accelerate our progress. We had proceeded for about two miles, when we suddenly heard what seemed to be the sound of human voices; but a sharp turn in the road prevented us from seeing very far ahead. 'Rebecca' now suddenly flashed across our mind, and for an instant we were undecided whether to advance or retreat. With as much self-possession as we could muster, we paused for a short time to deliberate as to the best course to adopt. We were unarmed, but to retreat at that hour of the night appeared simply impossible. Should the sounds proceed from an outlying band of Rebeccaites, it was highly probable we should be stopped; as it was reported they had on several occasions lately, levied 'black mail' on such unlucky individuals as had fallen in their way. They had also recently, we had reason to believe, had a skirmish with the soldiery, and it was likely that their 'Welsh blood was up'. Such and similar ideas flashed across us, and we now fervently wished we had taken the farmer's advice and remained at Blaen-Twrch-Uchaf for the night. We blamed ourselves for undertaking such a rash freak as to walk at night unarmed and alone, whilst the country was in such a disturbed state. However, it was now too late to repent or indulge in vain regrets, and we at length determined to brave the encounter, if to such it came, in the best way we could. Our plan was to walk quietly on until we could, unobserved, reconnoitre the enemy, and then to rush past them at the top of our speed. We had now nearly reached the turn of the road, and halted for a moment to listen again for the sounds that had so lately arrested our attention. We could hear nothing, however; all appeared as still as death, save the gentle murmuring of the neighbouring river. As soon as we had cautiously reached the turn, a scene presented itself which required all the nerve we could muster, and for a moment had nearly upset our self-possession. We found ourselves in the immediate presence of the dreaded 'Rebecca'. Within less than twenty paces, at least twenty tall dark-looking figures lay basking in the moonlight on the road-side, prepared, as we supposed, to dispute the road with every passer-by. We had come upon these men so silently, that we must have taken them by surprise as we rushed past with head-long speed. We were tolerably agile then, and being in good training, we managed to get over the ground with marvellous celerity. At first we fancied we heard the sounds of pursuit, but we soon discovered that it proceeded from an over-excited imagination; and by the time we had reached the bridge leading over the river, we discovered no signs of 'Rebecca'. Here, as well as we can remember, the mountain road joins the regular turnpike road to Llandovery. To our great relief, we soon afterwards heard the sound of horses' feet rapidly approaching, and presently an orderly and two other mounted dragoons came up. They halted as soon as they perceived us, and we then gave them information of what we had seen. We found, from their account, that it was quite true there had been a toll-gate riot on the previous day, and several parties of Rebeccaites were supposed to be still lurking in the neigh-bourhood. These men were out on patrol. Having thanked us for the information we had given, they trotted off towards the scene of our encounter. What were their subsequent adventures we never heard. The sequel is soon told. We arrived safely at our quarters about half-past twelve a.m., mentally resolving henceforth to avoid the perils of a lonely walk at night amongst Welsh wilds, and more particularly, to be careful in avoiding for the future another interview with 'Rebecca'.

John Henry Cliffe. *Notes and Recollections of an Angler* 1860

18. *The Sacking of Carmarthen Workhouse*

Monday proved to be a glorious June day. In the early hours small groups were to be seen coming from the hill farms and the villages and merg-ing on Newchurch, at a spot where the roads from Tre-lech, Talog, Blaen-y-coed and Conwil joined. Soon the narrow lanes were thick with people. The magistrates were now aware of what was going on, and J. Lloyd Davies, to give him his due, had the courage to ride out to

Newchurch accompanied by Captain Evans of Pantycendy, the blustering opponent of the tithe and the poor law, but they failed to dissuade the crowd from proceeding. They had to listen to a list of grievances regarding the tolls, the tithe, the poor law and church rates, which the Rebeccaites were determined to lay before the magistrates. The two men did succeed in persuading them to leave their firearms behind, and these were stacked up in a house in Newchurch. Then, having formed up in some sort of order, the vast concourse moved on, and entered Carmarthen appropriately by the Water Street gate. First came the band; then the men on foot, one of them bearing a placard with the words: 'Cyfiawnder a charwyr cyfiawnder ydym ni oll' (Justice, and lovers of justice are we all); then the horsemen. As is usually the case, it is difficult to determine the numbers present, but a conservative estimate would place them at three hundred on horseback and two thousand on foot. Among the former, John Harries was conspicuous. Contrary to popular tradition, only one rider was disguised; possibly he symbolised Rebecca. He wore a woman's clothes and had long ringlets of horsehair. The future historian, Alcwyn Evans, was present, as a boy of fifteen, watching the procession. As the fantastic horseman passed he winked at the boy, who recognised him as Mike Bowen of Tre-lech.

The behaviour of the crowd was quite orderly, and the route taken entirely discounts the theory that an attack on the workhouse was intended. For the procession turned westwards towards Picton's Monument, where it was joined by a contingent from St. Clears, then went down to the Quay, came back up Castle Hill, went along Spilman Street and around St. Peter's Church, on to the Cross (Nott's Square), and into the Guildhall Square. It had thus perambulated the whole town before reaching the Guildhall, where the resolutions were to be presented to the magistrates.

But here things got out of hand. The procession had been joined by unruly elements from the town who poured out of the congested back alleys and the slum houses along the quay. Many of them were fishermen who, on occasion, had had a taste of workhouse fare. These linked arms at the head of the procession and led it on to the workhouse. There they called on the frightened master to surrender his keys in order to let all the paupers out, and he complied. The mob then rushed into the courtyard and broke into the house. Frances Evans, a farm servant from the parish of Newchurch, who had recently given birth to her illegitimate child in the workhouse, led them in. She did a wild dance on a table in the hall as she urged the men upstairs. The noise was deafening as they shouted and smashed the furniture and threw the bedding out of the windows, while the children screamed in terror in the schoolroom. Suddenly there came a cry: 'the soldiers are here'.

For the dragoons were on their way to Carmarthen under the command of Major Parlby. They had been misdirected at Pontarddulais (possibly intentionally) and this had caused them some delay. But a despatch from William Chambers, senior, informed them of what was taking place, and they rode on furiously through the broiling sunshine. They galloped over the bridge and up into the town, scattering the amazed bystanders. A local magistrate had joined them. It was long remembered against him that he had shouted to the dragoons to 'slash away' and that Major Parlby had told them to take their orders only from him. Their arrival at the workhouse led to a scene of indescribable confusion. The mounted rioters stampeded wildly up Pen-lan Hill behind the workhouse. Others, including John Harries, were trapped in the courtyard. Some scrambled over the walls, abandoning their horses, which they were afterwards afraid to claim, and among these was Mike Bowen, with his curls in his pocket. The board, with its noble device 'Cyfiawnder', lay symbolically trodden underfoot by the dragoons. Hundreds of demonstrators scattered in all directions, over hedges and ditches, through fields and woods. Fifty years later, the widow of Michael Bowen had not forgotten her husband's ashen face when he returned home.

In the workhouse yard the horse of one of the dragoons fell dead from exhaustion, and another died the following day, for they had covered the last fourteen miles in an hour and ten minutes. While the soldiers rested, the magistrates immediately began the examination of some sixty prisoners taken in the workhouse. They committed a number to gaol while others were bound over to appear if required. At the Summer Assizes a true bill was found against twelve men, but their trial was deferred and they were remanded on bail. Among them was John Harries, and it is noticeable that his bail (£200 with two sureties of £100) was twice that of the others. It was not until the following Spring Assizes that they were brought up for trial with the other Talog rioters, when Lloyd Hall and Hugh Williams appeared for their defence. Harries was then sentenced to a year's hard labour, and five other men to eight months' hard labour, but the remainder were discharged. For by that time the authorities were taking a very lenient view of the disturbances.

David Williams, *The Rebecca Riots*

19. *Class Hatred in Carmarthen*

They say that the class-war is a product of modern Bolshevism and world-wide restlessness, but it certainly existed in Carmarthen town in the 'eighties. It was really an adventure of perilous possibilities for the large family coach to pass through Priory Street, the long thoroughfare that enters Carmarthen from the Abergwili side. Old George, the coachman, really dreaded it, I know. Two or more of us boys were usually seated in the rumble behind, and we had to bear the brunt of the running attack made by the wild unwashed urchins who pursued the carriage, shrieking, swearing, spitting and throwing mud at it as it passed along the street. When we rode our ponies into town, we had to run a veritable gauntlet of young ragamuffins bent on frightening our mounts and doing us some vague injury. The walk into Carmarthen by the mill-leet was almost as dangerous. On one occasion I was struck in the forehead by a large stone hurled by a lusty youth. Down I went to earth like a nine-pin, but fortunately the cad felt alarmed by the success of his shy and ran away. In a very short time I had a bump the size of an egg on my forehead and a splitting headache, but otherwise I was none the worse for the assault. But I never walked alone into Carmarthen after that. Perhaps it will be thought I am exaggerating; but I assure you I am not. I remember one day the county-court judge, Mr Beresford of Alltygôg, was hit in the eye by a stone thrown by a St Peter's boy (as they call those born at Carmarthen within sound of St Peter's bells). And on another occasion, a snowy winter's evening, the closed carriage was passing through Priory Street bearing my cousin, Miss Gertrude Lewis-Lloyd, on a visit to Bryn Myrddin. As the vehicle neared the Old Tree a huge snowball filled with a sharp, jagged stone was flung with great violence at the carriage, breaking both windows and just missing the lady's face by a few inches. Even the mild optimism of my grandfather was upset by this incident. I remember his handing round the formidable-looking missile next day for our inspection at breakfast, before he despatched it with a note of remonstrance to the Mayor.

Herbert M. Vaughan. *The South Wales Squires* 1926

20. *Latter-day Pirates*

Below Llechryd Bridge however, where the river is classified as tidal, there is no restriction and five pairs of coracles are worked on a part-time basis in the picturesque Cilgerran gorge. The coracle men there use both the traditional, armoured coracle net and the now illegal set nets for catching salmon. The gorge is an ideal place for using illegal equipment, for it cannot be reached by road or footpath. A newspaper

report, for example, notes that for the period June-October 1969, 81 illegal set nets laid by 'latter-day pirates' were removed from Cilgerran gorge. The set net (*rhwyd fach*) is a single unarmoured net 18 feet to 50 feet long, usually of fine mesh attached to the river bank by means of a light stone, and the other end is spread out as far as it reaches into the river. Lead is fastened to the foot-rope and corks to the headrope. The net is usually placed in the water by a coracle man and it can only be used in fairly still water. 'Although corks are attached to the top of the net,' says the 1971 *Report of the South West Wales River Authority*, 'there are sufficient weights on the bottom to sink the net below the surface.' In 1970 over 100 of these illegal nets were removed by water bailiffs dragging the river at nights.

J. Geraint Jenkins, *Nets and Coracles*

X

Work & Play

1. *Devils in Goggles*

I had been travelling for some miles through the soft Carmarthenshire country when, topping a hill, I saw lying before me a black town with smoke over it and chimneys rising above long streets of grim, slate-roofed houses.

Wales is so beautiful and so unspoilt that one's first industrial town is rather a shock. This town looked like a crazy intrusion. It stood up, rather horrible and gaunt, but all round it was open country. I passed groups of men in blue suits with cloth caps on their heads and neck-cloths round their throats. The mark of the town was on them. The stamp of the machine was on them. I stopped one group in order to hear their accent . . .

We talked about weather, work and industrial depression; and I was impressed, as I was to be impressed so often in South Wales, by the gentle manners and the air of good-breeding which distinguished these men. Certain industrial areas in England which have shut out all beauty from the lives of men have, not surprisingly, bred a sullen and unpleasant type of worker, but these Welshmen were quick, intelligent, well-spoken, humorous and kindly. So much I could tell in five minutes. And looking back on this, my first meeting with the South Wales worker, I realize that my first impression was accurate.

*   *   *

It is about 10 p.m. The town of Llanelly is going to bed, but the Steel Works which feed the Tin-plate Works are well on into the night shift. You can see the glow of its furnaces for miles. There are four furnaces in a row. When their doors are lifted for six inches you back away and hide your eyes from the white heat of the liquid steel.

The men who tend the furnaces look like devils as, grasping long shovels, they move about, pitch-black against the orange glow. A queer thing that might have flown in the darkness straight from hell glides and twists about like some immense bat. It is an electric furnace feeder. It runs on overhead rails, and is driven by a man who guides it among the assembled devils with the skill of a taxi-cab driver in Piccadilly.

At the end of the feeder is an object rather like one of the big hydraulic buffers from Euston Station. The feeder swings round to where a line of railway wagons has deposited a pile of scrap metal – bits of battleships, perambulators, iron bedsteads, and all manner of worn-out things. The buffer picks up an iron cage full of metal, the feeder swings round and glides to a furnace, the door opens, the heat comes leaping out, the battering ram slowly enters the inferno and gently tilts the metal into the seething horror of white-hot steel.

For one moment you see a slab of armoured plate, a bit of bedstead and a bicycle wheel trying hard to maintain their identities in the heat; then slowly they lose colour, sink, and are lost in the bubbling steel . . . So a furnace accepts a mouthful of food.

'We're going to tap No. 1 Furnace . . . Come along and see it!'

At the end of the line No. 1 Furnace is ready and waiting. I am given a pair of blue glasses. The devils who creep cautiously up to within twelve yards of No. 1 Furnace also wear blue glasses. No man could face the open door and gaze with unprotected eyes on a bath of sixty-five tons of molten steel.

Through the glasses I see a moving, bubbling cauldron of white-hot soup. The steel is boiling. Sometimes great chunks like pink icebergs fling themselves out of it for a second and sink again. The thing is like a star in flux, like matter being forged in heat, like the beginning of a world. When the surface of the steel is even it ripples like a pond. Breaths of something hotter than heat seem to pass trembling and shuddering over it. Now and again horrid, obscene eyes open and shut on the steel pond, winking terribly, soundlessly.

A devil in goggles creeps to the furnace with a twelve-foot pole. He thrusts it into the steel. He moves it about. He withdraws it. A sample of the steel is taken and examined. Yes; the furnace is ready to be tapped.

At the back of the furnace men are working in terrible heat to release the sixty-five tons of steel. It will run down an inclined way into a huge cauldron. Through the darkness of the immense steel works glowing red-hot ingots, weighing twenty-four hundredweight, go swinging through the air. Over to the right you can see a red-hot rail shooting backwards and forwards under the rollers.

'Stand back, there!'

Suddenly the darkness is lit by a brilliant light, showers of sparks arch themselves, and a hissing stream of liquid steel comes gushing from the furnace to fall into the cauldron. As it spills over the iron rim of the cauldron it looks like pinkish milk; as it settles it is a beautiful incandescent tangerine colour. The power locked up in it is terrible. If it disobeyed the devils in goggles and burst its red-hot banks, we should be dead or maimed for life in two seconds. The heat of it as we stand twenty yards away is almost unbearable.

The molten steel rises slowly in its giant pot. A scum forms on it. Sparks skate over it. Bubbles of steel open and shut their eyes. The stream of red-hot metal ceases. The sparks give one last firework display and sixty-five tons of steel for salmon tins have been safely decanted . . .

Through the darkness fly the cranes bearing red-hot obelisks. At any moment something molten may fly out of the night and miss you by yards. Now and then, just as you are about to put your foot on something, you recoil, feeling a breath of heat on your face.

That is a steel works at night.

H. V. Morton, *In Search of Wales*

2. *Gocses and Shol*

The cockle gatherers of the Burry Inlet start from their homes on the ebbing tide and this may well be before dawn breaks. Fleets of rubber-tyred carts make their way through the village streets and across the inhospitable, windswept salt marshes towards the beach, a distance of two miles or more from the villages. The journey across the beach may be one of considerable peril, especially at night or in foggy weather. The rapidly flowing streams or 'pills' that flow across the beach may be treacherous and can spell doom to horse, cart and cockle gatherer.

Each woman after arriving on the beach selects her section and begins to gather cockles. There are no set rules as to where the cockle women pick the shellfish: anywhere will do as long as it is not in front or behind another picker. Cockle picking is entirely a hand process and the picker is armed with a small knife with a curved blade about six inches long that is used in the right hand to break the surface of the sand, thus exposing the cockle beds. The knife, which is often shaped from an old sickle blade, is known as a *scrap* in Penclawdd and as *y gocses* in Llansaint and the handle of the tool is either bound with twine or a piece of rag to make it more comfortable for use. In the cockle gatherer's left hand is a hand rake (*cram* in Penclawdd, *rhaca gocs* in Llansaint). This is used for drawing together the cockles into heaps and for this the rake is usually transferred to the right hand. The heaps are then transferred to a sieve or riddle that is placed slightly behind but between the legs of the gatherer. It will contain, sand, empty shells, as well as live cockles. The sieve with a mesh of ¾ inch is then shaken back-wards and forwards and from side to side, so that all undersized cockles fall through the mesh. The sieve has a diameter of about 18 inches and is wired like an oblong-meshed builder's sieve; that is generally preferred to square-meshed sieves. Most of the equipment required by the cockle gatherers is locally made. The *scrap* is usually shaped from an old sickle and the blade turned to an S-shape under the heat of a fire, while the *crams* are made by blacksmiths; each one made specifically for an individual cockle woman. Although ordinary builder's sieves are used today, until about thirty years ago the sieves were made by the cockle women themselves or by specialized sieve makers (*gwilodwr* – *gwaelodwr* – bottomer in Llansaint). Baskets for carrying cockles and for washing them were, until recently, produced by village craftsmen, while the sacks used for carrying the cockles from the beaches were obtained from local farmers.

After sieving cockles, the shellfish are washed in a convenient pool or 'pill' and the harvest placed in sacks ready for transporting back to the village. When donkeys were used for transport, the sacks had to be sewn with needle and twine to prevent the fish from spilling out on the journey back from the beach. Two bags of cockles were slackly sewn together and slung over the donkey's back and the gathering equipment was then placed on top of the sacks for transporting. Although donkeys are still used by the Llansaint women mainly because the beaches of the area have much soft sand (*trath shinc*), at Penclawdd carts are used exclusively for transport. A few two-wheeled carts were used by the Llansaint women for transporting cockles from Ferryside beach in the 1920's but they were soon abandoned as unsuitable.

The life of a Carmarthen Bay cockle woman is not an easy one, for she has to be out on the beach in all weathers and at all times of the year. Constantly bending over a cockle bed is tiring work and the shaking of the sieve to get rid of sand, empty shells and undersized fish demands considerable energy. The old cockle women always wore many layers of clothes: an elastic edged cap or 'pixie' covered with a shawl (*shol drath* – beach shawl) tied around the neck ensured that the head was protected. A sack apron was considered essential and this was inserted between the legs and pinned at the back and had the appearance of a pair of trousers. Woollen cardigan, one or two flannel shirts, woollen underpants, a shirt and one or two flannel petticoats with knee boots completed the ensemble.

J. Geraint Jenkins. *Cockles and Mussels from Folk Life*,
Vol. XV, 1977

3. THE COLLIER

When I was born on Amman hill
   A dark bird crossed the sun.
Sharp on the floor the shadow fell;
   I was the youngest son.

And when I went to the County School
   I worked in a shaft of light.
In the wood of the desk I cut my name:
   Dai for Dynamite.

The tall black hills my brothers stood;
   Their lessons all were done.
From the door of the school when I ran out
   They frowned to watch me run.

The slow grey bells they rung a chime
   Surly with grief or age.
Clever or clumsy, lad or lout,
   All would look for a wage.

I learnt the valley flowers' names
   And the rough bark knew my knees.
I brought home trout from the river
   And spotted eggs from the trees.

A coloured coat I was given to wear
   Where the lights of the rough land shone.
Still jealous of my favour
   The tall black hills looked on.

They dipped my coat in the blood of a kid
   And they cast me down a pit,
And although I crossed with strangers
   There was no way up from it.

Soon as I went from the County School
   I worked in a shaft. Said Jim,
'You will get your chain of gold, my lad,
   But not for a likely time.'

And one said, 'Jack was not raised up
  When the wind blew out the light
Though he interpreted their dreams
  And guessed their fears by night.'

And Tom, he shivered his leper's lamp
  For the stain that round him grew;
And I heard mouths pray in the after-damp
  When the picks would not break through.

They changed words there in darkness
  And still through my head they run,
And white on my limbs is the linen sheet
  And gold on my neck the sun.

Vernon Watkins

4. *Maws and Rennets*

Cheese. – The Britons probably learnt the process of cheese-making from the Romans;* the Welsh term, *caws*, and the Irish *caise*, implies it. The Welsh *ymenyn*, the Cornish *manyn*, and the Armorican *amanen*, are terms quite independent of the Roman *butyrum*, or the Greek *boutyron*, which seems to have been used by them more as a medicinal liquid, than an article of culinary utility.

The cheese of South Wales is mostly for home use, and made from skimmed milk. The agent in curdling the warmed milk consists of various preparations of calves' maws, called by the Welsh *cywair* (rennet).

In most parts the mawskins are prepared by the butchers: cleaned, but not washed with water, salted, and dried upon a twig bent in the shape of a paper kite; and sold by them according to the size, from 1s. to 2s. each. Part of this dried skin, in proportion to the quantity of milk to be curdled, is put to soak in warm water over night, to be used next morning.

The rennet is prepared in various ways; the best mode I found, is: To clean well the maw, then return the curdle taken out of the maw, into its old situation, with a handful of salt, and new milk: in one day after-

---

* Strabo, if we recollect well, accuses the Britons with being *barbarians*, because at the Roman invasion, they were not acquainted with the art of making *cheese* (G.M.).

wards boil a gallon of water, and put therein a sufficient quantity of salt, with a glass of brandy: the rennet is to be deposited in this pickle for use. – *Vale of Towy*.

Gwallter Mechain, *Agriculture in Wales*, Vol. 11

5. *Lime Kilns*

The limestone quarries of Carmarthenshire have always been primarily concerned with producing limestone for burning or for use in building or road metalling. The industry, with one or two exceptions, was made up of small lime-burning units which suffered recurring periods of depression particularly during the 1920s and 1930s. In parts of the county there is evidence of ventures which failed to survive in the ruins of lime kilns.

The parish of Llandybie in Carmarthenshire has had long associations with lime burning which stretch back to the building of castles within a few miles of the parish during the twelfth and thirteenth centuries. At the beginning of the nineteenth century it was described as the 'prevalent manure' which was '. . . furnished in largest quantities by the quarries at the western extremity of the Black Mountains, in the parishes of Llandeilo fawr and Llandybie'. At this time, too, lime was generally used for whitewashing the exteriors and interiors of buildings in the area.

About the middle of the nineteenth century improved methods of farming and the coming of railways led to an increasing demand for lime, and lime burning developed on a large scale one mile to the north-west of the centre of the town. The first kilns at Cilyrychen were designed by an ecclesiastical architect, R. K. Penson. The foundations were laid in 1856 and the design of the structures which followed was true to the architect's style. By 1900 there were nine kilns in operation. They were built into sloping ground to facilitate their charging from above.

Carmarthenshire generally, abounds in ruined lime kilns. During the nineteenth century many kilns were built to burn limestone which was so easily available in outcrops. When the costs of working the raw material began to rise it became the practice to abandon the site, choose another, and build new kilns closer to the limestone. There are, therefore, the ruins of many 'typical' lime kilns in the county. In 1964 a member of the South East Wales Industrial Archaeology Society decided that an example of this industrial structure, which is also found in its 'typical' form in other parts of Wales, should be recorded. The site is near the village of Banc-y-Mansel a distance of about seven miles south-east of Carmarthen.

D. Morgan Rees, Industrial Archaeology in Wales

6. *The Black Ox Bank*

This bank, which has always been locally known as the 'Black Ox Bank', on account of the notes having been embellished on the left hand side with an engraving of a Welsh black ox, was established in Llandovery in 1799 in premises known as the King's Head, where it remained for many years. Its founder was David Jones, the great-grandfather of Mrs Davies-Evans of Highmead, co. Cardigan. He was the son of Evan John, a farmer near Llandovery, and was one of a large family. David Jones had, therefore, to rely almost entirely on himself, and the result of his enterprise and industry is a striking example of what has been done, and still can be done by steady application to business. He started business at the early age of 15 years. He later on married Anne, the daughter and heiress of Rhys Jones of Cilrhedin, who brought her husband a fortune of £10,000. This portion in conjunction with the capital he had already made, enabled him to found the bank at Llandovery in 1799. He was then about 40 years of age, and the enterprise

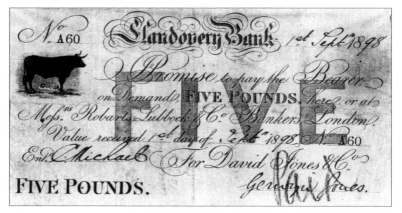

under his auspices proved a profitable venture. He was justice of the peace for co. Carmarthen, and in 1825 was sheriff of the same county.

After the death in 1839 of David Jones (the founder of the bank at Llandovery), the banking business was carried on by his grandsons, the sons of John Jones. The elder brother, David of Pantglas, continued the Llandovery Bank, while his brother William and John respectively, founded branches at Lampeter and Llandilo, under the title of 'David Jones & Co.'

The Black Ox Bank was one of the earliest banks established in Carmarthenshire, and in the number of its branches exceeded the scope of any of the other private banks of its period in the county. Its career, although it was no doubt affected by the financial crisis in 1825, was remarkably prosperous, and this is clearly indicated by the fact that its founder, David Jones, although he started with little more than the proverbial half a crown, yet at his death left a considerable real estate, besides £90,000 in Consols and £50,000 in cash at the bank. There was probably no bank of its era which enjoyed more local credit than the Black Ox Bank. A story has been handed down which strikingly illustrates the confidence placed in it. At the period when runs on banks were occurring all over the country, a timid client entered the Black Ox Bank to withdraw his money. The bank, in anticipation of a run, had just received a consignment of Bank of England notes, and the cashier on receiving the cheque handed over to the client Bank of England notes for the amount. The depositor, however, refused to accept the notes tendered, and demanded instead notes of the Black Ox Bank.

Francis Green, *Transactions of the West Wales Historical Society*

7. *School Holidays at Bryn Myrddin*

I doubt if there is a more *historical* view in all South Wales. Southward, Carmarthen town stands out conspicuous in the valley with the stumpy tower of St. Peter's against the skyline, and from the top of Merlin's Hill itself one can see Llanstephan Castle outlined against the sea. Just below the drive one catches glimpses of Abergwili Palace and the attractive pools called the Bishop's Pond, where as boys we used to fish by the hour for perch and tench. Here I spent many years of my boyhood, and I know I love the sweet vale of Towy better than my native Tivyside. Are not, at least to a man, the scenes of our boyish holidays the most sacred and precious of all remembered scenes? The luxuriant pastures, the woods filled with bluebells, the little trout streams, the meadows of hay where the corncrake complained all night, the trim Carmarthenshire farms, these are the things my memory loves to dwell on.

A great joy it was to be called very early on some dark morning in the Christmas holidays, to eat breakfast by candle-light, and then to ride in the wan foggy atmosphere of the breaking dawn up to some moorland stretch, where a band of squires and farmers was collecting for a day's sport. Sackville Gwynne, of Glanbrane, then living in Quay Street, Carmarthen, was always a prominent figure at these gatherings with his beloved greyhounds. Almost as exciting was a big shoot of rabbits on Merlin's Hill, which adjoined the grounds of Bryn Myrddin. On these occasions we used to help the keeper and our elders by catching the wounded rabbits or by knocking them on the head with our sticks. Once a school-friend, a town-bred boy, stayed with me at Bryn Myrddin and participated with gusto in one of these rabbit drives. At the opening of the following term it was the custom for us all to write an essay, 'What I did in the Summer Holidays'. So my friend filled his essay with a highly coloured account of the rabbit-shooting on Merlin's Hill. Our housemaster, a sentimental Radical of the Manchester School, was disgusted beyond words at the bloodthirsty description. – 'And pray, sir, where did all these horrors take place?' he demanded angrily. 'Oh, when I was staying with Vaughan!' came the innocent reply. And my house-master, who had never liked me, henceforth hated me in consequence with an unending hatred.

Herbert M. Vaughan.
The South Wales Squires 1926

8. CYWYDD TO DISGRACE A MILL

Here is a cywydd to disgrace a mill

The blessed nobleman, merry thick-naped,
from the religious house of jovial men,
made a harsh complaint, the treasure of a proud muse:
God, no man was born of like fame;
you are a brave and valiant poet,
with every good quality I hear of:
there is to you a mill in Cydweli:
it is little profit to claim it.
For what reason, without proof,
did you assert that I, a man of consequence,
from the sad virgin, on a hill yonder,
did get to know of your toll and did deceive you?
The hand-mill used to crush it,
but it does not crush as much as the crow would chew;
and it was my oath, and my hand,
which I could take at the feet of Elli,
that not half the corn of my crop
was coming to it,
nor white barleycorn, nor ears of wheat,
nor rye, woe that which would be in its state;
nor equal share or portion of oats,
nor small peas, nor beans a month since,
nor flour, nor one florin
in its part, more than a cupful to us.
For two months, if you were fated to be
with your bed on its roof,
it is unlikely, by Derfel, that you would see
it making grey the hairs of your hat:
nor dust there, we testify,
nor blemish on a pleat of your gown,
nor hearing, nor seeing the form
of a chaff-heap, nor the sound of women.
Where there was the sifting of wheat,
there is green clover and dew;
the wild garlic is where the stream was,
my lord, along its dyke;

there is matter, not from the grains of the corn,
as a mound about its spindle:
the two stones are as tranquil
as trees that would be on its wall.
You are strong, may you utter a word,
that it get three ages of the dry land.

Ieuan Tew, † *Llanstephan* ms 134, 183

9. *Danyrallt Timber*

'The barn at Danyrallt above the house is so old, that there is no tradition when it was built, but Thomas Lloyd the Admiral's Grandfather raised the walls and put on the present roof. There used to be a high square tower adjoining it, under an arch of which was the S.E. entrance to the upper floor of the barn. The upper part of the tower was used as a Dove Cot. The Admiral removed this tower entirely. Vaughan Lloyd cut the timber upon Tir Mawr and Cae Bychan farms and he cut Allt y Meibion on the demesne and sold the trees for £1500 which money he lost cockfighting in Glamorganshire. Llwyd Dewi grove was cut by Mr Vaughan of Golden Grove (who sold the farm to Admiral Lloyd) when Jack Twmas Sion was about 18 years old and the trees were sold to James Thomas, grandfather of the present tenant (James Jones 1840). The old Grove Allt y Meibion extended formerly from the Penylan road down to the private road from Cae Llyn Llygad to Danyrallt and reached as far as the old Clump of Scotch firs in Cae Yscybor, and was cut and sold by Vaughan Lloyd to Rees Jones tanner of Dolgarreg with the above mentioned timber. The Admiral then caused the roots to be taken up and the ground to be enclosed and planted as it is now, which work H. R. Lloyd, Clerk, repaired and renewed with entirely new hedges of which thorn and hazel and fresh trees where there were blanks (1835 and 1836). Cae Dafydd Ddu wood was planted about 10 years after Allt y Meibion and the beech upon the demesne in the hedges were planted seedlings by Jack Twmas Sion in the bottom of the Orchard whence they were transplanted out to their present sites. The Silver and Scotch firs (except those which stood in Cae Yscybor) were brought on horseback from Rhyd Odyn by the tenant of the Velin Isaf and planted in Coed y Felin Issaf Coed Croftau and Allt y Meibion when Jack was 9 or 10 years old. The two poplars in Cae Main were planted (about the year 1780 by the Admiral's gardener who lived at Bryntwedog [now destroyed]. The horse chestnuts (one only of which is now standing, the smallest of the lot) were planted in Ystradaufach by Vaughan Lloyd.'

The above Memoranda were taken down from the old man's mouth* in 1835-1836 by Rev. H. R. Lloyd and copied in here from the original papers in 1840.

Francis Jones, *Arch. Camb*, 1972

10. *Nigarly at work*

Pontarlleche July 2nd 1827

We the under named do agree to and with Benjn Brigstock agent to Mr Wm Bottomley Mirchamb of London to Remove and Convey the whole or as much as he may wish to send of the Oak Timber Bought by him of John Wm Lloyd Esq. in the Parish of Llangadock from the place where they now lay unto such wharf or wharfs or other landing places as Mr Bottomley or his agent may Direct at Carmarthen at and for the sum of ten pence per foot Girt Measure, and we do allso agree to draw such trees as Mr Bottomley does wish to have sided to the saw-pits, and also where the trees do lay so as the Hewers cannot conveniently

---

* Jack Twmws Sion.

hew them we also agree to draw them to such places as they can hew them and to do this so as the Hewers does not lose their time By our neglecty into the above named ten pence per foot, to the true performance of all those Covenants we bind ourselves Severaly Collectively and Seperately under Penalty of one Hundred Pounds each, and to continue Nigarly at work till the whole of the work is finisht.

Witness to the reading and fully	Thos. Jones his	✗	mark
Explaining of all the Conditions	Benjn Jones his	✗	mark
Here in Contained and allso to	Griffith Jenkins his	✗	mark
the	John Parry his	✗	mark
Signing here of			

Benjn Brigstock

it is allso agreed that the same shall be settled for every month. But that five Pounds shall be left in hand to each Team till the whole of the work is Compleated to be paid by Bills at two months as witnessed and signed by the above names.

Benjamin Brigstock. *Agreement for timber hauling at Danyrallt* 1827

11. *Loggers at Pibwrwen*

The river Towy, which borders the western side of our parish, was much used for shipping during the last century, and consequently the inhabitants of Croesyceiliog and the farms along the river bank had a great deal to do with this form of transport.

Ships passed up and down, transporting miscellaneous cargoes of tea, sugar, flour, etc., to the store-houses on the Quay-side of Carmarthen. Steamers on the other hand, with a heavy cargo of timber, were too big to go all the way up to the Quay-side; the furthest point available being 'Pwll-du', a deep whirlpool near Pibwrwen. Here the steamers stopped, and the logs were thrown on to the bank. Later they were tumbled to the river to form rafts. The skilled men in charge could be seen jumping from log to log, pushing them with their poles to move them on, until at last they reached the Quay-side of the town, where there was a large Saw-mill on William Joseph, the Timber Merchant's, yard, on our side of the Towy.

Ethel M. Davies, *The Story of Llandyfeilog Parish*

12. *Ship-launch at Abermarlais*

After keeping the gate for three years I took a lease in Llandeilo Fawr and built a house, which I got licensed as a tavern for my daughters to keep; I myself went on carrying wood as usual. Now it happened that the merchant at Abermarlais had built a small ship of about thirty or forty tons. He had built it in the wood about a mile and a quarter from the river Tywi, which was capable of floating small vessels as far as Carmarthen. However, it was made too heavy to be drawn to the river in the manner in which the man intended it should. He had resolved that the people should drag it there by way of sport, and had caused proclamation to be made in the parish churches that on such and such a day a ship would be launched at Abermarlais and that food and drink would be given to everyone who should come to lend a hand in the work. So there were broached four hogsheads of our measure in Denbigh, but two of the southern measure, and a great ovenful of bread was baked, and plenty of cheese and butter bought and meat cooked, for the more respectable people. The ship was provided with four wheels, or rather four great rolling-stocks, fenced about with iron, with great big axle-trees in them, and well greased against the appointed day. I had been loading in the wood that day, and sending the team forward I stopped to see the business; and a pretty piece of business it turned out. All the food was eaten, all the drink drunken to the last drop, the ship drawn about three roods and then left in a deep ditch. By this time night was coming on, so the multitude went away, some drunk, some hungry for want of food, but the greater part laughing as if they would split their sides. As for the merchant, he cried like a child, bitterly lamenting the act of folly which he had committed, and at length told me that he should have to take the ship to pieces before he could ever get it out of the ditch.

I told him that I could take it to the river, if I could but get three or four men to help me, whereupon he said that if I could but get the vessel to the water, he would give me anything I asked. He earnestly begged me to come the next morning if possible. I did come with the lad and four horses. I went before the team and set the men to work to break a hole through a great old wall which was, as it were, before the ship. We then laid a piece of timber across the hole, from which was a chain to which the tackle, that is, the rope and pulleys were hooked. We then hooked one end of the rope to the ship and set the horses to pull at the other. So the ship came out of the ditch prosperously enough;

and then we had to hook the tackle again to a tree which was growing near, and by this means we got the ship forward. But when we came to soft ground we were obliged to put planks under the wheels to prevent them sinking under the immense weight, and when we came to the end of the foremost planks we put the hinder ones before and so on, and when there was no tree at hand to which we could hook the tackle we were obliged to drive a post down to hook it to. So from tree to post it got down to the river in a few days. I was promised noble wages by the merchant, but I never got a farthing in the end but promises and praises. Some people came to look at us and gave us money to get ale, and that was all.

Twm o'r Nant, † Autobiography

13. Blow The Wind Southerly

The Towy is one of the best rivers in the principality for angling, not only because its banks can be approached without the usual intercessions which on the banks of other rivers too often interrupt the sportive step of the angler, but for the quantity of its fish, which consist of Salmon, Sewin, Trout, Eel, Pike, Lamprey, Carp, Tench, Perch, Flatfish, Minnows, and an occasional intruder such as the Sturgeon. It can be angled from its source to the sea, and would be one of the most prolific rivers in Europe if properly preserved.

> When the wind is in the South
> It blows your bait into a fish's mouth,

and when a cloudy day sets in with a fair breeze, a fine basket of fish is to be met with.

William Davies (Gwilym Teilo),
Llandeilo Fawr and Its Neighbourhood

14. Gwernogle Leopards

While fishing this stream (the Marlais), in the summer of 1828, the author experienced a pleasing instance of the simplicity of manners and genuine hospitality that distinguishes the peasantry of the agricultural districts of Wales. In crossing the mountain, at the foot of which the Brechva stream murmurs over its rocky bed, and precipitates itself in a hundred little cascades towards its junction with the Cothy, he was espied by a farmer, apparently engaged in collecting his cattle, that had strayed over the unbounded right of pasture attached to the mountain farms. The temptation of examining a stranger, obtaining an insight into his pursuits, destination, &c. was too strong to be resisted in a country where so little occurs to interrupt the monotony of rustic life, and where the dress and appearance of an Englishman furnishes conversation to a whole district for many days. The man, accordingly, quitted his occupation, and with hasty strides came up, just as we had cast our flies upon the surface of a beautiful little pool, the basin of one of those tiny cascades just mentioned. The first throw was successful; a brace of trouts, yellow as gold and spotted like a leopard, rose, one to each fly, or rather sprang out of the water and caught them ere they fell. The simple Welshman, delighted at this capture, and at the dexterity with which he considered it was effected, left his cattle to wander *ad libitum*, and solicited permission to carry our fishing-pannier and landing-net, and in fact, remained until evening; by which time the former contained an excellent dish of fish. After being regaled at his farm on some excellent substantial fare, we presented the contents of the basket to his children, and continued our route to Brechva; with difficulty escaping from our host's pressing invitation to pass the night and the next day under his roof.

As the angler, when in this neighbourhood, will be compelled to sleep at Brechva, he will do well to sally forth, before sunrise, the following morning, and fish the Cothy (which runs about a quarter of a mile from his inn), just at the spot where these united streams flow into it. He cannot fail of sport; there are always trout, and salmon too, on the feed there: as he passes through the meadows, he will see the former, in the pools of the brook, a dozen together.

George Agar Hansard. *Trout and Salmon Fishing in Wales* 1834

15. *The Tank Pool*

Although the M and M was remarkably free from any accident throughout its history, still Mr Jones had some thrilling experiences in his time. The greatest undoubtedly was when the boiler of his engine, the *Carmarthen*, burst at Maesycrugiau in the year 1890. He was working a mineral train at the time . . . The force of the explosion may be gathered from the fact that 12 cwt of the boiler was blown 400 yards into the River Teify where it is still to be seen when the river is low. The chimney was hurled into the fifth waggon from the engine. Mr Jones and his fireman had miraculous escapes, their injuries being slight. Mr Jones' cap was blown off his head and he never saw it again.

The implication that the driver and firemen were in the immediate vicinity when the explosion occurred contradicts the stories told locally – for 90 years after the event, people still talk about it as if it had happened the day before yesterday. One version is that they were having a sly drink in the nearby pub when the boiler blew up. Another, more colourful yarn is that news reached their ears – and they were both keen fishermen – when a friend was playing a big salmon in the river below. They ran to the scene, neglecting the engine with its banked boiler in their excitement. To this day, the spot where the boiler plunged into the river is known as Tank Pool.

Herbert Williams, *Railways in Wales*

16. *Sturgeon at Towy Castle*

In days gone by, farm labourers and other men in the neighbourhood spent much of their spare time fishing in the Towy, and the most frequent catch was a type of flat-fish known as 'Fflwcs'. The method of catching them was by stabbing the fish with long-handled forks or spears. On one occasion, back in June, 1896, when the late John Davies, New Inn, was out fishing with some friends from the Rhondda, they were greatly startled at finding a large, cartilaginous sea-fish beating in a shoal near Towy Castle. Discovering that it was a sturgeon, they called for assistance, and a number of coracle men came with all possible speed. The tide was out and the water shoaly. Throwing their nets over the fish, they attempted to capture him, but he broke three nets and upset two coracles. Then the men jumped forward, took a firm grip of the royal visitor's tail, and succeeded with much effort in dragging him ashore, although the fish still struggled for a considerable time. With infinite trouble, ropes were put round his head and tail, and the monster towed. The huge fish was placed on the roof of an outbuilding at Croesyceiliog, so that the villagers could inspect him. Then it was taken to Mr Bland Davies' shed on the Quay-side for exhibition at a trifling charge. On being measured, the fish was found to be 8 ft. 4 ins. in length, and 3 ft. 4 ins. in girth, whilst its weight was 320 lbs. It was exhibited to a large number during the day, about £7 being taken in coppers by the lucky captures. The following day the carcase was sold for 5/-, and taken to Cardiff for exhibition.

Ethel M. Davies, *The Story of Llandefeilog Parish*

17. *It Came As A Big Surprise*

There is an Angler's Prayer you still come across occasionally, painted on old mugs in fishing inns. It is a bit like a river itself, the couplet meandering towards a tired rhyme:

> Lord, grant that I may catch a fish so
>   big that even I,
> When speaking of it afterwards, may
>   have no need to lie.

This is an account of a man 'an excellent angler, and now with God', as Walton put it, who did just that. He caught a fish so big it would have needed two large men, their arms fully outstretched, to give cynics in saloon bars even a hint of its dimensions.

But he did more than that. He went fishing for salmon one day and caught something so peculiar, so far removed from even the footnotes of angling in Britain, that a grown man who was present ran off across the fields. Nobody would have thought it at all odd that day if the fisherman had been found trying to look up his catch in the Book of Revelations.

It needs a photograph. The fisherman is dead. His friends are beginning to die. If a photograph had not been taken few people would now believe what happened. A hundred years ago, ballads and hearsay would have wrecked it on the wilder shores of myth. As it is yellowing cuttings from the local paper, almost crumbling into carbon, are slowly unfolded from wallets. A print is unearthed reverently from under a pile of household receipts. It was on July 28, 1933, that Alec Allen caught his fish, but even that has been elbowed into myth. His obituary (far from the national press) says that it was on July 9. *The Guinness Book of Records* says that it was July 25. But the one contemporary cutting had no doubts. It was July 28. Appropriately it was a Friday.

Royal Sturgeon, caught by Alec Allen in the river Towy at Nantgaredig, length 9' 2", grith 59", weight 388 lbs. 25 July 1933.

The photograph is extraordinary. Allen, a short man in a Fair Isle pullover and baggy trousers, leans against a wall beside a trestle. It is a typical Thirties snapshot slough. His hands are in his pockets. There is a cigarette in his mouth. But of course you notice all this a long time afterwards, because of the thing dangling from the trestle.

At first it looks like the biggest herring in the history of the sea. It towers over the man by a good four feet. It is a fish certainly, but the head ends in a dark snout. The body appears to be armoured. The surroundings, a farm gate, the field beyond, underline the oddness. In a farmyard a man is posing beside a thing the size of a basking shark. Alec Allen had caught himself a Royal sturgeon in the River Towy, at Nantgaredig, near Carmarthen. It was nine feet two inches long, had a girth of 59 inches, and weighed 388 pounds.

Allen was a commercial traveller from Penarth in Glamorganshire. He was a well known sportsman and hockey referee. In later life he was to referee Olympic matches. But he was then in his early forties, one of that oddly innocent breed who figure in Saki and Wodehouse, but who latterly seem to have become as extinct as the Great Auk, the sporting bachelor. His great delight was fishing, but in him it was more than a delight.

His great friend was Alderman David Price of Nantgaredig, who died last year aged 74. He had known Allen all his life. All they had ever talked about, he recalled with wonder, was fishing.

In 1933 Allen was traveller for a firm of fishing tackle manufacturers. His father, also a great fisherman, was a traveller for a wallpaper firm. Father and son somehow contrived it that they could travel together in the same car. Both their commercial beats were West Wales, but a West Wales wonderfully concentrated between the rivers Wye, Teify and Towy. When their friends talk about the Allens it is with amusement. It was notorious that their business rounds were engineered for fishing.

Off-stage Hitler was ranting, Stalin drawing up lists of victims. Ramsay MacDonald droned his platitudes, and the dole queues lengthened. But in West Wales the Allens went their way, in a car full of tackle and wallpaper, their itineraries perfectly arranged to end in fishing inns beside rivers. The thing has an idyllic quality. It may have been a bit tough on you if your wallpaper shop was nowhere near a river, but nobody seems to have complained. In time the son succeeded the father as wallpaper salesman, but the itineraries did not change.

The two had rented a stretch of the Towy since 1928. This included some of the deepest pools in the river. But the summer of 1933 had been dry, and the water level was low. Walking by one of the pools that July Alec Allen noted enormous waves suddenly cross it. It puzzled him but at the time he would have discounted any suspicion that they had been made by a living thing. After all it was 15 miles to the sea, and tidal water ended two miles lower down.

A few days later Allen returned to the pool. It was evening and he had a friend with him, Edwin Lewis of Crosshands. There was a third man, his name lost to history, watching on the bank. Allen began fishing. It was a quiet evening. But then he felt a slight tug on his line. He pulled on it but to no effect.

Alderman Price was fond of telling what happened next, 'Alec used to tell me that he thought he'd hooked a log. He couldn't see what it was, except that it was something huge in the shadows. Then the log began to move upstream.' A faint smile would come over Price's face.

'Now Alec knew that logs don't move upstream.'

Allen had still no idea of what was in the river. A more imaginative man might have become frightened at that stage. His line was jerking out under a momentum he had never experienced. In the darkness of the pool he had hooked something which moved with the force of a shark.

He played it for 20 minutes, letting the line move out when it went away.

When it came back he retreated up the bank. But there was no channel of deep water leading away from the pool. If there had been, no salmon line made would have held his catch. Then he saw it.

Suddenly the creature leapt out of the water. Maddened, it crashed into a shallow run. It was there under them, threshing in the low water. Allen was confronted by a bulk that was just not possible. The sightseer ran shouting for his life.

But Lewis ran forward with the gaff. He stuck it into the fish, but the fish moved. It straightened the steel gaff. Then the great tail flicked up and caught Lewis, and threw him into the air on to the bank. Just one flick, but it nearly broke the man's leg.

There was a large rock on the bank. Allen dropped the rod (it had been a freak catch, the hook snagging in the fish's head, a sturgeon having no mouth) and tugged at the rock. With it in his hands he waded out, and dropped it on the head, lifting it again and pounding at it.

The creature began to die. The two men looked down at it. Neither had any idea what it was.

But in death it provided them with an even greater problem: how were they to get it out of the river? Allen ran to a nearby farm. There then occurred one of those rare moments which cannot help but be pure comedy. Allen asked could he borrow a horse and cart. The farmer, naturally, asked why. Allen said he had caught a fish.

It ended with farmer, farmer's friends, dogs, horse, cart and all going back to the bank.

'I can remember it now,' said Alderman Price. 'Alec came running to my house. I had never seen him so excited. All he would say was, "Well, I've caught something this time that you'll never beat." I went back with him. They'd pulled it up on to the trestle you see in the photographs, and the news had got round. People were coming in cars and in carts. They were ferrying children across the river.

'It had these big scales, I remember. Very slimy. It was a sort of black and white in colour. No, I wasn't frightened.' He was in the habit of pausing at that point. 'It was dead.'

As the anglers gathered it was determined that the thing out of the river was a sturgeon. Vague memories stirred. Was it not the law that a sturgeon was the King's prerogative?

A telegram was sent to Buckingham Palace inquiring after the King the next day. A stiff little reply came the same day, that the King was not in residence. Such trivia did not deter a man who had hooked the biggest fish in recorded angling history. Allen sold the sturgeon to a fishmonger from Swansea for two pounds ten shillings.

That worked out at something like a penny ha'penny a pound, and this at a time when Scotch salmon at Billingsgate was fetching two and six a pound. More than 40 years later Allen's friends, who had helped him load the thing on to the train, were still bitter about the deal.

There had been so much caviar in the sturgeon that some of it had fallen on to the farm yard where it was eaten by those of the farmer's pigs with a taste for the good life. History does not relate what happened to the pigs subsequently. But selling the fish did get rid of one problem. There were no refrigerators in the Valley, and 388 pounds of sturgeon was a lot of fish.

Allen fished on until his death in 1972 at the age of 77. In photographs the lean figure became stocky. Spectacles were added. Catches got held up regularly to the camera, something he could never have done that wild July night when he was content just to pose beside his fish. So did he consider the rest of his fishing life to be a sort of epilogue?

Brian Rudge, who now runs the fishing tackle firm on whose behalf Allen meandered through West Wales, knew him well. 'I think he saw the incident as more of a joke than anything. He wasn't a man who was easily impressed. I think, you know, that as far as he was concerned it was a bit of a nuisance. He was out salmon fishing. The sturgeon had got in his way.'

Alderman Price heard Allen talk about it a few times. 'It was usually when he heard anglers going on about their catches. He wasn't a boasting man but sometimes he couldn't resist saying, "Well, I suppose this would be the biggest fish I ever caught." And then of course they'd say, "Good God".'

Yet outside the valley and angling circles it was a small fame. There was no mention of it in the national press that July.

It was a small item even in the *Carmarthen Journal*. The august organ rose to its greatest heights of sensationalism. "Two anglers had an exciting time while fishing in the River Towy," the report began.

In March, 1972, Allen died suddenly at the home in Penarth he had shared with a spinster sister. But there was a passage in his will which surprised his friends almost as much as the catching of the sturgeon. Though he had talked little about the incident, he left instructions that his body be cremated and the ashes put into the river at the spot out of which he had pulled Leviathan.

'I called on David Price one day,' said Ronald Jones, the former Chief Constable of Dyfed, and another of Allen's friends, 'and said what a pity it was about Alec. "Aye," said Dai, "I've got him there on the mantelpiece." It was the casket, you see. We were all surprised. Nobody's ever heard of anyone wanting that done before.'

'I suppose it was a romantic touch,' said Brian Rudge, 'but he wasn't the sort of man who'd like people to gather round a grave.'

It was a grey wet day when they put the ashes into the water. A dozen of his old friends, contacted by phone or letter, gathered on the bank. No clergyman or minister had agreed to take part, their religion not recognising a river as consecrated ground.

Despite the hymns in the rain, it would seem to have had pagan overtones. Among the first things a people names are rivers. River gods are the oldest. A man who had pulled out of a river its largest living thing would seem to be assuaging something very old in having himself put back in its place.

'We said the Lord's Prayer,' said the Chief Constable, 'as we committed the ashes to the waters he'd fished for 50 years. But then as the wind carried them I saw a trout leap into the air just where they were drifting.

'And I said to Dai: "Look, Alec's there".'

Byron Rogers.
The Daily Telegraph Magazine, No. 600, June 11, 1976

18. *Bridge Adventure*

Oct 22, 1846

Very High flood. Part of the centring (of Llandilo Bridge) carried off. There were five men on it at the time and they were all precipitated with the falling timbers into the flood. Two were taken out immediately; one got up by a parapet of the old bridge, and one was carried by the river on some of the timbers to Cilsan where they were got out much exhausted.

Thomas Jenkins, Diary

19. *The Carmarthen Eisteddfod c.1451*

The profusion of itinerant bards continued to cause embarrassment to their patrons and, in 1402, during the reign of King Henry IV, Parliament enacted a law to get rid of 'many diseases and mis-chiefs which have happened before this time in the land of Wales by many wasters, rhymers, minstrels and other vagabonds', so that they would not be a burden on the country. Welsh poets were thus classified with vagabonds and beggars and liable to be put in the stocks or thrown into jail. Reputable poets had to find ways and means of protecting themselves against such punishment and this was achieved through a system of graduation and by the granting of licences to go on bardic circuits. Licences were occasionally granted at wedding feasts: Tudur Aled had his first degree as a bard conferred on him at a marriage feast at the hall of Ieuan ab Ithel Fychan of Tegeingl. The licence granted to Gruffudd Hiraethog, bard and herald, to go on circuit was signed by James Vaughan, Hugh Lewis and Lewys Morgannwg in 1546, and is still in existence. But the rules and regulations governing the craft of poetry were formulated at eisteddfodau, such as the eisteddfod held at Carmarthen c.1451, and the first to be described by that name.

The Carmarthen eisteddfod was not so much a competitive event as an occasion for tightening the control over the bardic orders. It was held under the patronage of Gruffudd ap Nicholas of Dinefwr, the most powerful figure in West Wales in the middle of the fifteenth century. One report states that the event was spread over three months at Gruffudd's castle at Dinefwr; others maintain that it lasted two or three weeks and that it took place at the New Town, Dinefwr.

The main prizes were carried off by men from Tegeingl. The prize for the best harpist, a silver harp, was awarded to Cynwrig Bencerdd of Holywell, and a silver tongue was awarded to Rhys Bwtting of Prestatyn, the best singer to the accompaniment of the harp.

Gruffudd ap Nicholas judged the poets and awarded the silver chair to Dafydd ab Edmwnd, a gentleman-poet from Hanmer in Flintshire. Ieuan Llawdden, a native of Loughor, and other poets from South Wales, accused Dafydd of having bribed Gruffudd ap Nicholas, but ab Edmwnd's competence was beyond question. He was not only a master craftsman but also a poet of considerable vision and imagination who sang mostly of love and beauty and, in particular, of the loveliness of women. The nun he compared to a summer moon, with the concealing night her habit:

> I leuad haf ail wyd di,
> A nos gudd yn wisg iddi.

Of him it has been written that 'he touched a word as though it were the leaf of a rose or the string of a harp.'

The chair was awarded to Dafydd ab Edmwnd not so much for the beauty of his poetry as for his revision and modification of the twenty-four metres, which had been established during the previous century by Einion Offeiriad and Dafydd Ddu Athro from traditional forms that had been evolved from the sixth century onward. He introduced further complexities, such as double rhyme in certain metres, and invented two new measures which interlocked rhyme and *cynghanedd* to the point of absurdity and which were hardly ever used except as exercises or tests for poets at subsequent eisteddfodau. He also brought stricter control over the intricate rules relating to *cynghanedd*. The proposals aroused considerable controversy and there were objections to them from the poets of South Wales, but Dafydd ab Edmwnd succeeded in persuading his fellow bards to accept the modifications.

Dillwyn Miles, *The Royal National Eisteddfod of Wales*

20. *The Dowsers of Llanelly*

Now, suppose we admit that the diviner *does* consciously move the rod. There is nothing to prevent him moving it *anywhere*, at *any time*, and under any *condition*; therefore it could not be relied upon as indicating the presence of subterranean streams, and the validity of the rod's action would soon receive its death-blow. But the *true diviner* does nothing of the kind. His love is in his work – the rod is sacred to him. With measured and noiseless tread he enters the vestibule of nature, whose architect and builder is God; whose ceiling is the canopy of heaven, its furniture the grand old forests, the adamantine rocks and everlasting hills; whose ornaments are the winding rivers, the foaming cataract, and the bubbling brooks; its music the song of birds, the hum of the busy bee, old ocean's ceaseless roar, the deep bass of his thunder, and the zephyrs among the stately pines; whose curtains are the clouds, draped in crimson, purple and gold, and tipped with the colours of His glory; whose carpet is woven in the Creator's loom; whose shuttle never ceases its race; whose border is fringed with flowers of every hue; whose messenger is the swift-winged lightning; whose light is that glorious orb the sun, suspended in the dome of the celestial vault, surrounded with myriads of clusters of scintillating stars, the fairy lamps of heaven. He takes his rod, he listens for the call-bell of the crystal stream; he awaits the finger of Nature to touch the key of the fountain of dewdrops, to vibrate the string of the rivulet as it rushes beneath him to old ocean's depths. He watches for the turn of that delicate galvano-meter, whose dial is figured by the Creator; whose indicator points to infinity, greatness, majesty, and power. Finally, he feels the pulsations, the tremblings, the vibrations of the tiny current of this mysterious energy as it passes through the mystic cable – the vast ocean of ether. The message has flashed! He pauses; the work is accomplished. He is satisfied it is correct, knowing that the laws of the Mighty Builder of this enchanting temple *never fail*. He relies on the instrument, whose designer and maker is God; and the monitor within whispers to him in sweet and solemn cadence.

J. F. Young and R. Robertson.
The Divining Rod 1894

21. THE OLD VALLEY

At dawn through the wintry February fog
when Aman's tide was up to its tricks
and the sharp morning breeze about to shear
the woolly mists around the slopes of Garth,
I walked to the mine over the valley road,
my heartbeat as loud as a hammer's thud.

A word with the fireman as I took my place –
'All safe and well at the old coal face?'
Into the level with its network of beams
to walk the longest mile of my life
and arrive lead-footed at the end of the road;
then off with my jacket and shirt and vest,
loud raucous singing filling the air,
as I took pick and shovel to start my shift.

There's a Lass from the Hendy whom I'll win hook or crook
Heave ho! Out with the coal!
Her voice is as sweet as the sound of the brook
Heave ho! Out with the coal!
The sunshine tangles with the tresses of her hair
her footsteps are as lively as the hind on the hills.
Alas! her tongue's sharper than the salt of the sea.
Heave ho! Out with the coal!

The collier from Betws has his eye fixed on her
   Heave ho! Out with the coal!
His love for the lass like an ache in the heart
   Heave ho! Out with the coal!
Paradise for him is to wait her approach
'neath the ash of Hafod by the gate of the grove –
and taste the honey on the lips of his love.
   Heave ho! Out with the coal!

Come all Saints' Day with its mists and rain
   Heave ho! Out with the coal!
The flame of love shall be a ring on her finger.
   Heave ho! Out with the coal!
At the feet of old Turcan in a small cottage there
we'll weave our dreams in front of the fire
and turn all life's woes into a wonderful song.
   Heave ho! Out with the coal!

Amanwy, † from *Yr Hen Gwm*

XI

Everyday Life

1. REV. ELI JENKINS, MORNING PRAYER

Dear Gwalia! I know there are
Towns lovelier than ours,
And fairer hills and loftier far,
And groves more full of flowers,

And boskier woods more blithe with spring
And bright with birds' adorning,
And sweeter bards than I to sing
Their praise this beauteous morning.

By Carreg Cennen, King of time,
Our Heron Head is only
A bit of stone with seaweed spread
Where gulls come to be lonely.

A tiny dingle is Milk Wood
By Golden Grove 'neath Grongar,
But let me choose and oh! I should
Love all my life and longer

To stroll among our trees and stray
In Goosegog Lane, on Donkey Down,
And hear the Dewi sing all day,
And never, never leave the town.

Dylan Thomas, *Under Milk Wood*

2. *Costume and Custom*

The old Welsh costume, folklore and custom have survived longer in Carmarthenshire than perhaps in any other county of West. The steeple-crowned beaver hat, now practically extinct, was often to be seen in the neighbourhood of Carmarthen as late as 1890, and the older women often affect the *pais-a-gûn bâch*, the frilled mob-cap and the small plaid shawl of a previous generation. Curious instances of old Welsh superstitions are to be found amongst the peasantry of the more remote districts, particularly in the lovely country in the valleys of the Towy and Teifi, where belief in fairies, fairy-rings, goblins and 'corpse-candles' still lingers. The curious mumming, known as 'Mari Lwyd' (Blessed Mary), in which one of the performers wears a horse's skull decked with coloured ribbands, was prevalent round Carmarthen as late as 1885. At many parish churches the ancient service of the 'Plygain' (a name said to be a corruption of the Latin *pulli cantus*) is held at daybreak or cock-crow on Christmas morning. A species of general catechism, known as *pwnc*, is also common in the churches and Non-conformist chapels. The old custom of receiving New Year's gifts of bread and cheese, or meal and money (*calennig*), still flourishes in the rural parishes. The 'bidding' before marriage (as in Cardiganshire) was formerly universal and is not yet altogether discontinued.

Encyclopaedia Britannica (13th Edition) 1926

3. *Good Health*

When you rise from your bed, walk a little, then stretch your limbs by putting your head to your neck, that will strengthen the body, and bending the head will make the spirit run from the stomach to the head and from the head when you go to sleep, it will fall to the body again.

In summer, bathe in cold water, that will keep the heat in the head and from that the appetite is roused.

After that, wear fine clothes, because men's mind rejoices in fine things and the heart exults.

After that dry your teeth with the bark of dry hazel, so they will be thence the brighter, and your speech will be clearer and the breath sweeter.

Also stand once in a while, because that will do much good and open up the dura mater, and strengthen the neck, the colour of the neck will be the fairer, the arms will be the stronger and improve the sight and strengthens the memory.

Converse and walk about with men as has been your wont; practise eating and drinking in moderation, indulge in a fair share of eating and of horse riding, because that will strengthen the body and break the wind in the stomach. And man will be the swifter and the stronger, and his stomach will be the warmer, and his sinews the more supple.

When you take food, take that which you like best of all and particularly sour bread. And if you eat weak foods, it will be easier for the stomach to digest it. But if you eat two kinds of food, weak food and strong food, eat the strong food first, since the bottom of the stomach is warmer than its top, because it is nearer to the liver, from which the heat comes.

When you eat, do not eat to satiety, leave some appetite. Do not drink water with your food because it will cool the stomach and prevent it from digesting the food and quench the heat; and if you must drink water, drink but a little and that of the coldest water that you can find.

When you finish eating, walk evenly along soft ground. When you wish to sleep do not sleep overmuch, rest for an hour on the right side and then turn to the left and finish your sleep. If you feel pain in the stomach, put on many clothes to take the heat of the stomach and drink warm water. And that will cause you to vomit the disease which may be in your stomach.

Walking a lot before food warms the stomach; walking much after food makes the stomach deteriorate, because from exertion it falls to the bottom of the stomach without being digested, and many sicknesses arise. Sleeping before food makes man thin, sleeping after food makes man strong.

Night is colder than day and for that reason the stomach digests better in the night than in the day, since the colder the weather is the better the stomach digests, since the heat sinks from the limbs above the stomach.

If a man is used to eating twice a day and then eats but once, that harms the stomach. If a man is used to eating once a day and that is changed to another time, that will harm the stomach. But if the need arises that the time must be changed, let him get accustomed to it gradually.

Also do not eat until the stomach is empty. You can recognise that from your desire for food and the fluidity of the saliva.

If you eat without desire for food the natural heat will freeze and if you eat when you have a desire for food, your nature will be as hot as fire; and whosoever does not take food then, his stomach will fill with sickness which will cause a headache.

The Physicians of Myddfai †

4. *Not an easy patient*

September 9, 1730.

	£	s.	d.
For dressing her mortify'd elcer upon hur lege, and den it from stinkin, with spirits of chamfire, tinct, myrhe, an udder dings praper for 49 tims. 15 tims it cost me 2s. 6d. evry tim, before I cowd get the stinking flesh away, and the oder 34 tims	3	1	6
For lancin and scallin the boune	0	10	0
For ungts. ols, and linimt, to anointe the stinking lege	0	7	6
For pills aurea guilded with goulde	0	7	6
For drams and cordiolls for her and hur companeons	0	7	6
For lodgen, care, and attendance upon hur	1	12	6
For runnin away, and hindrin me to have tim to make hur cure to perficteon	2	10	0
For envy, hatred, and mallis, and ill-will in spaaking, uttrin, and purnouncin sevrall reflections, and fuls stores uppon me and my hous	1	12	0
For brekin my glas in the glas windows, with hur hors is nos	0	1	0
	£10	9	6

John Torbuck. *A Collection of Welsh Travels
and Memoirs of Wales* 1749

5. BEFORE YOU GO COURTIN'

Get a godly wife of the right faith,
Christ's faith, agreeable, unstubborn;
in one bed will never agree
two who believe differently.

Seek a wife of chaste parentage,
sex will drag to wicked doing;

unless she's kept from harm by God
she'll slip just where her mother did.

Seek an amiable, neat, affectionate wife,
don't fancy a filthy girl;
it's sad and cold, tame and tedious
loving somebody who's odious.

Seek a silent wife, of good feelings,
tame of nature, brief in tale-telling;
worse than drips, worse than a she-bear,
worse than a viper is a scolder.

Seek a skilful wife, wise and virtuous,
she'll raise you to lead your people,
she will fill your every corner
and she'll make your heart a dancer.

Seek a lovable wife and able,
a gracious one and comforting;
the bed's cold, the board is poor
where the wife doesn't sweep the floor.

Seek one decent in her smile,
not too young and not too old;
if old, too cold, her cough will kill you,
whilst the other will disturb you.

Seek an obedient one like Sarah;
seek one courteous like Rebecca;
seek a loving one like Rachel
and as clever as the mother of Lemuel.

Seek her gracious, lovable, lovely,
cleanly, holy of clean life,
modest, proper, of good manners,
she's worth in wealth more than three manors.

Vicar Pritchard

6. *Bowen of Trelech and Bettws*

The Rev. John Bowen, Vicar of Trelech, Co. Carm, until 1753 when he was succeeded by the Rev. Benjamin Morgan, M. 23 May 1730 Anne, only child of Thomas William, owner of *Plas-y-Parcau* in Trelech. She is said to have borne 20 children. She had entered the church to be married to John Thomas Glanrhyd, when Bowen gave her a wink, and continued to whisper in her ear, that he wished himself to be her husband, whereupon she refused to marry Thomas, and a few weeks later was married to the clergyman. Among their children were:

> Easter, Thomas, Margaret, John Bowen, Ann, Paul Bowen, Barnabus, Tamerlane, Mary Abigail, Isabel, Rosamund, Gamaliel, Olive, Gamaliel, Thomas.
>
> *NLW Ms. 12357, Fol. 1192*

7. *Neighbourly Disputes*

There is much to be said for the annual ceremonial still followed in some parishes of 'beating the bounds', in which numbers of boys are led over the parish boundaries, the exact extent of which are then impressed upon their young minds by such expedients as standing them on their heads at doubtful or ill-marked points. The fruits of such primitive methods are possibly to be observed in the following extract, recording a Llanarthney Vestry meeting in the year 1799, in which Mr John Jones is ordered –

'to get Old Persons to view the Turnpike Road leading to Cwm-mawr, that was indicted on this parish upon their Oaths, and get a Magistrate of Road to receive the Oaths of the said persons, and to get the said persons to the next Qtr Sessions, to prove said Boundary upon the whole expence of the parish.'

There was a distinct prevalence of leg trouble in the village of those days, and we find that in the first Vestry of the year 1800 a decision was arrived at –

'to allow Daniel Lloyd 12s. per week, and to get the said Daniel Lloyd to Carmarthen before a surgeon to have his advice whether he can cure his sore leg or not.'

We cannot help thinking that most of the (un)-neighbourly disputes which to-day come before rural magistrates would be avoided under some such system as was practised by the old parish Vestries, as witness the following:–

'Thomas Jenkins, Overseer, to get the Iron pot from Wm. Clement and his servant maid, which was the property of the late Jno. Morgan, pauper; in cause that he shant have it peaceable he is to get a warrant go have the same on the expence of the parish.'

The first hint of really serious trouble comes in the report of a Vestry held in October, 1800, in which we read that –

'John Thomas, Church warden, is to go with Thos. Jenkins, Overs'r, to Borogh Money towards paying the poor, in case that the rate is too short.'

Our modern Roads and Bridges Committees could certainly learn much from these people of another age, who took upon themselves the whole of the work pertaining to the control of the district in which they lived. On October 23rd, 1800, the Llanarthney Vestry agreed:–

'With Thomas Harry, Mason, for making a new Bridge over Arbont Road for £4 13s. 6d., the said bridge to be from out to out, 16 feet; butments 2 feet 6 inches high to the springing of the arch; side walls 9 feet 6 inches high . . . to be completed before the 24th day of December next, or forfeit half a guinea; the said Thomas Harry is to keep the said bridge in good repair for 4 years for the same money, and he is to have the whole payment when finished, according to agreement.'

Rev. J. Jenkins, *Llanarthney, The Parish, its People and Places*

8. *No Sunday School Clothes*

David Davies, farmer, *Dolaugleision*, near *Llandilo*

There are upwards of 100 children in this immediate neighbourhood between the ages of 7 and 16 who attend neither day-school, Sunday school, nor place of worship. I have working for me as a farm-servant – David Davies.

William Davies (his examination)

I am sixteen years old; my mother is at the iron-works at Merthyr; I have never been inside a school or chapel; I do not know who to pray to; I do not know what becomes of people when they die; I don't know where my father is ('wn i ddim' was the constant answer to each question); I know what to steal is – taking a thing and not taking it back; those who steal are transported; it is more wrong to kill a man than a bird; those who kill a man are hung; I have heard of God; I know nothing about him; I am afraid to die; I don't know why I am afraid; I think I have a soul; I don't know what a soul is, nor whether it is different from the body; I never expect to see my father again; getting drunk is drinking ale; this is wrong; it would be wrong even if it were my own ale and no one saw me, and I was sure not to be found out; if I locked myself up in the dark no one could see me; I have heard of the devil; I know nothing about him; I have heard of him when people swear; I wish to go to school; I should like to learn to read; I have no fit clothes to go to the Sunday-school in (he was nearly naked in his rags); I can count. (The following questions I give along with the answers.)

How many people are there in this room? – Six. How many fingers have you? – Twenty (the Welsh word is the same for fingers and toes).

If I was ill I should not know who to pray to, to make me well again; I have never heard of heaven; I have heard of hell, but I don't know when; heaven is the best of the two, but I don't know why. (The boy's uncle is a farmer in the parish of Talley, paying 50/- a year rent.)

William Davies, Nov. 1846

Cwm Ifor School – This school is held in a room over the stable of the Baptist chapel. I visited it on the 10th of November. On my riding up to it, about 10½ a.m. there was a noisy rush of children to the door. From an urchin (who could understand hardly a word of English) I gathered that the master was away. I sent for the person in charge of the school, and presently a young man, staying in the village, from Merthyr, and deputed to fill the place of the master, who was gone to a wedding at Cwmdu for the day, made his appearance. No instruction was being given except in reading and writing. I heard three of the children read very indifferently from one of the Chambers' Miscellanies. I saw nothing to distinguish this from any other worthless village-school. The knowledge of English possessed by the pupils may be estimated from the fact that the boy who officiated as spokesman answered my question of 'When would the master be there?' by answering '*twelve*,' '*two*,' '*three*,' successively; besides '*yes*' to every other hour of the day which I suggested. On my asking him 'how long he had been at school?' he said *twenty-three,* the meaning of which rejoinder I could not discover. It could not have expressed his age, which was not more than 11 or 12.

Commissioners of Enquiry into the State of Education in Wales,
The Blue Books, 1847

9. THE PAUPER'S GRAVE

See! Where yonder yew is frowning,
How a green mound's daisied head
Gently lifts for quiet crowning
By Eve's hand dew-diamonded.
Yet its verdure tender-tinted
That should pious tendance crave,
Passing feet have crushed and dinted –
Ah! 'tis but a pauper's grave.

Hirelings, from the workhouse, bore him
To this lonely churchyard bed;
When the earth they shovelled o'er him,
Not one pitying tear was shed.
All his years with want he wrestled;
Life to him no joyance gave;
Yet, at peace, he now lies nestled
In a pauper's lonely grave.

Yon rough headstone, rudely carven,
With two-lettered epitaph
By an old boy mate of Arfon,
Now is lying cleft in half.
When the sweet Flower Sunday roses
All above the churchyard wave,
Whose shall wreath their fragrant posies
Pitying round the pauper's grave?

No fond Muse of marble rounded
Guards his dust in mute despair
O'er his resting-place green-mounded,

Time ere long shall urge his share
One with earth, from sight 'twill perish,
Lost in dark oblivious wave;
But an Angel's care shall cherish
Even then the pauper's grave.

Ioan Emlyn

10. IOAN EMLYN

Not for him the Muse which weepeth,
  Carved in marble rich and rare;
Even now time's ploughshare creepeth
  Through the grass which groweth there.
  O'er the place where he is sleeping
    Soon will roll oblivion's wave:
Still God's angel will be keeping
  Ward above the pauper's grave.

Trebor Mai

11. *Sospan Fach*

Llanelly's industries suffered various vicissitudes, but always succeeded in adapting themselves to changed conditions. The famous Dafen Tin-plate works were first erected in 1847, and began work the following year. It was the tin-plate industry which gave rise to Llanelly's 'anthem': *Sospan Fach* (Little Saucepan), heard wherever a Welsh football team is playing.

Curiously enough, the song is not a local product, and many people have claimed to have composed the verses. The famous Welsh bard, Mynyddog, published his third collection of poems in 1877, and one of those, *Rheolau'r Aelwyd*, includes the lines which form the basis of *Sospan Fach*. At the end of the nineteenth century, Llanwrtyd Wells was a great resort of the Llanelly tin-platers, and a Swansea eisteddfodwr and bard, Talog Williams, who was staying there in 1895, added a chorus in response to the popular demand. A student from Bangor either composed or produced the tune from memory. Four other 'nonsense' verses were added, and the whole was revised by Talog Williams, and the tin-plate workers sang it there and on their return to Llanelly. Various people have confirmed Talog's claim to be the author, but it was disputed by the Rev. D. M. Davies, Congregational Minister at Waunarlwyd, who said he did not claim them originally because he was ashamed of them. G. Brynallt Williams (Brynallt), a Llanelly man, went carefully into all the claims made and the evidence in existence, and whilst admitting the difficulty of deciding between two such claimants, thought that the weight of evidence was in favour of Talog as the author of the additional verses. He also examined all the many claims made in connection with the tune, and came to the conclusion there was reason to think it was a very old Welsh tune to which the words were fitted. Whatever the truth of the matter, there can be no doubt whatever that it has become so indissolubly associated with Llanelly that the mere sound of it makes every Llanelly man who has settled elsewhere feel homesick, whilst its rousing chorus stirs even the most sluggish blood of those unfortunate enough to have been born outside the town.

Maxwell Frazer, *Introducing West Wales*

Mary-Anne's finger has swollen,
And David the servant aint well.
The baby in the crib is crying
And the cat has scrammed little Johnnie.

Chorus
Little saucepan, boiling on the fire,
Big saucepan, boiling on the floor,
Dai bach the Soldier, little Dai the Soldier,
With the tail of his shirt out.

12. *Demand for a Commission of Inquiry into the State of Education in Wales*

In submitting to the House a Motion to address Her Majesty to institute an inquiry into the state of education in Wales – he might truly say neglected Wales – he felt that he had undertaken a duty, which ought to be performed by a Member representing some part of the Principality, whose local knowledge would enable him more forcibly to point out the great destitution existing in that country, of means for educating the industrious classes of its people; but he should be able to lay before the House such information from sources which could not fail to claim attention, and to convince them that education was in a greatly more neglected state in Wales than any other part of the United Kingdom.

The people of that country laboured under a peculiar difficulty from the existence of an ancient language. The gentry and educated class universally speak English, as well as generally the inhabitants of towns; while the farmers, labourers, and other inhabitants of the rural and mining districts speak the Welsh language.

This being the language of the poorer classes important works in literature have not for ages been produced in it, neither have scarcely been translated into it from other languages any works in literature, the arts, and sciences, especially on those important branches of them, mechanics, chemistry, agriculture, and it may be said useful knowledge generally; consequently although equally industrious with their English neighbours, the Welsh are much behind them in intelligence, in the enjoyment of the comforts of life, and the means of improving their condition. This is universally attributed by intelligent Welshmen, as well as Englishmen and foreigners who have been amongst them, to the want of an English education, which all the common people are most anxious to obtain; but the means afforded to them is lamentably deficient.

In many parishes there are no schools; and where there are schools, it is not uncommon for the schoolmasters to be ignorant, uneducated men, and incapable of giving instruction; of this he could furnish numerous proofs; but he would not weary the House, as he only asked for inquiry, which would bring to light an extent of educational destitution in Wales that would call for the interference of the House and the Government.

Inquiries have been made into the state of education in every part of England, Scotland, and Ireland, under the authority of the Committee of Council for Education, and most elaborate reports had been made by the gentlemen appointed; much valuable information was also obtained from the Inspectors of Factories, the Poor Law Commissioners, and Inspectors of Mines, on the state of education in England; but only one parish in Wales had been visited and reported upon. Why had Wales been thus neglected in so marked a manner? He was sure no satisfactory explanation could be given.

William Williams, M.P., reported in *Hansard* 1846

13. *Cartridges, Paints and Groceries*

Red House was a very large and flourishing business. There was a licence to sell wines and a good stock of these always, and also a licence to sell gunpowder. Ready-made cartridges from Kynochs had only recently been introduced, but many farmers still preferred to make their own. There was shot of many different weights in little drawers; powder was sold by the ounce, together with empty cartridge cases and wads to separate the powder from the shot and top wads to seal the cartridge after the shot had been put in. The gunpowder was kept in a locked cupboard and a police inspector came from time to time to see that stocks were kept under lock and key.

Paints and varnishes were kept in the 'paint room', and local painters would go into it and mix their own paint, weigh it and pay for it or have it booked. Ready-mixed paint was a thing of the future. We had a five hundredweight keg of white-lead-in-oil, and smaller quantities of red-lead-in-oil. The basis of all paints was ½lb. of white-lead rubbed down with equal parts of oil and turpentine to make 1lb. of paint. All shades of pink to red were made by adding more or less red-lead, yellows by adding yellow ochre, and browns by adding brown umber. Venetian red was also used, and lamp-black for black paint. There was an ultramarine blue-in-oil for all blues and this, mixed with yellow, made all greens. It was very necessary when embarking on any painting job to estimate correctly how much would be needed, since it was not at all easy to match the colour in another batch.

At Christmas, Miss May Hughes, Jack Hughes's sister, took over the dressing of the windows, and there was a huge display of Tom Smith's crackers, almonds, raisins, nuts and other Christmas goods. On the first floor was a room which was known as the Japanese. This was actually a room in the adjoining house, but a door had been made so that it could be reached from the drawing-room. It was filled with Japanese tea-sets and ornaments, very much in fashion then. Mrs Hughes and Miss May looked after this department and sold mostly to invited customers.

The shop also stocked many veterinary preparations, linseed cake for cattle, and 'greaves' for fox-hounds. But the busiest part of our trade was undoubtedly grocery. Llandeilo was a very prosperous market-town in the 1900s, and much of the shop routine was directed to preparing for Market Day, on Saturday. Each day some particular commodities were packed in readiness for Saturday. Thursday morning was always spent in making up the order for Dynevor Castle. This was huge – involving 14lbs of each sugar, crystallized, lump and demerara, 7lbs. of rice, 4lbs. of Patna rice, 2lbs. of mocha coffee, 2lbs. of plantation coffee, tapioca, sago, ground almonds, candles, Sunlight soap and Christopher Thomas's bars of soap, boot polishes, brass polishes, currants, raisins, sultanas and so on and on. It took most of the morning to get ready. It was addressed to the housekeeper or to the Hon. Miss Gwenllian Rice.

There were orders too from other big houses, from Mrs Peel of Danyrallt, from Taliaris, Golden Grove and lesser houses. There was just the beginning of a change occurring. Some large London stores like Whiteley's and Harrods, had begun to send out lists of high-class groceries and other goods, offering free delivery on orders of £10 or more. This – the very beginning of mail-order trade – slowly diminished the business placed locally and led to the decline of local shops.

John Miles Thomas, *The Llandeilo Apprentice*

14. Triads

The three fires kindled by a person on his own land which are not cognizable in law are: a heath fire from the middle of March until the middle of April, and the fire of a settlement kiln, and the fire of a settlement smithy nine paces from the settlement with a broom or turf roof on it.

Three birds whose worth the king is entitled to have wherever they may be killed: a peregrine falcon, a goshawk, and a raven; the owner of the land on which they are killed is entitled to fifty pence from the person who kills them.

Three vermin whose worth the king is entitled to have wherever they may be killed: a beaver, and a marten, and a stoat; because from them are made the collars of the king's garments.

Three birds which are not to be killed on the land of another person without his consent: an eagle, and a crane, and a raven; whoever kills them let him pay fifty pieces of silver to the owner of the land.

Three things for which, if found on the road, no answer need be made to anyone: a horse-shoe, and a needle, and a penny.

Three persons whom the king is not to sell: a thief, after he has been sentenced to the gallows, and a waylayer, and the traitor to a lord.

Three casts for which nothing is paid: one at a stag in corn, and at a dog in corn, and at a wild colt in corn.

Three private conversations which the king is entitled to have without his judge: with his wife, with his priest, and with his physician.

There are three legal needles: the needle of a queen's serving-maid, and the physician's needle to sew up wounds, and the chief huntsman's needle to sew up torn dogs. The worth of each of those, four legal pence.

There are three secrets better to be disclosed than to be concealed: treason and losses to a lord, and ambushing, and a person killing his father, if it be disclosed in confidence.

There are three one-footed animals; a horse, and a grey-hound, and a hawk. Whoever breaks a foot of one of them let him pay its complete worth.

Three timbers which every builder upon open land is to have from the person who owns the wood, whether the woodman be willing or not: a roof-tree, and two roof-forks.

Three things which are not paid for although they be lost in a lodging-house: a knife, and a sword, and trousers.

Hywel Dda, *The Law*

15. *Down the Gwydderig*

Turn your eyes on the other side, down the steep below, there you see rural beauty in all its native simplicity. White cottages spot the thickly-peopled vale; clean and healthy peasants, with their wives and lovely children, tending their flocks, their gardens, and pastures, where eternal spring seems to reign. The rivulet keeps them so constantly watered, that every thing appears as if it sprang up spontaneously.

In this sweet valley is plenty of wood, and the streams are feathered with alders down to the very edge of the water. The trees that ornament the dwellings of the cottagers protect them, 'in summer's heat', from the rays of the sun, and 'in winter's cold' afford them plenty of firing. They use the clear rivulet for their bath, their drink, their looking-glass.

Added to this, before you, as far as they eye can stretch, is a long ridge of mountains, many of them partly cultivated, some barren, and some covered with woods of such a length and thickness as in England we have no idea of.

In short, this must undoubtedly be one of the most beautiful and finest roads in the kingdom. It was made by a society of gentlemen, to prevent the necessity of going over Trecastle mountain, one of the highest and most dreary in South Wales. Not the least curious and admirable part of this road is their having thrown arches over the gullies, made in the sides of the mountain by the winter torrents; and wherever the natural surface of the ground rises or falls abruptly, the ascent or descent is in this manner diminished.

I must now quit these charming scenes, to give you an idea of Llandovery; though an account of it may be comprized in very few words.

Llandovery July 23

It is the meanest and dirtiest town I have yet seen in Wales. We are at breakfast in a room, that looks into the market-place; and there being a fair held to-day, my surprize is very great, instead of seeing peasants walking barefoot, dirty, and poorly clad, to find a hundred or two of women all on horseback, and most of them in an uniform dress, which is a blue cloth jacket and petticoat, and black beaver hat. The neatness and decency of this is a striking contrast to the gay and tawdry cottons worn by English women of this order; for these, I understand, are little farmers wives, who are come to Llandovery fair to sell their corn.

Not far from hence is a castle called Caer-Kenin, which is a very beautiful ruin; but we have not time to turn aside to take a near view of it. Adieu.

Mrs Mary Morgan. *A Tour to Milford Haven* 1791

16. *A Hibernian Town*

I am bound to say there is a marked Hibernian air about the place Llandovery, which may be described as of a mottled pink and somewhat dissipated complexion for the most part. A couple of streets and as many thousand inhabitants would, I fancy, describe its general bulk with sufficient accuracy. But really this is all of no importance. It is not well to jeer at these little country towns like a cockney out for a holiday, who writes them down as 'God-forsaken holes', if people are not tumbling over each other on the pavement at midday and there is no variety show in the evening. Llandovery is the trading mart of a large agricultural district and has its appointed days of animation and money changing. Seedy as these unpretentious streets may look, they have seen gay times in their day, and raked in money plentifully, and even yet there is both mirth and money going at the appointed seasons. Once upon a time too, before the days of railroads, when country society was less complex and roving and did all its frolicking at home, Llandovery, I have been told, was the scene of balls and routs, where fair women and brave men gathered from every part of the Vale of Towy. Times have changed all over Britain in this respect, not wholly perhaps for the better. Llandovery, at any rate in these days, does not look as if it could stand the strain of a smart modern gathering, but it looks like cattle and sheep, all over and from one end to the other. But Llandovery has really other claims to fame, the most immediately urgent being its possession of one of the two schools in Wales which take modest rank among the now numerous public schools of Britain. Its buildings, standing amid pleasant grounds outside the town, with their playing fields spreading out towards the Towy, give some distinction and, I have no doubt, more substantial advantages to the place. The Head Mastership of Llandovery school, moreover, has often proved a stage on the road to a Welsh bishopric. But I have not nearly done with Llandovery. A well-known printing press, for instance, existed here at one time, and turned out among other volumes the *Mabinogion* of Lady Charlotte Guest.

A. G. Bradley. *Highways and Byways*
in South Wales 1903

17. *The Welsh School-master*

In the memorable year 1688, being an hundred years after the *Spanish Invasion*, and twenty years before this present year, as may appear by the most exact calculation, a person, whose goodness is greater than my deserts, preferr'd me to the school of *Llandwwfwrhwy*: at my coming to the town, I found persons of all sorts and sexes, men, women, and children; and that day (as I shall always remember) there was a woman brought-to-bed of seven live children, which dying soon after, were put into a tray, being half boys and half girls, *viz.* three boys and three girls, and one hermaphrodite. I could not but wonder how persons should be so prolifick, in so barren a place; for the town was surrounded with large mountains, nor did you *come into it any way upon arable land*; for there is but one way to the town or parish, and that was not convenient for a coach and six horses to turn in. This is all expressed in the very name of *Llandwwfwrhwy*, for *w* is significant of a mountain, and the more *w*'s there are in a town's name, the more mountains about it. Now there are few towns in *Wales* without a *w*. The name of the very country itself beginning with it, shews it to be the predominant letter of the nation. Now *w* in this town's name being four times multiplied into itself, produces *w* four, or the fourth power of the root *w*, which is equal to *w*. Mountains quadratically multiplied into *w*. Mountains which makes a power of mountains. The word *Llan* is the same that the *Scotch* and *Irish* pronounce *Clan*, which signifies a company of people of the same lineage; and, indeed, I found in this town, not only all of them a-kin each to the other, but likewise to all *Welshmen* besides: and, which most surprized me, as they said, were all gentlemen. The word *dwarf* is not unlike in sound and significance to the English word *tuff, ruff, gruff.* The word *rwhwy* is likewise the same as the *English* word *crooked* or *awry*, so that the pedigree of the name of *Llandwwfwrhwy* being thus explained, it appears to be a town encompassed with mountains, with a rough crooked way leading to it.

These mountains *seem to be nothing else but a* composition of such hard, rocky, marmoreous, flinty, lapideous, stony, scrofulous, torry, cretaceous, obdurate, petrifactory, intractable, indissoluble; and, in a word, mountainous matter, as the Deluge could not carry, nor the rains, for many infinite numbers of years, (although *gutta cavat lapidem*) be able to penetrate, nor, indeed, cause such an impression upon them, as they might become fit for plowing or pasturing.

When I came to the school, I found but four that could read without book, and never a one but one that could write, and he could not write neither, for he had neither pen, ink, nor paper, nor his father before him; but I, and my usher, who is my wife, by great industry, increased my school to six, all the most considerable persons of the parish sending their sons and daughters to us; so that then I had two that could read fair, two that could not read, and never a-one that could write; and, by the mathematicks, it's easy to calculate how much they improved: it is remarkable, I had never a scholar under two years old, nor any much more than thirty, though I have in other places known several that have been upwards of forty. As my scholars were preferred to shoes and stockings, they went off; so that, as I remember, at one triennial visitation of the Bishop's, the schoolmaster of Llandwwfwr-hwy being called, was asked by the Bishop how many scholars he had? I answered, I had none; for, by great industry, I had so accomplished them, that their parents, by my advice, according to their capacities. had thought fit to provide for them in the bordering counties, some to feed sheep, and some to steal them.

'R.P.'
John Torbuck, *Some Natural Observations made in the
School of Llandwwfwrhwy*

18. *Litigious Monkeys*

The attendance at Fairs & Markets in these parts is astonishing. You would suppose, at the times these are held, that the whole Country had risen en masse & were come for mutual barter. They depend entirely upon these times for the vent of their goods & the supply of their wants. And as a Welshman is naturally a light-hearted social Being he generally adjourns from the Market-Cross to the Ale House & stays 'till he is more indebted to his Horses head than his own for his safety home. This accounts for the number of Ale Houses in every petty Town. In Llandovery, which consists of little more than two small streets, I reckon'd 23 of these houses.

There are houses of a still more ruinous resort & equally abundant in this Country – the offices of Attorneys. No monkey is so litigious as a Welshman. He is at good with all the world except his next neigh-bour – but there his love of a law-suit gets the better of him: & he will absolutely in the night make a gap in his own fence for his neighbours cattle to come in, that he may have the pleasure of suing him for a trespass the next morning. In the small Town of Carmarthen there are one or two & thirty Attorneys.

George Capper, *Journal* NLW Ms. 21235B,
NLW Journal XIII, 1983

19. *Brembutter & Lamb*

In this part of Wales five horses are sometimes yoked into one plough, and seldom fewer than three in a cart. Hay and pasture seemed abundant, and observing the rich dairy lands, with cows up to their knees in grass, we were prepared to find the butter pre-eminent here, which it always is, though never presented except with a *soupçon* of salt. As Welsh loaves, however, are baked without any, and taste what the Scotch would call very *wersh*, the balance is preserved, and their bread and butter when united are not much more salted than our own.

The Welsh mutton can be as tough as any other, and the best generally walks off to the London market; but at some principal inns, where the landlords had farms and fed sheep themselves, it was admirable, and of so small a breed, that the lambs might almost have been chickens.

Catherine Sinclair, *Sketches & Stories of Wales & the Welsh*

20. *Blunted Hunger*

Newcastle is a pleasant village: at a decent inn here, a dog is employed as turnspit; great care is taken that this animal does not observe the cook approach the larder; if he does, he immediately hides himself for the remainder of the day, and the guest must be contented with more humble fare than intended. The neighbouring peasantry live chiefly upon a coarse kind of black bread, very disagreeable in taste and appearance.

Unless there is a certainty of reaching Carmarthen before sun set, I would, by all means, recommend this village as night quarters: the difficulties and dangers we underwent by contrary conduct, were too unpleasant to risque repetition. Carmarthen is a very handsome town, and the Ivy Bush, a large inn, seemingly much frequented; it is, however, a fort of Hobson's choice.

At Llannon, much dirt and little provision is to be had: the cook on our arrival here was in the suds, and, with unwiped hands, reached down a fragment of mutton for our repast: a piece of ham was lost, but after long search found amongst the worsted stockings and sheets on the board: A little child was sprawling in a dripping pan, which seemed recently taken from the fire: the fat in this was destined to fry our eggs in. Hunger itself even was blunted, and we hastened to Swansea, leaving our delicacies nearly untouched. I devoted my attention to a brown loaf, but on cutting into it, was surprised to find a ball of carrotty coloured wool; and to what animal it had belonged, I was at a loss to determine. Our table cloth had served the family for at least a month, and our sitting-room was every where decorated with the elegant relics of a last night's smoking society, as yet unremoved.

Henry Wigstead,
Remarks on a tour to North and South Wales in the year 1797

21. *Laugharne on the Dry*

Gaining the summit of this hill, a grand display of scenic beauty is unfolded; the Bristol channel, and the adjacent country, appears widely stretched to observation, with the town of Laugharn below, at the foot of the declivity.

Laugharn is a neat, compact, seaport town, of small importance: in a situation the most retired imaginable, and is therefore seldom visited by strangers. It lies in no direct road to any place of consequence, neither are the accommodations, I have reason to suspect, inviting. To prevent that disappointment in others, we ourselves experienced, it should be stated, that although the place is literally crowded with petty alehouses, not one of several at which we enquired, could furnish even a mug of ale, with the exception of one rather better than the rest, to which we were at last directed under the dignified appellation of 'the tavern'. When malt is dear they abstain from brewing in this place.

Fatigued as we were, the sight of a drove of cattle bathing in the sea, began at last to inspire a hope that we could not be far distant from some village, and which we accordingly observed soon afterwards: a cluster of cottages rising upon a small patch of land in the midst of an arid solitude. These were the habitations of fishermen. Further on we reached a farm house, at which we were regaled with a bowl of milk, and oaten cake, just warm from the griddle; a breakfast, at three in the afternoon, not of the most sumptuous nature truly, but of which we had no reason to complain, because it was the best the house could afford. Cheese and butter, with barley bread, potatoes, and buttermilk, comprising the usual routine of the family provisions, even in this respectable establishment.

E. Donovan. *Descriptive Excursion through South Wales* 1805

22. *A pint for a Brown Study*

Our place of descent in Llandeilo was the White Horse, an old inn that had its entrance under the stone arch opposite the Cawdor Arms. Like the old market-town inns in general, it had clean stables and a river-pebbled stableyard to keep the carriages. The ostler was paid threepence or sixpence for the stall for the horse, and every respectable man called something 'for the sake of the house'. I was never in this old inn since those early days. But next time I go to Llandeilo, all being well, and if I have time to spare and a few pennies handy, I shan't be much surprised if I go into the White Horse and call – for the sake of the house – for half a pint of beer for a brown study of days gone by, and if I chance there upon worthy company it might even rise to a pint before my departure.

D. J. Williams, † *The Old Farmhouse*

23. *Civilised & Conversible People*

I carefully avoid entering into any Discourses of Antiquity, as what the narrow Compass of these Letters will not allow.

Having thus touch'd at what is most Curious on this Coast, we pass'd thro' the Land of *Gowre*, and going still *West*, we came to *Caermarthen*, or *Kaer-Vyrdhin*, as the *Welsh* call it, the Capital of the County of *Kaermardhinshire*.

This is an Antient but not a Decay'd Town, pleasantly situated on the River *Towy*, or *Tovy*, which is Navigable up to the Town, for Vessels

of a moderate Burthen. The Town indeed is well Built, and Populous, and the Country round it, is the most Fruitful, of any part of all *Wales*, considering that it continues to be so for a great way; namely, thro' all the Middle of the County, and a great way into the next; nor is this County so Mountainous and Wild, as the rest of this Part of *Wales*: but it abounds in Corn, and in fine flourishing Meadows, as good as most are in *Britain*, and in which are fed, a very great Number of good Cattle.

The Chancery, and Exchequer of the Principality, was usually kept at this Town, till the Jurisdiction of the Court and Marches of *Wales* was taken away. This Town was also famous for the Birth of the old *British* Prophet *Merlin*, of whom so many things are fabled, that indeed nothing of its kind ever prevail'd so far, in the Delusion of Mankind, and who flourish'd in the year 480: And here also the old *Britains* often kept their Parliament or Assemblies of their Wise Men, and made their Laws. The Town was fortify'd in former times, but the Walls are scarcely to be seen now, only the Ruins of them.

Here we saw near *Kily-Maen Llwyd*, on a great Mountain, a Circle of mighty Stones, very much like *Stone-henge* in *Wiltshire*, or rather like the *Rollrych Stones* in *Oxfordshire*; and tho' the People call it *Buarth Arthur*, or King *Arthur's Throne*, we see no reason to believe that King *Arthur* knew any thing of it, or that it had any relation to him.

We found the People of this County more civiliz'd and more courteous, than in the more Mountainous Parts, where the Disposition of the Inhabitants seems to be rough, like the Country: But here as they seem to Converse with the rest of the World, by their Commerce, so they are more conversible than their Neighbours.

Daniel Defoe, *A Tour Thro' the Whole Island*
of Great Britain

24. *Llandovery Station*

There are two fast trains up in the day, starting from Swansea, and stopping only at the principal stations. The early train starting from Swansea at 6.30 a.m., picks up and puts down Llanelly passengers at Pontarddulais Junction and, with another stoppage at Pantyffynon, reaches Llandeilo, where the first train from Carmarthen is met. At Llandeilo a number of men are now employed in constructing new points, laying fresh rails and new sidings to accommodate the extra traffic, and the traveller from Carmarthen, thoroughly aroused and pleased by the early morning ride through the Vale of Towy, is surprised to find the dull, forlorn station at Llandeilo looking quite gay and lively with business. An extraordinarily civil [railway] guard, attired in the smart uniform of the London and North Western Company, is at great pains to find out where you are going, puts your luggage in the van and yourself in a through carriage, one of a train of eight or nine, and in two seconds you are off at a good speed. Everything seems fresh to one accustomed to the local lines. The carriages are strange, many of the officials new and obliging, the speed delightful considering that you are on the Vale of Towy [line], and despite glimpses of such familiar places as Glanbrydan and Taliaris, you can scarcely persuade yourself that you are not somewhere else, until you pull up at Llandovery, without any intermediate stoppage. Here a new platform and fresh works of various kinds are in course of procedure. Leaving Llandovery, we enter upon the twelve miles of railway recently opened, and which connects us with Llanwrtyd. The ride is short, but abounding in scenes of great beauty. The country on the right, face to the engine, is perhaps as finely diversified as any part of South Wales. Charming snatches of landscape, enticing valleys, and magnificent, thickly wooded hills flit past in rapid succession. So does the half-finished station at Cynghordy, about four miles from Llandovery, and in a few minutes we arrive at the splendid valley spanned by the wonderful viaduct. It is owing to the immense amount of work required on this fine structure that the opening of the line has been delayed. Some idea may be formed of the appearance it presents when we say that it is nearly 1,000 feet in length, and 109 feet high. The line of railway is carried over the chasm on a series of eighteen arches about thirty-six feet wide, and formed, not of ordinary stone, but of immense iron girders, placed on the top of a series of massive pillars built of stone from the Dunvant Quarry, near Swansea. This piece of work was commenced in March of last year. A good view of the viaduct may be obtained before reaching and after passing it, and while crossing it delightful views are to be seen up the valley, both ways. About three miles on we take a grand sweep round into a tunnel, nearly three quarters of a mile long. Then comes the fashionable watering-place, Llanwrtyd, which competes with Llandrindod for becoming the Cheltenham of the district.

The Welshman, June 26, 1868

25. *Madam Bevan's Scratcher*

I have never seen that huge straw receptacle for feathers anywhere but in the Carmarthen Museum. But in spite of the size of Mari Lwyd, the 'cawlin,' and the coracle, sufficient space is allowed for the exhibition of some very charming old pictures from which we could gather an idea of what Carmarthen was like when General Picton met his friends upon the Parade. Naturally, all our most serious-minded Cambrians kept their eyes well glued to the glass cases, and consequently saw a fine collection of Bibles, amongst them being Tyndal's Bible of 1597. They saw also in those cases many links with Welsh worthies of the past, which were decidedly interesting, though perhaps – if it could have found a voice – such a relic as the nasty looking knife of Twm Shôn Catti might have told so unpleasant a tale that even strong-minded archaeologists would have been glad to stare instead at the 'Toddy Implements', cup-shaped ladles suggestive of jolly evenings, huge log fires, and the singing of sporting ballads.

And when thinking of some of those special links with the past seen on that happy August afternoon in Quay Street, I clearly recall how in spite of the crowd I had the chance of gazing with great enjoyment at a small object which, according to the chief custodian of the Museum, was once 'Madam Bevan's Scratcher'. The name of this elegant little article came as something of a shock to me, for having always heard much of the famous Madam Bevan of Laugharne, the immensely benevolent and able ally of Griffith Jones of Llanddowror, who in the eighteenth century devoted both her time and her money to the advancement of the Circulating Charity Schools in Wales, I found it difficult to visualize that well-born lady making use of the dainty little ivory hand attached to a long handle of whalebone. Fortunately, the 'Scratcher' was by no means the only object which was exhibited to us in connection with the generous-hearted Madam Bevan, for we saw her teapot, her card-case, her candlestick, her prayer-book, and best of all we were allowed to look at a manuscript book entitled: *Mrs Bevan's Dispensatory for the Poor*. As a frontispiece, the book contains a curious little picture depicting persons of different ages sliding and falling upon ice, while underneath is written 'Exercise ceases to prove a Blessing when an imprudent use of it is indulged, otherwise Health and Pleasure always attend it'. Having read so far, twenty pages are found to be filled with prescriptions and scraps of information supposed to be specially useful to poor persons, such as that a child of three years may have two *ounces* of blood taken from him or her, but a child under three years must be treated with leeches. What I wonder would the promoters of Infant Welfare Clinics say to that? In a note attached to a prescription against the bite of a mad dog, she states that it had never been known to fail if taken in time.

The *Dispensatory* also reveals the fact that Madam Bevan could prescribe for a mysterious complaint called the chin cough and also knew how to treat 'hysterics'. Possibly on such occasions the 'Scratcher' came into gentle use.

Evelyn Lewes, *Out with the Cambrians*

26. HALLS

You were our one and ninepenny pleasure palaces
in the villages of the Valley
offering your celluloid narcotics every night
in your velvet dusk,
and taking us on three-hour trips
far from the grip of the Black Mountain.
In you we sank,
extinguishing the lamps of our cares
promptly at seven, and letting the silver needle of the screen
inject the warm forgetfulness
into the veins of the brain.

You were the Wednesday night theatres of our winters
in the Valley
when we forgot the America of our dreams
after your stages had turned into Welsh kitchens,
and when the talented old companies of Dan Mathews
made puppets of our emotions,
compelling them to dance to the strings of their skill.
You were the warm courts
of our harmless eisteddfodau and old-fashioned concerts
giving your patronage
to the rural culture which lasted
in spite of iron and coal
in the villages of the Valley.

Baroque boxes,
halls of red brick and grey plaster,
posters of blue and yellow shouting welcome,
your colours continue to warm
the canvas of memory.

Bryan Martin Davies †

27. Welsh Traits

My speculations on the friends and acquaintances I hoped to make in Wales ended most happily. I had not expected to be at once so much 'at home' as I felt myself when I arrived at my journey's end, nor had I anticipated the warmth and friendliness of manner that characterise the Welsh, who are neither distant nor cold, but easily approachable. Two Englishmen meeting for the first time, chill one another by their formal bows and salutation. There is rarely that heartiness which, almost without words, speaks a welcome, but, on the contrary, an air of inquisitiveness, which seems to say, 'Who, and what are you? can one make your acquaintance?' A Welshman is unlike this. I would not accuse my countrymen of possessing less cordiality than their neighbours; but the spring from which it flows is more remote, and there is greater difficulty in getting at it: that of the Welsh, like their mountain streams, gushes out at once, and you are delighted with its freshness. They are very hospitable, moreover, and welcome you, by deeds as well as words, to their firesides.

The greatest impediment to a knowledge of such of the lower class as retain the peculiarities of race and country, exists in the difficulty of their language. Many of the cultivated Welsh know, comparatively, nothing of their native tongue, though it is absolutely essential to an acquaintance with the poor; and some, even, pride themselves on this ignorance. Strangers suppose that the pertinacity of the Welsh in not answering their question, proceeds from obstinacy, or unwillingness to oblige; and it has been asserted that they will neither direct a traveller nor converse with him. This is not the case; the truth being that they cannot, if they would, speak English. Many, even as far south as Carmarthenshire, are as ignorant of it as of the continental languages, – nay, I believe they would understand French better, on account of the identity of many of its words with the Welsh. It is true that, since English has become universal in the higher classes, and in those of the middle ranks who come into connection with them, the Welsh language has greatly degenerated, and many words, though pronounced with a most guttural accent, are nothing but English; still, among the native peasantry, particularly those who dwell in the mountains, there are numbers who speak their fine ancient language in its original purity.

As I believe we often gather, from the simple notions of the poor, both new ideas and distinct and near views of things, I felt, at first, much vexed at the difficulty of making myself understood. There was, however, generally some one in every party of two or three who spoke English, and acted as interpreter to those who did not; whilst others would know a few words, which they managed to employ so advantageously as to hold a short conversation with sufficient ease, and evidently with much pleasure.

My first acquaintances were a company of labourers employed in digging a pond on a gentleman's grounds, near a very pretty oak and fir wood: some were knee-deep in mud, others were wheeling away barrows full of it; but all stood still, simultaneously, at the appearance of a stranger. I asked a casual question of a little round-faced man with red cheeks, and an eye twinkling with more drollery than I can describe. He looked at his companions, shook his head, and uttered something in Welsh ending in 'seisoneg,' which meant 'I have not much English.' A tall, gaunt, upright man came to his assistance, as did one or two others, allured to a few minutes' idleness.

Anne Beale. *Traits and Stories of the Welsh Peasantry* 1849

28. *A Language full of Liquids*

There is a vast deal of business done in the town of Carmarthen which makes it very lively; and the number of elegant carriages that pass through it every day is surprizing.

We marvelled much at meeting more gentlemen's carriages from Hay hither, than we did in Berkshire, Oxfordshire, Gloucestershire, or any of the very thickly inhabited counties. This may be accounted for, perhaps, by the taste that now obtains of making the tour of Wales, and of going to some fashionable bathing-place upon this coast.

It is astonishing to see the crowds of people there are in this place on a market-day. Literally speaking, the principal streets, and the lanes that lead to the butchery and the corn-market, are as full as in London at

high change; and you may really walk upon the people's heads. It has been a great source of amusement to me today to stand at the window, and see and hear with what eagerness the country women talk to one another in Welsh. No doubt all the scandal of their village is discussed at these weekly meetings.

The Welsh language delights my ear exceedingly; and nobody will deny that I have a musical one. Far from being harsh and discordant, as many people would persuade us, I think it very much like the Italian. It abounds in *i* and *o*. Very many of their names of places and people terminate in *i*. Besides this affinity to that elegant language, a great many of their names, which have not that termination, are very melodious, and are full of liquids.

Mrs Mary Morgan. *A Tour to Milford Haven* 1791

29. *Pencader Wisdom*

'My Lord King,' [said the Old Man of Pencader to Henry II] 'this nation may now [1163] be harassed, weakened and decimated by your soldiery, as it has so often been by others in former times; but it will never be totally destroyed by the wrath of man, unless at the same time it is punished by the wrath of God. Whatever else may come to pass, I do not think that on the day of Direst Judgment any race other than the Welsh, or any other language, will give answer to the Supreme Judge of all from this small corner of the Earth'.

Giraldus Cambrensis, *The Journey Through Wales*

30. THIS LAND OF MINE – A PRAYER

O God, let not this ancient tongue decline
  In Libanus, Pant-teg and Bwlch-y-corn,
Nor ever let these hallowed shrines of Thine
  Be trampled by the feet of Saxon scorn.

Our fathers gathered here Thee to meet
  In weather fair and foul, in play and toil;
They laid their joys and sorrows at Thy feet,
  Their sacred ashes sanctify the soil.

Herein today in peaceful sleep they rest
  From Pen-y-bwlch, Llainbatis and Llwyn-gwyn
Protectors, guardians of their country's best
  Together lowly laid with kith and kin.

Here fragrance from Thy altars once ascended
  In soothing strains and holy lays of love,
And here soft showers from Thy heaven descended,
  Refreshing dewdrops of Thy Holy Dove.

Some distant day, if so Thy laws demand
  The door must close on mankind's destiny,
Let this, the language of my native land,
  Escort their souls into eternity.

W. Leslie Richards †

XII

Wildlife

1. POEM IN OCTOBER

A springful of larks in a rolling
Cloud and the roadside bushes brimming with whistling
   Blackbirds and the sun of October
      Summery
    On the hill's shoulder,
Here were fond climates and sweet singers suddenly
Come in the morning where I wandered and listened
    To the rain wringing
     Wind blow cold
  In the wood faraway under me.

Pale rain over the dwindling harbour
And over the sea wet church the size of a snail
   With its horns through mist and the castle
     Brown as owls
    But all the gardens
Of spring and summer were blooming in the tall tales
Beyond the border and under the lark full cloud.
    There could I marvel
     My birthday
  Away but the weather turned around.

Dylan Thomas, from *Poem in October*

2. *Tâf Estuary Birds*

The estuary down-stream from Laugharne is important for wildfowl
and waders, and is best viewed during periods of neap tides, particularly following high water. There are two main access points, both on
the west bank. A footpath runs south from opposite Laugharne Castle,
along the estuary or through the woods, but later along a seawall which
one can follow for about one and a half miles to Ginst Point. When the
Ministry of Defence Proof and Experimental Establishment at Laugharne
Burrows is engaged in firing, red flags indicate that entry as far as the
Point is prohibited. Nevertheless, good view of the estuary may be
obtained from the seawall nearer Laugharne. At weekends and in the
evenings it is generally possible to drive to Ginst Point by following the

unclassified road, the A4066 west of Laugharne. Once at the Point a visitor is advised to move up river and, if necessary, walk out across the *Spartina* saltings and cockle beds to the water's edge. Caution should be exercised when the tide is rising as the many channels fill quickly and one could easily become trapped.

Large numbers of oystercatchers feed on the cockle beds throughout the winter months. Other waders which appear in good numbers include dunlin, ringed plover and redshank, the latter seeming to be especially frequent in the narrower muddy section near to Laugharne. Shelduck are present virtually throughout the year, while during the winter mallard and teal are especially numerous. There are also small numbers of other duck like wigeon, pintail, shoveler, goldeneye and red-breasted merganser, the latter lingering well into the spring and may possibly breed shortly. Cormorants, probably from the large colony on St Margaret's Island, Pembrokeshire, can always be seen feeding in the estuary, while some roost on the cliffs below Craig Ddu and on the sand banks at Ginst Point. Unusual visitors recorded on or close to the Tâf estuary have included bittern, spoonbill, surf scoter, Bewick's swan, Montagu's harrier and avocet. A snow goose in September 1972 was probably an escapée.

David Saunders, *A Guide to the Birds of Wales*

3. *Porpoises in the Tâf*

Tave River being navigable as far as St Cleers Bridge (but farther by Boats) & Carthginning a little farther Yn Ye church. At present have Salmons & Sewing (Gwangaid) & mullets also heretofore, Enlarging their Walks out of ye sea, taken in them by Fishermen, drawing a net between 2 Corracles; each of Ye Portreeves paying yearly Chief-rent for Liberty of Fishing & Freedom of the Waters.

In Ye year 1660, or some years after I cannot positively name the year, a great number of Porpoise-Fish being seen to swim up Tave were chased up the same with stones thrown unto Ye River. These fishes being so chased arrived at a deep pool then of that River, by Ye side of Gweirglodd Chwareu aforementioned, called Pwll y Myled, where & near which they were at last totally destroyed by Ye Multitude of People flocking thither from all parts of Ye Neighbourhood, with such Instruments as came first to hand. Abundance of Ye which were lost in Ye

Action & buried in that Pool Wch since is become firm ground on Laugharn side; that River forsaking its ancient Channel, having by Degrees broken unto a small Ditch wch (being at first made for Defence of that meadow while the Hay grew) could & was easily stept over at that juncture.

Edward Lhuyd. *Parochialia* 1660

4. *Beavers*

The Teifi has another remarkable peculiarity. Of all the rivers in Wales, and of those in England south of the Humber, it is the only one where you can find beavers. In Scotland, or so they tell me, there is again only one stream where beavers live, and even there they are rare . . .

Beavers build their castle-like lodges in the middle of rivers. They have an extra-ordinary method of conveying and carting timber from the woods to the water, for they use other beavers as waggons. The beavers of one team gnaw down the branches, and then another group has the instinct to turn over on their backs and to hold this wood tightly against their bellies with their four feet. Each of these last grips a branch in its teeth which sticks out on either side. A third group holds tightly on to this cross-branch with its teeth and pulls the animal in question along backwards together with its load. Anyone who witnesses this manoeuvre cannot fail to be impressed. Badgers use a not dissimilar device when they are cleaning out their sets, which they arrange to their satisfaction by digging into the soil and scraping at it with their paws. It is remarkable that in both species of animal there are to be found slaves which are prepared to accept a debasement of their natural habits and to suffer at the same time a certain wear and tear of the skin on their backs.

There in some deep and tranquil bend of the river the beavers piece together with such skill the logs of wood which form their lodge that no drop of water can easily enter and no storm however violent do harm to it or loosen it. They have no reason to fear any attack, except that of us human beings, and even we must bring our weapons shod with iron. When they are building a lodge, they bind the logs together with willow-wands. The number of storeys placed one above the other varies according to the rise in the water-level which they foresee. They plan their construction so that it just protrudes from the water, with connecting doorways inside to lead from one storey to another. Whenever they have decided that it is necessary, they can keep a lookout from the top and watch the rising waters when the river is in spate. As the years pass and the willow-wands keep on growing, the lodge is constantly in leaf and becomes, in fact, a grove of willow-trees, looking like a natural bush from the outside, however artificially constructed it may be within.

The beaver can remain in the water as long as it chooses; and when under the water it can hold its breath, as do toads and hairy seals, which last creatures mark the ebb and flow of the tide by the alternate smoothness and roughness of their fur. These three species of animals live indifferently under the water or in the air. Beavers have short legs, a broad body and no tail to speak of, or at the best very short ones, and they are made rather in the shape of moles or badgers. It is worth noting that the beaver has only four teeth, two at the top of the mouth and two below. These teeth are very broad and sharp, and the animal uses them to cut with, as if they were an adze. Near their lodges they build underground hiding-places in the river-bank, carefully protected retreats which they dig into the dry earth.

Giraldus Cambrensis, *The Itinerary Through Wales*

5. *The Last Wolf, the Last Wild Cat*

The last wolf in Wales was killed at Teague's valley nr Amroth, 1576. Its pads were kept by Sir Herbert Eccles at Island House, Laugharne. The last wild cat in Wales seen at Llethr Mawr Taliaris (c.1650?)

Richard Fenton. *Tours in Wales* 1806

6. *Mammalia of Carmarthenshire*

As far as I know, the County cannot lay claim to any rare Mammal, for the Pine Marten, which used to be found in its wilder parts, has, I believe, ceased to exist there, the last specimen having been shot near Kidwelly some years ago.

The Polecat, Badger and Otter are still fairly common even in the neighbourhood of Carmarthen; and we have most, if not all, of the commoner land Mammals, such as the Hedgehog, Mole, Shrew, Fox, Stoat, Weasel, Squirrel, House Mouse, Brown Rat, Wood Mouse, Field Vole, Water Rat, Hare, and Rabbit.

The Dormouse appears to be rather local in the County. I found a colony of these pretty little animals two or three years ago in one of our fields at Oaklands.

The Water Shrew probably occurs, but I have never seen one here myself, although I have come across it more than once in Breconshire.

I only know of two species of Bats – the Long-eared Bat and the Pipistrelle.

With regard to the Cetacea, the Porpoise is seen not uncommonly in Carmarthen Bay; and some years back a Whale, of what species I cannot say, came ashore near Ferryside.

T. W. Barker,
A Handbook to the Natural History of Carmarthenshire

7. *Flora of the Limestone Ridge*

From Carreg yr Ogof a gullied slope sinks westward into the deep-cut, tree-shadowed gorge of the Sawdde Fechan where the rocks are draped with multitudinous mosses and liverworts and where, even in mid January, you will find hard shield-fern streaming down its shapely, winter-green fronds. In dark ravines the limestone makes itself felt through the plant life rather than by showing itself obviously. But further west the nude rock is reasserted on the grand scale where the medieval castle of Carreg Cennen perches high on a line of bold cliffs. Here grow distinguished plants – western spiked speedwell and wild chives; squinancywort (*Asperula cynanchica*); burnet rose (*Rosa pimpinellifolia*) which is rare inland in Wales; another lime-loving rose, *Rosa micrantha*; and round-podded whitlow-grass (*Erophila spathulata*). The trees include yew, hornbeam and a whitebeam (*Sorbus rupicola*).

The limestone persists in its narrow westward line and you pick up its influence clearly in the upper reaches of the Loughor River around Llandyfân and Llandybie (which has a colliery to remind you that on the Carboniferous Limestone the Coal Measures are usually not far away). In this region it is mainly in woodlands and old quarries that botanists make their best finds. Near Carmel, for instance, is a wood with lily-of-the-valley, herb-paris and a superabundance of woodruff. Near Porth-y-rhyd there is green helebore and the rare goldilocks aster

(*Crinitaria linosyris*). The Cwbin area has herb-paris in woodlands and southern marsh-orchid in wetlands.

A butterfly worth noting along this stretch of the limestone is the marbled white, a rather mysterious insect in the sense that while its food (common grasses) and its apparent habitat requirements (rough pastures, slopes and clearings) are so universal, it is everywhere local. Though I suppose it is best known on the chalk downs of southern England it is not a strict calcicole. For between Carmarthen and Swansea (this region is its Welsh stronghold) it spills over into Coal Measure habitats also.

William Condry, *The Natural History of Wales*

8. IN BLAEN TREN

The tops of trees are a park for birds,
a green web though 'tis New Year's eve,
fresh saplings covering the bank,
they are a bed of green-tipped hyssop,
and savory all over the hillside,
young oak trees all from their root
to the sky, not one of them crooked,
oak saplings a hundred acres in all,
a bed of green chives as well.
A field is had among green trees
a field of mighty trees and shrubs
and in the field, by the hundred thousand,
brushwood like Brazil-wood was found . . .

This year there's in Blaen Tren
the forest of Nien like the ash of the Land of York.
The frith is the safe way,
the frith will produce much fruit –
acorns without either great heat or blight,
other kinds of nourishing masts,
swarms, bees' nests by threes
and their graves in Bydder brushwood,
roebucks, does, by tens
there, stage below Pencarreg.

These are the trees where hawks are bred,
where there are copses for blackbirds,
a place for herons' nests in summer,
a place for squirrels all through winter,
where I see Rhys ap Davydd
loading wine in the wooded grove,
where Thomas and his people were,
where Rhys is:

Lewys Glyn Cothi, †
from *In Praise of Rhys ap Dafydd of Blaen Tren*

9. *Testaceology of Pendine Sands*

Returning through Pendine we struck down towards the sea coast, and after a time descended into a frightful sandy desert, the arid boundary of that part of the great bay of Caermarthen, which extends from the rocky shore of Tenby, with little interruption, to the point of Laugharn.

The ebbing waters of the bay had left the beach uncovered to a boundless extent. We traversed its sands under the reverberating heat of a fervid mid-day sun, without the possibility of obtaining the least refreshment, not even of water, to allay our excessive thirst. This was indeed a day of toil, though with the naturalist I may be disposed to think it well rewarded by the acquisitions our walk enriched us with.

The sands were bestrewed with a greater variety of uncommon shells than I ever remember to have seen at any one time upon our most productive shores. There were several distinct parallel ridges of shells, that extended for miles along the beach, all of which had been apparently washed out of their native beds in the sands by the preceding tide. Shells of the solen genus were the most abundant. Of these the species *Siliqua* were numerous, and of an uncommon size. *Vagina*, another of the larger kinds, were scattered among the rest, and likewise *ensis*: that rare species, *legumen*, were plentiful here, beyond conception; and *pellucidus*, was sparingly sprinkled with the others. Many curious shells of the *Tellina*, and other genera, were also lying about the shore . . .

About the loose sands that lie between the cluster of cottages above-mentioned, and the point of Laugharn, the shells of *mactra lutraria* occur in the greatest profusion; a proof the most convincing that this curious species, which the English conchologist has hitherto esteemed so greatly for its rarity, is one of the most abundant shells upon this coast. The children amuse themselves in gathering the valves of this shell in heaps, and strewing them along the foot tracks leading to the town: an amusement not devoid of some utility, since the sands are so light and dry in this part as to afford at best but very tedious walking without them.

E. Donovan. *Descriptive Excursion Through Wales* 1805

10. WINTER

Keen is the wind, bare the hill, it is difficult to find shelter; the ford is
    marred, the lake freezes, a man could stand on a single stalk.

Wave after wave covers the shore; very loud are the outcries
    before the heights of the hill; scarcely can one stand up outside.

Cold is the bed of the lake before the tumult of winter;
    the reeds are withered, the stalks are broken, the wind is
    strong, the wood is bare.

Cold is the bed of the fish in the shelter of the ice, the stag
    is thin, the reeds are bearded, short is the evening, the trees are
    bowed.

Snow falls, white is the surface, warriors do not go on
    their foray; cold are the lakes, their colour is without warmth.

Snow falls, white is the hoarfrost; idle is the shield on the
    old man's shoulder; very great the wind, it freezes the grass.

Snow falls on the top of the ice, the wind sweeps the crest
    of the close trees; fine is the shield on the brave man's shoulder.

from *The Black Book of Carmarthen* †

11. SPRING

Now Spring runs tip-toe on the scene,
And leaves its mark, a grace serene,
Here on artful compassed pitch,
There by careless stream or ditch.
Hid in this tremendous plot,
Frost and cold and storm forgot,
Lies doubt – a cob-webbed passing fear
That night's chill hand may re-appear
To pinch the children of the day
Before the sunbeams have their play,
Before the Orange-Tip is seen
And Primroses on hedgebanks gleam.
If, good Lord, thy hand be stayed,
Just here, where this thy subject prayed,
Then my small head will glad be made.

Gilbert Chaldecott

12. *Pencarreg Kettle-hole*

Llyn Pencarreg is a kettle hole lake near the Teify between Llanybydder and Lampeter, which is reached from the A485 at Pencarreg village.

Although the numbers of waterfowl occurring here are not large, it is, nevertheless, of local importance in Carmarthenshire, and in hard weather provides a refuge for birds arriving from farther east. Mallard, tufted duck and pochard breed and all are numerous in winter, while less regular visitors include goldeneye, goosander, whooper and Bewick's swans with smew and black tern particularly noteworthy occurrences. The first twite to be recorded in Carmarthenshire was seen here in January 1962.

David Saunders, *A Guide to the Birds of Wales*

13. *Heronries*

HERON. *Ardea cinerea L.*
Crëyr; Crëyr glas; Crachadingdong or Crychydd.

Barker called it fairly common. In the *British Birds* census of heronries, 1928, five existing and two extinct heronries were recorded for the county. The latter, at Llwynwormwood Park, near Llandovery and Coed, near Carmarthen, remain untenanted. Of the former, occupied in 1928, the largest was at Llanmiloe, Pendine, which then held 20 nests. After some fluctuations up to a maximum of 25 nests in 1937 and 1939 it has since steadily decreased, probably due to disturbance caused by firing at the Ministry of Supply Experimental Establishment. In 1946 there were only six nests and in each year afterwards up to 1951 only a single nest, since when it has been abandoned. These herons seem to have dispersed to various scattered sites but all of them appear to have been given up and it now seems clear that the Llanmiloe heronry has been transferred to Craig Ddu, across the Tâf estuary opposite Laugharne. Here in 1945 there were at least three occupied nests in stunted hawthorns on the low cliffs, in 1946 there were possibly six nests and each year afterwards up to 1950 about three nests. During this period isolated nests were reported also near Coomb and near Banc-y-felin in 1951. Meanwhile, coincident with the dwindling of Llanmiloe, a new heronry was being established at Gwempa Wood, Pont-Antwn, about ten miles eastward, and possibly began in 1940. It contained 4 to 9 nests, 1940-45, perhaps 15 nests in 1946 but dwindled to 9 in 1947, seven in 1948 and three in 1949 and 1950. It is interesting to note that this is quite close to the site of the former heronry at Coed mentioned above. However, this site has now been abandoned and the birds appear to have joined up with the others at Craig Ddu where, in 1953, there were 25-30 occupied nests, possibly even 30-35 nests, as they are difficult of access and hard to count.

Davies referred to 'a splendid heronry' in Dynevor Park, 'scores of herons', at the west end of the Deer Park. It is still marked as The Heronry on the six-inch Ordnance Survey map and was probably the fore-runner of the present Aberglasney, Broad Oak, heronry, though the actual site may have changed more than once since Davies' day. In 1928 it was designated Aberglasney (Golden Grove) and then held about nine nests. At Broad Oak there were about 18 nests in 1948, 25 in 1949, 20 in 1950, 25 in 1952 and 18 in 1953.

At Neuadd Fawr which, in 1928, held eight nests there were six in 1948 with an offshoot of three nests in a new site. In 1949 there were 13 nests, all at the new site, 10 in 1950 and eight in 1953. This heronry has had a somewhat chequered history. E. Cambridge Phillips recorded (*Zoologist*, 1882, 3rd ser. vol. VI, p. 217) that it was formed '15 years ago' (i.e., about 1867) from the desertion of the heronry at Llwynywormwood (elsewhere said to have occurred about 1870) which split into two parts. The larger part went to Neuadd Fawr, about seven miles northwards, 'now about 100 birds' he said, and the smaller part about the same distance eastwards into Brecknockshire. If, as he suggested, Neuadd Fawr held 50 pairs in 1882, it has much diminished since. Possibly tree-felling in the first world war may have been one cause; certainly tree-felling in the second war, followed by a violent storm in the spring of 1947 which blew down trees and destroyed nests, caused the removal to the present site.

Castell-Gorfod, St Clears, which had one or two nests in 1928, is now extinct, the trees having been felled. Ystrad, near Llandovery, as in 1928, still had a single nest in 1950 but it is not, perhaps, always tenanted every year. Of other, hitherto unrecorded heronries in the county it is said that there used to be a small one in Glan-yr-Annell Park prior to 1926; perhaps the result of disturbance in another heronry during the first world war. At Cwm Farm, Nantgaredig, two or three pairs are said to have nested since 1935 until the wood was felled during the last war; two nests were built nearby in 1948 but the site was deserted in the same year. Another unsuccessful extension was at Llanybydder, probably an offshoot from Highmead, Cardiganshire; occupied in 1947, 2-3 nests in 1948 but the trees felled in 1949.

There is an interesting record of a Heron, taken during hawking in Norfolk and ringed and released, which was said to have been shot on the Cothi, below Llansawel, on Jan. 7th, 1835. The ring was inscribed 'Major Wilson, 66 – Didlington, Norfolk, 1832' according to the *Carmarthen Journal*, Jan. 2nd 1953. A contemporary account, quoted from an unnamed Bristol newspaper, appeared in the *Bury and Norwich Post* of Mar. 11th 1835, but gave the year on the ring as 1822.

Geoffrey C. S. Ingram & H. Morrey Salmon.
A Handlist of the Birds of Carmarthenshire 1954

14. CYWYDD

(To ask for a goshawk showing part of its
nurture and maintenance)

. . . I am a man with a lake nearby
where live the ducks of Caeo land,
The abbot of all grammar,
a healthy place in the fair land of Llechau;
Huw has a splendid hawk if it could be obtained
(Huw is the shepherd of hawks).
A round bird with a strong fist
which would become a goshawk is my request,
its crooked beak is like a bow,
and talons like a fish-hook . . .
Ashes are not good for its eyesight,
neither does it like fire or smoke;
it is nursed on the glove,
and keeps its body healthy on fresh meat;
no foods enter its mouth
which go into the salt.
If it is on a perch for a long night
it always goes for the owl.*
A shape has been put upon a grey friar
the same as on a hawk I would imagine,
it wears feathers like a clean-shaven pate,
a grey cap over a wide pate . . .

If a goshawk, without any excuses,
I shall receive, a load on the back of my hand,
Huw Lewis of the line of Llywarch,
from Caeo to Môn, you will get a steed.

Ieuan Deulwyn †

---

* bittern.

15. *Kite: Milvus ictinus*

I am told on good authority that a pair or two still exist in the upper Towy Valley. Mr Jeffreys has had some sent to him occasionally, but they are becoming rarer every year. The following notes by Mr Browne as to its former distribution in the county are interesting: '1859'. The Kite used to breed many years ago regularly in the Iscoed woods near the Ferry, as I have been told by some of the old inhabitants: it is now very rarely seen and it never breeds. Two were seen about two years since – 'a farmer shot at one and wounded it, but did not succeed in killing it.' 'September 28, 1859. John Wilkin told me that he saw a Kite near his forge on this day.'

T. W. Barker.
A Handbook to the Natural History of Carmarthenshire 1905

16. *The Red Kite*

The red kite, though its nests are in trees down in the valleys, is a moorland feeder for much of its time. With its lightweight body carried on broad shapely wings and with a long, full, forked tail for buoyancy, the kite floats and wheels with the utmost grace over the uplands, making buzzards look heavy. If you watch through binoculars you can see how a kite's wing selects and uses each tiny current of air by bending and widely parting the long sensitive ends of the primaries. At the same time the chestnut tail turns sharply to reach steep angles with the plane of the wings, so enabling the bird to turn in astonishingly small circles and also to change in a flash from near immobility to being an earthward flung dart almost too swift for the human eye to follow.

By such steep plunges the kite seizes most of its prey – the voles, shrews, moles, birds and lizards of the upland sheepwalks. Occasionally kites pick up snakes. So much so, according to a nineteenth century egg collector, that he advised people climbing to kites' nests to 'beware of half-killed adders'. A surprising comment, for Welsh kites generally are not famous for snake eating. Still, it is known that individual kites sometimes specialise in bringing a particular type of prey to the nest, it may be crows, magpies, black-headed gulls or young rabbits. So why not adders in some place and year when they happened to be plentiful?

Always to be compared are the fortunes of kite and buzzard, for both had become scarce by 1914. How can we explain the buzzard's success alongside the near failure of the kite? Is the buzzard a stronger, better adapted species (whatever such terms mean)? Perhaps a key factor is the extent to which buzzard and kite populations have been reinforced from time to time by immigrants from abroad. We have no proof, yet it is possible that buzzards regularly come here from the Continent. But until recent years most observers would have doubted that there was any interchange of kites between Wales and the Continent. All that was known was that in some years a few kites, presumed to be young, wandered away in autumn over Offa's Dyke into Shropshire and Herefordshire or south into Somerset, Devon and Cornwall. Whether any went as far as the Continent and back was and still is unknown. Then in 1972 a young kite that had been ringed in Germany was found dead in Radnorshire. How significant was this? Was it or was it not an isolated freak? I think most people have assumed it was not and that it indicated that Welsh kites are at least sporadically in touch with those of the Continent. If so this was the final blow to the old theory that the Welsh kites, being an isolated relict group, were doomed to extinction because enfeebled by inbreeding, a theory that in any case had been losing ground for many years.

A frequent question is: why did the kite survive in just one area of south-central Wales? I think travel-writer A. G. Bradley had the answer back in 1926 in his book *The Wye* where he described these central Welsh uplands: 'a glorious solitude spreading from far away in the south up here to the foot of Plynlimon and covering many hundred square miles of crag and torrent, of heath and bog and green sheepwalk. Here the kite, the buzzard and the raven are making their last stand. And this because there are scarcely any keepers, the grouse being too few, and no people but sheep farmers whose scattered homes lie for most part near the outer edge of the waste'. So it is the comparative scarcity of heather and grouse that made this part of Wales a unique area where the kite could hold on until conservationists, in 1903, began to stand up in the bird's defence. Since then, with many ups and downs, kite protection has been continuous, having as two of its chief aims the thwarting of egg collectors and the persuading of local countryfolk that kites, being rare, beautiful, fairly harmless and very Welsh, were eminently worthy of respect.

Though our kites spend so much of their time in the lonely moorlands they are not really shy of man. Kites in the Middle Ages scavenged in the streets of London. In modern Wales they regularly visit the rubbish dumps of a couple of towns and everywhere they accept whistling shepherds, barking dogs, tractors and sheep lorries as part of everyday life. They have been seen circling inquisitively over sheepdog trials, country funerals, picnic parties, naturalists' field outings and many similar gatherings. What they do not like, however, is disturbance at their nesting sites and it is vital that bird watchers and photographers do not intrude on them. Even without human interference, the kite's breeding success is poor enough. No reason is known for this but perhaps conditions are in some subtle way not completely right for it. Certainly its habit of nesting so early – a fortnight or more before the buzzard – often exposes its eggs to keen frosts which may account for many failures. Maybe the truth is that the kite has chanced to survive in a district where it was always least successful, a part of Britain too cool and too wet for it to do anything more than hang on precariously as it still does.

William Condry, *A Natural History of Wales*

17. *Strange Birds*

There is the solitary owl, the lover of ruined habitations but here find shelter in the cliffs, where several are found. The sea-parrots, called puffins, roam about the rocks and inhabit the cliffs in spring and summer. They are beautiful birds; their beak or bill, like that of a parrot, is a lovely red, their plumage black and white, their wings beautifully variegated with green, red, and blue. The sea-paranets or pananets, a kind of wild duck, called also St George's duck, breed in Caldey island; come before storms; are seen about the sands; their bill like the duck's. Their beauty arises from the mixture of colours on their wings. At the Bigning they keep some paranets. The pewit is seen about the Pendine Burrows. The puits or purs, a bird of the size of a goldfinch, visit the coast of Pendine and other parts of this coast in winter. In very cold weather, frost and snow, they are in flocks on the sands. Wild ducks abound. The wherly or whorly-whit hounds have been seen in Pendine in the village. They are not much known, so I could get no account of them but that they came in flocks. The curlews lay their eggs in the sands, and are seen only in the evening and night, summer and winter, when their sweet short whistle is pleasant to hear. The heron is always found at the Whityard, a stream running along the sands. The pewit, I should have said, is called the green plover, and lays its eggs on the sands. I have said before that the prawns here are remarkably fine; shrimps not so fine as those of Laugharne. The fowls are very fine.

Mary Curtis,
Antiquities of Laugharne, Pendine, and their Neighbourhoods

18. *The Other Merlin*

The little merlin, though harassed on keepered moors, survived far better than the harrier but for unknown reasons has declined all over Wales this century even where not molested. Mainly a ground-nester its strongholds have always been the heather areas which provide deep shelter for its eggs and young. On grassy moors where ground cover is sparse it has learnt to breed in old crows' and magpies' nests in isolated hawthorns, coniferous windbreaks or in high-level oak woodland. Usually wild and unapproachable, the merlin is always a good bird to see, however briefly, as it flickers fast and low across the moors or round the heathery crags (for it occasionally nests on cliff ledges like a peregrine). Sadly today merlins are faced by another threat: the increasing popularity of falconry has put a considerable cash value on them and anywhere in Wales their broods are likely to be filched by the unscrupulous.

William Condry, *A Natural History of Wales*

19. *Birds of the Gwendraeth Estuary*

The Gwendraeth Estuary has recently been established as one of the most important estuaries in Wales for waders. This would probably not have come to light without the formation of the 'Llanelli Naturalists' Society' which provided the necessary impetus for much of the recording work carried out. Particularly helpful was the joint BTO/RSPB 'Birds of Estuaries Enquiry' which has revealed that the estuary ranks about fourth in importance in Wales. The richness of the avifauna is a consequence of the variety of estuarine habitats to be found and birds favouring saltmarsh, mudflats or rocky stretches are all catered for with extensive areas of each.

The area covered in this report is bounded roughly by Pembrey Forest and a poultry factory to the south and the main Swansea-Fishguard railway line to the north. It extends westwards as far as the dunes of Towyn Point and the rocks of Salmon Scar Point, where the Gwendraeth, Towy and Tâf estuaries share a communal head as they enter Carmarthen Bay.

Starting at the south-western most section of Towyn Point, there are areas of low dunes, rough grassland and ungrazed marsh. This is in the hands of the Ministry of Defence who use part of it as a bombing range. The major roost of the estuary is located here and so visits are most rewarding at times of high tides. Oystercatchers predominate with up to 9,000 present in the autumn while other typical waders include large flocks of Dunlin, Ringed Plover, Curlew, Turnstone, Bartailed Godwit and Greenshank with smaller numbers of other species.

The area is outstanding for waders and rarities such as a Buff-breasted Sandpiper in 1975 (another in 1977), a Baird's Sandpiper in 1976, a Little Ringed Plover in 1977, and an Avocet which remained throughout the winter 1975-76 have all put in an appearance. Gulls and Cormorants, the latter probably originating from the nearby St Margaret's Island Colony, can both be exceptionally numerous. Ducks, however, tend to be rather scarce, although Eider and Red-breasted Mergansers are often seen in good numbers. Birds of prey regularly include Merlin and Peregrine, while Hen Harrier and Short-eared Owl, surely overlooked in the past, are now regular winter visitors to the area.

Some interesting species breed or presume to breed at Towyn Point. It is an important site for Ringed Plover which have become very much disturbed elsewhere. A few pairs of Lapwing and Redshank also breed but the Oystercatcher, despite the proximity of an abundant food supply, has only been proved to nest on one occasion, namely in 1969, when two nests were discovered. In 1974 and probably in 1975 and 1976 up to four pairs of Black-headed Gull bred, this being the only known site in the county. Their close relatives, the Terns, are frequently seen over the low dunes throughout the summer although there has never been any evidence of breeding. Disturbance by bombing or more probably by numerous foxes may deter them from doing so. The creation of a small pool, perhaps with a few small islands, might lure the Terns into breeding as well as being a great attraction to waders.

Working east we come to the huge expanse of heavily-grazed Kidwelly Marsh which is intersected by a network of channels and small pills. During exceptionally high tides of 8 metres or over (Llanelli) it becomes completely flooded, causing many birds to be driven ahead of the advancing water up to the Banc y Lord, allowing close views of waders. The most numerous of these are Golden Plover and Lapwing, often forming large mixed flocks. Greenshank and Spotted Redshank are commonly seen in surprising numbers, with Little Stint, Whimbrel and Ruff also regular autumn visitors. Green and Common Sandpipers often occur in the pills and can be very numerous on migration.

The occurrence of rarer species, here or on the adjacent poultry farm, are always a distinct possibility as the last three years have shown. In 1974 Little Egret, Spotted Crake, Gull-billed Tern and White-rumped Sandpiper were all recorded. Another White-rumped Sandpiper, a Rough-legged Buzzard and an immaculate White-winged Black Tern in full breeding plumage were visitors in 1975, while in 1976 Wood Sandpiper, Grey Phalarope and a further Gull-billed Tern were seen. The following year an astounding number of Wood Sandpipers showed up as well as a Little Ringed Plover, both these species being very scarce in western Britain.

Between the Gwendraeth Fawr, which enters the estuary at Commissioner's Bridge, and the Gwendraeth Fach entering above Kidwelly Quay, there is an area of saltings. These extend along the northern shore where extensive mudflats are to be found. Oystercatcher, Redshank, Dunlin and Curlew gather in large flocks on the exposed mud and may be viewed at low tide from Kidwelly Quay. There are some rocky pools, too, which prove very attractive to the outstanding number of Greenshank and Spotted Redshank.

Visitors here have included Ruff, Curlew, Sandpiper, Dowitcher and Little Gull, while at least one Marsh Harrier turned up in the autumn of 1976. This is also a good spot to see Red-breasted Mergansers and Shelducks in some numbers.

Salmon Scar Point is an extensive rocky area at the mouth of the estuary with an abundant supply of mussels and other shellfish attracting feeding waders and ducks. A summering flock of a few hundred Oystercatchers can be seen here, although as stated earlier, they do not breed in the vicinity. The passage brings a multitude of these birds as well as many Turnstone and Curlew which feed on the mussel beds when the tide is out. As high tide approaches the birds usually fly to roost over at Towyn Point, but sometimes remain if the tide is not too high. Numbers of the commoner ducks, Mallard and Wigeon, are not normally large, although the scarcer Red-breasted Merganser and Eider often reach impressive figures, while Scaup and Velvet Scoter are occasionally identified. Red-throated Divers have been seen from here and may be more regular than the few records suggest. Rarities seen at

Salmon Scar Point in the 1960s included Stone Curlew and Little Ringed Plover, while more recently Roseate Tern and Red-necked Grebe have put in an appearance.

Mention must also be made of the localities surrounding the estuary as there is much movement between these and the estuary itself.

South of Towyn Point, renowned for their botanical richness, lie Towyn Burrows and Pembrey Forest which back onto the huge expanse of sand known as Cefn Sidan. Numerous Oystercatcher, Dunlin and Sanderling occur on the beach, while a massive flock of Common Scoter moult and winter offshore. A large concentration of ducks, such as this, is of course under high risk from oil pollution and all too often oiled corpses are washed ashore. Sea watching can be good here with Gannets, Shearwaters, Terns and the occasional Skua present during the autumn. Rarer gulls have been seen amongst the commoner species, with Sabines, Mediterranean and Glaucous Gulls all recently identified.

Prior to the construction of Pembrey Airfield, now the site of a poultry farm, 400-500 Russian White-fronted Geese used to winter on the marshes there. Disturbance caused the geese to desert the area to which they have become only very irregular visitors. Nowadays the fields are the haunt of Golden Plover, Lapwing, Common Snipe and often Ruff, while several small pools have been constructed attracting scarcer species, including Wood and White-rumped Sandpipers. Large Finch flocks roam the fields in the winter, often with many Bramblings present. Cirl Bunting, Tree Sparrow, Turtle Dove, Great Grey Shrike and Water Pipit are some of the more interesting passerines seen fairly recently.

East of the estuary is a system of lowland fields, known as Kidwelly Flats, which are liable to flooding during very high tides or after persistent heavy rain. On such occasions, waders and ducks soon utilise the new feeding areas. Even when not flooded the fields often hold considerable numbers of Lapwing, Common Snipe, Golden Plover and other waders, such as Redshank and Dunlin, which are usually more strictly estuarine. Shoveller are fairly regular here, while on the rarer side, Gadwall have also been recorded.

As might be expected there are many threats to the wildlife of the area. A huge holiday site complex of many caravans and chalets has been built on the north side of the estuary near Salmon Scar Point, and brought with it the pressures of the holidaymaker. Birds feeding on the mussel beds are subject to continual harassment from mussel pickers while numerous speedboats race up and down the estuary causing much disturbance to the birds roosting at Towyn Point. Kidwelly Marsh is heavily shot over with consequential disturbance, not only to the ducks, but also to the large wader flocks present in autumn and winter. Impending threats include proposals to operate dredgers on the estuary and to develop a marina at Kidwelly Quay and the Country Park.

The need for reserves has surely become vital if this extremely valuable area is to be preserved. The Towyn Point roost, with its birds of prey and breeding Ringed Plovers and Lapwings should certainly be under protection. Kidwelly Quay, being such an important feeding area, also merits reserve status, as does Kidwelly Marsh. Establishing a protected area would be an important step in helping people to appreciate more fully the wealth of birdlife to be found.

E. J. Smith, *Birds of the Gwendraeth Estuary*

20. OLD TREES OF PENLAN PARK

But Oh! How lately grey are
The brave old trees become
Aged, and withered bare, and
Stripped of their huge canopy fair;
The storm on its mammoth trek,
And the winter's blustering cheeks
Whistling its furious tune
Till they shudder within their strength,
Intent on uprooting them flat to the ground,
Venerable trees of Penlan Fawr.

But they are giant men,
And strongly they'll defy;
They'll withstand both storm and wind,
And the tempest wild with boldness;
Brave they stand, although so swift
The whirlwind – ripping with its gale!
But as to the blast of its brass
They dance in the storm!
Impressive concerts the tempest holds
Sometimes in the trees of Penlan Fawr.

Gwilym Teilo, † from *Hen Goed y Benlan Fawr*

21. *The Sewin*

This fish is also in abundance in this river (The Towy) during the months of April and May, (and indeed as early as March), when it weighs from five to six pounds; and it is most singular, and worthy of notice, that not a single fish is of less weight than this. Those that are able seem to return in June. In the latter end of June, July and August, those that are caught by netting and angling, average in weight from 1lb to a 1½1b. In September again we are visited by a quantity of Sewin, with their coats tinged with an iron red colour, all the males have the 'crook' at the lower jaw, and all are in good condition, and weigh from four to six pounds, and spawn in October, November and December following. The Sewin is not to be found in all the Welsh rivers. Geographical and Geological position seem to have something to do with them. Jones in his *History of Brecknockshire*, p. 16, notes this also in these words, 'The Sewin is not found in any of the rivers of Brecknockshire, except the Tawe, and is not seen in any river running in this county from East to West, but in all those flowing in a westerly direction.'

Gwilym Teilo, *Llandeilo Fawr and its Neighbourhood*

22. *Aurora Borealis*

I was called out of my house with great urgency and alarm; the whole sky was red, pale blue, yellow, purple, ruddy; the colour of blood, of the dawn, of porphyry, of amber; all the colours of the rainbow, and like to it with the one exception that the whole sky was dancing and playfully interweaving, as if to provoke shock and fear in the guilty part of the world, but indescribable and glorious joy in the inheritors of eternal life.

William Williams, Pantycelyn. *The Light in the North* 1774

23. *Ghastly Weather*

Abergwily Palace, 20 May, 1867

I am really saddened by this mysterious preter-natural weather like a long-protracted semi-eclipse accompanied by a strange ominous stillness. I am sure that the birds all feel the depressing influence. You hardly see, still less hear any. If a rook is to be seen it is evidently only some very pressing business that has brought him out of doors. I could fancy anything ready to come, an earthquake, or a collision with some strange body crossing our path. We have had a little rain, but not followed by any sunshine, and I am sure that the clouds mean something more than that; the air, however, is warm enough to enable me to feed my geese in perfect safety.

Did you know that the iceberg hypothesis has been recently superseded by another? That it is supposed there have been shoals of meteoroliths a few millions of miles off revolving round the sun and intercepting its beams? Certainly this morning the state of the sky quite corresponded with that hypothesis, the appearance being very like that of a partial eclipse.

Connop Thirlwall. *Letters to a Friend* 1882

24. LIGHT IN A DARK WOOD

Through the chill dusk of the wood
I stumbled, and urged my way;
Small creatures, unloved, and misunderstood,
Darted and fled in dismay.

Suddenly one clear beam
Pierced, like a lance, through the dome;
It made a snug little home, –
A lodge of light, still as a dream:
It brought a reviving cheer
To that noisome haunt of fear.

Lord, I would be such a ray, –
A token of wider day:
A ray of peace in the world's black strife;
A ray of warmth on a rain-drenched day;
A ray of song on a sun-lorn way:
A ray of God through the deadly Tree,
That made night at noon on Calvary.
When its brief, glad shining, Lord, is done,
Let the ray come home again to the Sun.

Elfed, *Songs of Assisi*

XIII

Husbandry

1. THE FARM IN HIGH SUMMER

All the sun long it was running, it was lovely, the hay
Fields high as the house, the tunes from the chimneys, it was air
   And playing, lovely and watery
      And fire green as grass.
  And nightly under the simple stars
As I rode to sleep the owls were bearing the farm away,
All the moon long I heard, blessed among stables, the night-jars
   Flying with the ricks, and the horses
      Flashing into the dark.

And then to awake, and the farm, like a wanderer white
With the dew, come back, the cock on his shoulder: it was all
   Shining, it was Adam and maiden,
      The sky gathered again
   And the sun grew round that very day.
So it must have been after the birth of the simple light
In the first, spinning place, the spellbound horses walking warm
   Out of the whinnying green stable
      On to the fields of praise.

Dylan Thomas, from *Fern Hill*

2. *Scything*

The hay was heavy with dew, and with each sweep of the scythe a green
wave broke over the curved, shining steel. Swish, then forward again with
the left foot, a long rhythmic sweep of the arms, and another swathe
lay darkly green at one's feet. The eight mowers moved in an oblique
line across the steep field below our house; no one spoke, and the only
sound to be heard was the swishing of the scythes through the short,
thick hay, and the laboured breathing of the older men. High above us,
revelling in the morning sun, a lark linked and looped its song in the
wind-freshened air. The countryside, as yet, was not quite awake from
its summer-night sleep. There was still a soft mist rising along the Sawdde.
The woods, too, were half draped in mist and stood almost black against
the sunrise. Six miles away, the rocks of the Van showed only a jagged

shoulder through the cloud that had draped it since the evening before. Apart from this one cloud, the sky was clear. Down in the valley, from the direction of the squire's, the ratchetting whirr of one of those new mowing machines could be heard. Up here with us at Trewern, it was impossible to use a machine on our steep fields: it was scythe work all through the harvest . . .

The sight of the field was a joy to me. The mowers were moving like one, and the rhythm was the rhythm of the countryside. The sun was bright on the poplars at the end of the field, and the tiny, trembling leaves were twinkling like bits of glass. The heavy, fragrant smell of bruised grass and hayseed rose in the air. Seeing a molehill in front of me, I pressed instinctively on the heel of my scythe, and the dew-shining point of my blade missed it finely. Then on again, left foot forward, the backward swing to the right, then the sweep forward, and the purple and red clover flowers settling so gently on the flat of my blade. So we worked, aiming to account for a quarter of the field before breakfast, the dew wet and sparkling on my oiled boots, the hay flowing backwards over my scythe, and the sun flashing steely-blue fire from the whetted edge of my blade.

Now we were working back across the field. I could feel the sun on my back. How father could wear his waist-coat and thick flannel shirt I could not understand. He would have it that flannel kept the sun off his back. For myself, I preferred the old print shirts which mother had washed and washed until they were as thin as butter muslin.

In front of us, the sun caught the white-washed walls of the house. From the chimney an upright spiral of blue wood-smoke twisted up. Luck was with us this year; a fortnight of this weather and we would be finished with the hay. Of course, we would have to return the help of Cefn Wern and Berthlwyd. Moc, too, would need a hand. But Justin would be help enough for Moc. They always worked with a ten-gallon squatting on its end in the shadow of the hedge.

Soon, the mist disappeared from the river, and along the hedge rows the heat-haze shimmered. And still the green-dark hay flowed backward in waves over our scythes. Step by step the mowers darkened the sunlit field with row after row of heavy swathes.

'Halt, then!'

Father laid his scythe flat on the ground and straightened his back. He eased himself backwards a few times to relax and loosen his loins. One by one, the mowers tested their edges. Eli pressed his flat, work-callused thumb against his blade. A deft pinch, and the steel sang with a thin, pinging noise.

Again the oblique line moved across the breast of the field. I could feel my shirt sticking to my back. Soon, tiredness would set in; aching, cramping tiredness, the thigh muscles pulling, and a line of pain across the small of the back as if a rope of iron were biting into one. Still, I kept in step. I kept the same distance between Jack Berthlwyd and myself. That was all that mattered, to keep my distance constant between him and myself.

Thoughts came and went through my mind in measured succession, moving almost with the rhythm of my arms. A step forward again . . .

And with the blood pounding in my ears and the sun-dazzle on the poplars rippling like water, I scythed and dreamed of her loveliness and kept my place behind Berthlwyd without knowing half the time that I was doing so.

By eleven o'clock we had nearly finished the field. Twm was still leading. For once he had discarded his fancy waistcoat, and his shirt had almost worked itself out of his trousers. Justin was scything easily and keeping up a conversation with Moc. Once or twice father called on him to moderate his language. A blister broke between my fingers and I felt the bite of the sweat as it ran over the sore. I watched father's back. Was it possible, I wondered, that there was still enough vanity in him not to call for a rest? No one spoke now, even Justin and Moc were quiet, the sun was getting high and the butterflies in the clover were like flashes of sudden, spasmodic brightness. I looked at the sky from under my sweat-stinging eyebrows. It was pale and milky with heat, only in the distance, over the far-off mauve of the Van Rocks was it blue. When a little breeze came over the field, it came like a puff of heavy warmth, and all the time the hayseeds clung to the sweat that formed in heavy drops on my upper lip. The vast heat added distance to the hills, and the scythes cut monotonously into the standing hay. Some day the harvest would be over, but the thought of September with its crisp dew in the morning and its evening mists along the river was too far in the future.

Richard Vaughan, *Moulded in Earth*

3. *An Hour on the Hay: killing, cutting, reaping...*

In recollecting the harvest in the old district at that time, there are many interesting things relating to harvesting which should be 'recorded in the memory and kept', as they say. As a rule, there would be plenty of hands available for the work on the small farms of the locality, as everyone helped one another. There was help for 'killing the hay' (*killing hay* would be the term every time and not cutting hay). I well remember seeing as many as eight, and ten, long scythes killing hay on the top of Gwaun Cwmgarw, everyone coming there for free, except for a bit of food, and a sip to drink. The scythes followed each other, and each killed his own 'swath', but not all swaths were equally clean. There were those who killed cleanly, and some who killed very untidily, as there was pressure to keep pace with the leading man. There was usually one poor killer there as a rule, and they'd shout at him, 'Kill cleanly, boy; look at the uncut hay behind you.' He replying, quite unperturbed, 'What's losing a bit of hay beside losing company?'

There was plenty of help to harvest it after killing it. Girls and women, usually, would handle the *rake*, and harvesting the hay, making it into *swathes* to begin with, then into *cocks*, then cutting it to harvest it and carting it to the *stack* in the sledge-cart.

'Can we risk *cutting* the hay?' they'd say in unsettled weather. That is, to break it out of the *cocks* for carting, and not to cut it with the long scythe – *killing* it with the scythe every time . . .

There was no shortage of fun and games beside hard work at hay harvest. 'An hour on the hay' was a term with *meaning* to it. If a boy, who was not too keen to offer help with the harvest, turned up at a hayfield where a couple of lively, strong girls happened to be working, he'd have 'an hour on the hay' before getting out. They'd catch hold of him, get him on the ground, with a pile of hay on him enough to smother him, and it would cost him a lot of sweat and toil to escape with his life. If the boy could overcome all the girls, woe to them!

There were notable customs concerning the corn harvest also, more important than in relation to the hay harvest, perhaps, in particular with regard to 'reaping wheat'. Usually, every one of the farmers of the locality kept one field of wheat, something this generation knows nothing about! The 'corn reaping' was an important affair on every farm – very important on the odd one where there was a bit of wealth, and plenty of beer prepared.

'Reaping corn' they did and not killing as they killed hay. The wheat was too valuable to kill! In the first years I can remember, they reaped all the wheat with reaping hooks. Hands familiar with the hook could reap very cleanly and pretty quick too. The 'scythe with a cradle' came to reaping subsequently, and a man familiar with the scythe with the cradle was able to cut clean and lay the valuable straw and the precious ears tidily. The wheat was bound in sheafs and placed in *stooks* the same day on the field.

After finishing, before leaving the field, the best, or the worst stacker, I can't remember which, had to be carried; but I do remember well, it was quite a job to lift him onto your shoulders, if he was a strong lad, but having hoisted him, a victorious cheer would rip through the air.

Watcyn Wyn, † *Memoirs*

4. *Liming Days*

A great deal of the talk in the harvest fields had reference to liming days and the fine exploits of men and teams. I gathered that they were stirring days, much prepared for and looked forward to in their early years. It was only on such occasions that the waggoners as they raced along the roads could show the mettle of their teams. There seemed to have been a liming season and at such times all the farmers made for the lime-kilns of Llangyndeyrn and Llandebie. The author of the history of the latter parish says it was nothing to see fifty carts drawn up awaiting their turn. They did not go in convoys, the idea was to avoid the convoy, at least on the way out, for the main thing was to be first at the kiln. One of my uncles was noted for the fine staying qualities of his team. Farmers from our parish started so as to reach the Carmarthen turnpike gate as the clock struck midnight. Having paid once, they were then covered for the next twelve hours. A string of carts with excited horses pulled up here waiting for the hour to strike. Then the race began, but there was one drawback: it was an indictable offence to drive two horses through the streets from the cart. They had, therefore, to dismount and run with their horses.

Carmarthen town in its long history must have been roused from its sleep more than once by the sound of horses' hooves, and many echoes must have been awakened as these carts rumbled over its narrow cobbled streets accompanied by the shouts of the drivers, the clanging of heavy chain traces, the tramp of hooves and the equally heavy tramp of hobnailed boots. These noises have long died away and nothing can again disturb their echoes. The journey home was more leisurely, and at the Rock and Fountain, the home side of Carmarthen, man and beast had a rest. Here were extensive stables sufficient to accommodate two dozen horses.

D. Parry-Jones, *Welsh Country Upbringing*

5. Compensation for livestock

CATS

The value of a cat which guards a king's barn, if it is killed or stolen: its head is to be put downwards on an even clean floor, and its tail is held up, and wheat is poured about it until the tip of its tail be covered. Unless the grains can be obtained, its value is a milch sheep with her lamb and her wool. The worth of another cat is four legal pence.

The attributes of a cat and of every animal the milk of which people do not drink, are valued at a third of its worth, or the worth of its litter.

Whoever shall sell a cat, let him guarantee it free from caterwauling every moon, and that it do not devour its kittens, and that it have ears, eyes, teeth and claws, and that it be a good mouser.

GEESE AND HENS

A goose is two legal pence in value; the nest of a goose, two legal pence; a gosling under its mother's wing, is a curt penny in value. When it leaves her, a legal penny; in August, its value is two legal pence.

A cock or a hen, is a curt penny in value.

SWINE

A porker, in its litter, is a legal penny in value. From the time it goes out until it ceases to suck, two legal pence. When it ceases to suck, it is four legal pence in value until the feast of St John of the swine. Thence until the first of January, it is ten legal pence in value. Until the same feast of St John a second time, twelve legal pence; and then the life is two thirds more in value than the flesh. Until January the first it is thirty pence in value; and then the flesh is worth two thirds more than the life. There is no legal worth on a young pig until it is a year old; and it assumes the law of a large sow.

Every thing upon which no legal worth is set, is to be appraised according to the law of Hywel.

Whoever shall sell swine is to guarantee them free from quinsy for three days; from the strangles for three months; and that they do not devour their young; and if they devour them, let him restore the third of their value, and let [the seller] guarantee their wholeness always.

If swine kill any person, let the owner of the swine pay the *galanas* of the person, if he acknowledge the swine.

For a stud boar is to be paid a boar with a sow on either side of him.

Hywel Dda, *The Law*

6. *White Park Cattle*

One of the oldest breeds of cattle in the British Isles, long-horned, White Park (though often dappled faintly) with black points, is to be found at Chillingham in Northumberland, Chartley, Cadzow, Vaynol and Dynevor near Llandeilo.

10. THE SHEARING

Shear them the fourth or fifth return of morn,
Lest touch of busy fly-blows wound their skin.
Thy peaceful subjects without murmur yield
Their yearly tribute: 'tis the prudent part
To cherish and be gentle, while ye strip
The downy vesture from their tender sides.
Press not too close; with caution turn the points,
And from the head in regular rounds proceed:
But speedy, when ye chance to wound, with tar
Prevent the wingy swarm and scorching heat;
And careful house them, if the low'ring clouds
Mingle their stores tumultuous: thro' the gloom
Then thunder oft with pond'rous wheels rolls loud,
And breaks the crystal urns of heav'n; adown
Falls streaming rain. Sometimes among the steeps
Of Cambrian glades (pity the Cambrian glades!)
Fast tumbling brooks on brooks enormous swell,
And sudden overwhelm their vanish'd fields:
Down with the flood away the naked sheep,
Bleating in vain, are borne, and straw-built huts,
And rifted trees, and heavy enormous rocks,
Down with the rapid torrent to the deep.
  At shearing-time along the lively vales
Rural festivities are often heard;
Beneath each blooming arbour all is joy
And lusty merriment. While on the grass
The mingled youth in gaudy circles sport,
We think the Golden Age again return'd,
And all the fabled Dryades in dance:
Leering they bound along, with laughing air,
To the shrill pipe, and deep-remurm'ring-cords
Of th' ancient harp, or tabor's hollow sound.

John Dyer, from *The Fleece*

11. *Dynevor's Gardens*

The gardens at Dynevor are charmingly embellished with fine old yews, cut and carved on the fashion of King William's time, and sub-divided with walls, built in open arches, which produce a very light and cheerful effect. The green-houses are superintended by a first-rate gardener, who turned out, of course, to be Scotch, as wherever any one enters a particularly well-managed garden, he might safely address the superintendent in the northern salutation, 'Hoo's a' wi' ye?' . . .

The fashionable but inoffensive affectation at present is to profess an extravagant passion for flowers. No one should be able to exist a day without heliotropes and geraniums; and it would be more tolerable to dispense with a dinner than with a bouquet. In Germany, peasants who can afford a garden, always appear in church carrying nosegays, to show that they are persons of property; but young ladies now, whose whole estate is in a flower-pot, cannot be seen without as many camellias and hyacinths daily as would fill a conservatory, and employ half-a-dozen gardeners. At Dynevor there ought to be none of the modern parvenu flowers, such as dahlias, cactuses, chrysanthemums, and calceolarias, all distinguished foreigners, newly imported, and generally received with ecstasies of admiration; but in such an old Welsh scene, we expect to find only the native families of lilies and hollyhocks –

'The vulgar wallflower, the smart gillyflower,
The polyanthus mean, the tribe of single and of double pinks.'

Here roses were in the highest perfection – by no means a frequent sight now; for there appears considerable reason to apprehend that the respectable old race of hundred-leafed and cabbage roses, and others with a pedigree as ancient as those that fought for the houses of York and Lancaster, will soon become extinct, and give way to the more showy, but far less estimable, monthly and Chinese tribe.

The rose of Damascus is one of the most beautiful kinds; and Sir John Malcolm mentions – what may be an inducement to their culti-vation that in the east, he has seen excellent tarts made of the leaves; though in this country a cook would give up his place if asked to try the experiment.

As it is said in heathen mythology, that all roses were originally white, till Venus accidentally pricked her feet with thorns, and stained them red, perhaps Flor had the jaundice when they became yellow; but roses are very rare yet of that hue, and all attempts to make them perfectly black have hitherto been failures; though everywhere our complaisance is put to the test by the exhibition of some which profess to be a match for ebony. The gardener here has not yet adopted the new fashion, so prevalent elsewhere, of training rose bushes into trees. Many varieties are now engrafted on the top of a tall straight stem, and they consequently branch out in all directions, looking so much like an umbrella, that any one caught in the rain would be much tempted to pull it up by the roots. The effect of this artificial engrafting is neither natural nor graceful, having no recommendation but novelty; and when I see these imitation trees in preparation, with a string attached to every branch, and not a twig left to nature, they often remind me of modern education.

Miss Catherine Sinclair.
Sketches and Stories of Wales and the Welsh 1860

12. *Bees*

A queen bee is twenty-four pence in value. The first swarm is worth sixteen pence; the second swarm, twelve pence; the third swarm, eight pence. The swarm which comes from the first swarm is twelve pence in value; the swarm from the second swarm, eight pence; and in that value they remain until the feast of All Saints. Every swarm from before August until after the feast of All Saints is of the same value, namely twenty-four pence. If a swarm go out after the first of August, it is a wing swarm, and is only four pence in value until the first of May.

A queen bee after the first swarm goes from it, is twenty pence in value; after the second swarm goes from it, is sixteen pence in value; after the third swarm goes from it, is twelve pence in value. The worth of a bee-hive is two shillings. The worth of a hive in the woods, two shillings. If a hive be stolen, and the tree in which it is be cut, the worth of the tree along with the worth of the hive is to be paid to the lord of the land. Whoever shall find a hive, if he show it to the owner of the land, is to have four pence and his dinner, or the wax. No swarm is of more value than four pence until it has settled down for three days, in calm weather; a day to find a place, a day to remove, and a day to rest. Whoever shall find a swarm on the land of another person, is to have four pence from the owner of the land if he insists on having the swarm.

Hywel Dda, *The Law*

13.   THE VIRTUES OF LEEKS

It is good to drink the juice against vomiting blood.

It is good for women who wish to have children, to eat the leek often.

It is good to take leeks and wine for snakebite or the bite of any other animal.

A plaster of leeks and honey is good for a wound.

The juice of leeks and the milk of women is good for an old cough.

The juice of the leek and the gall of goat and honey in three parts is good for deafness, and that to be put hot in the ears or in the nostrils.

Leeks are good for pain in the head.

Leeks and wine are good for pain in the kidneys.

Leeks are good for making bones knit and to bring boils to a head.

If leeks and salt are put against a wound, they will make it close up straightaway.

If the leek be eaten raw, it will cause drunkenness.

It will strengthen people who have haemorrhages.

It will combat flatulence of the intestines.

Leeks are dangerous for the stomach, whether they be taken boiled or raw, because they cause looseness of the sinews, and smoke from them rises to the head and damages the sight and causes people to have horrific dreams unless lettuce or poplar or suchlike be eaten to modify them.

The Physicians of Myddfai †

14. *The Golden Grove Tradition*

Some of the best timber in the county stood on the Golden Grove estate, the largest in West Wales. For several generations the Vaughan family had endeavoured to conserve their timber resources. The leases of many of their tenants included agreements to plant a number of oak and ash saplings annually. As early as 1608, Sir William Vaughan (1577-1641), the agricultural and colonial pioneer, had advocated the planting of trees and the making of orchards among his methods for improving agriculture.

The third and last Lord Carbery had taken a special interest in the woodlands of his estate. On his death in 1713, he was succeeded in the inheritance by his daughter, Lady Anne Vaughan. Shortly afterwards she married Lord Winchester, son and heir to the Duke of Bolton. The marriage was an unhappy one and could have proved disastrous to the estate. Winchester was a spendthrift and a profligate who regarded his wife's estate and especially the valuable timber on it as a ready means of paying off his heavy debts. But Lady Anne, true to the family tradition and loyally supported by her Vaughan cousins, resolutely opposed the felling of woodlands in the vicinity of Golden Grove. These, she stated, made 'the Beauty and Ornament of the Seat', and added that as she had at heart the preservation of a home which had been so long in the family she would not dream of doing anything 'which may tend to its Ruin and Defacement'. However, she permitted the cutting down of trees in woodlands surveyed and marked out in her father's time, but continued the policy of systematic replanting.

Her distant cousin, John Vaughan of Shenfield, Essex, whom she had chosen to be her heir, had good reason to applaud the wisdom of his predecessors in respect of afforestation. When he took possession in 1751, a survey of the woodlands was made. Mature and older trees were earmarked for felling, and for the most part were replaced by saplings. In some areas the land was added to farms for arable and pasture purposes. In 1756, when the price of wood was steadily rising, John Vaughan advertised in *The Whitehall and London Evening Gazette* that, 'A large quantity of full-grown Timber fitting for shipping' was to be disposed of. This brought several enquiries, among them one from a leading English timber merchant, Robert Chitty of Sussex. Soon, he came down with his agents to inspect the timber. After many months of hard bargaining, in which Chitty found Vaughan as tough a business man as himself, an agreement was signed. This covered the sale of 6,620 trees, mainly oaks and elms, to be selected by Chitty 'out of a greater number' in the parishes of Llanfihangel Aberbythych, Llandeilo Fawr and Llangathen, for the sum of £10,300. As the annual rents from the Golden Grove estate amounted to a little over £3,000 when John Vaughan inherited it, the policy of afforestation in previous years paid high dividends. He also sold considerable quantities of rough timber and hollow trees to the Carmarthen iron-master, Robert Morgan, for conversion into charcoal fuel for his group of furnaces.

Chitty's task of felling the selected trees, digging up roots, clearing the ground, tidying up and making good any incidental damage was to be completed within five years. His felling, sawing and carting tackle arrived by sea at Carmarthen. With the aid of expert coracle men, Chitty and his workers floated the timber to Carmarthen along the Tywi. There it was stacked on the quay ready for export to Milford, Plymouth, Portsmouth and London. Some barges and smaller boats were constructed on the banks of the river below Golden Grove during these operations. Chitty also used some of the timber to build a vessel called *Golden Grove* at Carmarthen. When this and another ship *Rose* sailed for Plymouth laden with timber, he had a second ship on the stocks ready for launching as soon as the construction work had been paid for. Unfortunately, Chitty appeared to have run short of money during the timber deal, and there was trouble in securing full payment. John Vaughan's son Richard also complained to his father in London of the damage done to trees, fences, gates and pastures on the estate by Chitty's workers and said that the family's tenants 'have greatly suffered'. Richard who succeeded John Vaughan in 1765, was a popular, kindly landlord who was much more lenient with his tenants in respect of arrears of rents and manorial obligations than his imperious, exacting father. He took an interest in agriculture at his home farm and carried on the family tradition of afforestation.

His son John, the last of the Vaughans, inherited the estate in 1780. Reference has already been made to his enthusiastic encouragement of the new agriculture and his love of gardening. In addition, he added to his woodlands. In 1781, he purchased 5,000 saplings from a London nursery and continued to plant many more during his lifetime. He also appointed woodwards to look after the young trees, to mark timber suitable for felling and to check the widespread pilfering of wood by townsfolk and villagers. Charles Hassall in his *General View of Agriculture in the county of Carmarthen* (1794), commented upon the excellence of woodland culture in the area . . . 'of which the extensive and valuable woods about the seats of Lord Dynevor, Mr Vaughan of Golden Grove, and several other gentlemen afford ample proof'.

Though the Golden Grove estate was heavily mortgaged partly as a result of encumbrances inherited from the problems created by Lady Anne Vaughan's grasping husband, and partly by his own inability to cut down on an expensive mode of living, John Vaughan steadfastly refused to sell the old oaks which grew in the parklands of his ancestral home. Several efforts to induce him to do so were made by government contractors.

A. G. Prys-Jones,
The Story of Carmarthenshire

15. RHYDCYMERAU

Planted in whips are the trees of the third war
On the land of Esgeir-ceir and the meadows of Tir-bach
Near Rhydcymerau.
I remember my grandmother at Esgeir-ceir
Sitting beside the fire pleating her apron;
The skin of her face as yellow as the Peniarth manuscript,
And the Welsh on her old lips the Welsh of Pantycelyn.
A piece of Puritan Wales from the last century she was.
And my grandfather, though I never did see him, was
A 'character'; a little creature, lively, tough, a wag,
And fond of his pint;
A fugitive from the eighteenth century was he.
They raised nine kids,
Bards, elders and Sunday school teachers,
Leaders in their own little circles.

My uncle Dafydd it was who farmed Tir-bach,
A rustic bard and a local rhymester,
And his song to the bantam cock was famous in the parish:
'The little cock scratching
This end, the far-end of the garden.'
To him we went on summer holidays
To shepherd sheep and to compose lines of cynghanedd,
Englynion and eight-line verses on the eightseven measure.
He also reared eight children,
And the eldest son a minister with the Calvinistic Methodists,
And he too poetised.
There was in our family a nestful of poets.

And by now nothing's there but trees,
With their impertinent roots suckling the old soil:
Trees where community once was,
Forest where there were farms.
Southern English slang where poetry and theology once were.
The barking of foxes where there were cries of children and lambs.
And in the darkness right in her middle
Is the lair of the Saxon Minotaur;

And on branches, as if on crosses,
Cadavers of poets, deacons, ministers and Sunday school teachers
Bleaching in the sun
And being washed by the rain and dried by the wind.

Gwenallt †

16. *Weather Prognostications from Cilycwm*

If the New Year begin on a Thursday, this produces a long winter, mostly dry with cold winds, yet wholesome and healthy; the summer – great part of it – temperate, tho' in harvest time much rain will fall, with thunder and lightning, doing much mischief (by the over-flowing of the rivers and land floods) to the corn, yet there will be no want of plenty: murmurings and discontent will be among some people, and mischief may ensue thereon: people much given up to vice, particularly that of whoredom; taxes will decrease and trade revive: for the most part, the season will be healthful, but many troubled with catarrhs, asthmas, and consumptive coughs in the fall of the leaf, and most part of the winter, to their no small affliction; yet fewer die than last year.

If the sun shine clear and bright on Christmas Day (Old Style) it promiseth a peaceable year, from clamours and strife, and fore-tells much plenty to ensue: but if the wind blow stormy towards the sun-set it betokens sickness in the spring and autumn quarters.

If it be lowering or wet on Christmas or Innocents-Day, it threatens scarcity and mortality among the weaker of young people, but if the day will be very fair it promiseth plenty. If January 25th (Old Style) be fair, it promises a happy year; but if cloudy and rainy otherwise.

If New Year's Day (Old Style) in the morning open with dusky red clouds it denotes strife and debates among great ones; and many robberies to happen that year. Or if the wind blow aloft, great stirs will vex the world; and if dark clouds do muff the sky, then fowl and cattle oft will die that year.

Mark the sun rising, and if it look broader than usual, then many moist vapours are gathering from the sea; the air is thickened and the sun-beams diffused in it makes the face of the planet shew greater than usual; and in a little time you will see clouds muster, and spread over the face of the heavens, and the air densing into a watery body, and if this happen in hot weather, *viz.* Summer or autumn, violent showers will fall, but of no long continuance; but if in winter or spring, settled rains, but more moderate.

If the sun rises with a bluish circle inclining to white, the air is gross, rain will soon ensue.

The sun setting in a black cloud, and diffusing or spreading its beams palish to North and South, prognosticates a rainy night and morning.

The sky of a dusky red in the morning and the sun rising pale, an overcasting will soon ensue and rain quickly follow upon it, attended with whisking winds.

The often-shifting of the wind is a sign of rain, especially in winter and spring.

Many small clouds at North-West in evening shew that rain is gathering and will suddenly fall. The moon's horns blunt at its rising three days after the change, denotes rainy weather for that quarter, but the other quarters – seasonable weather.

The stars seeming bigger than usual, pale, dull, and not twinkling shew the air is thickening to rain, which will soon fall.

Many stars appearing in the night, seeing a greater number than usual, then wind east in summer fore-shews sudden rain.

If the moon blushes and is redder than usual, winds are engendered, and storms will arise.

Chaff, leaves, thistle, down, or such light things, whisking about and turning round, fore-shew tempestuous winds.

William Augustus (Wil Awst).
The Husbandman's Perpetual Prognostication
for the Weather 1794

XIV

Rivers & Lakes

1. *Source of the Towy*

This noble river takes its origin from an immense bog in a wild and desolate region, upon the mountains separating Cardiganshire from Brecknockshire. The stream called the lesser Towy or Towy Vechan, rises to the westward, from a branch of the same bog, and joins the greater Towy after a course of a few miles, at a place called Moel Priscoe, where are the first habitations upon the river, consisting of two shepherd's huts, containing the old shepherd and his wife, their children and grand children, with every appearance of health and contentment, in defiance of the disadvantages and hardships to which their situation upon a bleak and dreary mountain exposes them. But such is the power of habit, that contentment, the greatest of sublunary blessings, may be found under circumstances which the generality of mankind would conceive calculated to excite nothing but despair. Hospitable to the extent of their ability, they offer to the stranger the best of their store, sweet milk, excellent butter, and oat cake; a repast not to be despised after having braved the keen blasts of a district so elevated.

The course of the river is south easterly as far as its junction with the Towy Vechan at Moel Priscoe, where it turns to the southward, and rushing over its rugged bed for some miles, now glides almost imperceptibly along, then bounding over the rocks, receives the waters of innumerable rills and brooks, descending from the clefts in the hills on either side, with an occasional solitary cottage seated upon the banks. Hitherto this celebrated river may be crossed on foot in many places, till a picturesque bridge formed of a single plank and hand-rail, thrown from rock to rock, presents itself, and affords some relief from the sameness of the bare hills and broken craigs by which its channel is confined. This bridge deriving its name from that of a neighbouring farm, is called Pont y Cledach. The river is now still more obstructed by rocks, and the track on its eastern bank becomes precipitous and difficult. The country continues equally dreary and desolate, till upon turning the point of a rock, a scene bursts upon the sight with the effect of electricity . . . so sudden, so instant is the transition from savage wildness to a view romantic in the highest degree. A farmhouse, called Vanog, is situated on the western bank of the river, enveloped in wood, crowned by a majestic rocky hill; the mountain on the opposite side, almost perpendicular, is covered with trees of various kinds. The river, raging over the rocks, roars through its gloomy bed in some places near a hundred feet below the surface, but entirely concealed by the profound depth of its channel, and the luxuriance of the foliage upon its banks, with hills folding over hills in the distance; and this contrast, produced by the advance of one single yard, after having traversed a dreary waste for several preceding miles, may easily be conceived capable of producing an effect that no one, unless totally insensible to the beauties of nature, can pass without admiration.

Leaving the farmhouse, Vanog, on the right, the track crosses the Camdwr, a few yards above a waterfall of considerable height, which meets the Tywi, as it again emerges from its Acherontic pass. The scenery from this point of junction, looking up, is highly gratifying; presenting the woods of Vanog on either side, with the river foaming down the rocks as it escapes from its dismal passage, and the whole crowned by rugged mountain forms towering in the distance. From hence the vale, now near a quarter of a mile in breadth, is chiefly occupied by meadow land, till the mountains again approximating, shut in the channel of the river, which sweeping to the westward round Cerrig Tywi, approaches Ystrad Ffin.

L. G. Wood. *The Rivers of Wales* 1813

2. *Towy*

The Towy, which is one of the finest rivers in Wales, rises in one of the wildest parts of Cardiganshire, and winds, like a silver serpent, on the bosom of those fertile meadows immediately below the Town; and after a westward course of about 27 miles, reaches Carmarthen, where it becomes navigable, and after taking a more southward course, it arrives at its 'home' – the grand reservoir of all rivers near Llanystyffan. The Venerable Arch-deacon Williams states that in Roman times this river was called *Tobi-og*, 'and if,' he says, 'we strike off the case termination, we shall find that word *Tobi* represents, as closely as a Greek could express it, our Towy, which in old and purer form, would be *Tov-ui*. Prior to the introduction of the Railroad into Llandeilo, the greatest portion of its commerce with London and Bristol was shipped by traders to Carmarthen, and forwarded from thence by carriers, which plied regularly, at a charge of 9*d.* per cwt. There are three bridges over the Towy within short distances of each other, namely: – the County Bridge, before alluded to in a former part of this work, the Railway Bridge, and another lately built by A. J. Gulston, Esq., close the Railway Station, which is very commodious for communication with the population of the part of the locality, called *Dyffryn Ceidrych*, as it shortens their route a good mile to the Town.

Gwilym Teilo, *Llandeilo Fawr and its Neighbourhood*

3. Towy's Tributaries

A little hour, I came to Llandovery. I passed over a brook called Gwdderig, whose course was not long ere it came into the Towy, not far from the town of Llandovery.

Not far off this brook I came over the Brân River that riseth about twelve miles off, and cometh hard by the foot of Llandovery Castle.

And even almost hard by it passeth over the little brook of the Dyfri, running through the middle of the town of Llandovery. So that the castle hath on the one side Brân river, and on the other Dyfri Brook.

Brân a little beneath the castle, and also Dyfri goeth into the great river of Towy.

Llandovery is a poor market, much standing by repairs that carry fish from the quarters of Carmarthen to the lower parts of Wales, hath but one street and that poorly builded of thatched houses. To the townlet belongeth one church within and another a quarter of a mile outside the town.

Passing out of Llandovery within a two furlong length I rode over the river Towy, the which there oftentimes drowneth in winter diverse many for lack of a bridge, and thence I came to Abermarlais three miles off I passed over two brooks whereof one was called Mynnys.

Marlais Brook maketh no great course, but coming through the park that he giveth name unto goeth into Towy. In (Aber) Marlais park is a well-favoured stone place moted, new mended and augmented by Sir Rhys ap Thomas. There now dwelleth Thomas ap Jones an esquire.

The ground between Llandovery and Abermarlais is well wooded.

I learned in Llandovery that the Towy commeth by Llangurig in Powisland in the Lordship of Arustle and that his head is not far from thence (false – Leland).

Coming from Abermarlais a couple of miles towards Carmarthen I saw on the right hand about three miles off a desolate Priory of white canons, commonly called Talley *alias* . . . (Tal-y-Lychau).

Again forward two good miles I rode forward into a great bottom wherein ran the pretty river of Dulais and so into Towy.

But ere I came into the vale I espied on the right hand the Castle of

Dynevor by estimation about three miles off from the banks of the Towy.

From this Dulais about two miles further I passed over another called Myddyfi . . . and three or four miles beyond that I rode over another rivulet called Dulais that goeth into the Towy hard by Duplwyn Castle.

Dryslwyn (as I learned) is as much as to say a place full of difficulty and encumbrance to pass through.

About three miles beyond this I passed over a great bridge, under the which runneth the fair river Cothi and not very far into the Towy.

And so through a little valley, with hills being on each side onto Abergwili about three miles or more where is a fair collegiate church of prebendaries belonging to St David.

And a mile thence to Carmarthen.

John Leland. *The Itinerary in Wales* c. 1536-39

4. DRAYTON'S WATERS

As *Towy* doth entice: who setteth out prepar'd
At all points like a Prince, attended with a Guard:
Of which, as by her name, the nearest to her of kin
Is *Doethie*, tripping down from *Berwyn's* rushy Llyn,
Through *Esgair* running out, with *Pysgotwr* to meet
Those rills that Forest loves; and doth so kindly greet,
As to entreat their stay she gladly would prevail.
Then *Tranant* nicely treads upon the watery trail:
The lively skipping *Bran*, along with *Gwydderig* goes,
In Towy's wandering banks themselves that scarcely lose,
But *Myddyfi*, with *Llechach* and *Sawdde* soon resort,
Which at Llangadog grace their Sovereign's watery court . . .
. . . Now Towy toward her fall (Llangadog over-gone)
Her *Dulais* forward drives: and *Cothi* coming on
The train to overtake, the nearest way doth cast
Ere she *Carmarthen* get: where *Gwilly* making haste,
Bright *Towy* entertains at that most famous town
Which her great Prophet bred who Wales doth so renown:
And taking her a harp, and tuning well the strings,
To Princely *Towy* thus she of the Prophet Sings.

Michael Drayton, from *Polyolbion*

5. Pysgottwr

The river Pyscottwr rises in the mountains to the westward, and in its course falls into the Dethia, about a mile west of Cerig Tywi: the latter river takes its origin from Llyn Berwin, north of the source of the Pyscottwr. The most considerable stream with which the preceding part of the Tywi has been augmented is the Camdwr, flowing from the same range of mountains, and emptying itself into the Tywi, a little below Vanog.

From hence, the Tywi rolls between stupendous mountains to Pen y Garreg; and, about a mile farther on the eastern bank, stands a good house, called Nant y Mwyn, belonging to Lord Cawdor, and inhabited by the manager of his lord-ship's extensive lead mines, which are within a short distance of the house. Nearly opposite to Nant y Mwyn, a picturesque foot bridge, leading to Pwll Pradog, crosses the Tywi. The vale now exhibits abundant marks of cultivation and increasing population; and the river, continuing to ripple over its pebbly bottom for about a miles, takes a fine sweep to the westward; then resumes its deep and rocky channel, adorned with a profusion of wood overhanging its banks, and enlivened by the verdure of extensive meadows on either side, but more particularly on the eastern; which, together with the lofty rock, Craig y Mwyn, in the distance, affords a scene highly worthy of notice.

As the adjacent country assumes now a less romantic character, the beauties of the river exhibit different, but not less interesting, features. The air of wildness and impetuosity, which marked its passage through its native hills, gradually softens as it advances into the more level vale, through which it afterwards winds its course; and changes imperceptibly into an aspect of greater grandeur and majesty, which astonishes less, but perhaps pleases more.

Thomas Rees. *The Beauties of England and Wales* 1815

6. The Drove Sets Out

On the following morning after an early breakfast, Edgar and Llewelyn saddled their horses, and rode out into the cold shadow of the hills, the morning air was crisp and keen and they cantered side by side along the road to Cwrt y Cadno.

For the first few miles the thudding hoof-beats of the horses mingled with the tumbling music of the river in its rocky gorge beside the track. There were places where the rough road followed tunnels of branches from the trees that grew on either side of the way. At other times the track climbed and clung to the open hillside giving splendid views of the greening valley with the giant hills that grew ever steeper as with each mile of splendour the valley closed about them.

This was the southern gateway to the wild and lonely sheep land of Elynedd, over which the Cardigan drovers would soon be wending their solitary way. In the face of the natural beauty of the closing hills, the two brothers cantered on in a state of happy contentment.

They followed the narrowing valley of the Towy glen until it swung sharply to the right by a spectacular gorge towards the ancient hiding-place of Twm Shôn Catti, the Welsh Robin Hood of an older age.

The greening hills carried their dead red bracken of the previous year, high up to the edges of the rocky scarp that lined the mountain crests, and the fresh scent of the sodden moorlands came to meet them on the wind. For every mile of their journey, the music of the crashing rivers grew louder in their ears. Some hint of the spell of Elynedd came down through the Towy gorge and Edgar Morgan turned to his brother.

'Ever been up that way, Llewelyn?' he asked. 'We'll be going up there for ewes when we get back from London, if we ever do get back,' he added with a twinkle.

Normally when drovers took fellow travellers on their first journey to London, their grim tales of the dangers of the road assumed alarming proportions. But Llewelyn knew that he would be wasting his breath if he tried to frighten his brother.

While they forded the main river and paused to give the ponies time to drink, Edgar looked into the wild glen of the Towy, and the high sheep walks that rose beyond it. Their route lay back to the left of the gorge and they climbed steadily towards the cradling hills of the Cothi river. White clouds rode by across the blue vault of the sky and their shadows went beneath them over the hills and valleys. From the climbing track they watched the ever-widening panoply of mountain grandeur spreading out below them.

On the other side they heard the falling of the head-waters of the Cothi crashing along a deep ravine of oak woods. From all directions the roar of hidden rivers thundered through the trees.

Then they followed a long descent to the floor of the valley, where all the foaming rivers of the mountain were merged into the gentle winding

Cothi. Three miles further on, they came to Cwrt y Cadno and the end of the first half of their journey.

Roy Saunders. *The Drovers' Highway* 1959

7. *William Edwards of Dolauhirion Bridge*

From where we stand on the road Dolauhirion just looks like any other old and well-built road bridge round these parts.

Now we'll get through this hedge and slip down through a few nut bushes and brambles to river level. Mind how you go – it's a bit muddy down this bank. Someone has been down before us, quite a few hob-nailed boots have worn this track down and now we can see the Towy no wonder at that either. Look down stream the – Black Pool, one of the biggest Salmon pools around here and not unknown to boys of the local College who know how to swim . . .

And now for the bridge itself. See anything unusual in its construction? Yes! that's right, you've spotted the large circle on either side.

In my ignorance I've always referred to those circles as something designed to carry flood water through to relieve pressure on the arch. Even now I'm not sure they wouldn't save this ancient edifice during a super spate, but they do seem a long way above bank level.

Another mile or so up stream there's an identical bridge but a bit narrower and over a deep gorge – the circles being yards above any flood you could imagine.

Now here's a thing that will intrigue you a bit further. On the far side of the Towy about due south of Llandovery there's a derelict but still very stately old Mansion named Cilgwin. Covering a small stream which runs through a meadow below Cilgwin Mansion there's a bridge not more than cart's width and about twelve feet long, which is an exact model of Dolauhirion – the bridge we're gazing at now.

Where is this leading us to? Why, back to about the middle of the eighteenth century! About that time there lived a bridge building genius if ever there was one – William Edwards who was born about 1719, the son of a farmer in Glamorganshire. He started by restoring stone walls on his father's farm, then blossomed out by helping neighbours with their repairs. After that he studied local stone-masons at their work and eventually became so efficient was offered a contract to build a road bridge over the Taff at Pontypridd and began his first big enterprise in 1746. This bridge consisted of three arches.

Unfortunately for Edwards, nature entered into the ring and by creating a sudden but severe spate in the head waters of the Taff ended the architect's labours in a few hours.

Edwards' contact saw to it that he should maintain his bridge for a definite period, so he had to begin all over again. This time he designed the bridge in one high arch. Just as he had finished the arch and removed the centre, but before the parapets were finished, the weight of the bridge ends forced the keystones out of place and again his labour was wasted.

But Edwards, not unlike the spider, started again and relieved pressure by making three circles, each one larger than the other, at either side of the bridge and won the day. As far as I know, his original bridge still stands. Anyhow, it looks as though Dolauhirion might last a lot longer than you or I.

Lawrence C. Hill, *The Vale of Towy*

8. *Deceptive Waters*

When we were about to set off from Llandovery, Mr M – enquired about the height of the river Towy, which he well remembered to have been nearly fatal to him some years ago. They informed us, the rains had swollen it very much, and recommended to us to go three miles round, rather than ford it. For this I was very strenuous, and Mr M – kindly complied with my request. I am, you know, extremely fearful of water; and the rivers in this country have a remarkable deception in them: they are transparently clear, and have such a smooth pebbly bottom, that you may count every stone in them; and you think by stooping a little you can gather up the polished variegated ones in your hands. But alas! if any unwary damsel or inexperienced stranger should be tempted to beguile their way by such an innocent recreation, they would find themselves fatally mistaken; for these rivers are sometimes so dangerously rapid, that they might be hurried down the stream, and never more heard of.

Mrs Mary Morgan. *A Tour to Milford Haven* 1791

9. *Vale of Towy*

We on our cycles can glide at leisure down the long descent, though on the opposite side of the gorge from the railroad track, to the levels of the Brân valley. We see the woodlands of Glan Brân, once a seat of the Gwynnes, and still descending, with the green uplands of the forest of Cil-y-cwm rolling skyward on our right and the last spurs of the Epynt on our left, pass Cynghordy, and are again in touch with humanity, though of a Carmarthenshire type, for the county line crosses the top of the pass. There is a market somewhere in the Vale of Towy nearly every day in the week, and rustics of various ages and both sexes, mounted on ponies or afoot, are setting their faces down the valley of the Brân. Mowing machines are rattling through the meadow grass, and cultivators are running up the red turnip drills, steered by musical hinds, who are waking the echoes, not as the passing Saxon might suppose, with the ancient strains of Wales, but with those more probably of last Sunday's hymn, at Cynghordy chapel. Great oak and ash trees shake their canopy of leaves above our heads. High banks of ferns and foxgloves, capped with lush growths of willow, birch and brier-rose, border the road. Bright tinted homesteads peep shyly through the thick foliage with which provident tenants long dead and gone have surrounded them, to the great comfort doubtless of their descendants in these warm southwestern valleys.

Llandovery stands, not literally at the head of the vale of Towy, but near where that river, after a twenty mile course through mountain gorges and narrow valleys, meets the Gwydderig and the Brân in a more spacious country, running thence for nearly thirty miles to the tidewater at Carmarthen, amid scenery of a different class and with a temper more suited to its changed surroundings.

Famous in Welsh life, Welsh history, and Welsh song is this Vale of Towy. Putting aside Glamorgan, who turns her great humpy back towards the rest of Wales, and hugs her fatness and her treasures between the mountains and the sea-coast, the Vale of Towy is the heart of South Wales as Carmarthen is its capital. In the days of the Welsh princes it was the political centre of the southern kingdom, and, save Glamorgan, a province unto itself from earliest times, the richest or at least the most distinguished strip of old South Wales. Here, as was natural, men and consequently warriors were thicker on the land than elsewhere, and here was a rallying point for the native chieftains of the south in their long struggle with the Anglo-Norman power. Glamorgan fell under Norman rule in the person of Fitzhamon and his twelve companion knights in the days of Rufus, as Brecon and Radnor succumbed to the sword of Bernard de Newmarch. But Carmarthen and the Vale of Towy kept the native interests alive, and the Norman from all serious footing, till, simultaneously with North Wales and Llewelyn, it fell before the invincible Edward, and, happily for itself, jumped at once from a native province into a royal county. As arms and men and flocks abounded here in the days of the Plantagenets, so, for the same reason do country houses, prosperous or ancient families, and fine farms distinguish the Vale of Towy at this time above most parts of South Wales. Something of what the Vale of Clwyd is to the north that of Towy is to the south, though, strangely enough, while the former was till quite recent times the peculiar stronghold of the old Anglo Norman families, the latter has boasted a larger share than common of the ancient Welsh blood among its ruling class. Yet in both these notable tracts the Welsh language holds its own among the tenantry with tolerable obstinacy.

A. G. Bradley. *Highways and Byways in South Wales* 1903

10. RIVER SAWDDE

When I step thimble heeled at an end of day
Sound of water Sawdde water pricks my ear,
A spreading dynamo sheer over all stone
Except for the round ribbed ones to wash it by.

Never trunk of tree on a sunken 'twmpath'
Met man or bill or hedging glove as I was there,
No smell no taste no speaking cold by people with a bell
In the finished disc of moon could but resemble

The next line open in wind tremble, heart whole being
Up the hillside moving as if telltale fingers
Were uncoffined at some thread; a mascot falls in love.

What it is to have water running near one's own house
With eels in it – alone – real – a one-syllabled water language.
Those town fellows have borrowed beetles in their shoes!

Keidrych Rhys

11. *Gwili, Cothi & Gorlech*

The river Gwili issues from Llyn-hir, or Pib Mountain. Its course, which is very circuitous for many miles, is singularly beautiful, as it runs rapidly in a channel confined by lofty hills, which are covered with groves of oak, exhibiting a succession of romantic scenery rarely to be met with in an equal space. In its passage it receives the following brooks, namely, the Cafras, the Nantbendigaed, the Duad, the Cynwil river, and some lesser streams; and passes by Floswion, Glangwily, the churches of Llanllawddog and Llanpumsaint; the iron-works at Cwm-dwyfrân, and leaving Cwmgwili on its northeastern bank falls into the Towy at Abergwili.

The river Cothy rises in the mountains, not far south of the source of the Pyscottwr, and descends through a region even more wild and desolate than the early course of the Towy; till, like the latter river at Ystrad Ffin, it is accompanied by scenery both sublime and romantic; and receiving the tribute of many lesser streams, pursues its course, leaving the lofty Cynvil Gaio on the east, to the pleasing village of Llansawel; and meeting another river from the north-west, enlivens the beautiful grounds of Edwinsford. Talliaris park, the seat of Lord Robert Seymour, is in this neighbourhood. The mansion is spacious, and commands a magnificent view of the Black Mountain, &c. from its south front. From Edwinsford, the Cothy flows through Abergorlech, when it is joined by the Gorlech, from the north-west, and receiving other small rivulets from the same side, rolls under Cothy bridge, and falls into the Towy.

L. G. Wood. *The Rivers of Wales*, Vol.II 1813

12. PRAYER FOR A TYWI BRIDGE

There will be a tide out of the sea
and a full flow of water from the mountain.
She had, these are the characteristics
 a peculiarly generous custom:
What her flood takes from one region,
she gives it to the other.
She is a housewife after this
with her housewifery over foam.

Her flood bears on its breadth
Corn and hay to the weir;
thence removing to the sea
the oaks between her two sides;
uprooting, felling the trees
and overwhelming the bushes.
Below the houses Tywi shows
how wide her mantle is.
Mother of floods of seething shallow brooks,
the swelling sea of many streams,
daughter to the river of Jordan,
a surging sea greater than Noah's flood.
It is a strait over meadow land,
it is a street hindering me . . .
I do not like, any more than the sheep,
a short narrow necked coracle and boat.
It is my intention one day, diligently
to travel there over the mountain.
Oh God, may He grant long life to the two,
if He wills it, may he give an age to me as well,
And still in our own time
may God bring a bridge over Tywi.

Lewys Glyn Cothi,
from *In Praise of Llewelyn and Henry ap Gwilym of Llangathen*

13. *Abergwili Beetles*

With the imagination wound up, on a near approach to Merlin's hill, and the evening just closing, it was very easy, by the aid of the poets, to believe, that I saw the magician at the entrance of a cave.

My wrapt imagination dwelt upon these scenes, combining the faint shadow of what I saw by the dim light of declining day, with the stories I recollected, till we had nearly reached the village of Aberguilly; when I was awakened from my delightful reverie by an object that startled me exceedingly. I had never in my life seen any thing that wore such an appearance; nor could I at all conceive or guess what it was. Four very gigantic figures, perfectly black, occupied the whole road, and moved with an even but quick pace towards us. I thought I could discern feet and legs like men's; but the upper parts were spread out three or four feet wide into a shapeless trunk, without arms or head. I did not long remain silent, but earnestly enquired what these frightful creatures were. Mr M –, well acquainted with such appearances, told me, they were men with their boats upon their backs, which is the Welsh manner of carrying them, after they have been fishing in the Towy for Salmon. By this time we were nearly come up to them; and I then became apprehensive, lest the horse should be as foolish as his mistress had been. But he, not having filled his imagination with legendary tales, let them pass close by him, without even laying his ears close to his head. This certainly shewed a wonderful degree of either philosophy or dullness in the animal, but I could not discover which. We passed through the village of Aberguilly, which is within a mile and a half of Carmarthen, where stands the bishop of St David's palace; but it was so dark, we could see nothing of it.

We were very much struck with the appearance of the flames and smoke, which issued from the furnace belonging to the ironworks at Carmarthen. It exhibited as grand a spectacle as I ever beheld; and in a place so surrounded with mountains, a stranger, entering it, as I did, in the dusk of the evening, must conceive there was a volcano in the neighbourhood.

Mrs Mary Morgan, *A Tour to Milford Haven*

14. *Coracles*

Although the coracles of the Tywi and the nearby Tâf are somewhat similar in shape, the Tâf coracle, designed for use in a fairly narrow, swiftly flowing stream, is heavier than the Tywi variety. Instead of the wattled gunwale of the latter, it has a planked gunwale. The Tâf coracle is sharper at the fore end and flatter at the other, and usually weighs about 33lb compared with a maximum weight of 28lb in Tywi coracles. During a recent fishing season, when a Tâf licensee was unable to make a coracle for his own use, a Tywi coracle from Carmarthen was borrowed for the season. The Tâf fisherman was not happy with the design and performance of this vessel on the river and he soon reverted to the traditional coracle built by the craftsmen of Lower St Clears, specifically for the Tâf . . .

Coracles are also found on the Tywi, where twelve are licensed to fish for salmon in the river below the town. In the eighteen-sixties, according to the *Commissioners Report on the Salmon Fisheries*, no fewer than '400 men . . . supported themselves on the salmon and sewin fisheries'. The report continues: 'To a poacher (a coracle) is invaluable . . . The coracle man is often lawless and always aggressive, he poaches private waters for years and claims a prescriptive right; he uses violence if he is very strong, he threatens if his opponent be not so much weaker than himself as to make violence unsafe . . . working without noise and at night and scarcely visible, they are difficult to detect, and if detected, almost impossible to capture, for a few strokes of the paddle will always place the river between the poacher and his pursuer'.

The authorities, even in the eighteen-sixties, were critical of the coracle as a fishing craft in non-tidal waters, for although 'in tidal waters they are a perfectly fair and legitimate engine . . . in the fresh and non-confined portions of the rivers, they are very destructive . . . if a fish shows himself in the day, his capture that night is nearly certain. Perfectly portable, the coracles are put in the river at the end of the pool, containing the fish, and it is swept again and again, if necessary until he is caught'. The twelve pairs in use today between Carmarthen Bridge and the sea represent a considerable reduction in numbers since the nineteen-twenties, when in 1929, 25 pairs were licensed to fish from coracles. By 1935 the numbers had declined to 13 pairs 'under stringent regulations and subject to a licence fee of four guineas' . . .

On the Tâf, a short swift river that flows into Carmarthen Bay near the village of Laugharne, two licensees are still allowed to fish from

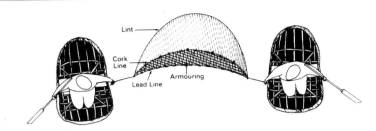

coracles. The fishermen based on the village of Lower St Clears are part-time workers and operate at night during the months of June and July only. In the early nineteenth century, the Tâf fishermen were regarded as very efficient and one observer 'saw for the first time, those feats of dexterity which are required in the management of such a capricious vessel', despite the fact that he was familiar with other coracle-men 'of the Towey and other rivers'.

J. Geraint Jenkins, *Nets and Coracles*

15. *Coracles at Croesyceiliog*

Coracle fishing has now died out at Croesyceiliog, but it is well that some information concerning the old traditions and habits of these fishermen should be preserved. It was customary to wait at a certain point for the twilight, to start fishing, and this was called 'clyfwchwr'. Then the fishermen made for the pools, the following being the names of those bordering our Parish. Pwll Pibwr (where the brook Pibwr discharges itself into the Towy); Gwar Garw; Cwcwll (meaning hood or cowl); Gwar ucha Pwll Du (the upper shallow of Black Pool) near Pibwrwen; Pwll Du (this dark or shaded pool stands under Green Castle, and is noted for its ghosts, and for being the spot near which one of Lewis the Timber Merchant's ships got wrecked); Gwar isha Pwll Du (the lower shallow) near which pool carts proceeded to the lime quarries; Brig y Gwter (this was one of the fishermen's landing-places, and close by is the huge boulder known as Gwely Tomos, upon which, tradition says, that a certain Thomas slept and got drowned by the incoming tide); Gwar Bach y Gored (meaning a weir for taking fish). This used to stand near Towy Castle, and consisted of poles driven into the ground, joined by woven twigs, and facing the tide in the shape of a V. Here fishermen stood in boats, ready to catch fish thrown back by the on-rush of the tide against the weir.

Ethel M. Davies, *The Story of Llandyfeilog Parish*

16. *A gleam of spears, a murmur of arrows . . . a fair face*

Twenty miles from the sea, a little river leaves an underground lake, flows through a cave, and falls radiant from the darkness among steep rocks, and takes a course like a man's thoughts when they have the joy of an unknown impulse and no certain aim. There, the river always talks of Spring. It winds and studies all the country round, – castle and farm and inn and old graves, – with many sharp digressions, which I suppose it could not have done without, any more than I in a similar case. Now it shines and curves gently and looks over its bank at the cattle, and now, changing its voice, it is gloomy and intent among mossy stones, and now it leaps and is all foam over a ladder of crag. Suddenly it enters a steep, wooded valley, and falling over a perpendicular cliff it is richly embowered, and always remembers Summer and begins to please the trout where it swirls with shuddering foam or runs swiftly in the middle, and gloomily and slow under the alder roots. But in the wood, where birch and oak and hornbeam stand over it, it gains a look of great and growing age which mountain rivers have, and a shadow besets its cheerfulness, so unlike the happy prime of English waters among cowslip meadows. When it leaves the wood it is a masterly, full-grown stream that can turn a mill-wheel. Then it begins to pause in deep pools under shadowy bridges, where the otter slides for a moment over a slippery ledge and then can hide his path for fifty yards. There the girls stand and dip their vessels, and think for a minute while the vessels fill, and raise them again, spilling some, and show that the black water can shine as when it left the mountain ten miles away.

Leaving a hamlet near one bridge, the river runs through such a lonely land that even on stormy nights it is heard only by the groups and groves of oaks that guard the stony and tussocky pastures. Here and there, on either hand, a brook adds a murmur to its music. A throbbing flock of lapwings for ever wheels and gleams and calls over it. The royal fern basks on its edge. And there Autumn abides.

When it reaches the next village, the river is so yellow and poisonous that only in great floods dare the salmon come up. There, with two other rivers, it makes a noble estuary, and at the head of that estuary and in the village that commands it, the old and the new seem to be at strife.

On the one hand are the magnificent furnaces; the black, wet roads; the ugly houses, that have the one pleasing virtue of not pretending to be anything else, with their naïvely chosen names, such as Bryn Gwyn Bach and Mazawattee Villa; the cheap and pretentious chapels; yet all of them filled with people bearing the old names, – the women called Olwen, Myfanwy, Angharad, – loving the old songs, theologies, histories.

On the other hand, there is the great water, bent as if it were a white arm of the sea, thrust into the land to preserve the influence of the sea. Close to the village stands a wooded barrow and an ancient camp; and there are long, flat marches where sea-gulls waver and mew; and a cluster of oaks so wind-worn that when a west wind comes it seems to come from them as they wave their haggish arms; and a little desolate white church and white-walled graveyard, which on December even-ings will shine and seem to be the only things at one with the foamy water and the dim sky, before the storm; and when the storm comes the church is gathered up into its breast and is a part of it, so that he who walks in the churchyard is certain that the gods – the gods that grow old and feeble and die – are there still, and with them all those phantoms following phantoms in a phantom land, – a gleam of spears, a murmur of arrows, a shout of victory, a fair face, a scream of torture, a song, the form of some conqueror and pursuer of English kings, – which make Welsh history, so that to read it is like walking in that place among December leaves that seem never to have lived and been emerald, and looking at the oaks in the mist, which are only hollows in the mist, while an ancient wind is ceaselessly remembering ancient things.

Edward Thomas. Beautiful Wales 1905

17. A Towy Flood

July 18th

The wind had got up a little in the night and there had been a slight shower but it was fine and clear when we got up and had our breakfast. About ten it began to thunder and gathered up quickly into a storm. We retired inside the tent, making everything as watertight as possible and it rained in torrents, but the thunder and lightning didn't seem very close. It cleared a little by twelve, and we crossed the river and walked up the hill opposite – it did not look very promising with the thunder rumbling among the hills and heavy clouds banking up.

At midday it fairly began again and there was nothing to do but sit inside the tent, and once there we expected the whole thing to collapse at any minute! Still, it was quite dry inside in spite of great hailstones which fell and we thought *must* split the fabric. About 2.30 the water began to pour in through the back of the tent, and after heaving everything, rucksacks etc, to the highest part to avoid the stream of water we scrambled out and found the river was rising rapidly and torrents of water from every surface of the hillsides pouring into it.

It was impossible to get help from Nant Neuadd as it was across the river so I dashed up the hill to the road to try and get help on our side. I left Margery taking what she could to the nearest rocky piece of ground. The road was crossed by cascades of water from the hills and in places where there had been a landslide. Just as I reached the road there was a big one on the other side of the river, almost on top of our tent. It is a strange sight to see a whole piece of the hill subside, and leave a great scar on the face of the green hillside. It was very difficult to see much in the storm but I found I had to cross a fair-sized stream on our side of the river but the road was built up and had iron railings on each side so I crossed easily, wading to my knees.

After about a mile the thunder started again. I pushed on as I thought I must be as near the farm as to go back, but almost at once my path was blocked by a rushing stream and a landslide. I felt rather in despair as the thunder and lightning were terrific again and the flashes and the clap instantaneous, but there was nothing to do but to go on, as it was all bare mountainside without cover of any sort or kind.

Soon after, I came to Pant-y-clwydau, a very wild little place perched up on the hillside. I found the whole family in a great state of alarm at the storm; the water was pouring through the kitchen and out through the door and down the steep steps to the road, like a waterfall. They could hardly speak English but I made the man, Mr Roberts, understand we wanted help to get our things under cover and somewhere to dry ourselves. He at once offered all he had, but explained there was no fire as the water had put it out! He came with me at once, the heavy rain was easing and it soon became a steady drizzle. When we reached the stream where I had waded across he seized my arm and refused to allow me to cross saying, when I protested that I must get back to the other lady, that she was most certainly drowned already – and there was no use two being drowned!

We were joined there by the farm man from Nant Neuadd who had been sent to tell us that they had a room and fire, etc, all ready for us there. He had been unable to cross close to us and had come up above the farm, to cross the Towy by the bridge between there and Pant-y-clwydau. He agreed that it was not possible to cross our stream yet and explained that it would run down sufficiently to cross by the rail in about a quarter of an hour, saying that the little streams would empty themselves; but he didn't know how much the river would rise.

While we stood there the cart bridge that we had crossed by was swept away, turning completely over as it went, cutting him off completely from the farm. We could see bushes, trees and sheep going down with the flood. Three or four sheep came down our stream, one poor thing struggling which they managed to reach, but it was dead by the time they got it out. When we crossed eventually and hurried along to Margery, it was to find her safely on the rocky piece of ground with all our possessions spread around her, calmly rolling up the tent ropes as if there had been no such thing as the storm, while the ground below where the tent had been was awash, the river having risen ten feet!

We heard afterwards that it had risen twenty feet in all and three bridges went, leaving the Towy without any bridge at all for about fifteen miles. [Llandovery bridge was damaged and there had been a collapse in the Sugarloaf railway tunnel]. The general agreement was that there had never been such a storm.

Dorothy Raikes, 1926 Diary: The Open Road

18. *Isambard Kingdom Brunel's 'White Bridge'*

On December 13, 1844, a bombshell was dropped by *The Carmarthen Journal* when it was revealed that Brunel's South Wales railway [GWR] would pretty well cut off Carmarthen for navigational purposes. This was confirmed in a letter of December 20 from Brunel's solicitors. It can hardly have placated the townsmen's worst fears when it was reported that although the intention was to impede navigation of the river as little as possible

> 'in a great national undertaking like the present, it was impossible, *alone*, to consider the interests of a particular town.'

Carmarthen was in uproar. Thankfully, Brunel also wrote to the Burgesses, a letter which was characteristically brief and to the point, and saved the day.

> Dear Sirs
> I propose to cross the Towy by a swivel bridge or drawbridge of dimensions amply sufficient for any vessel capable of reaching Carmarthen, and trust this assurance will prove satisfactory to the parties interested.
>
> IK Brunel

Terrence James. *The Carmarthen Antiquary XXII*

19. *Grant Respecting the River Towy and its Fisheries*

Know all those who now are and those that are to come that we Henry de Lancaster, Lord of Monemue of Kidwelli and of Carmarthen have given and granted and by this our Charter have confirmed unto Cadwgan ap Griffith le Latimer, all the land with the meadow and with the Fishery in the water of Telby (Towy), and with all their appurtenances: the which we Richard de la Mote held of us upon the water of Towy in our lands of Kedwelli: to have and to hold of us and of our heirs and of our Assigns all the aforesaid Land, Meadow and Fishery with all their appurtenances, to the aforesaid Cadwgan and to his heirs, of his body lawfully begotten, freely, wholly, well and in peace for ever; after the decease of Isabella Verk Rosser, who was the wife of the aforesaid Richard: the aforesaid Cadugan and his heirs of his body lawfully begotten, paying yearly to us and our Heirs, or to our assigns six shillings and eight pence sterling, at the feast of Saint Michael and doing the Services due and accustomed in like manner as the aforesaid Richard and the aforesaid Isabella have done before the making of this our Charter. And we and our Heirs, all the aforesaid land and Meadow and Fishery with all their appurtenances will warrant to the aforesaid Cadugan and to his Heirs of his Body lawfully begotten, for ever, in the form before mentioned: In witness of which thing, we have put our Seal to this our Charter: These being witnesses, Robert de Cautelous, now our Steward of Kedwelli and of Caruwathlan; Sir Morice of Llanethli: now our Receiver of Kedwelli and of Carnuwathlan, Davi Malessant, Phelipe Hervey, Cadugan ap Griffith, Willym ap Adam, Ievan ap Incas, and others. Given at our Castle of Kedwelli, the tenth day of the month of May, in the sixth year of the reign of King Edward the son of King Edward (10th May 1313).

Translated from the Norman French,
Carmarthen Record Office

20. TOWY

Past Carmarthen
the Towy promises sea
miles before the castle of Llanstephan
or the station at Ferryside.
Sand-strips finger the river
and hold banks of heron, gulls,
parading the brief islands before
the incoming of the tide.
Pasture land
rich from the hoarding of the river
feeds cattle, slow as statues.
Time crumbles the banks

sudden away under calves;
the water floods over the field
a conquering army.
Like a clock the tide regulates life:
the hawk feeds from the sky
the same shadow of necessity;
salmon swim old, known ways to the sea.

Tony Curtis

21. *Pink Freshwater Pearls*

The history of pearl fishing in British rivers goes back to Roman times.
Suetonius in his *Lives of the Caesars* contends that the presence of pearls
in freshwater mussels was instrumental in inducing the invasion of 55
B.C. A paper by Thomas Pennant in 1777 reveals that as many as
sixteen small pearls had been extracted from a single Conway mussel.
The mussel was called 'cregin dilyw' in Welsh and 'kregin diliw' in
Ireland – 'deluge shells', for they were usually found washed up after a
flood.

The existence of the pearl mussel in the larger South Wales rivers has
been catalogued as follows:- 1888 in the Cleddau, 1891 in the Ely and
in 1902 in the Towy at Llanarthne and the Teifi at Maesycrugiau. To
date, no historical reference to the presence of pearl-mussels in the Tâf
has been discovered but such mussels have been, and still are being caught
by fishermen using worm as bait for salmon, sewin and trout. In fact,
the pearl-mussel must cohabit with fish in the same water in order to
complete the parasitic phase in its life cycle. The fry, or the very imma-
ture pearl-mussels, attach themselves to the gills of fish and live as
parasites for some two to five weeks. Having completed this phase the
young mussel detaches itself from the host and falls to the river bed
to fend for itself. The mussel appears to show a preference for certain
species of fish – some contend that trout are their natural host. Minnows also provide an easy anchorage but it is not certain whether sewin
or salmon perform the host role under natural conditions. These fish
species are to be found in the Tâf, whose water is deficient in lime salts
– another essential prerequisite for the survival of the pearl-mussel.

Specimens were retrieved from a pool on Pentrecwn Farm, Llandeilo
in September, 1973 just a week after a severe flood in the Towy. The

adult shell varies a great deal but is usually long and oval, black in colour and about four to five inches long. Pearl-mussels are also present in the Tâf at numerous places and recently have always been in evidence in the vicinity of the weir at the milk factory in Whitland.

Pearls may be pink, white or brown. They are formed by an outpouring of nacre from the mantle to surround a foreign body or damaged portion of flesh. It is in this way that the marine oyster also forms its pearls. A pearl from a mussel caught in the Tâf by Mr Walford Harris at Tynewydd Farm, Whitland in 1922 was mounted on a ring for his wife – fifty years after its capture – in December 1972. It is a good specimen, pinkish white in colour, rounded symmetrically on its upper portion, but slightly flattened at the base. It is 10.8 mm. in diameter and weighs, according to the Kunz gage, 35 grains. It is difficult to appraise its value on account of its uniqueness.

During the decade 1926 to 1936 a group of Scotch pearl fishers paid annual visits to the Tâf during July and August when the water was low and the fishing was relatively easy. They were probably a syndicate from the Stirling area but the party also included some fishermen from Perthshire. Their itinerary was, from all accounts, well organised. They travelled widely in England and Wales and covered the rivers in a rough rotation. They retained the services of an advocate to challenge any cases of interdict brought against them in the courts to prevent them fishing, but the outcome of the action was often immaterial. By the time judgment was given sufficient time had elapsed to allow them to 'clean' up the river in question.

Two methods of fishing were employed in the Tâf. One involved the use of a dredge net drawn between two small craft which from a description given by Mr T. H. David could well have been the Scotch 'box' – a small type coracle. The other method required the fisherman to wade in the river using a pole five to six feet long with a cleft extremity for retrieving the quarry from the river bed. The mussels, once entrenched on the end of the pole, were transferred to a bag carried over the shoulder. The use of a sighting tube with a glass window facilitated the locating of the mussel on the river bed – a variant of this device was held by the fisherman. In the deeper pools the pole method would still be used, with the operator lying flat over the side of the 'box' craft.

However the mussels were caught, they were brought to the bank for shell opening. Small mounds of opened shells were a common sight along the Pentrehowell stretch of the Tâf above the confluence with the

Hydfron in midsummer; they would be removed later in the year by flood water. The Scots were extremely reticent and divulged little to the local populace about their pearl haul. Pearls were their only interest, for they discarded the flesh of the mussel and the mother of pearl shells, although the latter were being used for button manufacture at the time.

Trevor Jones, from 'Perlau Tâf', *The Carmarthenshire Historian*

22. AFTER GOING BEYOND TALLEY ABBEY IN OCTOBER

Was ever valley road so full of sound
And mellow sweetness as the league I came
Between the mountains to enchanted ground
Burnt warm and wondrous by autumnal flame?
Along that road I could have sworn I heard
Ap Gwilym, lithe and laughing, in the brake,
Calling on Morfudd – and for Morfudd's sake
Outpouring songs of passion, like a bird.

And then at eve, when drooping dusk drew near,
I sat with neighbourly, moss-rooted trees
And watched the moon that bathed in Talley mere,
And heard, dim-wafted on the downward breeze
Across the stubbled fields, from hill to hill,
The echoing orisons that still
Lie captive in the heart of moor and stream,
And saw the singers, darkly as in a dream . . .
The pilgrim bands who passed the abbey door
Chanting their sorrows centuries before.

And to the uplands, where in days of old
The Romans ranged the secret hills for gold,
I turned and looked – and saw, in moonlight gay,
October, that red fox with tail on fire
Who makes the woodlands blaze from shire to shire,
Turn in his tracks and swiftly steal away.

A. G. Prys-Jones

23. *Llyn-y-Fan Fach*

In a hollow at the base of the highest pinnacle of the Black Mountain, called the Van or Beacon, is Llyn Van, a fine lake of beautifully transparent water, in the form of a parallelogram, nearly a mile in length, and about ninety-six feet in depth. The sombre aspect of the dark red precipitous rocks that form the eastern boundary of this extensive sheet of water, and the general air of sterility which characterises all the surrounding objects, are finely contrasted with the high state of cultivation which embellishes the lower grounds of its vicinity. Though the situation is so elevated that the snow remains unmelted upon the shore for the greater portion of the year, this lake abounds with trout and eels of superior quality. When a strong breeze ruffles the surface of Llyn Van, the rise of the fish is almost incredible, and can be compared only to violent rain, or the effect that would be produced by casting handfuls of gravel upon its surface. We once spent an entire day on its wild, rocky shores, and were, for that period at least, perfectly satiated with sport. The trout threw themselves out of the water in sommersaults, by hundreds at once; and the effect was most singular, as their golden spotted sides flashed and glittered in the sunbeams that occasionally broke through the gloom which overspread the atmosphere. Fortunately for the lover of angling, from the shallow rocky bottom of this lake near the shore, it is useless to attempt dragging with a net; while its great depth towards the centre, would render any similar method of fishing equally unprofitable, even could a boat be conveyed to the lofty rugged mountain hollow in which it is situated. The trout are therefore propagated in immense numbers, undiminished by the successful devices adopted for their destruction in waters less difficult of approach, and they consequently, for the most part, die of old age; very few persons being willing to encounter the toil and fatigue of the ascent. In the grousing season, a tent is generally erected on the shores of Llyn Van, and the sportsmen occasionally vary their pursuits, by angling when the breeze is sufficiently strong for the purpose. In stormy weather its surface is greatly agitated, and the fish are then often thrown ashore in considerable numbers.

George Agar Hansard.
Trout and Salmon Fishing in Wales 1834

24. *Little Van Pool*

The Little Van Pool lies in a fine Cwm beneath a precipitous concave wall of old red sandstone towards the summit of Carmarthen Van. This stone also forms the bed of the lake, which is bare of weeds of any kind. The food supply is poor and although trout are fairly numerous, they average only about five to 1lb. It seems from a MS. of the late seventeenth century, referred to under Llyn-y-Fan Fawr, that food must then have been abundant in this water, for it mentions the abundance of 'troutes' which were 'dayly taken here in greate store.'

'There is allso a greate Poole on each side of't which makes it most dreadfull presenting Death on all sides . . . which Pools, are worth ones noteing, the one called Llynllwch Sawthey (i.e. Llyn-y-Fan Fâch) for its abundance of fish of all-sortes (but more to be wondered at) especially for its troutes which are dayly taken here in greate store, but this poole is in Carmarden-shire, the other of a contrary nature in this County called of the Hill Llyn-y-fan-hir (i.e. Llyn-y-Fan Fawr) hathe no fish attalle in't neither will any fish being put into it live, but as soone as they have tasted of this water turne up there Silver Bellies and suddenly dey . . . it's much greater than the other Poole and a large parte of the rock stood shelveing over it which about Ano Doni 1687 on Saterday December the tenth . . . fell downe into the Poole makeing the water overflow all the land about it doing great mischief to the Country, and caused the river Uske to breake over its banks in a most dreadfull manner.'

(British Museum Harleian MSS No.7017)

. . . It is difficult to account for the change that has taken place. It may be mentioned that eels have for long been very numerous here.

During the partial drainage while the dam was being built nearly 300 were caught, and 100 to 150 years ago it was a practice with local farmers to fix basket traps under small waterfalls below the lake at night. In this way some colossal eels were caught, local tradition says up to 10 feet in length.

Apart from fishing, this lake is, by reason of its associations, one of the most interesting in Wales.

Four miles away lies the village of Myddvai, where dwelt about the middle of the thirteenth century, the celebrated Rhiwallon and his sons, physicians to Rhys Gryg, Lord of Dynevor Castle and Ystrad Towy.

They were ancestors of the long line of the Physicians of Myddvai, which ended in Rice Williams, M.D., of Aberystwyth, who died at the age of 85 on May 16, 1842.

Adapted from Frank Ward,
The Lakes of Wales

25. *The Bishop's Pond*

The *Bishop's Pond*, or Old River as it is sometimes called, marks the course of the Towy at the close of the last century. During hard frost, it is much frequented by skaters. The diversion of the river from its old channel at this place occurred on the occasion of a great flood on the night of Llanybyddyr fair, July 17, 1802, during the episcopate of Bishop G. Murray. Previously coals used to be conveyed by boats from Carmarthen to Abergwili Palace, there being then a short canal from the Towy, crossed by a bridge, called Pont Groca. Traces of the canal remain.

William Spurrell, *Carmarthen and its Neighbourhood*

26. *Exploring Llygad Llwchwr*

9th   Made a coffin for Richard Davies's son, aged 5 years, who died of scarlet fever. Wood and labour 8/-. Made a coracle that may be taken to pieces and made up again, for Llygad Llwchwr cave. Cost 10/6d.

10th   Went, together with B. Morgan, Dd. Lewis, John Thomas, Walter Jones, Puddicomb and Owen Jones to Llygad Llwchwr.* Entered the cavern at 8½ a.m. and after turning to the left at right angles to the main branch and getting down over the rock by the rope-ladder over the stream, we made up the coracle and proceeded down the stream over very deep pools through several magnificent caverns where man never dared go before. Came out to daylight 1½ p.m.

---

* The Revd. Lewis Price's Guide to Llandilo' 1883 says of Llygad Llwchwr cave . . . 'in the interior of this wonderful cave there is a large pool which, some years ago, afforded much amusement to gentlemen residing in the neighbourhood, who undertook the difficult task of contructing a coracle suitable for wading it, and which was left there for the amusement of others, until it got unfit for any longer use'.

14th   Went to Llygad Llwchwr cave together with Revd. John Lewis, Messrs. D. Lewis, R. W. Lewis, H. Bundy and J. Roberts. Left coracle inside. Entered 10 a.m. Out 4 p.m. Thermometer in the shade outside 68 deg. Water 49 deg. Quantity of water discharged per minute 450 ft. – 28,325 lbs. – 12 tons 11 cwts. 12 lbs. – 45 hogsheads. Holywell discharges 84 hogsheads per minute.

23rd   Edward Price, Thomas Jones and self went at 6 p.m. to Llygad Llwchwr to see if the coracle, left there by me some years ago, was in a fit state to make use of. Found it completely decayed. Returned home 1 a.m. 24th.

The Diary of Thomas Jenkins of Llandeilo 1826-1870

27. Potholing in Llygad Llwchwr Cave

A squeeze through a gap at the top of the wall built across the entrance leads to a series of right angle bends. A low, muddy chamber offers a choice of two ways which join later. At the next junction, there is a choice of three ways. The two passages on the left lead to the 'First River Chamber'. The upper passage should be used in order to protect the formations. In the River Chamber, a traverse, high on the right, leads across the river to a pleasant grotto, whilst upstream a duct of 3 ft. makes a short cut to the 'Second River Chamber'. Back to the junction, the way on is via the right hand passage, this leads to a fine stalagmite pillar; the passage becomes lofty, but soon closes down to a muddy crawl into the Boulder Chamber. A lower series can be explored, under the floor, but the way on is over the boulders at the far end. Keeping left for 10 ft. brings one to the 'Parting of the Ways'. The left hand passage leads through a pool which must be waded, to the 'Second and Best River Chamber', where a 20 ft. ladder admits one to the mud banks of the river, with stalactite curtains and grottoes reached by roof traverses. The right hand passage leads to the 'Third River Chamber' where a 15 ft. ladder descent leads to the river with no way of keeping dry. The 'Fourth and Last River Chamber' marks the end of the cave for the non-diver.

Llygad Llwchwr is a confusing cave, with many junctions, so it is as well to use a survey on a first trip.

The entrance to this cave is just above the resurgence of the River Loughor, near the village of Trapp. This is probably one of the largest resurgences in Great Britain, but the water works take most of the water through six 10 inch diameter pipes and only a small proportion now goes over the notched weir. The entrance has been fenced in by the water works authority.

The cave has always been open, the earliest known visit was by Jenkins in 1841.

The cave consists of an extensive system of dry passages, opening on to four river chambers. There are a number of fine formations. The four river chambers are connected by sumps with two standing sumps. The underground river resurges from the 7th sump. The Terminal or 8th sump was examined by Balcombe and others in the 1940s. It was dived by C. D. George and B. De Graaf on 10th July, 1960 using 100% 0^2 for 320 ft. with three air spaces.

In 1970 John Parker passed a 470 ft. long sump and discovered a 400 ft. long, well decorated passage.

Tony Oldham.
The Caves of Carmarthenshire 1975

XV

Estuary & Coast

1. *The Dead child*

Only the steady creaking of a flight of swans disturbed the silence, labouring low overhead with outstretched necks towards the sea.

It was a warm, wet, windless afternoon with a soft feathery feeling in the air: rain, yet so fine it could scarcely fall but rather floated. It clung to everything it touched; the rushes in the deep choked ditches of the sea-marsh were bowed down with it, the small black cattle looked cobwebbed with it, their horns were jewelled with it. Curiously stumpy too these cattle looked, the whole herd sunk nearly to the knees in a soft patch.

This sea-marsh stretched for miles. Seaward, a greyness merging into sky had altogether rubbed out the line of dunes which bounded it that way: inland, another and darker blurred greyness was all you could see of the solid Welsh hills. But near by loomed a solitary gate, where the path crossed a footbridge and humped over the big dyke; and here in a sodden tangle of brambles the scent of a fox hung, too heavy today to rise or dissipate.

The gate clicked sharply and shed its cascade as two men passed through. Both were heavily loaded in oilskins. The elder and more tattered one carried two shotguns, negligently, and a brace of golden plover were tied to the bit of old rope he wore knotted round his middle: glimpses of a sharp-featured weather-beaten face showed from within his bonneted sou'wester, but mouth and even chin were hidden in a long weeping moustache. The younger man was springy and tall and well-built and carried over his shoulder the body of a dead child. Her thin muddy legs dangled against his chest, her head and arms hung down his back; and at his heels walked a black dog – disciplined, saturated, and eager.

Suddenly the older man blew through the curtain of his moustache as if to clear it of water before speaking, but he thought better of it after a quick glance round at his companion. There was no personal grief in the young man's face but it was awe-struck.

An hour later the two men had left the sea-marsh behind them: they had reached higher ground where a lofty but tangled and neglected wood traversed a steep hillside. So soft was this south-western Welsh climate, and so thick the shelter of all that towering timber round, that here a glade of very old azaleas planted in a clearing had themselves grown almost into gangling trees and dripping rhododendron-scrub had spread half across what had once been a broad gravelled carriage-drive.

Richard Hughes, *The Fox in the Attic*

2. LLANSTEPHAN

A ship lies foundered in the bar,
   These many years;
To keel and chain and wave-worn spar
   Sea-rust adheres.

The castle on this flowery Head,
   Empty and grey,
Seems waiting for its warriors dead, –
   Dust, dust are they!

The sea around the foundered bark
   Still ebbs and flows;
High in the blue a brown-winged lark
   Carolling goes.

Let no ill fate unlink the chain
   Of Nature's power;
Nor ancient woe nor new-born pain
   The Spring unflower . . .

Oh! it is well that seas should flow,
   Tho' anchors rust;
And it is well that summers glow,
   Tho' hearts be dust! . . .

On Towy's flood the evening falls,
   Larks are asleep;
And o'er the crumbling castle walls
   Dark shadows creep.

Hark! from the shadowy sea beneath
   What murmurs come?
From shadowy walls what night-airs breathe,
   Which day made dumb? . . .

The moon was silvering the sea
To Gower's head:
It shone, as tho' there could not be
   Anyone dead.

Elfed, from *Llanstephan*

3. *Encroachment at Laugharne*

It is difficult to decide to what extent the sea has receded and encroached at Laugharne; the accounts are conflicting, but I give them. It is certain the sea broke in at the Salt House on the marsh facing Ferryside, and that the land there extended four hundred yards out before the sea came in; did it, before this encroachment, come as far into Laugharne as it does now? It would seem not. I was told by an old inhabitant, whose family had been here for generations, that the marsh was reclaimed from the sea about four hundred years ago by a Dutchman, as I shall mention presently. Tradition says the sea came up to Duke's Bottom, at the hills in Pendine, and to Coigan, and the rocks along to Laugharne; there are facts that prove it. There was once dry land on Cefn Sidan between Ferryside and the marsh at some period. Thomas Prout, an old inhabitant of Wiseman's Bridge, near Sandersfoot, told me there was a tradition that the old town of Laugharne stood on Cefn Sidan; this is very likely to have been confused with the old town of Ferryside, which stood between the Ferry Point and Laugharne Burrows. The old inhabitant I have just mentioned, who is eighty years old, gave me this account, which he had from his father and grandfather, who both held farms on the marsh. That Dutchman, he said, was the first to shut out the sea and put up banks. He first banked in that part by the Sand Hills. He reclaimed a good deal of it. The sea had previously been receding. He made that road from Kingaddle straight down to the Sand Hills, and pitched it. He lived in Laugharne, and spent much money in the place. A tradition exists of a Dutchman, named Von Dono, living here. He introduced the Dutch one-handed plough, which ceased to be used about thirty years ago. His mantle, which was very handsome, was preserved in Laugharne Church, as well as Gui de Brian's. Much fine pasture land is still covered by the sea. He gave me this account of the sea breaking in by the ancient Salt House; it stood near the Cockle Bank, about thirty yards from it by the sands at the Upper Marsh. About 130 years ago the sea broke in, and rose to a great height, he said; and his grandfather, Mr John Morris, a farmer, residing at Brook Farm, on the estate of the Upper Marsh, rescued the inmates of the Salt House. He swam to them on his horse. They escaped from the top windows and were all saved. The walls of this house are to be seen when the tide is out; and this is the ancient one; that which stood till 1873 by the bridge over the hill was more modern. I have it, upon what would be considered good

authority, that, about ninety years ago, it was dry land from the Castle to Bach Point; that it was all grass and shady with trees, the stumps of which remain. Patches of grass are visible now at low tide. This is confirmed by others; and an old inhabitant, eighty years old, deceased these four years, told me he remembered a house being built with one of the trees. Another, who is now seventy, says that when he was a boy the sea never came up to the Strand House on the strand, nor to Island House, as it does at present, and that there was not so much mud as now, and the land here was firmer. I have, in Part I, mentioned the quay wall and the ballast posts that were here once. A person of middle age, and another much older, says, that at spring-tides the sea always came into the town past Island House up to the old Porch House in Wogan Street. One of the fishermen of Laugharne tells me the sea is now rather receding at Laugharne and encroaching at Pendine; it is certainly receding at the bottom of Laugharne Marsh where the Wit-y-yerd, or Whityed flows, for the residents of Honeycors say, that forty years ago it came at high tides over the marsh opposite Brook, two fields from the road; a bank was put up to keep it out. James Wilkins, an old man, who was gardener to the Laugharne family of the Castle, tells me that in the gardens of all the houses at Gosport which look upon the strand, and also in the gardens of the houses on the opposite side of Gosport, passing down to that called 'The Horse Shoe', and to Stonyway, there is sand if you dig four feet down; that it is like that at the sea, only a little darker, which shows that the sea washed over them once. There is the same kind of black slime found in the bed of the river Coran all the way up to Horsepool, which is seen where the sea washes on the strand.

Mary Curtis,
Antiquities of Laugharne, Pendine and their Neighbourhoods

4. OVER SIR JOHN'S HILL

. . . The Heron and I,
I young Aesop fabling to the near night by the dingle
Of eels, saint heron hymning in the shell-hung distant
Crystal harbour vale
Where the sea cobbles sail,
And wharves of water where the walls dance and the white
    cranes stilt.
It is the heron and I, under judging Sir John's elmed
Hill, tell-tale the knelled
Guilt
Of the led-astray birds whom God, for their breast of whistles,
Have mercy on,
God in his whirlwind silence save, who marks the sparrows hail,
For their souls' song.
Now the heron grieves in the weeded verge. Through windows
Of dusk and water I see the tilting whispering
Heron, mirrored, go,
As the snapt feathers snow,
Fishing in the tear of the Towy. Only a hoot owl
Hollows, a grassblade blown in cupped hands, in the looted elms
And no green cocks or hens
Shout
Now on Sir John's hill. The heron, ankling the scaly
Lowlands of the waves,
Makes all the music; and I who hear the tune of the slow,
Wear-willow river, grave,
Before the lunge of the night, the notes on this time-shaken
Stone for the sake of the souls of the slain birds sailing.

Dylan Thomas, from *Over Sir John's Hill*

5. *Mr Morgan Meets Tragedy*

The Burry Inlet, on the south coast of Wales, looks its best from the sea. At least so thought Mr Morgan, as he sat in the sternsheets of his boat, a fishing line between his fingers, while his son, Evan, pulled lazily over the still water.

In truth the prospect on this pleasant Autumn evening would have pleased a man less biased by pride of fatherland than Mr Morgan. The Inlet at full tide forms a wide sheet of water, penetrating in an easterly direction some ten miles into the land, with the county of Carmarthen to the north and the Gower Peninsula to the south. The shores are flat, but rounded hills rise inland which merge to form an undulating horizon of high ground. Here and there along the coast are sand-dunes, whose grays and yellows show up in contrast to the green of the grass-lands and the woods beyond.

To the south-east, over by Salthouse Point and Penclawdd, Mr Morgan could see every detail of house and sand-dune, tree and meadow, lit up with a shining radiance, but the north-west hills behind Burry Port were black and solid against a setting sun. Immediately north lay Llanelly, with its dingy coloured buildings, its numberless chimneys and the masts and funnels of the steamers in its harbour.

It was a perfect evening in late September, the close of a perfect day. Not a cloud appeared in the sky and scarcely a ripple stirred the surface of the sea. The air was warm and balmy, and all nature seemed drows-ing in languorous content. Save for the muffled noise of the Llanelly mills, borne over the water, and the slow, rhythmic creak of the oars, no sound disturbed the sleepy quiet. Morgan leaned back in the stern-sheets, gazing out dreamily on the broad sweep of the Inlet and the lengthening shadows ashore . . . To any one attempting navigation in the Burry Inlet the tides are a factor of the first importance. With a rise and fall at top springs of something like twenty-five feet, the placid estuary of high water becomes a little later a place of fierce currents and swirling eddies. The Inlet is shallow also. At low tide by far the greater portion of its area is uncovered, and this, by confining the rushing waters to narrow channels, still further increases their speed. As the tide falls the great Llanrhidian Sands appear, stretching out northwards from the Gower Peninsula, while an estuary nearly four miles wide contracts to a river racing between mud banks five hundred yards apart.

Mr Morgan took the paddles, and heading the boat for the northern coast, began to pull slowly shorewards . . . The two had left Burry Port on a flowing tide and had drifted up the Inlet to above Llanelly. Now the tide was ebbing, and they were being carried swiftly down again. Mr Morgan reckoned that by the time they were opposite Burry Port they should be far enough inshore to make the harbour.

Gradually the long line of the Llanelly houses and chimneys slipped by. Evan had clambered aft and at intervals he felt with the hand of an expert the weighted lines which were trailing astern. He frowned as he glanced again at the two mackerel. He had had a good many fishing trips with his father during the holiday and never before had they had such a miserable catch. How he wished he could have a couple of good bites before they had to give up!

The thought had scarcely passed through his mind, when a line checked . . .

Freeman Wills Crofts. *The Sea Mystery* 1926

6. *Giant Conger Eels*

Telpin used to be the great spot for catching conger eels. The whole shore is covered with huge rocks, and under the rocks were pools, in some of which the congers stayed between tides. I have caught a little one a few times, but some men skilled at the work, using a barbed crook, occasionally caught six footers, and I have seen some as big as that. It was said that they barked like dogs, but I never heard them. They were vicious brutes with razor-sharp teeth and could give a terrible bite. Of course there were the usual fishermen's yarns, and Luther Phelps always told how a conger bit the toe of his boot clean off. His toes were saved because he was wearing a big pair of somebody else's cast-offs. Now *wasn't* that lucky! Luther fished for anything, anywhere, and I never knew him spoil a good yarn for want of a bit of imagination. All the same, congers had and still have vicious bites.

H. V. Fletcher, *The Coasts of Wales*

7. VIEW FROM LLANSTEFFAN

Stand on this rock.
Look over there, south by south-east.
There the *Paul of Hamburg* slid
down to the everlasting feast
of cockles and mussels,
the waves' yeast

and the storm's kitchen.
Now enswathed in the watered skeins
of long Cefn Sidan,
fitted forever to the grains
of the saffron sands,
the hulk remains

forfeit to Wales.
It came in peace, but the bay's jaw
bit it – like a flurried bird
pulled under for the old pike's maw.
Beware, then, you who want to come
and play at war.

Raymond Garlick

8. *The Burry Estuary Wrecks 1868*

One of the worst incidents of multiple shipwreck on the coast of Great Britain, excluding of course military engagements, took place on the North coast of the Gower Peninsula at the mouth of the Burry Estuary on the night of January 22nd, 1868. Several days prior to this date, the Gower had been ravaged by Westerly gales, but on the 22nd the winds had blown themselves out and the sea became calm. The disaster which was about to occur involved vessels setting out from the Port of Llanelli, their Masters and crews happy in the knowledge that the fierce Westerly gales had at last abated.

Llanelli in those days was a busy little port, even though the sand bar at its approaches proved a somewhat dangerous obstacle. It was indeed this sand bar, on that calm, practically windless evening, which was to bring doom to many of the vessels as they set out on the ebb tide. Although the wind had abated almost to nothing, unknown to the Masters of the vessels the bar was still in tremendous swell. The vessels, nineteen in all, proceeded down the Burry Estuary in convoys of four bow to stern, and towed by tugs. The vessels were the *Eliza* of Jersey, the *Mary Anne* of Amlwch, the *St Catherine* of Fay, the *Amethyst* of Dublin, the *Huntress* of Workington, the *Jeune Celine* of Jersey, the *Ann* of Barnstaple, the *Sophie* of Regneville, the Pilot cutter *Ceres*, and several other small ships. The whole convoy ranged from 20 tons upwards to 400 tons.

Things began to go wrong soon after the tugboats cast off their towlines. The sea was running a heavy swell and, there being hardly any wind to catch the sails, the vessels all began to drift. Some drifted on to the bar and were severely buffeted by the sea against the sand. Those which managed to be swept off the bar found that the inrush of water through their stoved-in hulls was far too much for the pumps to handle and they soon began to sink. The vessels which missed the bar completely, found themselves driven onto the beaches where the heavy seas soon began to break them up. In a very short time, four ships were on the beach at Llanmadoc only yards from each other, and five or six lay wrecked in Broughton Bay.

Control of the vessels was such an impossible task, that several of them collided. Captain Thomas Roberts, Master and owner of the Llanelli brigantine *The Brothers*, found his vessel with several others of the same tow, in a position which he himself thought was clear of the bar. His towline was cast off, and soon afterwards, to his horror, he realised that he was drifting towards the shore. At eleven o'clock at night, *The Brothers* struck the bar. Shortly afterwards the crew observed another vessel, which they recognised as the *Roscius* of Llanelli, approaching them completely out of control. The vessels collided, the *Roscius* being badly holed. Her crew together with the pilot, eight men in all, jumped safely to the deck of *The Brothers* whilst the two vessels were interlocked. Another vessel, the brigantine *Jeune Celine* was soon observed, her Master desperately calling for help.

The Brothers at last cleared the bank, left the *Roscius* to the mercy of the seas and managed to get afloat again in deep water. Captain Roberts decided to drop anchor, but all too soon realised that too much water was seeping through his vessel's battered hull. The anchor cable was cut, and the vessel allowed to beach herself. Her crew, along with the men from the *Roscius* decided to seek refuge on the hulk lightship in Broughton Bay, where they found the crews of several other vessels clinging on for dear life. In the darkness the men could hear cries of help coming from vessels out on the bar, vessels which were slowly breaking apart, spilling their crews into the dark seas.

A survivor from the *Ann* of Barnstaple related how the heavy seas had knocked the vessel's mainmast out when she was at the Burry Estuary approaches. The vessel drifted into Broughton Bay along with several others. 'When we left Llanelli, we thought it was all smooth, as it had been calm all day.'

When daylight finally appeared, it disclosed the gruesome fate of the convoy. Llanmadoc and Broughton sands were strewn with wreckage and cargo, and even worse, many bodies lay in stark evidence upon the yellow sand. Several of the vessels were salvaged and one, the *Elizabeth* of Barnstaple, put in to Tenby severely battered after her ordeal.

Eighteen lives were lost that night, and of vessels lost with all hands were the *Waterfly*, the *Jeune Celine*, the *Huntress*, the *Amethyst* and the *Mary Fanny*. The *Mary Fanny* was later salvaged from where she ran aground in Rhossili and was rebuilt. She sailed for many years afterwards until she was sunk by a German U-boat in 1918.

P. H. Rees, *Gower Shipwrecks*

9. The Wreck of the Teviotdale

The inhabitants of Croesyceiliog were greatly stirred in 1886, when the ship *Teviotdale* sank on the Cefn Sidan sands. Many of the menfolk and farmers along the river bank who possessed boats, set out to explore the lost cargo, and on finding that it was timber, made a special effort to salvage some for their own use. Rowing their boats upstream, they made rafts of the floating wood, and after many such journeys some of them acquired enough timber to erect new out-buildings, etc., for themselves. At low tide the old wreckage is still visible to those travelling on the railway.

Ethel M. Davies, *The Story of Llandyfeiliog Parish*

10. *The Hatchet Men of Pembrey*

Pembrey men, it is said, are called the 'Bw'elli Bach' – The Small Hatchets, and the explanation given to me for the name was that it is a reference to the little axes that some of the village men carried when they went to look for wrecks – and it was subtly suggested to me, also, that these men were not above trying to entice ships onto the rocks and the sand at treacherous Cefn Sidan, by showing lights in their houses, and even on the Church tower itself. Across from Pembrey of course are Cefn Sidan sands that were the cause of destruction to many a ship, and death to many a seaman and traveller as the gravestones testify. I remember as I went on my way down the Bristol channel on a fishing trip in the Atlantic with Captain Brown how he showed me Cefn Sidan and told me tales of the devastation that these sands have caused.

In the Church graveyard the three fellows showed us a stone that chronicled the shipwreck of *Jeune Emma* on November 21st, 1828. All the passengers and crew were lost, but for six sailors.

Among the passengers was a Colonel Coqueline and his daughter Adeline – 'Niece to Josephine, Consort to that renowned individual, Napoleon Buonaparte', according to what is to be seen on her gravestone.

Aneirin Talfan Davies, † *Crwydro Sir Gâr*

11. *Looting near Cefn Sidan*

My Lord,

I believe the melancholy duty devolves upon myself of first informing you that on the 19th day of this month, the Barque *Brothers* bound from Bahia, South America to Liverpool, of 370 tons burden, and of which a Mr Williamson of Liverpool was Owner, was wrecked on Cefn Sidan Sands (near the town of Kidwelly), Carmarthen Bay – and that of the Crew, which consisted of sixteen men, only one person, the Carpenter, was saved. The Vessel was laden with Cotton Wool, Hides, and Buffalo Horns and, I learn from the deposition of the Man saved that she contained about 2000 bales of the Cotton, and 4000 Buffalo Hides. What particularly induces me to address your Lordship, is, the nearly total plunder of the Wrecked Vessel and her cargo by the Country People, for the wind then blowing hard upon the shore, nearly the whole of the goods and wreck were driven on Shore – between the Borough Town of Kidwelly, and the Village of Pembrey in the Parish of that name. I was not informed of this wreck until Saturday, the 21st inst. at about eleven o'clock a.m. – by the Collector of the Customs, when I immediately rode to the Scene of the Wreck, distant about twelve miles from the House, and as I followed the Sea-shore, I observed numbers of Country People employed in cutting open the Bales of Cotton which were lying in quantities along the shore of nine Miles in length, and carrying them away in Bags and Carts, etc. – as I approached Kidwelly, I informed the People, chiefly of that Town, engaged in breaking up the wrecked vessel with Saws, Hammers, etc. and conveying the Timber, etc. away in Carts – I warned the People, many of whom were Farmers of respectability of the consequences of this proceeding, but being alone, the Constable I had engaged being unable to keep pace with my horse, I did not succeed in deterring them from doing so – I have very highly to complain of the conduct of a Gentleman, who resided near the spot where the wreck occurred in refusing me the assistance of his carts and men to preserve some of the goods, etc. – for had I been made acquainted with the wreck on Friday morning, on which day, the chief plunder was committed, and had the assistance of the Gentleman I mention and the neighbouring Magistracy, some of whom resided within three miles from the Wreck and in sight of it, nearly the whole of the goods and wrecked Vessel might have been saved; whereas, in consequence of the want of co-operation I name, only about 109 bales of Cotton and a few hides have been preserved. Carts have been sent from a distance of twenty miles round, to convey away the Bales of Cotton, etc., and timber of the Vessel, but the Constables I had stationed along the Sands, from the length of the shore along which the goods were strewed, and the numbers of the People, were unable to prevent them from carrying them off, and I was myself assaulted by two Men, in endeavouring to do so, and apprehend the offenders. Some respectable farmers have employed Men to saw up and take off the Mast, bowsprit, etc., tho' some Men I placed to preserve them, gave the Parties notice that I had desired them to prevent their being taken away, and was that morning going to send timber carriages for them.

I regret to say that this is the third wreck that has occurred on these Sands within the period of one week – One Vessel of about 120 Tons was stranded opposite the Village of Pembrey on Monday last. She was laden with Oranges and Lemons bound from Seville to Glasgow but as I had timely information of the circumstance, as also, the Custom House Officials, we succeeded in landing most of the Cargo during the night with very trifling loss – One of the Justices of the Borough Town of Kidwelly picked up a Bag of Letters belonging to the *Brothers* which He has sent up to the General Post Office by direction of Sir F. Freeding –

As the number of the Offenders is so great, and many of them Persons of much respectability (large Farmers, etc.) I should wish to have the honor of your Lordship's instructions on the subject, ere I take steps in the business, as I stand alone, as a Magistrate in it. I have informations against many Persons of substance, for cutting up the Masts, carrying off bales of Cotton, the Ship's pumps, etc. and against an Iron Monger of Carmarthen, for actually having Carts to carry off Bales of Cotton to Carmarthen and other places. I venture to suggest to your Lordship, that unless some example be made of the Major Offenders, these disgraceful scenes will again occur, as Wreckers are frequently on this Coast and as I was myself this time *assaulted* in the execution of my duty, unless people be checked in their Lawless proceedings, there is no knowing to what lengths opposition may be carried, as They come prepared with short hatchets, hammers, etc.

Since writing this, a Gentleman is arrived from Liverpool on behalf of the Underwriters, and Owners; I went with him to the Town of Kidwelly, the Mayor of which granted a Search Warrant for the stolen goods. We found in one House some hides, and in a Farmer's Premises (within the Borough) some Bales of Cotton, three of which were concealed in a Potato Stack – besides three pieces of a Mast.

I am ready to furnish your Lordship with all the information with respect to offenders, I possess and awaiting your instructions, I have the honor to be, My Lord,

Your Lordships Obedt. Humble Servt.
J. H. REES
Magistrate

Killymaenllwyd,
near Llanelly,
Carmarthenshire
26 Decr. 1833.

The Carmarthen Antiquary 1960

12. *The Wreckers of Ragwin*

In the many years I wandered over these beaches there was, and it may still be there today, the wreck of a ship stuck fast in the sand near Ragwin. It stood far below high water and every tide covered it. The gaunt wooden ribs, which were all that were left of it stood bare and tall, weed and barnacle covered, hard as iron, like two long rows of sentinels, with the thicker heavier timbers of bow and sternpost one at each end. That skeleton had been there so long that nobody I ever met knew anything at all about it.

In the wide bay there were a couple of farms. There was a story that many years ago an old farmer and his wife lived alone in one of them, and they supplemented what they made on the barren land by wrecking. They had a son, but years before he had left home, and they had never heard of him since.

In stormy weather they would lure ships into the bay by putting out lanterns to look as if they were harbour lights. The ships were wrecked, and as the cargoes came ashore they reaped a harvest richer than they ever gathered from the land.

One day after a storm and a shipwreck they were walking the beach in search of what had been washed in, and they came on the body of a sailor, lying face downwards.

'He's alive,' said the old woman. 'I saw him move.'

The old man picked up a heavy rock. 'Dead men tell no tales,' he said and threw the rock down hard on the sailor's skull.

They turned the body over. It was their long-lost son.

H. L. V. Fletcher, *The Coasts of Wales*

13. *The Ferry House, Laugharne*

The ancient Ferry House was at Bottom Point; it is in ruins now. Here they ferried over to the part midway between the wood called Cwm Celyn and the small cottage just by the stream on the sea-shore; thence the road passed to the farm, Mwchau; afterwards turned up to Pentywyn, a farm above the Scar, and into the road which now goes to Llanstephan. On the cliff a small house is within the gates leading to

Glan-y-môr. Before it was built, a public-house, called the Ferry House, was here. The ancient Ferry House stood by the rocks and sea, on a line with the part where the stables of Glan-y-môr are, the Recess cottage alongside of it; a kiln stood by it.

It is in the memory of old persons, lately deceased, that the ferry boat was not in the request it is now; that they knew an old woman of the name of Bennet, who resided in this ancient Ferry House; they called her Betty Fordside, because the house was by the side of the ford. She was the ferry woman. She had a horse for carrying persons over to the Scar at low water; it went with them on its back; but to their misfortune, when the tide came in quicker than usual, the horse would have to swim to land and the riders sometimes to swim for their lives.

Once upon a time a Jew going this perilous course was drowned. She could have been stopped from this; for there was, as now, a ferry boat; but they were not very strict then. She must have carried on a good trade with her horse, for it took travellers by land as well as by sea. On Saturdays it was in tremendous request; every one wanted the horse to go to Caermarthen. She was verily besieged with applicants; plenty of intriguing carried on, and subterfuges resorted to, to induce her to let out the horse. The ferry boat belonged then to that Ferry House that I have mentioned as within the gates leading to Glan-y-môr.

The present Ferry House is a new one. The ferry is held between M. Jones, Esq., of Llanmiloe, and Mr Meares, to whom Plâs at Llanstephan belongs. The ferryman pays £3 3s. yearly to M. Jones, Esq., and the same to Mr Meyers, who holds the property on the Llanstephan side. By this Ferry House is a pool called Bunny Saer's Pool, after a man of that name, who was drowned in it; its water is 17 or 18 feet deep.

Mary Curtis,
Antiquities of Laugharne, Pendine, and their Neighbourhoods

14. TWMI

On the grey marsh Twmi lives,
His door ajar to the blue shore,
With nothing now to disrupt his nightly rest
But the tide coming in, and the tide's going out.
Very short is his journey,
Short is its turning that was just now so full;
From kitchen to door and from door to kitchen –
Like the tide coming in, and the tide going out.
But he remembers the whole journey,
Despite the shivering and crookedness,
And sometimes he relives his travels with relish;
And something like that is life, says Twmi
Some tide coming in, and tide going out.

Nantlais †

† Translators

Acknowledgements

For permission to reprint works in copyright the author and publisher thank the following copyright holders for items from titles listed here:

A. T. Arber-Cooke and the Friends of Llandovery Civic Trust Association for an extract from *Pages from the History of Llandovery* published at the Old Printing Office, and to the following publishers and copyright-holders for the relevant selections from these listed works:

B. T. Batsford Ltd. for D. Parry Jones's *Welsh Country Upbringing*.

Chatto & Windus Ltd. for Jacquetta Hawkes's A *Guide to the Prehistoric and Roman Monuments of England & Wales* and Hugh Casson's National Benzole Guides to *Follies* and *Monuments*.

William Collins, Sons & Co. Ltd. for William Condry's *The Natural History of Wales* published in their New Naturalist Series.

J. M. Dent & Sons Ltd. for Ernest Rhys's *Wales and England Wed*.

Faber & Faber Ltd. for Ted Hughes's *Collected Poems*, Vyvyan Rees's *Shell Guide to South West Wales* and also to Mrs Gwen Watkins for Vernon Watkins's *Collected Poems*.

The Gomer Press (J. D. Lewis & Sons) for Bryan Martin Davies's *Darluniau ar Gynfas*, D. R. Griffiths's *Caneuon Amanwy*, Raymond Garlick's *A Sense of Time*, Pat Molloy's *And They Blessed Rebecca*, D. Parry-Jones's *My Own Folk*, Kusha Petts's *A Necklace for a Poor Sod*, D. J. Williams's *Yr Hen Dŷ Ffarm* trs. by Waldo Williams, published by Harrap as *The Old Farmhouse*, Nantlais Williams's *O Gopa Bryn Nebo* and to their Gwasg Aberystwyth for extracts from *Songs of Assisi* by H. Elfed Lewis, and D. Gwenallt Jones's *Eples*.

David Higham Associates and the Trustees for the estate of Dylan Thomas for permission to include extracts from Dylan Thomas's *Collected Poems* and *A Portrait of the Artist as a Young Dog*, and Richard Hughes's *The Fox in the Attic*.

Robert Hale Ltd. for H. L. V. Fletcher's *The Coasts of Wales* and Bernard Knight's *Lion Rampant*.

William Heineman Ltd. for Eleanor Fairburn's *The Golden Hive*.

Michael Joseph Ltd. for Wynford Vaughan Thomas's and Alun Llewelyn's *Shell Guide to Wales*.

Methuen & Co. Ltd. for Maxwell Frazer's *Introducing West Wales* and H. V. Morton's *In Search of Wales*.

John Murray Ltd., Miss Katherine A. Thomas and the Estate of the late Ernest Thomas for Richard Vaughan's *Moulded in Earth*; and also for David Williams's *A History of Modern Wales*.

John Long Ltd. for John Capstick's *Given in Evidence*.

The University of Wales Press Board for E. G. Bowen's *The Settlements of the Celtic Saints in Wales*, Thomas Jones's *Brut y Tywysogion* and David Williams's *The Rebecca Riots*.

The author and publisher also thank the following for permission to use their copyright work in this publication:

Dr Rachel Bromwich, Lord Cawdor, Tony Curtis, Eirian Davies, Bryan Martin Davies, Mallt Davies, William Davies, Dafydd Evans, Dr Gwynfor Evans, Professor Simon Evans, Professor Ralph Griffiths, Ann James, Professor A. O. H. Jarman, Professor Dafydd Jenkins, Dr J. Geraint Jenkins, Professor Dafydd Johnston, Mrs D. Gwenallt Jones, Dr E. D. Jones, Major Francis Jones, Raymond Garlick, Bryn Griffiths, Mrs Margaret Lloyd-Johnes, Dillwyn Miles, Alison Morgan, Dr Derec Llwyd Morgan, Dr Prys Morgan, Miss Morfydd Owen, Tony Oldham, Kusha Petts, Douglas Phillips, A. G. Prys-Jones, W. Leslie Richards, Rev. Gomer M. Roberts, Byron Rogers, David Saunders, Mrs Irene Saunders, Dr H. N. Savory, Mrs John Miles Thomas, Peter Underwood, Huw Walters, D. Mervyn Williams, the Estates of D. J. Williams and Waldo Williams.

The author would also like to thank, for their special and invaluable help:

Elizabeth Bourner, Dr Rachel Bromwich, Wendy Bullen, Chris Delaney, Ann Dorsett, Professor D. Simon Evans, Mr Dafydd Evans, Dr Trevor Evans, Mrs Jenny Gammon, D. F. Griffiths, Ann James, Norah Isaac, Professors A. O. H. Jarman and Dafydd

Jenkins, Alwyn Jones, Dr Brinley Jones, Miss Eirwen Jones, Dr E. D. Jones, Ieuan Jones, Major Francis Jones, John H. Lewis, Thomas Lloyd, Dr Prys Morgan, Sally Moss, Morfydd Owen, Eluned Rees, Keidrych Rees, Rev. Gomer M. Roberts, Byron Rogers, W. Leslie Richards, Dr J. Beverly Smith, Gwyn Walters, Huw Walters and Rhydwen Williams.

The Editor of the *Carmarthen Journal* for 'The Dafen Murder' and Lynn Hughes's 'Life and Times of a Modest Hero'.

The Editor of the *Daily Telegraph Weekend Magazine* for copyright material by Byron Rogers.

The Editor of the *South Wales Guardian* for *Hen Ffynnon Llandyfân* by Gomer M. Roberts.

The Editor of the *Western Mail* for Wil Ifan's piece and for material by Lynn Hughes published in the *Weekend Magazine*.

The Cambrian Archaeological Association for items by Francis Green, Francis Jones and W. Llewelyn Williams from *Archaeologia Cambrensis*.

The Council of the Hon. Soc. of Cymmrodorion and the editor of the *Transactions* for H. M. Vaughan's *Cromwell in South Wales*.

The London Carmarthenshire Society for extracts from *A History of Carmarthenshire* by Sir J. E. Lloyd.

The editor of *The Carmarthenshire Historian* for 'Perlau Tâf' by Dr Trevor Jones, and Trevor Owen's own piece on Sackville Gwynne.

The Editorial Board of Folk Life for *Cockles and Mussels* by J. Geraint Jenkins.

The Director, British Geological Survey (NERC) for the Crown Copyright account of the Old Red Sandstone in T. Neville George's *British Regional Geology South Wales* (3rd Edn.) 1970.

The Librarian and the Editorial Committee of the *National Library of Wales Journal* for an extract from Mr D. Emrys Williams's article 'George Capper's *Journal*'.

The Editor of the *Bulletin of the Board of Celtic Studies* for the report on the excavation of Twlc y Filiast by H. N. Savory.

The Editor of *Carmarthenshire Life* for Lynn Hughes's 'Lunchtime Legend'.

For Picture permissions the Editor would especially like to thank the Librarian of the National Library of Wales for permission to use photographs from the D. C. Harries, Llandeilo, Collection; Ieuan Jones for access to his private collection of maps and engravings of Welsh topography; John Jones, Ruthin, for the Dylan Thomas photograph; Richard and Eiryl Firstbrook and Roger Vlitos for their photographic contributions, and Mr and Mrs L. Guilor for the photograph of the sturgeon; K. M. Lindslay for the 'Cockalorum' engraving; the Librarian and staff of Carmarthen County Library; the Curator and staff of Carmarthen Museum; the Librarian at Llanelli Borough Library; John Davies and his staff at Carmarthen County Record Office; Michael Francis at the National Library of Wales; the Curator and staff of the Glynn Vivian Gallery, Swansea; and the Director and his staff at the National Museum of Wales, Cardiff.

Finally, my sincere appreciation to Emyr Nicholas and his staff at the Dinefwr Press, Llandybie, for generous help and their infinite care in the production of this book.

Bibliography

ALED, TUDUR d. 1526
Gwaith Tudor Aled 2 vols. Ed. T. Gwynn
Jones, UWP, 1926.

AMANWY
– see Griffiths, David Rhys.

ap THOMAS, HOPCYN ap EINION
Iolo Mss. Taliesin Williams (ab Iolo).
The Welsh Mss. Society, Llandovery
1848.

ARBER-COOKE, ALFRED THEODORE
Pages from the History of Llandovery.
2 vols. Published for the Friends of
Llandovery Association at the Old
Printing Office, Llandovery,
1976.

AUGUSTUS, WILLIAM (Wil Awst)
*The Husbandman's Perpetual
Prognostications for the Weather.*
Printed by J. Ross, Carmarthen,
1794.

BARING GOULD, S.
& CHARLES CLARK
Lives of the British Saints Vol. IV (for
Hon. Soc. Cymmrodorion), 1913.

BARKER, T.W.
*Handbook to the Natural History of
Carmarthenshire.* (Privately published),
1905.

BEALE, ANNE
*Traits and Stories of the Welsh
Peasantry,* Routlege, 1849.

BEYNON, TOM
Cwm Sêl a Chefn Sidan, Llyfrau'r
Methodistiaid Calfinaidd, 1946.

BLACK BOOK OF CARMARTHEN
(13th Century) Anon.
Llyfr Du Caerfyrddin, Ed. A. O. H.
Jarman, UWP, 1983.

'BLUE BOOKS', (so-called)
*The Report of the Commissioners of
Inquiry into the State of Education in
Wales,* 1843.

BOWEN, E.G.
*The Settlements of the Celtic Saints in
Wales,* UWP, 1954.

BRADLEY, ARTHUR G.
Highways & Byways in South Wales
(Companion Vol.) Macmillan, 1903.

BRECHFA, IEUAN
NLW Ms. Llansteffan 7. p. 333.

BRIGSTOCK, BENJ.
Document in private hands.

BRUT Y TYWYSOGION Anon
*The Chronicle of the Princes: Red
Book of Hergest,* source. Trs. & Ed. by
Thomas Jones, UWP, 1952.

CAMBRENSIS, GIRALDUS
*The Journey Through Wales. Description
of Wales.* Ed. Lewis Thorpe. Penguin
Classics, 1978.

CAMDEN, WILLIAM
Britannia, 1610.

CAPPER, GEORGE
Journal. Ed. D. Emrys Williams.
NLW Ms. 21235B. pub. NLW
Journal XIII, 1983.

CAPSTICK, JOHN
Given in Evidence. John Long, 1960.

CASSON, HUGH (Sir)
Follies, Monuments. (National Benzole
Publications). Chatto & Windus, 1963.

CHALDECOTT, GILBERT
River Poems. (Privately published). J. D.
Lewis & Sons, Gomer Press, 1980.

CLARK, CHARLES
– see S. Baring Gould.

CLIFFE, JOHN HENRY
Notes & Recollections of an Angler.
Hamilton Adams, 1860.

CONDRY, WILLIAM
The Natural History of Wales. Collins
New Naturalist, 1981.

CROFTS, FREEMAN WILLS
The Sea Mystery. Collins, 1928.

CURTIS, MARY
The Antiquities of Laugharne, Pendine and their Neighbourhoods. Second Ed. 1980.
CURTIS, TONY
Album. Christopher Davies, 1974.

DAVIES, ANEIRIN TALFAN
Crwydro Sir Gâr. Llyfrau'r Dryw, 1955, 1970.
DAVIES, BRYAN MARTIN
Darluniau ar Gynfas. Gomer, 1970.
DAVIES, DUDLEY G.
The Boat-Race and other Poems. The Alden Press. N.D.
DAVIES, ETHEL M.
The Story of Llandefeilog Parish. (Privately published). Spurrell, 1953.
DAVIES, WALTER (Gwallter Mechain)
General view of the Agriculture and Domestic Economy of South Wales. Royal Comm. Land Report 1814.
DAVIES, WILLIAM (Gwilym Teilo)
Llandeilo-Fawr and its Neighbourhood Past and Present. (Privately published). D. W. & G. Jones, Llandeilo, 1858.
DDA, HYWEL *The Law* (anon).
Jenkins, Dafydd, ed.: *The Law of Hywel Dda, Selections from Welsh Medieval Texts*. 'The Welsh Classics'. Gomer, 1985.
Richards, Melville: *The Laws of Hywel Dda*. Liverpool University Press, 1954.
DEFOE, DANIEL
Journey through the whole Island of Great Britain. 1738.
DE PENHOUET, MAUNDET (incognito)
A Pedestrian Traveller. 1797.
DEULWYN, IEUAN
Gwaith Ieuan Deulwyn. Ed. Ifor Williams. Bangor Welsh Mss. Soc. 1909.
DINELY, THOMAS
The Account of the Official Progress of His Grace Henry the First Duke of Beaufort through Wales. 1684.
DONOVAN, E.
Descriptive Excursions through South Wales and Monmouthshire in the Year 1805.
DRAYTON, MICHAEL
Polyolbion. 1622.

DYER, JOHN
Savage's *Miscellany* 1726. *English Pastoral Verse*, ed. John Bull. Penguin, 1982.

EDWARDS, THOMAS ('Twm o'r Nant')
– see *Wild Wales* ch. 59 by George Borrow. Ashton, Glyn: *Hunangofiant a Llythyrau Twm o'r Nant*. UWP, 1948.
ELFED – see Lewis, H. Elfed.
'EMLYN, IOAN'
– see Jones, John Emlyn.
EVANS, CARADOC
My People. Dobson, 1915.
EVANS, GWYNFOR
(*Aros Mae*), *Land of my Fathers*. (Gwasg) John Penry Press, 1974.
EVANS, CONRAD
The Story of a Parish: Llanfihangel Abercywyn. (Privately published), 1975.
EVANS, DANIEL
Life and Work of William Williams, MP for Coventry and Lambeth. Gomerian Press, Llandysul, 1939
EVANS, WILLIAM 'Wil Ifan'.
Here and There. Western Mail Publications. N.D.

FAIRBURN, ELEANOR
The Golden Hive. Heineman, 1966.
FENTON, RICHARD
Tours in Wales. 1804-1813.
FISHER, J.
– see Baring-Gould, S.
FISHLOCK, TREVOR
Wales & the Welsh. Cassell, 1972.
FLETCHER, H. L.V.
The Coasts of Wales. Robert Hale, 1969.
FRAZER, MAXWELL
Introducing West Wales. Methuen, 1956.
FURNEAUX, RUPERT
Famous Criminal Cases. Alan Wingate, 1955.

GARLICK, RAYMOND
A Sense of Time. Gomer Press.
GEORGE, T. NEVILLE
British Regional Geology: South Wales. HMSO. 1976.

GILPIN, WILLIAM
Observations on the River Wye & Several Parts of South Wales in the Summer of the Year 1770. Pub. 1789.

GLYN COTHI, LEWYS
Ed. E. D. Jones. *Gwaith Lewys Glyn Cothi*. Vol. I. UWP, 1953.

GOCH, IOLO
Ed. Henry Lewis. *Cywyddau Iolo Goch ac Eraill*. Cardiff, 1937.

GREEN, FRANCIS
Trans. Hist. Soc. West Wales 1916.

GRIFFITHS, BRYN
The Mask of Pity. Christopher Davies, 1966.

GRIFFITHS, DAVID RHYS ('Amanwy')
Caneuon Amanwy. Gomer, 1976.

GRIFFITHS, RALPH
Gruffydd ap Nicholas and the Fall of the House of Lancaster. Welsh History Review. Vol. 13, 1965.

GWENALLT – see Jones, David G.

GWILI – see Jenkins, John Gwili.

HANSARD, G. A.
Trout and Salmon Fishing in Wales. 1834.

HARRIS, HOWELL
Diaries.
– see Beynon, Tom. *Cwmsêl a Chefn Sidan*.

HAWKES, JACQUETTA
A Guide to the Prehistoric and Roman Monuments in England & Wales. Chatto & Windus, 1976.

HILL, LAWRENCE C.
The Vale of Towy. Jakemans, Hereford, 1947.

HOOD, PAXTON
Christmas Evans, Preacher of Wild Wales. Hodder, 1881.

HOWEL, JAMES
Familiar Letters. Epistole Ho. Elianne, 1655.

HUGHES, LYNN
Hawkmoor. Penguin, 1979.
Christopher Davies 1979.
Twm Siôn Cati's Men (5th reprint of above). Gomer Press, 1983.
Unhappy Breed of Men, 'Dear Dynevor' (Privately published). J. D.

Lewis & Sons, Gomer Press, 1977.
Carmarthenshire Life, Nov./Dec., 2002.

HUGHES, PHILIP GWYN
Wales and the Drovers: The Historic Background to an Epoch. Foyles, 1943.

HUGHES, RICHARD
The Fox in the Attic. Chatto & Windus, 1961.

HUGHES, TED
Collected Poems. Faber, 1982.

IFAN, WIL – see Evans, William.

INGRAM, GEOFFREY C. and SALMON, H. MORREY
A Handlist of the Birds of Carmarthenshire. (Privately published). Narberth, 1954.

JAMES, HEATHER
Roman West Wales. Rampart Press, Carmarthen, 1972.

JAMES, TERRENCE *Navigation on the Towy*. Carmarthenshire Antiquary XXII.

JENKINS, J. GERAINT
Cockles & Mussels Folk Life XV. 1977.
Nets and Coracles. David & Charles, 1974.

JENKINS, J.
Llanarthney: the Parish, its People and Places. (Privately published), 1939.

JENKINS, JOHN 'GWILI'
Poems, 1920.

JENKINS, THOMAS
The Diary of Thomas Jenkins of Llandeilo 1826-70.
Ed. R. T. Jenkins. Dragon Books, Bala, 1976. NLW. 1983(?)

JOHN, BARRY
The Barry John Story: An Autobiography. Collins, 1974.

JONES, DAVID GWENALLT
Eples. Gwasg Aberystwyth, 1951.

JONES, D. E.
The History of the Parishes of Llangeler & Penboyr.

JONES, FRANCIS
Archaeologia Cambrensis 1967, 1968 & 1973.

JONES, E. VERNON
The Carmarthenshire Historian. Vol. IX. 1972.

JONES, JOHN EMLYN 'Ioan Emlyn'
Bedd y Dyn Tlawd.
JONES, IRA
Tiger Squadron. WH Allen, London,
1954. *An Airfighter's Scrapbook.*
Nicholson & Watson,1938.
JONES, TREVOR
The Carmarthenshire Historian. Vol. X.
1973.

KNIGHT, BERNARD
Lion Rampant. Robert Hale, 1972.

LAWS, EDWARD
A History of Little England Beyond Wales.
1888.
LELAND, JOHN
The Itinerary. Vol. I. Oxford, 1710.
LEWES, EVELYN
Out with the Cambrians. Williams &
Norgate, 1934.
LEWIS, H. 'ELFED'
Songs of Assisi. Gwasg Aberystwyth,
1938.
LLOYD, Sir J. E. (Ed.)
A History of Carmarthenshire. (2 vols.)
(Privately published by the London
Carmarthenshire Society). J. Lewis.
Cardiff, 1935.
LLOYD, THOMAS
Garden of Eden, Abergwili. Welsh
Historic Gardens Trust Newsletter
No. 8, 1995.
LHUYD, EDWARD
Parochialia. Ed. Gunter. *Early Science in
Oxford.* OUP, 1946. *Arch Camb.*

MABINOGION, THE (Anon)
Ed. Lady Charlotte Guest. Pub. for
Welsh Mss. Soc. by Longmans,
London and Tonn, Llandovery, 1849.
Ed. Gantz G. Penguin, 1976.
MALKIN, BENJ. HEATH
*The Scenery, Antiquities & Biography
of South Wales.* 1804.
MAI, TREBOR
– see Williams, Robert.
MAP, WALTER
De Nugis Curialium. Cymmrodorion
Record Series (pp. 101/2), 1923.

MARLES, GWILYM
– see Thomas, William M.
MEE, ARTHUR
Carmarthenshire Notes. Llanelly, 1889.
Caermarthenshire Miscellany, 1892.
MECHAIN, GWALLTER
– see Davies, Walter.
MILES, DILLWYN
*The Royal National Eisteddfod of
Wales.* Christopher Davies, 1978.
MOLLOY, PAT
And the Blessed Rebecca. Gomer, 1983.
MONMOUTH, GEOFFREY of
The History of the Kings of Britain.
Ed. Lewis Thorpe. Penguin, 1966.
MORGAN, D.
The Story of Carmarthenshire. Ed. Pub.
Co. Cardiff, 1909.
MORGAN, DEREC LLWYD
Y Tân Melys. Dryw, 1960.
MORGAN, 'Mrs' (Mary)
*A Tour to Milford Haven in the Year
1791,* pub. London 1795.
MORGAN, PRYS
The Eighteenth Century Renaissance.
Christopher Davies, 1981.
MORRIS, Sir LEWIS
The Works of Sir Lewis Morris. Kegan
Paul, 1904.
MORTON, H.V.
In Search of Wales. Methuen, 1932.
MURCHISON, R. I.
The Silurian System. 1839.

NANT, TWM O'R
– see Edwards, Thomas.
NICHOLAS, J. W.
The White Dove. Arthur Stockwell.
London, 1923.

O'DWYER, S.
*The Roman Roads of Carmarthenshire
and Pembroke.* Newtown, 1936.
OLDHAM, TONY D.
The Caves of Carmarthen. Privately
produced and published. Bristol, 1975.
OWEN, DAVID ('Brutus')
Yr Haul. Vol. IV. 1839.
See also Testimony to Commissioners of
Inquiry into the State of Education in
Wales. 'The Blue Books'.

OWEN, T. R.
Geology Explained in South Wales, David
and Charles.

PARRY-JONES, D.
Welsh Country Upbringing. Batsford, 1948.
My Own Folk. Gomer, 1972.
PETTS, KUSHA
Necklace for a Poor Sod. Gomer, 1970.
PHILLIPS, DOUGLAS
Beyond the Frontier. Christopher Davies,
1972.
PHYSICIANS OF MYDDFAI (Anon)
Meddygon Myddfai. Trs. John Pugh. Ed.
John Williams (Ab Ithel) Welsh Mss.
Soc. Llandovery, 1869.
PLINY
Natural History Vol. XXXIII. tra.
Philomel Holland. Adam Flip, London,
1634.
PRICE, FRED S.
A History of Talley and Caio.
Privately published. Swansea, 1934.
PRITCHARD, RHYS *Vicar Pritchard*
Ed. William Evans. *Pritchard's Poems*.
Carmarthen, 1771.
John Bulmer *Beauties of the Vicar of
Llandovery*. Holdsworth & Hall, 1830.
PRYS-JONES, A. G.
Poems of Wales. Basil Blackwell, 1925.
The Story of Carmarthenshire (2 Vols.).
Christopher Davies, 1952, 1972.

RAIKES, DOROTHY. *A 1926 Diary, The
Open Road*. (Privately published by
Alison Morgan, Maes Glas, Llanwrtyd
Wells, 2000)
REES, ERNEST
Wales and England Wed. Dent, 1940.
REES, P. H.
Gower Shipwrecks. Christopher Davies,
1978.
REES, THOMAS
The Beauties of England and Wales.
1815.
REES, VYVIAN
The Shell Guide to West Wales. Faber,
1963.
REES, WILLIAM (Tonn)
Verbatim Intro to *Meddygon Myddfai*
see *The Physicians of Myddfai* above.

RHYS, Sir JOHN
Celtic Folklore. 2 vols. OUP, 1901.
Wildwood House, 1980.
RHYS, KEIDRYCH
Under the Van Pool. Routledge, 1942.
RICHARDS, W. LESLIE
Adledd. Dryw, 1973.
ROBERTS, GOMER M.
Chwedlau Dau Fynydd. Dryw, 1948.
South Wales Guardian, 1976.
ROBERTSON, R.
– see Young, J. F.
ROBINSON, H.B.
The Life of Sir Thomas Picton.
Richard Bentley, 1835.
ROGERS, BYRON
The Daily Telegraph Weekend Magazine,
No. 600. June 11, 1976.
Meet the Family. Saga Magazine,
Oct. 2002.
ROSCOE, THOMAS
*Wanderings and Excursions in South
Wales*. 1844.

SALMON, H. MORREY
– see Ingram, C.
SAMUEL, WILLIAM
Llandilo Present and Past. Printed at
'The Welshman', Carmarthen, 1868.
SAUNDERS, BRUCE
Murder in Lonely Places. Herbert
Jenkins, 1960.
SAUNDERS, DAVID
A Guide to the Birds of Wales. Constable,
1974.
SAUNDERS, ROY
The Drovers' Highway. Oldbourne,
1959.
SAVAGE, RICHARD
Selected Poems.
SAVORY, H. N.
Bulletin of the Board of Celtic Studies.
Vol. XVI (iv) 1956. pp. 300-8.
SINCLAIR, (Miss) CATHERINE
*Sketches and Stories of Wales and the
Welsh*. 1860.
SPEED, JOHN
Atlas of Wales. 1726.
SPENSER, EDMUND
The Faerie Queene, 1590. Penguin.
Ed. P. Roche Jr. 1972.

BIBLIOGRAPHY 443

SPURRELL, WILLIAM
Carmarthen and its Neighbourhood.
1879.
SWIFT, (DEAN) JONATHAN
The Briton Described: A Journey thro'
Wales. 1738.
SIKES, WIRT
British Goblins. Samson Low, 1880.

TAYLOR, JEREMY
The Golden Grove. SPCK, 1868.
Holy Living/Holy Dying. Longmans,
1938.
TEW, IEUAN (fl. 1470)
NLW Llansteffan Ms. 134, 183.
THIRLWALL, CONNOP
Letters to a Friend. Ed. Arthur Penrhyn
Stanley. Bentley, 1882.
THOMAS, DYLAN
Collected Poems. Dent, 1952.
A Portrait of the Artist as a Young Dog.
Dent, 1940.
Under Milk Wood. Dent, 1954.
THOMAS, EDWARD
Beautiful Wales. A. & C. Black, 1905.
THOMAS (TOMOS), HOPCYN AP
EINION
Iolo Ms. Welsh Ms. Soc. Llandovery,
1848.
THOMAS, J. I.
A Laugharne Mixture. Lodwick,
Carmarthen, 1984.
THOMAS, JOHN MILES
The Llandeilo Apprentice. Lodwick,
Carmarthen, 1983.
THOMAS, WILLIAM
'Gwilym Marles'.
TORBUCK, JOHN
– see Swift, Jonathan, above –
A Collection of Welsh Travels and
Memoirs of Wales. (Pirated edn.)
1749.
TREMBLE, HENRY
Carmarthen Record Office.

UNDERWOOD, PETER
Ghosts of Wales. Christopher Davies,
1978.

VAUGHAN, HERBERT
MILLINGCHAMP
The South Wales Squires. Methuen,
1926. Golden Grove, 1988.
Trans. Hon. Soc. Cymmrodorion,
'Cromwell in South Wales', 1936.
VAUGHAN, RICHARD
(alias) Ernest Thomas. *Moulded in*
Earth. John Murray, 1951.
VAUGHAN, WILLIAM
The Golden Grove Moralised. 1600,
1628.
VAUGHAN-THOMAS, WYNFORD,
with Alun Llewelyn
The Shell Guide to Wales. Michael
Joseph, 1965.

WARD, FRANK
The Lakes of Wales. Herbert Jenkins,
1931.
WATKINS, VERNON
Selected Poems. Faber, 1967.
WESLEY, JOHN
Ed. A. H. Williams. *Wesley in Wales*
1739-1790. UWP, 1971.
WIGSTEAD, HENRY
Remarks on a Tour to North and South
Wales in the Year 1797.
WILLIAMS, DAVID
A History of Modern Wales. John Murray,
1950.
The Rebecca Riots. UWP, 1955.
WILLIAMS, D. J.
Yr Hen Dŷ Ffarm. Gomer/Gwasg
Aberystwyth, 1953.
The Old Farmhouse. trs. Waldo
Williams. Harrap, 1960. Golden Grove,
1987.
WILLIAMS, HERBERT
Railways in Wales. Christopher Davies,
1980.
WILLIAMS, ROBERT 'Trebor Mai'.
WILLIAMS, WILLIAM 'Pantycelyn'
Ed. Gomer M. Roberts. *Gweithiau*
Williams Pantycelyn (2 vols). UWP,
1964, 67.
WILLIAMS, W. LLEWELYN
Gwilym a Benni Bach. Hughes a'i Fab,
1897.
'*Slawer Dydd.* Llanelli, 1931.

WILLIAMS, W. 'Nantlais'
  O Gopa Bryn Nebo. Gomer, 1968.
WOOD, L. G.
  The Rivers of Wales (2 vols.).
  (Privately published.) London,
  1813.

WYN, WATKIN
  Adgofion. Cwmni Cyhoeddi Addysgol
  Caerdydd, 1907.

YOUNG, J. F. and ROBERTSON, R.
  The Divining Rod, Baker & Son, 1894.